# REMINISCENCES OF A SOLDIER'S WIFE

A SHAWNEE CLASSIC

A Series of Classic Regional Reprints for the Midwest

Mrs John A Logan

# REMINISCENCES
# OF A SOLDIER'S WIFE
## AN AUTOBIOGRAPHY

### MRS. JOHN A. LOGAN
*Foreword by John Y. Simon*

**ILLUSTRATED**

SOUTHERN ILLINOIS UNIVERSITY PRESS
*Carbondale and Edwardsville*

Foreword by John Y. Simon, copyright
© 1997 by the Board of Trustees,
Southern Illinois University
First published 1913 by Charles Scribner's Sons
All rights reserved
Printed in the United States of America
00   99   98   97      4   3   2   1

Library of Congress Cataloging-in-Publication Data
Logan, John A., Mrs., 1838–1923
Reminiscences of a soldier's wife  :  an autobiography  /
by Mrs. John A. Logan :
foreword by John Y. Simon.
p.   cm.— (Shawnee classic)
Originally published:  New York  :  C. Scribner's Sons, 1913. Includes index.
1. Logan, John A., Mrs., 1838–1923.  2. Logan, John Alexander, 1826–1886.
3. United States—History—Civil War, 1861–1865—Personal narratives.
4. Illinois—History—Civil War, 1861–1865—Personal narratives.  5. United
States—Politics and government—1865–1900.  6. Generals' spouses—Illinois—
Biography.  I.  Title.  II. Series.
E601.L87  1997
973.7'81—dc21                                          97-17322 CIP
ISBN 0-8093-2157-2 (alk. paper)

The paper used in this publication meets the minimum requirements of
American National Standard for Information Sciences—Permanence of Paper
for Printed Library Materials, ANSI Z39.48-1984. ♾

DEDICATED

WITH  UNDYING  LOVE

TO  MY

CHILDREN  AND  GRANDCHILDREN

# PREFACE

To tell my own story is to tell that of my famous husband, General John A. Logan. Our marriage was a real partnership for thirty-one happy years. I shared his thoughts and plans no less when he was a senator than when he was a prosecuting attorney in southern Illinois. We were working in the harmony of a common purpose, whether I was in the kitchen improvising a meal for his friends when he was running for the legislature, or entertaining in Washington after his fame was secure and his influence nation-wide. With him I witnessed the stirring events in which he was a leader on the borderland of the Confederacy, where he raised his Union regiment. We were together whenever possible during the war. I travelled with him on his political campaigns after the war. Thus I came to know not only the eminent soldiers and public men of his time, but the men in the ranks who believed in him and followed him, whether to Vicksburg and Atlanta or in his political battles.

Our tastes were the same; likewise our ambitions for the best attainments in life. We came of the same pioneering American stock. We were reared among the same surroundings of the Middle West when it was the frontier. After his death, my naturally active temperament and the inspiration of his career kept me in touch with the pulse of national affairs and brought me fresh acquaintances among new celebrities. When I think of the conditions which prevailed in my girlhood days in comparison with those of the present, I marvel how the span of one person's life can compass such changes.

MARY S. LOGAN.

# CONTENTS

## CHAPTER I

## CHAPTER II

## CHAPTER III

# CONTENTS

## CHAPTER VII

## CHAPTER VIII

## CHAPTER IX

## CHAPTER X

## CHAPTER XI

## CHAPTER XII

## CHAPTER XIII

## CHAPTER XIV

## CHAPTER XV

## CHAPTER XVI

# ILLUSTRATIONS

# ILLUSTRATIONS

# FOREWORD

Senator John A. Logan of Illinois died on December 26, 1886, in Washington, D.C., at the age of sixty. Thousands mourned the death of a Civil War hero, charismatic political boss, and icon to Union veterans. Logan had fought as a colonel in General Ulysses S. Grant's first battle at Belmont, later as a major general in Grant's Vicksburg campaign and in General William T. Sherman's advance to Atlanta. Union troops admired Logan's flamboyant style, recklessness in combat, and dramatic appearance, his dark complexion offset by an enormous walrus mustache. Postwar Republicans esteemed his relentless determination to uphold congressional Reconstruction, to support black civil rights, and to commemorate Northern victory.

Mary Simmerson Cunningham Logan, who survived until 1923, embarked upon a journalistic career, usually writing under the name Mrs. John A. Logan.[1] Mary Logan dedicated her long widowhood to preserving the fame of her beloved husband. The Logans' Washington home, named Calumet Place, eventually contained a memorial hall filled with pictures and mementos of John A. Logan. Mary took an active role in placing monumental equestrian statues of her husband by Franklin Simmons at Logan Circle in Washington and by Augustus Saint-Gaudens at Grant Park in Chicago.[2] She is best remembered for *Reminiscences of a Soldier's*

1. Before her *Reminiscences*, Mary Logan had written, compiled, or coauthored three books: *The Home Manual: Everybody's Guide in Social, Domestic, and Business Life* (Philadelphia: H. J. Smith, 1889); *The Part Taken by Women in American History* (Wilmington, Del.: Perry-Nalle, 1912); *Thirty Years in Washington* (Hartford, Conn.: A. D. Worthington, 1901). The latter was enlarged and reissued as *Our National Government* (Minneapolis: H. L. Baldwin, 1908). An earlier reprint of the *Reminiscences* omitted the first three and portions of the last four chapters. Mary Logan, *Reminiscences of the Civil War and Reconstruction*, ed. George Worthington Adams (Carbondale and Edwardsville: Southern Illinois University Press, 1970). Adams provides some useful notes.

2. George Francis James, ed., *The Logan Monument Memorial* (Chicago: University of Chicago Press, 1898).

*Wife,* serialized in *Cosmopolitan* immediately before book publication in 1913.

Those who joined Mary in veneration of her husband balanced others who condemned aspects of his career. Born deep in southern Illinois, in the region called Egypt (in part because of endemic prejudices against blacks), Logan had first achieved recognition in 1853 as a young Democratic member of the Illinois legislature instrumental in passing a bill that banned black migration into the state by providing heavy fines for responsible whites and additional fines for blacks who entered Illinois. As U.S. Representative, he strengthened his Negrophobic reputation by defending the fugitive slave law. A spokesman for the Southern wing of the Democrats, his loyalty to the Union remained in question for two months after the Civil War began.

Once Logan decided to fight for the Union, he rapidly rose from colonel to major general. When Major General James B. McPherson fell in battle before Atlanta in 1864, Logan was next in line to command the Army of the Tennessee. Overall commander Sherman, however, decided to assign command to a fellow West Pointer, Major General Oliver O. Howard, a decision heavily influenced by Major General George H. Thomas, another professional officer who distrusted Logan. Later in 1864, when Thomas ignored General Grant's orders to attack Confederate General John B. Hood at Nashville, Grant selected Logan to replace Thomas. Logan was on his way to assume command when Thomas finally attacked, won a smashing victory, and curtailed Logan's military ascent. Mary's account incorporates a postwar fabrication that Logan delayed his journey and sent a secret warning to Thomas of his imminent removal.[3] For the remainder of his life, Logan resented trained officers and celebrated the virtues of volunteers. His posthumously published *The Volunteer Soldier of America* (1887) sustained this fixation for nearly seven hundred tedious pages.[4]

During the war, Logan began a political hegira from ardent

3. James Pickett Jones, *"Black Jack": John A. Logan and Southern Illinois in the Civil War Era* (1967; reprinted, Carbondale and Edwardsville: Southern Illinois University Press, 1995), 242–43.

4. See Russell F. Weigley, *Towards an American Army: Military Thought from Washington to Marshall* (New York: Columbia University Press, 1962), 127–36.

Democrat to radical Republican. Running for congressman-at-large in Illinois in 1866, Logan was dogged with reminders of his Democratic past but prevailed by misrepresenting his record. Once returned to Congress, he excoriated the South and all who urged a lenient Reconstruction, especially President Andrew Johnson, whose impeachment trial he participated in managing. During two terms as U.S. Senator (1871–77, 1879–86), Logan achieved fame as a partisan stalwart, an assiduous spoilsman who despised civil service legislation, and a leader of the Grand Army of the Republic, a veteran organization that he manipulated as an arm of the Republican party. Logan had conducted a vendetta against General Fitz John Porter, dismissed during the war for alleged disloyalty, who later sought vindication. In 1880, Logan denounced Porter in a Senate speech that lasted four days. Logan's "greatest personal grief of his life" came when Grant later reversed his stand against Porter.[5] As vice-presidential candidate with James G. Blaine in 1884, Logan joined the first losing Republican ticket since 1856. Both Blaine and Logan sought to rally support by resuscitating Civil War issues, a practice known as "waving the bloody shirt." The first of his two mammoth books, *The Great Conspiracy* (1886), chronicled the Civil War in a frenzy of partisanship.

Defense of General Logan furnishes an unacknowledged subtext of his widow's book. Mary Logan joined other long-lived widows of the period such as LaSalle Corbell Pickett (Mrs. George E. Pickett) and Libbie Custer (Mrs. George A. Custer) in defending their controversial spouses. LaSalle Pickett lived until 1931, Libbie Custer until 1933. Both posthumously rewrote their husbands' letters before presenting them in print.[6] Mary Logan may have skirted the truth but never went that far. Nonetheless, biographers suspect that she carefully sorted and weeded the papers that she preserved.[7]

Married at age seventeen to a man twelve years older and already

5. J.F. Wilcox, ed., *Historical Souvenir of Williamson County Illinois* (Effingham, Ill.: LeCrone Press, 1905), 169.

6. Gary W. Gallagher, "A Widow and Her Soldier: LaSalle Corbell Pickett as Author of the George E. Pickett Letters," *Virginia Magazine of History and Biography* 94 (1986): 329–44; Edward G. Longacre, *Pickett: Leader of the Charge* (Shippensburg, Pa.: White Mane, 1995), xi; Shirley A. Leckie, *Elizabeth Bacon Custer and the Making of a Myth* (Norman: University of Oklahoma Press, 1993), 310.

7. Jones, *"Black Jack,"* 77.

embarked upon a legal career, Mary had never experienced independence until widowed. As a girl, she assisted her father with clerical work at the federal land office; after marriage, she did the same for Logan, gradually becoming more deeply involved in his law practice and political career. Always operating quietly, she covered her tracks too well to permit an assessment of her role in propelling Logan from an Egyptian backwater to national prominence. Clearly, however, the couple formed an effective political partnership.[8]

Mary Logan emerged from the shadows during her husband's campaigns for the U.S. Senate to beguile state legislators (the only voters in such elections) in parlors in a Springfield hotel. Gustave Koerner, himself a rival candidate in 1879, recalled Mary as "full of vivacity and in volubility of tongue she was the equal of the General himself," but "rather provincial and lacking the perfume of refinement." After Logan's death, Mary as "patron saint of the Grand Army of the Republic," sneered Koerner, should be "canonized as such, like Santa Barbara, who in all Catholic countries is considered the patroness of the heavy artillery." As a female in politics, concluded Koerner, Mary "ought not to be approved, much less admired."[9] No wonder, then, that Mary preferred to minimize her political role and to work behind the scenes.

In her *Reminiscences*, Mary continued her lifelong practice of celebrating her husband rather than emphasizing her own role in furthering his career. Occasionally, her prose becomes somewhat overwrought, as in her account of "General Logan's matchless genius, indomitable courage, and leadership of men—men who would have followed him to the jaws of death." When Logan campaigned in his former congressional district for Lincoln's reelection, "scarcely a dry eye was to be seen among the thousands upturned to him, their idolized leader in civil as well as military campaigns." Writing earlier, Mary stated that she had "made the best fight possible at home surrounded by very bitter political opponents, who sympathized very strongly with the Rebellion, and who, from

8. See Sandra J. Fenger, "Mary Logan: Nineteenth Century Feminine Politician," M.A. Thesis, Southern Illinois University, 1977.

9. *Memoirs of Gustave Koerner*, ed. Thomas J. McCormack (Cedar Rapids: Torch Press, 1909), 2: 522.

regarding General Logan as little less than an idol, became his bitter enemies." Mary "went through everything that a human being could endure."[10] Only later did she soften her portrait of wartime Egypt.

Logan's decision to fight for the Union distressed his own family. His mother reacted angrily and only one of his numerous siblings approved his course. During the campaign of 1866, Logan's sister publicly proclaimed her brother's initial wartime disloyalty.[11] Mary's father, John M. Cunningham, had attended a pro-secession meeting in Marion, and a younger brother, Hibert—Mary was the eldest of thirteen children—joined a company of Confederate volunteers who fought against Logan at the battle of Belmont in November 1861. In her *Reminiscences* Mary recalled her fondness for Hibert, "a dashing, thoughtless spirit," who, "in a mad moment," had "yielded to an impulse." Hibert redeemed himself in Mary's eyes by deserting the Confederacy in fall 1863 and serving on Logan's staff during the Atlanta campaign.[12]

Hibert died soon after the war and Mary drew close to the family of Logan's cousin, Cornelius Ambrosius Logan, who had died in 1853. Mary traveled with his daughter, the actress Eliza Logan Wood, and referred to Eliza's sister Kate as her own adopted daughter. Both Eliza and Kate died in 1872. Their brother Cornelius, for whom Logan secured an appointment as minister to Chile, later served as Logan's literary executor.[13] Mary had earlier lost an infant son. Her other son, John A. Logan, Jr., was killed in action in the Philippines in 1899. Only a daughter, Mary Logan Tucker, survived into the twentieth century.

The Civil War had torn apart both the Logan and Cunningham families. Mary's mother, who died in 1866 after nursing the family of one of the Confederate volunteers from Marion, receives almost no attention in the *Reminiscences*. Mary maintained a better

10. Wilcox, *Williamson County*, 169.

11. Arthur Charles Cole, *The Era of the Civil War, 1848–1870* (1919; reprinted, Urbana: University of Illinois Press, 1987), 402.

12. Ed Gleeson, *Illinois Rebels: A Civil War Unit History of G Company, Fifteenth Tennessee Regiment Volunteer Infantry* (Carmel, Ind.: Guild Press, 1996).

13. C. A. Logan, "Memoir of the Author" in John A. Logan, *The Volunteer Soldier of America* (Chicago and New York: R. S. Peale, 1887), 25–73.

relationship with her father, who died in 1873 in Utah, where he had gone with a patronage appointment from the Grant administration. Ruptured ties with the Logan and Cunningham families brought John and Mary closer, perhaps too close.

Mary wrote her *Reminiscences* to glorify her husband. Logan's modern biographer characterizes the book as "most deceptive," although "helpful in research" if "handled carefully."[14] This warning bears repeating. After Logan's defeat for reelection to the Senate in 1877, for example, Mary went to President Rutherford B. Hayes to solicit an appointment for her husband.[15] Mary omits this unsuccessful venture from her book but repays Hayes by calling him "the weakest man, save one, ever elected to the Presidency." Mary's background in political partisanship and journalism, combined with her ardent defense of her husband, ill-equipped her to pen an entirely trustworthy narrative. Nonetheless, because Mary wrote engagingly about the dramatic events of her husband's astonishing career, her account deserves a fresh audience.

JOHN Y. SIMON
Southern Illinois University at Carbondale

---

14. James Pickett Jones, *John A. Logan: Stalwart Republican from Illinois* (Tallahassee: University Presses of Florida, 1982), ix–x.

15. Ibid., 102–3.

# REMINISCENCES OF A SOLDIER'S WIFE

## AN AUTOBIOGRAPHY

### CHAPTER I

EARLY LIFE IN SOUTHERN ILLINOIS — SOUTHERNERS THE MAJOR-
ITY AMONG THE SETTLERS — ABSENCE OF FREE SCHOOLS —
POPULATION MAINLY AGRICULTURAL — WOMAN'S WORK ON THE
FARM — PASTIMES AND HOLIDAYS — QUILTING-PARTIES, CORN-
HUSKINGS AND APPLE-PARINGS — "TRAINING DAY" — FOURTH
OF JULY AND CHRISTMAS — CHURCHES INFREQUENT — PRO-
TRACTED MEETINGS AND REVIVALS — PROMINENT PREACHERS —
DOCTOR BASCOM, THE FRIEND OF CLAY — PULPIT DEBATES —
ORGANIZATION OF THE CAMPBELLITE CHURCH — TEACHERS
FROM MASSACHUSETTS — PROGRESS IN EDUCATION SINCE PIO-
NEER DAYS — WIDE-SPREAD IGNORANCE

I WAS born in Petersburgh, Boone County, Missouri, on
the 15th day of August, 1838, of Irish-French ancestry. My
father was a native of Lincoln County, Tennessee, but when
quite a young man migrated to Petersburgh, as an employee
of George P. Dorris, a merchant king of that day. Mr. Dorris had a dry-goods establishment in the town of Petersburgh,
where my father met my mother, Elizabeth Hicks La Fontaine. Grandfather La Fontaine was one of the French Hugue-
nots who settled in western Illinois and Missouri at a very
early date. My grandfather owned large tracts of land in
Missouri and many slaves. My Grandmother La Fontaine
was a cousin of General Sterling Price, of Mexican War and
Confederate fame. When my father and mother were married,

grandfather gave my mother, as a wedding-present, a colored man, his wife, and two children.

Soon after my birth, my Grandfather Cunningham, having liberated his slaves in Tennessee, removed to southern Illinois, and became urgent for my father to come to him to look after him in his declining years. Full of filial affection, father decided that he could not resist Grandfather Cunningham's appeal. He therefore disposed of his business, liberated his slaves, and returned to southern Illinois.

The country was new and population sparse; but my father, full of courage, made every effort to overcome all difficulties and hew his way to success. In his efforts he was ably seconded by my self-denying, loyal, and courageous mother, whose brilliant mind enabled her to devise ways and means of meeting every emergency. In a brief time my father became one of the most popular men in that locality, our home then being at Marion, Williamson County, where we resided during my childhood. Schools were very few, and we had only the advantages of itinerant teachers, who came and went periodically. Father and mother were so anxious for us children to be educated that they lost no opportunity of employing these teachers, as well as taking advantage of every other source of education for us.

Southern Illinois at that time was not so advanced in civilization as the far Western States of to-day. The wealth of the nation was not what it is at present. The earlier settlers of the border States and Territories of the West had not the modern inventions and improvements which have in later years so facilitated their settlement. The pioneers of the whole belt of country south of the Ohio and Mississippi Railroad had accomplished wonders in the matter of clearing away the dense forests, draining the swamp-lands of that locality, making large farms, and building up towns and villages. Still, under the methods then employed, it was a slow process, and they were far behind in matters of education and

progress. Free schools were unknown, much prejudice existing against the education of the masses, through the influence
of the Southerners, who were greatly in the majority among
the settlers. People from the slave States opposed education
on the ground that they could not "keep the niggers down
if they had larnin'." They considered illiteracy their surest
bulwark for the protection of their cherished institution.

With but one railroad—the Illinois Central—which runs
transversely through the whole length of the State, communication and intercourse with the world was limited. Agriculture
was the chief resource of the people. Every child was, to a
certain extent, a producer, and children had to work part of
each year before they had reached their teens. From early
spring until the crops were in and the grain harvested the
girls and boys had to assist in putting in the wheat and small
grain that must be sown in the fall, and in gathering and
garnering the corn and other products, and all without the
aid of machinery. There were no McCormick reapers and
harvesters, or Hough's ploughs and planters; but with oxen,
mules, and horses men and boys ploughed all day long, while
the women and weaker or aged men followed in the furrows,
dropping the seeds by hand. The harvesting was done with
cradle, scythe, or sickle, while men followed the skilful cradler,
and by hand bound the bundles of rye, oats, and wheat.
Others followed and shocked them in the fields till they had
passed through the "sweat" and were ready for the thrash-
ing-yard. Here was heard the stamp of many horses' feet,
tramping out the grain on the smooth yard prepared for the
purpose. The Ruths and Naomis were many, who gleaned
the fields carefully after the men, to be sure that, as nearly as
possible, every grain should be saved.

Besides the gleaning, the women and girls worked prodigiously to brew, bake, and cook for the harvesters, who went
into the fields at five o'clock in the morning. The women
had to rise long before that hour to give them their break-

fast. At ten o'clock came lunch, at twelve o'clock a dinner composed of every variety of meat and vegetables at their command, and at six o'clock supper for all the men who worked together in the harvest. Four meals a day cost these faithful women aching limbs and much fatigue that would now dishearten housewives. In addition, the young girls had to assist in carding, spinning, weaving, and making the clothes for the family, including those of the men. Ready-made clothes were little known even to well-to-do people. Such clothes were regarded with great contempt, as being made of "factory material" of inferior quality. "Very few pieces of factory cloth are a yard wide and all wool," would be said depreciatingly. After all this work, it was not an unusual thing to hear the thrifty housewives say: "I have done very little this year. I have made only so many yards of jeans, blankets, flannel, cotton cloth, carpeting, etc. Not by — so many yards as last year." Unless they could show an incredible number of yards of material manufactured, dyed, and then made into clothing they had not accomplished the full measure of their ambition.

It goes without saying that these women were more industrious, abler managers of domestic affairs, and better wives and mothers than a majority of the wives and mothers of this era. The multiplication of labor-saving machines and the introduction of luxuries which were unknown to our mothers have begotten a spirit of indifference and lassitude. Mothers now rarely feel it incumbent upon them to enlighten their marriageable daughters on the duties of wifehood and motherhood. Girls marry now expecting only indulgence from their husbands, and if children are born to them trained nurses are called to relieve the mothers of the care and responsibility of their babies. They are more interested in the preservation of their girlish figures after childbirth than in the welfare of their offspring.

Household duties devolved absolutely upon the female

members of the family, it being effeminate for any male member to perform any labor of a domestic nature. Many stalwart sons have stood idly by while their delicate mothers, wives, or sisters exposed themselves in inclement weather, milking the cows and performing the hardships which were considered woman's work. On the other hand, the men did not hesitate to insist upon the same mothers, wives, and sisters trudging up and down the rows, dropping and covering the corn with a hoe, or following the reapers, turning and raking the grain as it fell before the sickle. The blessed wives of pioneers fulfilled to the letter their marriage vows of devotion in "sickness and in health, for richer or poorer." They were handmaidens when the family were in health, nurses and ofttimes physicians when any of the family were ill; even undertakers when death visited a household, unless, forsooth, that office was performed by some friend or neighbor.

Ex-President Roosevelt's heart would have been delighted with the large families which were the rule, and not the exception, in those days. I have often heard mothers say they had no more trouble in caring for half a dozen children than for one because, in either case, it took all their time to look after the home and baby. When there were more than one the children took care of each other, and they could only give all their time under any circumstances. These children were reared by their own parents, and not by indifferent, ill-mannered, unscrupulous servants, whose influence is so baneful in many of the homes of to-day. They were taught self-denial, and to help themselves and their brothers and sisters.

I doubt seriously if there is now half the happiness among the people generally that there was in those pioneer days, when all worked hard, and all enjoyed the holidays and merrymakings together. Old and young joined in the sports and pastimes with an abandon of enthusiasm which springs from healthy minds and bodies that have not been satiated by too much leisure and overindulgence.

Amusements were often preceded by the accomplishment of something useful. If a piece of land was to be cleared, not infrequently the proprietor invited all his neighbors to give him a day of their services in felling and rolling the logs that he could not possibly handle by himself. If he had the money to pay men to assist him he could rarely get them, because there were few in the country who could afford to leave their own work to engage in the service of anybody for the low wages paid in localities where slavery did not exist. However, where persons had anything like a favorable standing in the community in which they lived neighbors would readily accept their invitation, and give an honest hard day's work to help each other with their clearing, harvesting, husking, or house-raising.

A few days before he was ready for the work the person desiring this assistance would mount a horse, and ride for miles from house to house, asking old and young men to come on a certain day to help him; and as the good wife had a very important part to play in preparing the feast for the occasion, the husband usually bore his wife's compliments to the female members of his friends' families and an invitation to them to come also. This invitation, these good women knew, meant that the wife wanted some assistance in her work.

The women held quilting-parties. A patchwork quilt was generally prepared thus for quilting: The lining was first laced in frames made for the purpose, the cotton laid smoothly over the lining, then the patchwork spread over and basted closely all around the edges. Then, with chalk and a line, the women marked out the designs for the quilting, fan-shaped figures being the most popular. After quilting one or two rows of fans, according to the size, the side frames were loosened, the quilted part rolled up, and the frame again fastened by placing a peg through the holes in the frames, thus allowing the quilters to reach another row nearer the centre, repeating the process until the whole of the quilt was quilted.

Among so many there were often drones, or unskilled needle-women. These went into the kitchen and helped the house-wife cook the dinner and supper, an indispensable feature of the occasion. The young people many times remained for dancing or games, according to the scruples of the persons giving the entertainment.

The "corn-huskings" and "apple-parings" were evening affairs. A company of young men and women, in an evening from six to nine o'clock, would husk a hundred bushels of corn, and peel many bushels of apples, peaches, or pears, for drying. The young men paired off, as they are ever wont to do, each inviting the girl he fancied to sit beside him. They talked, they sang, and merrily chaffed each other as they rapidly husked the corn. Every time a red ear was found a scuffle ensued, as the finder claimed a kiss from his partner, who, with becoming modesty, resisted the attempts to kiss her. All enjoyed the fun at the expense of the blushing girl, who was always captured, and could do nothing but surrender. The "fruit-parings" were characterized by the same jollity and good humor. After the work was over everything would be set aside, and the merriest dances indulged in, lasting till the wee small hours. These indefatigable people were as bright and ready for the fun at five o'clock in the morning as if they had neither worked nor danced a step. They would go to their homes and take up their duties the following day regardless of the fact that they had hardly slept an hour of the previous twenty-four. Toward the evening of the second day, however, they began to lag, and followed with avidity Franklin's maxim, "Early to bed," etc.

The harvesting was done in much the same way: neighbors going from farm to farm, joining forces and despatching the work with great rapidity, the lads having many a frolic with the lassies in the light of the witching harvest-moon.

In case of intermarriage between members of the more wealthy families a series of parties and banquets would be organized, and for a whole week following the wedding the neighbors would go from house to house, on horseback and in every conceivable vehicle, to attend the parties which were given for miles around. They gave themselves up to feasting, dancing, and merrymaking, troops of them staying all night at one house and the next day going to another, until they had finished their round of festivities.

New Year's Day, Washington's Birthday, Training Day, Fourth of July, or Independence Day, as it was sometimes called, Thanksgiving Day, and Christmas were each observed universally and with prodigality of preparation and earnestness.

New Year's Day was celebrated generally by dinner-giving, much feasting, and dancing-parties in the evening. The custom of making ceremonious calls on New Year's Day did not obtain in this country until later years. Usually the evening was taken up with social affairs as a finale to the festivities of the preceding holiday week.

Washington's Birthday had its annual celebration by banquets, which were great events. Eloquent and patriotic speeches were made in response to the toasts. Thrilling stories were told of Washington and the battles of the Revolutionary War. A grand ball invariably followed the banquets, either at the mansion of some private individual or in a hall, and was attended by the eligible society people of every community. Extensive preparations, consuming much time of the most prominent members of society, were made for these celebrations of the natal day of the Father of His Country.

Training Day, which usually occurred in midsummer, was anticipated with the wildest enthusiasm and outbursts of patriotism. The few who were descendants of the heroes of the Revolutionary War, or War of 1812, or had participated in the Black Hawk or other Indian wars were the commissioned and non-commissioned officers of what might be called the

State militia. They imagined that annual meetings were quite sufficient to cultivate the proper military spirit and keep aglow the fires of patriotism in the hearts of the people. They were thoroughly imbued with the belief that—"To fight

"Is the best office of the best of men;
And to decline when these motives urge
Is infamy beneath a coward's baseness."

They had implicit confidence in their prowess, and felt assured that, on their country's call, they could drop the plough-handles, or whatever vocation they had, pick up their guns as did the men of Concord, and rout any foe. They thought little training necessary for longer service.

When the day arrived, at an early hour the whole population gathered in the villages. Red, white, and blue calico was displayed in great profusion. Flags and bunting not being so plentiful as they are to-day, the ingenious people used every symbol of love of country which they could conceive. I have seen home-made flags, supposed to be the correct copies of the national emblem, with red, white, and blue stripes and gilt stars on blue fields. Those truly patriotic people were unable to remember correctly the arrangement of the colors in Old Glory—so familiar to every child of this age of patriotic instruction, flag drill, and with the emblem of freedom waving above every schoolhouse.

All the treasures which had been preserved in families whose antecedents had ever been in the service in any capacity were brought forth and displayed on that day. The "sword of Bunker Hill," and the rusty blades used in other engagements were brightened up. The guns and muskets were taken down from the racks made of antlers of the deer and elk, which were over the front doors of most homes. The guns or other implements of warfare were carefully cleaned and polished. Bullets were moulded by hand as if for actual warfare. Faded and moth-eaten clothes and sashes were donned with pride

by the scions of military heroes who figured in the early struggles of the republic. Drums and fifes which had been handed
down through at least two or three generations played a
conspicuous part in the marches that were the features of
the day, the shrill notes of "Hail, Columbia," "Yankee
Doodle," and "The Star-Spangled Banner" stirring the latent
patriotism in all hearts to the highest pitch. Falstaff's troop
presented no more ludicrous spectacle than did some of these
soldiers enlisted for a single day. I have vivid recollections of
seeing these parades. The captains of the companies, mounted
on fiery steeds unused to the sound of drum-beats and the
whistling of fifes, employed desperate efforts to manage their
horses as they rode up and down the crooked lines, shouting
meaningless commands to the embryo soldiers. The latter,
though hopelessly ignorant of tactics, were intensely in earnest in their manifestations of the spirit of patriotism.

Great rivalry existed among those who had, either by inheritance or experience, any knowledge of military tactics,
as to who should be the commander-in-chief on these occasions, and bitter feuds frequently followed Militia or Training
Day on account of the election of the commandant. The
commander-in-chief was usually elected by the company or
companies who belonged to the militia. Every one was glad
when the day closed without personal difficulties or collision
between the factions of the eligibles to the enviable position
of generalissimo. Late in the evening, exhausted by the heat
and fatigues of the day, they repaired to their homes to
discuss the glories of the display, and their individual experiences and opinions of the thrilling episodes that had occurred
during the momentous twenty-four hours.

No member of any family was left at home on Training
Day, as it would have been an evidence of unpardonable indifference to the future of the country. The female members
took special pride in the part their lords and masters had in
the mimic manœuvres. They prepared splendid feasts, which

were spread picnic-fashion under shady trees then adjacent to all villages and towns. At high noon everything was suspended for an hour in which to enjoy the feast.

The Fourth of July, Independence Day, was the occasion of all occasions for jubilation and patriotic demonstrations. There were mimic military parades, firing of cannon, hoisting of flags, orations setting forth the deeds of valor of our ancestors in achieving American independence, barbecues, and feasts for the multitude. Dancing in the evening and all manner of demonstrations illustrative of the freedom and the happiness of the people were in order.

After the harvest and garnering of the grain came Thanksgiving, observed always by a feast. Everything that flies in the air, swims in the sea, grows out of the ground, or upon tree or vine, contributed to the abundance laid upon the table for the Thanksgiving dinner. In almost every home family parties gathered together to utter their gratitude to a bountiful Providence, and to feast upon the good things set before them. It must be confessed that there was sometimes indulgence beyond the proprieties.

But the holiday of all the year was blessed Christmas-tide, extending from Christmas to and including New Year's Day. For weeks before parents and children would lay aside, with scrupulous care and great secrecy, all they could for Christmas; and none was so poor as to be indifferent to the influence of the pretty custom of remembering loved ones with some token at Christmas.

We have watched the simple folk in their preparations for this day with moistened eyes, because of the touch of heavenly love that pervaded all their efforts. They little knew themselves how much of the love divine was portrayed in their vigilant efforts and tender care to obtain something with which to gladden the heart of some one of their cherished circle. From the sturdy, thrifty father and patient, tireless mother to the generous, loving children, all were busy with plans and schemes to get the most and the best their scant stores could afford for Christmas morning, when, at early dawn, "Merry Christmas!" resounded through their homes.

We have seen children gathering nuts and carefully hiding them away; drying pop-corn ready to be popped white for the feast; selecting and putting away in the loft bright-red apples, to be given Christmas morning to father, mother, sisters, brothers, and friends. We have watched them awaken from their fitful slumbers, impatient to see what their gifts might be. Their fond mothers had perchance tucked them in their beds the night before with aching hearts, because they hardly knew how to provide satisfactory surprises for the early greetings of beloved children. Many a time these same devoted mothers have lighted the fire, and, while the children slept, have made sweet dough and cut with their dexterous hands "Jim Crows," elephants, horses, cows, dogs, cats, and every device that could be called an image of a man, beast, or bird, baked them and slipped them into the stockings of the little ones. These, ignorant of the latter-day sweetmeats and bonbons, were as happy to find the crude imitations of animate objects as if they had found the most dainty delicacies. In a brief time thereafter the children would devour the men and the menagerie with the avidity of veritable cannibals, all the while making merry with their happy songs and talk.

In families better situated in life, by dint of industry for days and weeks before, useful and ornamental presents were gathered together. Slippers, gloves, mufflers, and lap-robes were fashioned by mothers, wives, sweethearts, and daughters for fathers, brothers, husbands, and beaux; while these manly fellows were generous and thoughtful for those who loved them so dearly. The poor in every community were not neglected, but came in for turkeys, rare viands, and clothing.

The merchants in small towns were the only ones who dreaded the Christmas holidays, because of the troops of

children, some of them in their teens, going from shop to
shop crying: "Christmas gift! Merry Christmas!" and
expecting something from each merchant. Marbles, toys,
confections, ribbons, and trinkets were given sometimes,
greatly to the loss of profit by the proprietors. This custom,
through the increase of population, became such an intolerable nuisance that it had to be discontinued.

The tree was an important factor in the preparation for
celebrating the advent of Christmas. A fine evergreen, of
which there were giant specimens in the primeval forests
that surrounded every town and hamlet, was cut down and
brought to the largest private house, or to the church. It
was put in place in a box or mound, which held it firmly.
This foundation was covered with green boughs, or something representing grass. The decorations consisted of dried
grasses, tinsel thread, pop-corn strung on string, red and yellow berries gathered in the fall from the berry-bearing trees
in the forest, oranges, apples, lemons, and every variety of
bright-colored chenille and knitting-yarn.

If the tree was in a home, every member of the family, on
Christmas Eve, brought to the home their gifts, all wrapped
up and marked for the persons for whom they were intended.
Early Christmas morning, every one interested, including the
servants, assembled. The oldest man in the family was
dressed up in cotton batting or furs, and, wearing a mask
and a fur cap, played Santa Claus. When all were ready,
some one played a Christmas carol. Then Santa Claus, scis-
sors in hand, proceeded to cut off the presents from the tree,
and distribute them as they were addressed. The exclamations of delight with which the recipients received each parcel rings in my ears as I recall those happy occasions. After
every one had displayed his gifts, a sumptuous breakfast was
announced, and again all was merriment.

If the tree was in the church, the whole town joined in.
Every man, woman, and child was remembered and some-

thing provided for each out of the fund collected. The ministers announced the hour when all were expected to be present. They prepared an appropriate programme of recitations and carols, and closed with a benediction. For months good cheer and happiness seemed to follow such fitting observance of the anniversary of the birth of our Saviour.

A round of sleighing-parties, balls, candy-pullings, dinner-parties, and merrymaking consumed the whole time from Christmas Eve until January 2. Christmas Day was set apart for religious service, when the churches were decorated with evergreens and all the flowers possible to obtain. Among the vicious or lawless people it was a season of debauchery; tramping about over the neighborhood they went shooting, drinking, and yelling like heathen, whose pagan festivals were once observed during the winter season. The custom of decorating the homes seems to have been as old as time, and, in the scarcity of flowers in that climate, careful housewives used to gather and press the autumn leaves and grasses when they were in their glory, and then arrange them so effectively that they supplied every deficiency.

With me the memory of the Christmas holidays of my girlhood will ever be one of the most sacred and sweet of my life—from the larks of the school-children, when I was one of them, in barring in or out the teacher till he or she gave us a holiday and a treat, to the blessed Christmas morning, when we all flew into father's and mother's room screaming "Merry Christmas!" to find the thirteen pairs of well-filled stockings hanging round the broad old fireplace, and to receive the warm embraces of those revered and indulgent parents. I can never forget the happy time that followed in displaying our treasures, and in coming to the table to see father and mother open the numberless packages which we used to prepare for them. The hours we brothers and sisters spent in executing our surprises for father, mother, and each other, with the merry episodes, mishaps, successes, and pleasures, will cling to me evermore. The madcap fun that we used to have, sleigh-riding with the troops of boys and girls who were our friends; the overturning of the sleighs; the scrambling to pick ourselves up, and the hurrying and scurrying to get home all right for fear of the disapproval of father and mother! The merry dancing and candy-pulling, when, with ropes of candy, we used to lariat some favorite school-boy friend, and threaten his execution with the sweet cord, for some boyish prank he had played! How well I remember the sparkling wood-fire in the ample old fireplace, with rows of apples toasting before it, the great dishes of pop-corn, so white and fresh and tender, as it always is when popped in a covered kettle; the sweet, rich nuts and the amber cider for the evenings when we assembled in each others' homes for a good time, and to play games of forfeit and chance! For genuine pleasure, those times have never been surpassed by the stately occasions of maturer years, and, more than once, my heart has longed for a reversion of time, and a return of those happy days.

The churches were few, some denominations, notably the Baptist and the Methodist, having only monthly meetings, beginning on Saturday and sometimes continuing for two or three days and even longer, but always until and including Sunday night. Persons from all over the country attended these meetings, coming great distances on horseback, in wagons, or in any other kind of conveyance at their command, and frequently on foot. In such instances the care of the shoes was the first consideration. Men and women would walk barefooted until near the church, when they would sit down and put on their shoes and stockings in order to appear properly dressed on their arrival at church. Every one seemed to have some pride, and worked hard all the time in order to appear as well as possible, and to accumulate property and establish good homes. The claim that one generation accumulates for the next to spend has been exemplified in many instances among these worthy people, who struggled all their lives and passed away, expecting that their children would emulate their example. Unfortunately, the second generations have neither the energy nor the thrift to add to, or even to keep, their inheritance, and strangers now possess the homes of their ancestors. In August or September camp-meetings were held, always of two weeks' duration. Some denominations owned a tract of land in a good neighborhood. Here, different members of the congregation built log houses. Sometimes a series of these one-story log houses, now denominated bungalows, belonged to the more wealthy of the assembly. Into these the families moved, taking beds, bedding, cooking utensils, crockery, table linen, and everything necessary for a comfortable sojourn in the woods. Large quantities of supplies were provided, including pickles, sweetmeats, honey, delicious butter, hams, vegetables, the best bread, and everything those dear mothers in Israel used to know so well how to prepare.

Around a great square of ground, like the barracks of a military post, these long rows of log houses were built. In the centre was a large tabernacle or mammoth pavilion, which was nothing more than a spacious roof supported by strong columns made from the trunks of giant trees. Every inch of the space beneath was seated like a church, except that the seats were benches without backs. At the east end of these pavilions was a broad pulpit. Here services were held daily for two weeks. The morning meeting began at nine o'clock with an intermission of half an hour at ten o'clock, and rarely closing before twelve-thirty. In the afternoon at three o'clock there was another meeting, and the evening service started at seven and never ended before eleven o'clock at night. Great revivals attended these meetings, and, doubtless, many people were converted and thereafter led better lives; and yet it now seems incredible that intelligent people could have been impressed by the illiterate sermons and riotous services that often characterized the "protracted camp-meetings."

As a youthful participant, my sympathies were always deeply aroused for the poor women who were the hostesses on these occasions. Multitudes came from every quarter, and many times, as a child, I have wondered if some of the ministers would or could perform the miracle of the loaves and fishes, to feed the hungry legions who congregated around the tables of the much-imposed-upon householders. For months beaux saved up their best clothes, and the belles their choicest finery, for camp-meeting. The best horses in the whole region were pampered and groomed so that they could be ridden to camp-meeting, as if they were to be exhibited at a county fair. On Sundays the townspeople as well as those in the country, all went carrying great baskets filled with eatables, as if going to a picnic, and, after listening to the ten-thirty o'clock service, groups of people could be seen sitting all around under the trees, feasting and enjoying themselves as on a holiday excursion. They would then wander up and down the banks of the stream of water—a requisite of an eligible site for camp-meeting grounds—or visit at the different camps. They started to return to the pavilion at the sound of the horn for three o'clock service. If disinclined to attend a second service, they continued to stroll about enjoying the beauties of nature. Under such favorable auspices, the young people frequently indulged in flirtations, as it was difficult to resist temptations of this character with such an environment. Innumerable weddings generally followed camp-meetings. Whether this was the outcome of dwelling together in love and harmony, or whether they did not give themselves time at any other season to cultivate the affairs of the heart, I do not know. Sometimes it rained in torrents, and the discomforts the people endured were indescribable, and were enough to dampen the ardor of the most devoted lover or religious enthusiast. There are persons to-day, however, who look back upon these occasions and the associations around them with sacred reverence and hallowed memories.

Sometimes the ministers who conducted the services were very able men and devout Christians, who felt that to worship God in the temple of nature was the highest privilege that could be given mortals, and some of their sermons were real inspirations. Reverend Doctor Bascom, of Kentucky, the friend of Henry Clay, was one of the most eloquent divines I ever heard. It was never necessary to request quiet attention of the vast congregations which assembled on an intimation that he was to preach. Spellbound they sat and listened to him, and were always deeply moved by the sublimity of his eloquence. If the sermons were not of divine inspiration they were from a mind and heart of finer mould than is often seen in this age of better opportunities of speakers and preachers.

It is told of Doctor Bascom that, after he was made chaplain of the Senate, through the influence of Henry Clay, he was so much elated over the elevation to the position that his first sermon was a failure. Mr. Clay was much chagrined, but in no sense felt the keen mortification which Mr. Bascom himself experienced. He returned to his lodgings, and prostrated himself in earnest prayer to be forgiven for his vainglorious attempt to preach with "Mr. Bascom" uppermost in his mind. In the afternoon Mr. Clay sought his friend, feeling great solicitude lest he were ill as the solution of the fiasco. As soon as he entered Mr. Bascom's apartments, the minister came forward to greet him cordially, saying: "My friend, I know what brings you here. I know how completely I failed in my sermon this morning. I was preaching Mr. Bascom in all his glory, but wait until next Sunday, and I will preach Jesus Christ crucified, and you will have no cause to blush for me." And he fully redeemed his promise.

The gigantic form of Elder Heap looms up before me as I

look back through the veil of tears and time that has shut
out those familiar scenes. He was one of nature's noblemen,
and did the work of his Master most effectively.

Father Thatcher, that learned and eccentric Methodist divine, whose rugged character was reflected in a most remarkable physiognomy and physique, was another of that wonderful phalanx of men who preached and prayed and worked for
the church in those days.

Father Thatcher was always so absorbed with some theo-
logical question or in the study of the Bible which he invariably carried with him (and generally in his hand), that he
used to do some very funny things in his absent-minded way.
On one occasion he was attending quarterly meeting, and was
stopping with a good brother of the church near by. He had
ridden his old white horse, which he insisted should be turned
into a pasture. The horse got out and wandered off. Notwithstanding the fact that they all hunted for him, the old
white horse could not be found by the boys of his host's family. Father Thatcher had to preach that day, so he forgot
all about his horse being gone until, just as he was closing
his sermon, he saw the animal pass the church-door, going
down the road. Without finishing the sentence he was uttering, he called out: "Whoa, Gray! whoa, Gray!" and down
from the puplit and down the aisle, out at the door he ran,
calling "Whoa! stop, Gray!" until he reached the horse; then,
taking him by the mane, he led him to Brother Marvel's stable,
without remembering to go back and finish his sermon and
close the service. For some time the whole congregation indulged in roars of laughter, until a good brother, taking in
the situation, stepped into the pulpit and pronounced the
benediction. On another occasion, as Father Thatcher was
walking along the street, through the open door of a comfortable home he saw a good mother and daughters sitting sewing. He walked in, and they arose to greet him, but, without going through any ceremony, he dropped on his knees,

saying: "Let us pray." In kneeling, he turned around so that his face was toward the door. The family hurried to get on their knees. While he was praying fervently for them, opening his eyes and looking out of the door, he saw a person passing whom he wished to engage to do some work at the church. Calling him by name, he said, "Hold on there, I want to see you," and, suiting the action to the word, went out at the door and walked down the street with him. He did not finish his prayer, or again return, but left the family as much amazed at his abrupt departure as they had been at his call. Often, when his family were not on the lookout to tell him to come into the house on his return from appointments on his circuit, he would sit for hours in his buggy in front of his own door, where his faithful old gray had halted, absorbed in his Bible, oblivious to sunshine or storm, or to where he was. Once he lost his pocket-knife, which he used continually to sharpen his pencil, with which he made copious notes on the fly-leaves and margins of the books or Bible he happened to be reading. In closing his sermon one day with the following favorite stanza:

"Refining fire go through my soul,
    Scatter thy life through every part
And sanctify the whole,"

he called out with almost the same breath: "If any of you have found a six-bladed penknife, it is mine, and I hope you will bring it to me."

He always stopped with some member of his congregation in making his rounds. He appeared at the hour he chose, without any previous notice, announcing the moment of his arrival that he was hungry, or otherwise, and the hour he was due at the church, so that his host would know what he expected. His wonderful ability and marvellous understanding of the Scriptures drew about him large congregations of interested listeners.

The great debate between Campbell and Rice made the deepest impression upon the whole country, and caused a division in the Baptist denomination, and the organization of the Campbellite Baptist Church. Of this there were very many adherents in southern Illinois, my mother and father being among the number. In fact, at one time this church had many communicants in Kentucky, Illinois, Indiana, and Ohio. President Garfield was a minister of that branch of the Baptist Church.

The ministrations and labors of these early Christian preachers were not in vain, and no locality in any State has to-day better churches or more devout Christians than has that section, which was once the field of itinerants and without many spires pointing heavenward.

The constant demands upon old and young for manual labor left little time for the schools; therefore no attempt to have schools more than a few months in the year was made. They were, however, public-spirited people, and southern Illinois came in for her share of teachers sent out by the governor of Massachusetts at the request of the Western States in the early fifties. I owe a debt of gratitude to one of them for her faithful training when I was very young. The august "Board" who examined these teachers were the finest specimens of the "broad and comprehensive" type so graphically described by Mark Twain. Miss C. amused my good-natured father excessively by a description of her experience before the "School Board." Among other things I remember she was asked: "Which is the largest river in the world?" To this she replied: "The Amazon." Her interrogator frowned severely upon her, and asked: "Miss, what are you gwine to do with the Massassippi?" With consummate tact she quickly said: "I beg your pardon, I misunderstood your question. If you asked which is the largest river in the United States, the Mississippi, of course, and I am obliged for your kindness in correcting me." His vanity was satisfied, and she was voted the school, but not without another poser from one of the profound gentlemen. "Miss, is there anything impossible with God?" She replied: "Nothing." He rejoined: "Well, now, I would like to know how God or anybody else could put two mountains side by side without a valley between them!" She was warned not to "waste all your time over your books and a-larnin' the children, but get some of the wimmen where you stay to learn you to cook, and how to do something useful." She was a bright, pretty girl of twenty, of just the spirit to be thrown among these good-hearted people; and, before the term was out, she had captured the affections of every one, and was regarded as a veritable Minerva, not only by her pupils, but by everybody with whom she came in contact. She was the leader in all amusements and everything which tended to improve and cultivate the people. After a few years of effective work, she married one of the leading physicians of the community, and reared an interesting family who are much beloved because of their mother.

There were ambitious parents who sent their children away from home to school or employed teachers from the East to reside in the family and train the children. I have thought sometimes that these children with poor advantages accomplished more than some of the children of the present, who have had "education made easy." A people so heroic have kept pace with the march of time, and to-day every facility is offered for education in that community. Fine schoolhouses and good normal-school teachers are in every school district, their average scholarship being second to none in any of the States. They have nobly borne their part in carrying the burdens of church and state. On their country's roll of honor there are many familiar names of my youthful companions who, notwithstanding the vicissitudes and embarrassments that attended their earlier years, have arisen to distinction and leadership among the men and women of their day and generation. Magnificent, up-to-date schoolhouses, with all the modern appliances for the various departments, have taken the place of the log schoolhouses, with the cracks between the logs chinked with pieces of wood and plastered over with mortar or clay, to keep out the cold in winter. The puncheon floors have been relegated to the wood-pile, to be succeeded by hardwood or tile floors. Fine desks, with chairs attached, have succeeded the puncheon benches, relieving the children from the agony of sitting on high, backless benches, with their feet dangling inches above the floor. On dark days, and in the evenings when lectures or entertainments are given, electricity or gas floods the school-room with light, displacing the "tallow dips" and oil-lamps which were so inadequate that there was no alternative but to dismiss the school if the clouds obscured the sun.

Many ambitious students of that time did as Mr. Lincoln did—gathered up old boards and pieces of wood which had resinous deposits, saving them carefully to burn judiciously in a fireplace, thus furnishing light by which to see to read at night. It was no uncommon thing to see grown men and women lying flat on the floor to enable them to see by the blaze of the burning boards.

The majority were unable to read and write, some learning to write their signatures by copying them repeatedly—after they had been written for them—until they could sign their names to important documents. One dear old man by the name of Harper, who was quite wealthy, accomplished this feat, though he knew no other letters of the alphabet. Soon afterward he was asked by a friend to indorse his note, which he did. His friend defaulted on the note and Mr. Harper had to pay it. He was much outraged, and declared he was sorry he ever learned to write his name, and he could never be induced to write it again for fear of incurring obligations, saying he preferred to make his "mark."

# CHAPTER II

THE Mexican War of 1847–8 afforded many an opportunity to prove their patriotism and give vent to their adventurous inclinations. Communication with Washington was very lim- ited, but when it was found that volunteers were called for, as war had been declared with Mexico, astonishing numbers rushed into the towns to try to get on the rolls. I can just remember seeing my father borne aloft above the heads of the men who elected him captain of the company. He had enlisted to serve three years, or until peace was declared. He had been sheriff of the county, and probably was the most popular man in Williamson County. The moment he an- nounced his intention of going many more than he could enroll volunteered to go with him. The town of Marion, where we lived, was on that day thronged with people. As soon as the roster of a company was complete the men elected my father captain by acclamation. They seized him, and, to the music of a fife and drum, they hoisted him above their heads, and carried him around the court-house, shouting and huzzaing, regardless of his attempts to be put down. I remember how, on hearing the noise and music, my mother went to the door. Seeing father in his elevated position, she knew what it all meant and began to cry, while we children gazed wild-eyed, first at father and then at mother's tearful face, wondering what it was all about. As soon as father could get away, he came home to tell mother he was going to Mexico. All was commotion in the home for many days following. Father's company was made Company B, 1st Regiment, Illinois Infantry Volunteers. He was ordered to march his company to Alton, Illinois, where the regiment was to rendezvous. I shall never forget the pathetic scenes which occurred the day they left Marion to begin their long march, which ended in Santa Fe, New Mexico. The wives, daughters, and sweethearts of the one hundred and ten men came into town to say their good-bys. The morning was spent in the final preparations. After a twelve-o'clock dinner, at the sound of the drum and fife, the men stepped in line, and at father's command, "Forward, march!" they moved off like veteran soldiers, leaving aching hearts and tearful eyes behind them.

Arriving at Alton, father found his old friend and legislative colleague, Captain Hampton, of Jackson County, in command of Company H of the 1st Regiment. Father's men were from the counties adjoining Williamson. Captain Hampton's first lieutenant was John A. Logan, of Jackson County. My father was extremely fond of young Logan, as he was full of fun, of a genial disposition, brave as a lion, and delighted in adventure. An intimacy soon sprang up between my father and the young officers, especially young Logan, which grew stronger when, years after their return, Lieutenant Logan demanded that father should redeem his promise to give me to him as his bride.

I have often heard father and General Logan give thrilling accounts of their experiences in crossing the Great American

Desert on foot; of being chased by the Indians, the tortures of hunger, their devouring thirst while marching along the banks of the alkali streams, the waters of which they dared not drink. They were both deeply grieved that they did not reach their destination until too late to participate in any of the engagements of the Mexican War.

They had returned but a short time before the marvellous stories of the discovering of gold in California were started. Desirous of further adventure, many of those who had been to Mexico were wild to repeat their long march across the plains to California, my father among them. In the early spring of 1849 these daring spirits again assembled at Alton, Illinois, to join an overland train for Sacramento, California.

The season was dry, and the grass was very scarce and unusually short; hence but one-third of the party and but very few of the animals survived the three months they spent in making the long journey. The graves of their comrades marked the route they had taken over the Rocky Mountains and across the trackless desert. Then followed another three months of waiting before my father's letters reached us. I can to this day in imagination hear the sound of the long horn the stage-driver used to blow as he entered our town at the midnight hour twice a week. An old friend was postmaster, and would always open the mail to see if there were letters from California. I was then but twelve years of age, and yet at the first sound of the horn, in moonlight or darkness, I would rush out and never stop running till I reached the post-office, which was the residence of the postmaster. Sometimes I used to be almost frightened out of my wits by the bluff old driver, who would insist upon talking to me. In winter he wore an overcoat made of buffalo-skins and, to my childish eyes, looked as terrible as that animal. After weeks and months of anxiety and disappointment, at last the postmaster handed me letters for mother and myself. It seemed to me I never ran so swiftly before. Mother was almost overcome,

as she read page after page of father's graphic stories of all
that had taken place since he left us; of his disappointments
and successes; of the legions of seekers after gold from every
country on the globe; of his longing to return home and his
tender messages to us children.  No such long intervals between his letters again occurred, as the mails from California
subsequently came by sea around the Horn.  He remained
two and a half years, reaching home in 1853, soon after
Franklin Pierce's inauguration.

Shortly after father's return home he was appointed by President Pierce registrar of the land office at Shawneetown, Illinois.  It was an important appointment, on account of the
passage by Congress of the "Bit Act," which meant that actual settlers inside the radius of the district of which Shawneetown was the headquarters could enter one hundred and
sixty acres of land, at twelve and one-half cents per acre.  As
the time was limited for such entries, it was necessary for
father to assume the duties of the office as soon as possible.
We removed to Shawneetown, and father opened the land office
on the first floor of the large house he was able to secure as a
residence.  It was on the main street, which ran along the
banks of the Ohio River.  He had little leisure from his first
day as registrar.

The question as to where I was to be sent to school was
soon settled.  Father took me to Saint Vincent's Academy
near Morganfield, Kentucky.  Saint Vincent's was a branch
of the celebrated Nazareth Convent of Kentucky.  It was
then, and still is, one of the best schools in the whole country.  In the community where I had always lived there were
few Catholics, and no churches, monks, nuns, or priests.  I
was totally ignorant of the ceremonies and symbols of the
church and of the significance of the costumes worn by the
priests and nuns, and had consequently much to learn that was
not in the curriculum of the school.  I was in my fifteenth
year, but had had more experience in the realities of life than

many older girls on account of being the eldest of a large family, for whom mother and I had to care during father's absence in Mexico, and subsequently in California.

I can never forget the tremor which seized me when father and I entered the convent grounds. I saw the nuns walking about in their flaring white caps of the Order of Saint Vincent's, and their sombre black gowns. The priest, Father Durbin, was in his garden, walking up and down bareheaded, saying his prayers. The church was built in the form of a cross, and was gray with age. One arm of the cross was the convent and the other Father Durbin's home and study. The large cross over the front apex impressed me as being probably the one upon which our Saviour was crucified. Under the interlacing branches of the grand old trees we walked up to the entrance of the convent, my limbs shaking with fright. For once I was silent, as I could not have spoken had my life depended upon it. The bars and grates of the doors and windows suggested incarceration to my unsophisticated mind.

In answer to father's ring the angelic face of a sister appeared at the little grated panel in the door, and, upon father's announcing his name, she quickly unlocked the door and invited us into the parlor. Under the influence of her gentle manner and the immaculate appointment of the room, together with the bright wood-fire in the fireplace, I began to feel less frightened. After seating us, the sister withdrew to call the sister superior. Before Sister Isabella came in, I had scanned the pictures of Christ on the Cross, Saint Anthony, and other saints on the walls; admired the pretty rag carpet, old mahogany furniture, and literally everything in the parlor, down to the fine old brass andirons and fender. In a few moments Sister Isabella came in. She was short and very stout, had a jolly face, and the cordial greeting so important in a mother superior. She drew me close to her, and, in a voice of tenderness, welcomed me as one of her girls. I soon forgot my terror, and thought her cap and gown especially becoming to her.

After luncheon father completed all the arrangements for my remaining for the school year of nine months and took his leave, while I, with tearful eyes, was led by Sister Isabella into the convent proper, and introduced to some of the older girls, who acted as hostesses to the new arrivals. At first I was very homesick, but soon forgot my unhappiness surrounded by light-hearted companions and the good, kind sisters who were ever ready to comfort and cajole the homesick and unhappy.

To have any idea of the conditions at Saint Vincent's in 1854–5, it would be necessary to turn back the leaves of time for more than fifty years, and to realize that scarcely a single advantage which the pupils at Saint Vincent's now enjoy then existed. We were literally pioneers, and the opportunities we had were of the most primitive character; but, underlying them all was the lovely spirit of devotion, purity, and tenderness of the dear sisters, which made the simplest exercises beautiful and attractive.

In those days we had the cabins of the slaves in the rear of the main buildings of the school. I remember very distinctly some of the pranks in which Sallie Cotton, the Van Landinghams, the Cunninghams, the Lunsfords, the Spauldings, Annie Casey, Mollie Poole, Josie Goddard, Mary Kuykendall, myself, and a host of happy, unaffected, sweet girls indulged. We used to take our finery and deck out the pickaninnies and mammies in harlequin colors, and enjoyed seeing them sally forth to attend parties, religious meetings, and to make visits among their colored friends.

Memory brings back incidents in the lives of these slaves that are as vivid as if I had witnessed them yesterday. Nearly, if not all, of the negroes belonged to the slaveholders in the neighborhood. Among them was Uncle Harry, the overseer's best hand on the big farm connected with the convent. His wife, Aunt Agnes, was the head cook for the girls. We all loved Aunt Agnes, who slipped many dainties to her favorites. She and Uncle Harry had four or five little children. Her old master died, and the sons who inherited the slaves were reckless. They sold Aunt Agnes to some "slave-traders," who visited that part of Kentucky, picking up "likely niggers" to take them to the New Orleans market. Great excitement followed. Uncle Harry rebelled; the sisters pleaded with the buyers to let them keep her, but they heeded nothing. They came with a sort of grocery wagon, seized Aunt Agnes, tied, and bore her away. She fought them like a tigress and screamed as loud as she could. The children screamed and cried so that the girls discovered what was going on, and, before the sisters could stop them, they rushed out to rescue Aunt Agnes. Seeing them come pell-mell, the brutal men grabbed hold of her and tried to bandage her mouth. The sisters could not bear to hear her cries, and they, too, joined in the pleas for mercy for the poor, innocent creature who was being torn away from her husband and family. The men ordered the driver to whip up the horses, and they galloped away, Agnes's piteous cries reaching us above the clatter of the horses' feet. Sister Isabella led us into the church to pray for Agnes, while the tears were streaming down the cheeks of sisters and girls.

Uncle Harry was never the same. He was sullen and insubordinate to the overseer, who, he thought, had something to do with the sale of Agnes. Soon afterward he and the overseer had some trouble over something which the overseer had ordered Uncle Harry to do. The overseer struck Uncle Harry with a blacksnake whip, whereupon Uncle Harry went at the overseer with an axe, and came near decapitating him. From being one of the most docile, respectful negroes, Uncle Harry had become a veritable demon. Hearing the *mêlée*, Sister Isabella ran out to try to restrain Harry. He told her to go into the house; that he would not touch her, but he must be let alone. Our classroom was near Sister Isabella's office and study, and, hearing the loud talking, we ran out to see what the trouble was. I can never forget what a very demon incarnate Uncle Harry looked, as he stood there in a threatening attitude, every muscle tense, and his wild eyes on the alert for a sight of the overseer. We were, of course, frightened, but knew Uncle Harry would do anything for us because of our kindness to "Aggie," as he called his wife. Two or three of us walked up to him, and, taking hold of his hands, led him to his cabin, promising him that we would get Sister Isabella and Father Durbin to send the overseer away. We bathed his old black back with warm water, and Sister Genevieve brought soft linen cloths and soothing lotions to bind up the wounds made by the whip. Sister Isabella persuaded him to go to bed and stay in his cabin all day. The overseer was glad enough to take flight, and quiet was restored.

We engaged in frolics like most boys and girls who go away from home to school. Three or four of us used to take chances; sometimes they were rather hazardous. One of the graduates of my first year at school married during vacation and was a widow before we returned to school in September, her husband having been killed by an accident. She was a devout Catholic; he a Protestant, and could not, therefore, be buried in the consecrated ground of the cemetery which was near the church. The cemetery was enclosed by a zig-zag fence, and she had him buried in one of the outside corners of the fence. They made a rail pen over his grave. We Protestant girls thought it a shame that he should be outside, so, one night when we thought Father Durbin was away visiting the churches under his jurisdiction, we went up to the cemetery. Taking the rails that made the pen, we added another panel, which let the poor fellow's grave inside the sacred grounds. We were mistaken about Father Durbin's being away, and, in the morning, going out to walk, he discovered what had been done. He instituted an investigation, determined to punish the perpetrators of such an outrage. He counted without his host, and failed to find the culprits. He became satisfied the negroes did not do the mischief, but never thought of accusing the girls and finally concluded that it was the work of heretics, of whom there were many in the community. He made the negroes take down our fence and restore the pen over the outsider's grave. We kept still and escaped suspicion, waiting for an auspicious occasion to repeat the adventure. One Saturday night we again extended the fence and took the grave inside. Sunday morning when the people came to early mass and saw what had been done they were highly indignant, and were sure the Protestants in the neighborhood had done the shocking deed. Members of the congregation turned detectives, and sentinels were posted to watch for the marauders. We were afraid to attempt our experiment again, and were, therefore, obliged to let our friend's husband continue his eternal sleep in unhallowed ground. Years afterward I confessed to Father Durbin who the heretics were, and the dear old man insisted he suspected us all the time; but, as we were pretty good girls with all our faults, he granted us absolution. The sisters were shocked; but, as we had all turned out very well, they pardoned us, but prayed us never to tell that we could do such a thing with one of them watching over us all the time.

I remember that on one May-day all the girls got themselves up in their best clothes and escorted Sister Isabella to quite a high place up in the forest opposite the academy. Here we had built a throne, and, putting her on it, we crowned her the "Queen of the May" with so much enjoyment that we were all extremely happy. I can picture now how she looked sitting on her green throne in her uniform. A crown of flowers decked her cap, and a long rope of flowers hung around her neck and about her unsylphlike waist, with long ends hanging down the sides. We had made her a sceptre by twining flowers around a stick. This she wielded with much dexterity, directing the rendering of the programme of songs, recitations, and original poems, which we had prepared for the occasion. Sue Fletcher was a born poetess and had written a long poem which caused much merriment among us; Sister Isabella laughed as heartily over it as any of the girls. After sundown, we escorted her with mock solemnity back to the refectory, where she had ordered for us a lovely supper. It was truly a happy May-day.

We used to exercise by taking long walks in the woods; in the spring gathering flowers, in the fall gathering nuts. We hoarded up large quantities of nuts for the winter, as well as pop-corn and apples. We had many feasts on holidays and on stormy days, when we were not allowed to go out. We popped the corn, roasted the apples, cracked the nuts, and spent our time in feasting. These refreshments were often served at our impromptu dances on Saturday night, when Uncle Harry and his friend Jim played the fiddle for the girls to dance. We passed around the hat, and, I think, paid them the munificent sum of fifty cents apiece for music furnished for an evening's entertainment. Of course, we never danced until the "wee sma' hours," as they do in the present day, because taps were sounded not later than ten-thirty. Soon after the lights were out, and we were fast asleep, as few of us had any cares or anxieties to keep us awake after retiring.

I often recall the long dormitory with our beds side by side, and dear Sister Lucy at the end with her bed, table, and books, curtained off by white curtains. She was always within call of the girls of the dormitory. We were not saints, and we gave the dear sisters a good deal of trouble, like all mischievous, healthy, active girls have done since Mother Eve created a disturbance in the Garden of Eden.

Transportation being very difficult in those days, many of us spent our holidays at the academy, and employed our time in embroidering, knitting, repairing our clothes, and sometimes in feasting and dancing. We were allowed to go into the parlor to be introduced to the parents of the girls who came to visit them, and on these occasions we were coached as to the manner of entering the room, saluting the guests, and how to withdraw without betraying awkwardness. Sister Isabella gave us periodical lectures, especially if any of the girls had been guilty of violation of the rules of the academy. We used to enjoy the Sundays. After service we would go out on the lawn or to the window to watch the people who came to church at Saint Vincent's. Some of them were on horseback, some on foot, and others in every conceivable kind of vehicle of those early days. I remember, as if it had occurred yesterday, the visit of Bishop Spaulding and the great "to-do" that we made of his coming to Saint Vincent's. We all kissed his ring, and thought it was the greatest event of our lives. He of course made an address, which is supposed to have had a great influence over us, but I am afraid we did not remember long the many injunctions he laid upon us.

In those halcyon days, in addition to our studies and school drudgery, girls of sixteen and upward had to make their own clothes, including a graduation dress of sheer, fine muslin, together with the slip to wear under it. All this was made by hand, which meant many hours of careful sewing after school hours, on Saturdays and holidays (forgive the term, under such circumstances). They not only had to make their own clothes, but had to assist the sisters in making the white dresses for the ten or a dozen orphans whom the sisters had on their hands to clothe and educate. Good-natured, jolly Sister Superior Isabella would journey by water to Louisville, Kentucky, to buy the material for the dresses, together with many bolts of blue ribbon for sashes and bow-knots, which every girl was obliged to wear on commencement day. This was the one occasion of all the year when we laid aside our purple calico and white-apron uniforms. These, on May 1 annually, took the place of the black alpaca ones which we wore in winter.

The last few days before graduation day were bewildering with the multiplicity of things that had to be done at the last moment—final recitations for the elocutionists, rehearsals for the musicians, and the last reading of compositions which we innocently believed would startle the literary world if they could only appear in print.

I recall vividly the difficulties we had in preparing our final essays. "Fame" was my theme, and, as I read it a year or two ago, it sounded amateurish. I felt very proud of it then, and doubted seriously if any author had ever written so fine a production, as, after Sister Lucy had corrected it many times and I had rewritten it, incorporating her corrections, it seemed to me nothing could be more perfect. I remember the difficulty I had in getting a quill pen and selecting paper that was good enough, on which to inscribe this wonderful production. When completed, the essay was tied with pink ribbons, and every one was kind enough to say that it was one of the best. In the more than fifty years which have passed since I struggled over that composition I have discovered:

> "What so foolish as the chase of fame?
> How vain the prize! how impotent our aim!
> For, what are men who grasp at praise sublime,
> But bubbles floating on the stream of time?"

Memory carries me back to that bright morning in June, 1855, when our class graduated from dear old Saint Vincent's, when beneath the boughs of the majestic trees of the lawn a large platform had been erected and covered with a bright-green carpet. A fine piano was on one side, while a suitable place was arranged for the bishop and priests who were to distribute the diplomas, medals, and prizes. Seats were also arranged for the parents and visitors who attended. After a long programme of music, addresses, giving of diplomas, awards, and a benediction by the bishop, we marched to the long refectory, where a sumptuous repast was spread and enjoyed by all.

Trunks and belongings had all been packed, and we were not long in donning our travelling-dresses, and saying good-by to the sisters and members of the household of our Alma Mater. Youth is so full of spirit that our tears were soon dried, and we were all happy in returning to our homes and friends, to begin building castles in the air for the future, as girls are wont to do.

During my absence at school John A. Logan, mentioned as serving in the same regiment with my father, Captain John M. Cunningham, of the 1st Illinois Volunteer Infantry, came to Shawneetown, Gallatin County, Illinois, where we then resided. He was the prosecuting attorney of the third judicial district, and was obliged to attend the sessions of the circuit court. He was not long in renewing his acquaintance with my father, or in reminding father that he still expected him to redeem his promise, made while they were soldiering in Mexico, to give Logan his daughter Mary in marriage when she was old enough. Soon after I reached home father said he had made an engagement for me to meet young Logan, who was coming to Shawneetown to make a visit at our home. Having many young-men friends and associates of my own age, it never occurred to me that any one was likely to think of me seriously. Believing the visit to be intended for my father, I paid little attention to father's message. I was therefore greatly surprised when Mr. Logan put in his appearance, and assured me that his visit was intended for me. Though but seventeen, I began to realize that I was considered a young lady, and that my happy-go-lucky days were over. Notwithstanding the fact that Prosecuting Attorney Logan had to travel over sixteen counties which composed the judicial district, every two weeks found him in Shawneetown for a stay from Saturday noon until Sunday night, when he was obliged to leave and drive all night over very bad roads to be present at the opening of court on Monday. I had my share of attention from the young men of my acquaintance, and can not plead that I was indifferent to their attentions. Consequently I was not infrequently chided by father, mother, and Mr. Logan for being too much inclined to flirtation. However, in the few months of our courtship, we had a very happy time. To this day I marvel that a young man of Logan's rare ability, ambition, and mature years—he being then twenty-nine—should hazard his career by marrying a girl of seventeen.

My father had many friends in different parts of southern Illinois; the Logan family and a majority of young Logan's friends lived at a great distance from Shawneetown, considering the facilities for travelling. We therefore decided we would not have a big wedding, which in those days must be followed by a round of festivities, lasting sometimes a fortnight. At high noon, on the 27th of November, 1855, in the presence of a party of intimate friends and a number of Logan's associates at the bar, we were married by Hon. W. K. Parish, judge of the circuit court of the third judicial district of Illinois. After a bridal breakfast, accompanied by Judge Parish, Hon. W. J. Allen, Mr. Logan's law partner, Hon. N. C. Crawford, and my father, we departed for Benton, Franklin County, Illinois. The journey was made in buggies, two persons in each. The roads were almost impassable. At a little inn on the way to Shawneetown, in the small town of Equality, distant about twelve miles, Mr. Logan had made arrangements for the night. The innkeeper was much elated over the order which he had received, and he, his good wife, and their assistants had been very busy with their preparations for our entertainment. The house, with all of its old-time appointments, was in perfect order when we arrived, at about eight o'clock in the evening. The room to which my husband and I were assigned was most inviting, with its canopied bed and chintz bed and window curtains, snow-white bedspread and pillows, the feather bed making it necessary to have a pair of steps like those you see at Mount Vernon, for use in climbing into bed. The floor was covered by a pretty rag carpet, the toilet-table and dresser having fine white linen covers on them. As soon as we had removed the mud spatters, and made hasty toilets, we were ushered into the dining-room, where a feast fit for the gods was laid on the whitest of napery. The daintiest of cut glass and china, which had been handed down from colonial ancestors, and choice flowers, adorned the table. In those days a wedding or the entertainment of a bride and groom excited intense interest; hence these good people felt they must bring out their most valued treasures to suitably entertain our party. Many of the townspeople called during the evening to extend congratulations and express their good wishes. Early next morning we resumed our journey to Benton, which was to be our future home.

The road for the thirty-five-mile drive was as bad as it could possibly be. The weather was raw and cold, and we were delighted when, led by Judge Parish and Mr. Crawford, we entered Judge Parish's hospitable door at Benton, Illinois. Judge Parish and Mr. Logan were very intimate, and the Judge and his lovely wife had insisted that we should make our home with them until we should establish one of our own. Mrs. Parish had made preparations for us, and a large company had been invited for the evening, that Mr. Logan's friends should give us a cordial welcome. I soon felt quite at home with the people whom I was later to know better, and to love as my own kindred. We remained with Judge and Mrs. Parish for a few days, and then proceeded in a one-horse buggy to Murphysboro, Jackson County, Illinois, the home of Mr. Logan's mother. Many of the residents of Murphysboro were relatives of the Logan family, and we

Mrs. John A. Logan in 1858.

General Logan as Prosecuting Attorney in 1855.

had a very cordial reception, and were much entertained during our stay with Mother Logan.

Returning to Benton we remained with Judge and Mrs. Parish until our home was ready for occupancy. In the meantime my father and mother had sent our household goods to Benton. When we remember that everything at that time was transported by horses, mules, or oxen, we can imagine the tedious delays which frequently ensued. However, before the holidays we were ensconced in our own cottage and began life together. My mother had sent with our goods a colored "mammy," whom we called Aunt Betty. Aunt Betty was to be our maid of all work, and but for her I do not know how I should have gotten through with many domestic trials, as I was, in a measure, ignorant of the details of home and house keeping. Aunt Betty helped me out in my first experiences; but there being no colored people in Benton, she became, in time, very much dissatisfied, and returned to Shawneetown, leaving me to struggle through emergencies and domestic difficulties that multiplied rapidly. Many times without help, and with no confectioners, marketplaces, or groceries to which I could resort in such emergencies, I was obliged to draw upon my friends and neighbors to come in to aid me in the preparation of a meal for unexpected guests. As I discovered, we were supposed to extend boundless hospitality. Visitors and friends arrived unannounced, coming at any time that suited their convenience, without inquiring whether or not it was agreeable to us. They frequently brought children with them as, in that day, parents rarely had any one with whom to leave their charges when they wished to give themselves an outing.

These unexpected visitors always arrived in the early morning. You had to welcome them with a smiling face, notwithstanding the fact that your heart might sink within you. By eleven o'clock you had to go to your kitchen to begin preparations for the midday meal, the menu for which you had been mentally trying to arrange from the moment of the arrival of your unexpected guests. Fortunately, they were unconventional and followed you to the kitchen. You had to keep up a conversation with them, while you endeavored to think what it was possible for you to set before them an hour or two later. Older housekeepers had well-filled larders, but brides like myself were not so thoughtful, and often found themselves with an empty pantry. There were no markets, caterers, bakers, or greengrocers. The variety stores which carried everything from a pound of nails to lace and millinery, or from a peck of onions to dried beef and bacon, never had in stock what you wanted, or what was of the least use in emergencies. In such cases you had to look over your larder, through the smoke-house, dairy, or garden—according to the season—and get the best you had; your obliging guests, meanwhile, insisting upon helping you. They would pare the apples for the pies—if the dessert was to be apple pie, apple float, or Brown Betty—or hull the berries if small fruits were in season. They would shell the peas, or peel the potatoes, all the while indulging in animated conversation, peals of laughter emphasizing their enjoyment. If you were the hostess, you had to play the part of entertainer while standing over a hot stove, trying to keep in mind the numerous saucepans and drip-pans which were simmering in the oven or boiling on the stove lest they boil over or burn. You had to lay the table for adults and children, no matter how many, rushing meanwhile from the kitchen to the pantry lest something go awry. Many a hostess has collapsed as soon as her guests departed.

In my case, I quickly discovered that my husband's friends and acquaintances were equally unconventional, and expected him to invite them to dinner or to supper, and at times to stay all night when they happened to attend the courts, or come to town on occasions of political conventions. He never knew how many to expect, but, as soon as he found out how many were in town, would send me a note saying he was bringing ten or a dozen friends for dinner, adding tenderly: "Do the best you can, my dear, and I am sure everything will be all right." Imagine a bride of to-day so situated, and with no alternative but to find a messenger to send after some friend to come and help her out of her dilemma! Be it said to their credit, the friends were always ready to help. My mother had taught me to be somewhat provident in the matter of looking after the larder, which served me well in those days of real trial. Prompted by an insatiable ambition to be all that was expected of me by my husband's numerous friends, I triumphed over many otherwise painful experiences.

Notwithstanding the fact that I was but little over seventeen years old, I soon discovered that I was expected to know everything; to be an efficient milliner, dressmaker, and to assist in the work of an undertaker in preparing the bodies of the dead for their coffins. I was sent for almost daily to perform some of these offices, and shall never forget the terror with which I assisted in preparing the shroud which was used in those days for the dead. A lovely lady died very suddenly, and I was sent for. It was the first time I had ever touched a corpse, and, like all young people, I was frightened almost out of my wits. My blood ran cold, and I grew dizzy, and came near fainting. Remembering that Logan's wife must be equal to everything, I put aside my timidity, and having a real affection for the person, helped to my utmost. I was much gratified at having the friends report to my husband that I was very skilful, and that they would not have known what to do without me. As long as I live I shall remember, with the deepest gratitude and the tenderest affection, the devotion of these dear people who adopted me as the wife of their leader and hero. Sometimes my husband demurred against my undertaking to comply with the requests of these friends, when he knew my sympathies would be very deeply aroused or my ingenuity overtaxed. However, I insisted that I must at least try to do anything they wanted me to undertake. As I look back upon it now, I realize that, as is said in common parlance, I "put up many a bluff," and was only able to accomplish my task because of my devotion to my husband, and my pride in not wishing to be "found wanting." My husband was their idol and paid the penalty for their adoration by being obliged to take the lead in everything. He decided all controversies, wrote their wills, planned for the execution of all their projects, managed their political affairs. In a word, he was the leader at all times and under all circumstances. Notwithstanding all these responsibilities, we were repaid tenfold by their loyalty and devotion. We had many diversions and happy times, sharing in all their pleasures as well as in their sorrows. When my husband had to be away from home, I was looked after carefully and tenderly by neighbors and friends.

Franklin County was an important county in that part of the State. The people were for the most part agriculturists, and, as a consequence, had a fine agricultural association. Necessarily, they had to provide for an annual fair or exhibition of the products of the husbandman and housewife, the first one of which I attended about a year after our marriage. These fairs were interesting beyond description, both as to the people who attended them and the exhibits that were made. Men and women had here an opportunity to display the fruits of their special provinces, and the results of the year's experiments and labors. With untiring energy, much thought, and patient care, everything belonging to the animal and vegetable kingdoms, or to domestic and household art, was exhibited in the pleasant rivalry for premiums. Acres of ground, usually at the county-seat, were enclosed by a high board fence, that none might behold the wonders on exhibition without first depositing the fee at the entrance-gate.

Families generally provided themselves with season tickets for "fair week." The president, treasurer, and secretary of the agricultural association, who managed and conducted the

fairs, were men of unquestionable integrity and business qualifications. They spent much time and labor in forming the
committees and appointing the judges who were to make the
awards in the contests for the prizes in the various departments. The same officers had to provide for the payment of
the premiums that often aggregated many thousands of dollars in excess of the gate-fees. It required a voluminous
catalogue to list all the premiums offered for the best of everything—from a cucumber to a mammoth pumpkin or squash;
from a glass of jelly to a barrel of marmalade; from a ginger-
snap to huge loaves of bread and cake; from a dainty piece of
embroidery to innumerable patchwork quilts; from a yard
of flannel to yards of jeans and bright "bayadere"-striped
linsey dress-goods, and rag carpeting; from a lady's fan made
of the golden-bronze feathers of a turkey's tail to fly-brushes
from the glory of a peacock; from a breed of Brahma, Spanish, Shanghai, Cochin, or Dominique chickens to proud cocks
and blustering hens of every species; from goslings to geese
and swans; from ducklings to quacking ducks of all varieties.
Pigs, cattle, horses, mules, and every species of domestic animal preserved in the ark, and propagated since the days of
the flood, swelled the list competing for superiority. Fruits
and flowers in limitless numbers were brought and arranged
to the best advantage for competition, according to the taste
and tact of the exhibitor. Sometimes they assumed such
fantastic shapes that one was at a loss to recognize Nature's
most familiar productions. Elaborate conventional designs
of flowers and leaves would be wrought of all kinds of
seeds and grasses, and large panels would be carefully framed
and other devices made out of feathers, shells, and straws.

My husband and I were obliged to serve on the committees
of award for various departments, and congratulated ourselves
that we were made to feel we had made no enemies by the
decisions in which we joined. This was evidenced by the
number of prize vegetables and fruits which were left at our

home. We felt that these dear people appreciated the interest we took in these fairs.

Speeding their horses was especially exciting and brought the largest crowd of "fair week." There was especial interest in the equestrian contests, because couples of men and women from the country and town competed for the prizes. Fast riding, not unlike that of the "wild west," was considered evidence of the finest attainment in the art. Once, at a county fair, I witnessed a veritable John Gilpin ride in an equestrian contest participated in by six couples. Three of the couples were from the towns and three from the country. The young ladies and gentlemen from the town wore genteel riding-suits, one couple being arrayed in dark-green cloth, one in black, and one in dark-blue. The ladies wore stovepipe hats with long blue or gray tissue veils wound around them and tied in front—the fashion of that day. The country girls wore their summer dresses, ordinary hats, and riding-skirts made of light blue cottonade buttoned on over their dresses. One of them rode a light, clay-bank horse with white mane and tail. The rider had abundant bright-red hair, much color in her cheeks, and was a very large, fine-looking woman. She wore a white dress with a blue riding-skirt over it, and a broad-brimmed hat with green ribbons. Another of these girls wore a gingham dress of yellow with a blue riding-skirt. A white, broad-brimmed hat, with blue ribbons that hung down in long streamers behind, completed her costume. She was seated upon a white horse. The third girl wore a dress of some kind of dark goods, and had a bright-red ribbon on her hat. Like a statue she sat on a splendid, blooded bay horse that was at least sixteen hands high. The escorts of these blooming lassies were young men from the country who could ride like Comanches. The moment they were drawn up in front of the judge's stand to start, the most careless observer could see by the contemptuous expressions and sneers of the country riders that there was to be some reckless riding.

They started around the ring, but, before the quarter post was reached, the country couples began to pull their spirited steeds, while those from the towns quickened their pace in a dignified manner. By the time they reached the half-mile post they were going faster and faster, and as they approached the three-quarter post the country couples were leading the van. On they came, flying past the judge's stand, round and round again, the broad-brimmed hats with their streamers flapping in the wind. The contest rapidly narrowed down to the three country couples, between whom the rivalry grew closer and closer. On, on, they went, flying over the track, till the girl with the red hair was leading the race; her hat gone, her hair unbraided and streaming in the wind like the rays of a glaring red sunset that betokens a coming storm. The blue riding-skirt had become unfastened, and was flying in the wind like the sails of a yacht. The yellow horse, stretched to his full length, and his long tail sweeping behind, looked like a very demon as he came puffing like a bellows, round and round the third time, leaving everything, escort and all, far behind. The multitude of people had rushed to the edge of the ring, and were shouting, clapping their hands, and screaming like Indians. "Go it, Sallie!" "Go it, Liza!" "Go it, Yaller!" "Beat 'em, gals, beat 'em!" until everybody was wild with excitement. Betting was lively, and in the brief moments these reckless riders were flying around the track many dollars changed hands. Finally, hatless, skirtless, and with dishevelled hair, "Liza" reined her dripping, yellow horse in front of the judges' stand to receive the blue ribbon, while the spirited bay was given the red one. Then off the two went round again to display their trophies, and finish their victory over the "stuck-up town girls, who don't know how to ride nohow." Cheer after cheer greeted them as they galloped round the track and out of the ring triumphantly, while the town girls and their escorts rode away disgusted.

This is only an example of the many amusing incidents which occurred during our life in Benton. The cottage which was our first home, with its whole front blooming with the prolific sweetbriar rose, is still standing in Benton. The Illinois legislature recently passed a bill for the purchase, renovation, and preservation of our cottage home in Benton, Illinois, and the committee who have charge of the matter will make an effort to recover many of the articles of furniture, etc., which we used in this cottage, the whereabouts of which are well known to these old friends and their descendants. Around it will ever cling memories of our happy days, when we joined hands and hearts in performing every duty, and shared in the enjoyment of every pleasure when we started on life's journey together. In it our first two children were born. Unfortunately we lost our firstborn son. Our only living child, Mrs. Mary Logan Tucker, is now the comfort of my declining years.

I was forcibly reminded of the changes which time has wrought by the receipt of a letter some time ago from Mrs. Hettie A. Dillon, wife of Captain Dillon, of Benton, Illinois. Mrs. Dillon was then Miss Hettie A. Duncan, and was one of the "town girls" in the equestrian contest described in the foregoing, when she rode with General Logan's brother, William, both of whom were fine riders, but too dignified to descend to the Comanche style of their rivals from the country. The following extract will serve to show how much the town of Benton has progressed since the days of the war:

Recently a member of our Self Culture Club entertained us in her new beautiful home upon the site of the old Floral Hall where long ago exaggerated pumpkins, squashes, beets, and other farm products, with great bunches of zinnias, hollyhocks, and coxcombs, competed for blue ribbons. It seems rather an odd coincidence that in the spacious reception-hall a beautiful Carrara marble Ceres smiles from a wealth of fruit and flowers, illumined with tiny in-

First residence owned and occupied by General Logan, in Benton, Illinois.

candescents. The old race-track makes a fine drive. Where the judges' stand was is a lovely pergola. The stock pond in summer is a fragrant lily pond. It all makes a beautiful environment for my lovely friend.

# CHAPTER III

IT was while spending "court week" at Murphysboro that
I discovered I could write the blanks for indictments from
those the prosecuting attorney had prepared for criminal offences: viz., for selling liquor without license, gambling, assault and battery, petty larceny, and other violations of the
law. There were no such things as printed blanks like those
used to-day. Everything had to be written out with pen and
ink—a quill pen being generally used. I had worked in the
general land office for my father, and knew something about
business matters. As I had nothing to do while my husband
was in court, and he had to write out these indictments at
night, after the foreman of the grand jury reported them to
him, it occurred to me that it would be easy to write out a
number of each kind, thus relieving my husband of the me-
chanical drudgery of writing them at night. Being a swift
writer, I prepared a number one day, leaving a blank space
for the insertion of the name of the unfortunate offender.
Albeit more than fifty years have come and gone, I recall with

warm emotion the gratification I experienced when, after timidly submitting them to the prosecuting attorney, he pronounced them well done, and declared they would be of valuable service to him. It did not take him long to insert the names, and his work was ready for the next morning.

I was deeply interested in every case my husband had in court, and spent many hours reading law-reports and authorities, and marking decisions which bore upon those he might have to argue. I cut slips of paper, wrote across them the point made, and marked the most important paragraphs, which enabled him to get at the pith of the case without having to read pages of irrelevant matter. Through his experience as prosecuting attorney criminal law became a passion with John A. Logan, his practice and fame multiplying continually, until he was probably the most conspicuous lawyer south of Springfield in 1860.

As in all comparatively new States, Illinois had her share of litigations which attracted many of the brightest lawyers of the whole country. Among many others were Judge Sydney Breeze, Hon. Walter P. Scates, Hon. W. A. Denning, Judge James Shields, Hon. S. S. Marshall, Hon. W. K. Parish, General John A. McClernand, Hon. Lloyd Posey, Hon. W. J. Allen, Hon. John A. Logan, and Hon. John Doherty. Twice each year spring and fall terms of the court were held in the county-seat of each of the counties composing the judicial districts. The sessions of the courts were great events. For days before, extensive preparations for the entertainment of the people attendant upon the courts were made by private citizens and the landlords of the little taverns. The entertainment of the lawyers of the circuit was a matter of much importance, and nothing was spared that would contribute to their comfort.

Friends and tavern-keepers were each eager to have the judge and the lawyers at their board, that they might be regaled by the good stories that were told, and the brilliant

repartee in which they indulged over the high-noon dinner—
the court adjourning one hour for this purpose. Not infrequently the best points have been made in important cases
during this hour, when all joined in the most unreserved discussion of matters of litigation, politics, religion—everything
that is liable to arise in the scope of social conversation, the
judge laying aside the dignity of his office and entering freely
into the colloquies. Attorneys felt at liberty to put in many
points which would profit their clients, and which were, without seeming to be so, matters of special pleading. Sometimes
most amusing incidents occurred, betraying the tact and
sagacity of brilliant men in legal sallies. Some of the most
noted cases in criminal practice have been tried in these
courts. The eloquence of the lawyers of the day has saved
from execution many desperate criminals.

On one occasion, when Mr. Logan was defending a
young man being tried for murder, a lamb that had strayed
from the fold was chased by dogs into the park that encircled
the court-house. In its fright and endeavors to elude its
pursuers, it ran into the court-room, down the middle aisle of
the crowded room, and lay down at the judge's feet. Quick
as a flash Mr. Logan paused in his pleading and seized
upon the incident to the profit of his bitterly prosecuted client,
insisting that the innocent lamb had come to offer itself as
a sacrifice to save the life of the unfortunate prisoner. His
touching appeal so impressed the jury that the young man was
acquitted, while the judge announced the verdict in open
court, betraying much emotion, the whole audience and the
prisoner weeping like children.

In the evening lawyers, judges, and citizens congregated
together, sometimes to play poker, sometimes to smoke and
talk; discussing always every phase of the politics of the day.
It was a curious fact that the men of that time were, without
exception, thoroughly posted on political questions, and
while perhaps very partisan, they knew all about political

affairs, and espoused one side or the other with enthusiasm. An "independent" was unknown, and our modern "third-party men" would have had little encouragement from these intensely earnest people, whose politics were as much a part of their faith as their religion. Sometimes they carried their intensity so far that they came to blows over questions or individuals whom equally earnest opponents were espousing. On such occasions men fought each other like tigers: pounding, biting, cutting, and sometimes shooting each other fatally. Duelling was never recognized in Illinois, as it was farther south, but the equally barbarous practice of assaulting each other with knives, bludgeons, brickbats, pound weights, and any instrument of destruction at hand was freely indulged in. There was seldom a term of the court when there was not a murder case on the docket and always cases of assault and battery.

The judges and lawyers were obliged to travel in buggies or stages from one place of holding court to another, and any overland conveyance which they could obtain was gladly used. The distance was always from twenty-five to fifty miles, over the worst of roads, through the wind and rain of the spring and the bitter blasts of the fall and winter. My husband always insisted upon my accompanying him whenever it was possible. The taverns were invariably small and poorly furnished.

The court-rooms were circumscribed and densely crowded with people who looked upon the terms of court as their one opportunity to hear the arguments in litigation and the often eloquent speeches of the attorneys, together with the political discussions that usually occupied some hour during court week. Everybody's affairs were talked of. All the gossip of the country was retailed to the visitors who attended court. It was a luxury to the many who seldom saw newspapers and the monotony of whose lives was only relieved by these occasional recreations.

We remember how some of the lawyers were obliged to carry their law-books from court to court, as they could not depend upon finding authorities in every town. Law libraries were few and incomplete. One lawyer always carried a green-baize bag, in which were the books he was constantly quoting when he had a case. He would bring the bag into court every morning, and lay it on the bench or a table beside him, to show that he was well fortified. He was an Irishman, and would parry with his Irish wit the fun poked at him by his brother lawyers, always concluding with: "I've the authorities with me, will ye mind that, my fellows?" Many of the cases were most amusing and difficult of adjustment, as, for instance: a Mr. B, Sr., married the daughter of a widow who had property. His son, Mr. B, Jr., married his wife's mother; that is, he married the mother of his stepmother. Both mother and daughter had children, and got into litigation to establish the relationship of these children, their inheritance, and the division of the property. The father being son-in-law to his own son, his son's wife being his mother-in-law, and at the same time his daughter-in-law, while the father's young children were half brothers and sisters to their grandfather. The son's children were his grandchildren, and also his brothers and sisters in law, because they were his wife's half brothers and sisters. For years this case was on the docket. Argument after argument was heard by judge and jury without deciding the status of this much-mixed-up family, until the residue of the estate was absorbed by costs and attorneys' fees.

The digging and delving into facts and authorities, together with the earnest work that was unavoidable to attain success in any case, wonderfully developed these naturally able men. As a result, a galaxy of illustrious men were produced who have made an impress upon the nation as well as the State. The scene of Mr. Lincoln's early career was farther north in Illinois. The central and northern part of the State had its own bar of remarkable men whom I knew in later days.

The presidential campaign of 1856 was one of intense interest, far in excess of that of any preceding campaign. The Kansas and Nebraska trouble had brought out most conspicuously the subtlety of the slaveholder of the South and the no-longer-to-be-concealed fact that, in order to extend slavery into the Territories and to perpetuate that institution, they would not hesitate to overthrow every opposition, even to the destruction of the government and the disruption of the union of the States. Scarcely a man in southern Illinois was so ignorant as not to think he knew all about the important principles involved in the contest, and thought it was necessary for him to be on hand on all occasions when political affairs were discussed or in any way under consideration. Hence, at all public gatherings and meetings multitudes assembled, men and women flocking to a political demonstration as they would to a camp-meeting or to a circus. Before the hour for speaking or joint discussions these occasions were enlivened by processions led by bands of music, when often unique banners and devices were displayed. Among these, not infrequently, was a pyramid of seats arranged on long wagons, upon which would be seated young girls representing every State in the Union. The girls were dressed in white with red, white, and blue ribbons flying from their waists and shoulders. A goddess of liberty was placed in the centre. Her robe was made of the flag; red and white stripes in the skirt and a waist of blue studded with stars of gold or silver, while in her hand she carried a flag or sceptre, thus impersonating Columbia. These spectacles awakened the wildest enthusiasm, and the people became so absorbed that the girl representing a State immediately became its champion, together with all its interests and "isms," whatever they happened to be. Heated controversies often arose between Massachusetts and South Carolina before the fair representatives had laid aside the printed name of the States they represented.

Barbecues which would have done credit to the feasts of the days of Roman greatness were usually a feature of these political gatherings, whole beeves, sheep, and pigs being cooked to feed the multitudes. After butchering and quartering the animal, long pits were dug and filled with logs of wood. These logs were set on fire, and kept burning until the pits were quite full of live coals. Across these were placed iron bars, and on these bars were laid the quarters or halves of the animal. By a system of turning over and over, the huge pieces of meat were cooked to perfection, while chicken and other fowl were daintily broiled. Potatoes, both white and sweet, and green corn were roasted, and with the delicious bread baked in "Dutch ovens" of private families a feast fit for the gods was the result. In the groves of trees, always an indispensable adjunct for a barbecue, long tables were constructed, upon which were spread the viands, and around these the multitudes gathered. After enjoying the great feast, toasts and speeches were in order, and some as brilliant speeches as ever followed any banquet of the Gridiron or the Clover Club have echoed through the trees above these crude tables, eliciting shouts of applause from appreciative hearers. The crowd then congregated around the speaker's stand, erected sufficiently far away from the table and pits to keep the noise of clearing away of dishes and the last of the feast from disturbing either speaker or audience. Then began in earnest the business of the day in the discussion of political topics.

The Democratic party was very greatly in the majority in southern Illinois, and controlled all the party-machinery resources, having done so for years. It was not surprising, therefore, that the local as well as the national nominees were elected. The campaign of 1856 aroused the lethargic as never before. In the subsequent contests for the election of the legislators who were to vote for United States senator, there was even greater excitement, and more bitter controversy than had characterized the presidential campaign.

Lying as southern Illinois does—between Kentucky and Missouri—and having then a population strongly sympathizing with the slaveholders, the questions that had arisen would not down. Popular sovereignty, the motto of the State, under the leadership of Mr. Douglas, the champion of States' rights, had thoroughly impressed itself upon a large majority of the citizens south of the Ohio and Mississippi Railroad without it ever occurring to them to what extent this theory could be carried, or whither they were drifting in advocating this dangerous doctrine. Not one of the most earnest advocates of popular sovereignty, not even Mr. Douglas, who claimed the authorship of the bill, ever had a disloyal thought. They would not for one moment have sustained the theory that, acting under its tenets, a State had the right to secede; and yet secession was the logical sequence and result of the agitation of the question and theory of popular sovereignty.

As I look back over the past, I am glad that my husband insisted upon taking me with him, whenever it was possible, wherever he went. Therefore I was fortunate enough to witness the stirring scenes of those eventful days which prepared me for the memorable ones preceding and during the Civil War.

At the November election in 1856 my husband was elected to the Illinois legislature. He resigned his position as prosecuting attorney, greatly to the delight of the criminal class in the third judicial district. He had convicted so many during his term that he had become a terror to evil-doers.

Our little son, John Cunningham Logan, was but two months old when the legislature convened in January, 1857. I decided that it would not be wise to leave our comfortable home with a young baby to live in a hotel. Therefore my husband's brother, William H. Logan, who was reading law in my husband's office, stayed with me while Mr. Logan went to Springfield for the session of the legislature, which in those days was never of more than two or three months' duration.

The session proved rather an important one, my husband adding much to his reputation by his position on questions before that body. Among other things he arraigned Governor Bissell for violation of the statute which debarred from the position of governor any one who had given or accepted a challenge to a duel, Governor Bissell having years before participated in a duel.

The winter in Benton was very quiet, nothing occurring beyond the informal social affairs of a small town in the West during the fifties. Mr. Logan returned home for the spring term of the courts. He had many clients, and was quite as busy as when prosecuting attorney. Young as I was, I realized that my husband was destined to take an active part in political affairs, which were then becoming of more and more importance. I was therefore prepared for the nomination of Mr. Logan for Congress, and for his election in November, 1858. After the death of our first-born son, whom we lost when he was less than a year old, I resumed my wonted occupation of going everywhere with my husband. We knew the campaign was to be one of great excitement. Mr. Logan was in correspondence with the leading men of his party, including Mr. Douglas, W. A. Richardson, General Singleton, General Thornton, Mr. Shehan, the noted editor, and a number of others, and was advised of all the plans for carrying the State for the Democratic party.

Among other things Mrs. Douglas was to accompany the senator during the campaign in Illinois. Mr. Douglas had married the charming Adele Cutts, niece of Dolly Madison. She was one of the most queenly women of her day, quite as fascinating and captivating in her manner as her illustrious kinswoman. She was Mr. Douglas's second wife. She had all her life been associated with people of social and official prominence, and was eminently qualified for her position.

There was to be a conference with Mr. Douglas on his arrival in Chicago, which Mr. Logan agreed to attend. He arranged for me to go with him, that I might meet Mrs. Douglas. I was naturally delighted with the prospect of seeing so much, but trembled at the thought of meeting so many distinguished people, who to my unsophisticated mind were little lower than the angels. I feared Mrs. Douglas might consider me quite provincial, and too inexperienced to merit her attention. When I did meet her I understood why every one was charmed with her, and soon forgot my timidity. Mr. Douglas I had known before, as he had been a guest in my father's house, my father being one of his warmest supporters.

The interest manifested in political affairs in the campaign of 1856 was intensified by the issues involved in the approaching senatorial election. Illinois had in its list of public men some of the most brilliant in the whole country, and therefore in the contest for political preferment there was great rivalry. The parties had been the Whig and Democrat, with now and then offshoots from one or the other of these great parties under different names, and with various "isms" for a foundation. There were "Know-Nothings," with their anti-foreign proclivities; Abolitionists, with their antislavery principles; Kansas and Nebraska bill parties; and numerous other organizations, but at each election the great bulk of the population cast their votes for the candidates of either the Whig or the Democratic party. Through the bloody contest over the Kansas and Nebraska bills new "isms" had sprung up involving the question of States' rights *versus* national authority, making the division in the Democratic party wider than it had been hitherto. Mr. Douglas, as leader of the Popular Sovereignty party, had attempted to harmonize matters between the North and the South; consequently it was important, many thought, that he should be re-elected to the Senate. The State was thoroughly aroused. At every convention—county, legislative, and senatorial—instructions were given to the nominees of both parties as to whom the representatives and senators should support for the United States Senate, Mr. Lincoln being the choice of the Republicans, a new party, composed principally of men from the Whig and Abolition parties. Mr. Douglas was the choice of the Democratic and Popular Sovereignty parties. Long before Congress adjourned the excitement was intense.

Mr. Lincoln had been nominated by the Republican State Convention as their candidate for United States senator. Mr. Douglas's return to Illinois was impatiently awaited. Finally it was announced that he would return to his home in Chicago on Friday, July 9, 1858. Most extensive preparations were made to extend to him the grandest reception that had up to that time ever been given to any man. A large committee was appointed composed of the leading men of the city and State, Charles Walker being made chairman. This committee was composed of Hon. J. B. Vaughn, C. C. Marsh, Thomas Lanagan, D. A. Gage, D. L. Boone, Hon. Thomas Dyer, Andrew Harnia, H. T. Dickey, W. B. Scates, B. S. Morris, General H. L. Stewart, S. W. Fuller, Colonel E. D. Taylor, General Jacob Frye, Hon. Lambert Tree, J. A. McVicker, B. F. Bradley, Hon. W. W. Drummond, B. T. Caulfield, H. D. Calvin, Robert Healy, and others. These men invited prominent men of the State to assist in the demonstration, arranging for extra trains from every direction. A large delegation went to Michigan City to escort Douglas in triumph to Chicago. All along the route it had been arranged for the special train to stop, so that the great crowds of people might have an opportunity to see Douglas and allow him briefly to address them. On the arrival of the train at the depot in Chicago a multitude greeted him, and as the party drove from the depot to the Tremont House the crowd pressed around Douglas's carriage so closely that it was with difficulty the horses could move. Such cheering and huzzaing had never before been heard. Handkerchiefs, hats, and banners were waved, and every kind of demonstration that could be conceived was indulged in by the people. The city was elaborately decorated and brilliantly illuminated at night. Reaching the Tremont House, then Chicago's best hotel, appearing on a balcony on the Lake Street side, Douglas addressed the assembled thousands, Mr. Lincoln being among the number of hearers. The press contained a glowing description of the whole affair, which in those days was a marvellous one in point of numbers, character of the participants, enthusiasm, and grandeur of display. Now, alas! every trace of that momentous occasion has been obliterated by time and the great fire of '71, which destroyed all the landmarks, even the Tremont Hotel, that had been the headquarters of Illinois' greatest men and the rendezvous of politicians of all parties. Nearly all the conspicuous men taking part in that occasion are also gone, but few, if any, of the committee surviving.

I always like to think of Mr. Lincoln as he was in the days when I saw him with the eyes of an opponent. His awkwardness has not been exaggerated, but it gave no effect of self-consciousness. There was something about his ungainliness and about his homely face, even in a State of tall and ungainly men, which would have made any one who simply passed him in the street or saw him sitting on a platform remember him. "There ain't no one else and there never was any one jest like Abe Lincoln," as an old farmer said. His very awkwardness was an asset in public life, in that it attracted attention to him, and it seemed to enhance the appeal of his personality when he spoke. Any one who was introduced to Lincoln without ever having heard of him before, though the talk was commonplace, would be inclined to want to know more about him.

Douglas won your personal support by the magnetism of his personality. Lincoln did not seem to have any magnetism, though of course he had the rarest and most precious kind. He seemed able to brush away all irrelevant matters of discussion, and to be earnestly and simply logical. In fact, he had the faculty of carrying conviction. At a time when the practice of oratory as an art was the rule he was without affectation. The ungainly form, the bony face, the strong, sensitive mouth, the quiet, sad, and kindly eyes, were taking you out of yourself into unselfish counsel.

Give Mr. Lincoln five minutes and Mr. Douglas five minutes before an audience who knew neither and Mr. Douglas would make the greater impression; but give them each an hour and the contrary would be true. This does not mean that Douglas was not sincere. No man could be more patriotic or sincere than Stephen A. Douglas was. He was as earnest in his belief in the rightness of his position as Lincoln was in the rightness of his; and when he found that he had been in error no man of pride ever acted more courageously in admitting it.

Immediately after followed the first meeting of the campaign, Mr. Lincoln having spoken on the evening of the 10th, in Chicago, arraigning Mr. Douglas in the strongest terms. The friends of Mr. Douglas planned for a grand demonstration at Springfield on the 17th. On the morning of the 16th, on a special train, beautifully decorated, the engine bearing the motto, "S. A. Douglas, the Champion of Popular Sovereignty," a large committee with a fine band of music accompanied Douglas to Springfield. At every town en route flags were flying, cannons were booming, and immense crowds were gathered at the station. At Bloomington, where, after speaking, Douglas was to rest at the Loudon House for a few hours, there were five thousand people (a great number for those days) gathered at the depot. Douglas's appearance on the platform, to descend to a carriage in which he was to be driven to the hotel, was the signal for prolonged shouts. It was a difficult matter for the marshals to make way for the carriages that were to lead the procession, so many were determined to escort Douglas to the hotel. At seven-thirty in the evening he was to speak in the court-house square, the only place where the great multitudes could be accommodated or be able to hear the speeches. The whole city, especially the court-house grounds, was brilliantly illuminated, transparencies and gay bunting making it a resplendent scene. As Douglas reached the platform the cheering was deafening. He defended his position in Congress, appealed to the people to stand by him, and avowed his devotion to the Union and the government. The people applauded him vociferously. Mr. Lincoln made it a point to go to the Douglas meeting and to listen attentively. The following morning Douglas continued his journey to Springfield, where the demonstrations were even greater than they had been at Bloomington.

Up to this time Douglas had not replied to Mr. Lincoln's charges, made in his speech accepting the nomination of the State convention as candidate for senator, in which he said, in substance, that Douglas, Chief Justice Taney, President Buchanan, and ex-President Pierce had entered into a conspiracy to prevent and overturn the Constitution of the United States and establish slavery throughout the Republic. He arraigned them in the following forceful words: "I charge that the people had been deceived in carrying the last presidential election by the impression that the people of a Territory might exclude slavery if they chose, when it was known in advance by the conspirators that the count was to decide—that neither Congress nor the people could so extend slavery." In one of the speeches which Mr. Lincoln made after Douglas returned he said: "Judge Douglas has carefully read and reread that speech. He has not, so far as I know, contradicted those charges. In the two speeches which I heard he certainly did not. On his own tacit admission I renew the charge. I charge him with having been a party to that conspiracy and to that deception, for the sole purpose of nationalizing slavery."

Douglas was advertised to speak at Clinton July 27. The wide-spread publication of Mr. Lincoln's reiteration of these charges augmented, if possible, the desire to hear Douglas. An innumerable concourse of people, therefore, assembled at Clinton. The papers were teeming with the description of the arrival of the throng. From daylight in the morning they came into the town—on horseback, on foot, in every imaginable vehicle, on train, and every way possible. The fair grounds where the speeches were to be made were at least two miles from the railroad depot. It was said the procession reached from the station to the grounds; all conceivable devices in the way of banners, mottoes, and flags were carried in the procession, a remarkable feature of which was thirty-six ladies and gentlemen mounted on horseback, representing all the States in the Union. The goddess of liberty was represented by a beautiful young woman, wearing a dress composed of the Stars and Stripes. A liberty cap crowned her head, and she sat her charger like a veritable Joan of Arc, indifferent to the scorching rays of a midsummer sun, or the dust which was almost suffocating. As soon as Douglas began his speech all was quiet from the earnest desire of the whole multitude to hear him. After again going over the many questions involved, he replied to Mr. Lincoln's charges in these words: "I did not answer these charges before for the reason I did not suppose there was a man in America whose heart was so corrupt as for an instant to believe that such a charge could be true. I did not think that any man in America believed that Chief Justice Taney and his associates on the Supreme Bench, and two Presidents of the United States, to say nothing of myself, could be guilty of a conspiracy, involving such turpitude and such infamy. I had too much respect for Mr. Lincoln to suppose he was serious in making the charge. He says now that he did not know the charge was true when he made it; that he had no personal knowledge of the truth of it. I then asked him 'Why such a charge?' I reminded him there is as much corruption in making a charge without knowing it to be true, as there is in making one and knowing it to be false. It is as dishonest to charge that which you do not know to be true as it is to tell an open lie; and yet he now confesses that he made the charge against the judges of the Supreme Bench, two Presidents of the United States, and myself without knowing whether it was true or false. Mr. Lincoln can lay down that rule of action for himself in his conduct towards others which he thinks proper, but I should deem that I had forfeited my character as an honorable man if I should make a charge against him of moral turpitude without knowing it to be true at the time I made it." He further declared that he had never spoken to any member of the court on the subject of the Dred Scott decision; that the introduction of the Nebraska bill was prior to the decision, hence Douglas's part of the conspiracy was impossible; that Buchanan was at the court of Saint James when the Nebraska bill was introduced, therefore they could not have had a conspiracy over the question. Continuing in the most earnest strain, he spoke for two hours and a half, and still the crowd yelled, "Go on!"

Such strong language from such strong men, and the unmistakable determination on the part of each leader to carry the warfare to the bitter end, served to inspire violent antagonisms. Clubs were organized bearing the names of Lincoln and Douglas, and the famed "Wide Awakes" created great enthusiasm wherever they appeared. They were uniformed and armed with torches, and carried banners with pictures of their favorites, and mottoes of all kinds, and quotations from the speeches of their leaders. So numerous were the political meetings and so intense was the excitement, that people did little else but attend political demonstrations and talk politics.

Mr. Lincoln spoke in the evening to a large crowd who remained to hear him, Douglas being obliged to leave so as to reach his appointment at Monticello. Before going, however, he and Lincoln had a long interview to arrange about the famous joint discussions, Lincoln promising to advise Douglas as to time and places. They would necessarily have to begin at the close of the appointments already made by Douglas, which were to end at Ottawa, August 21, 1858.

At each of those places the demonstrations were unparalleled by anything ever known in the State, each place trying to outdo the other in the magnificence of its processions, decorations, and the enthusiasm with which the people showered honors upon the "Little Giant."

Very soon after the meeting at Clinton, through correspondence, they agreed as to places and dates for the joint discussions. They were to alternate in opening and closing. In the intervals each was to fill his own appointments at other places in the State. By looking over the list it will be seen they were in every section of the State, from one extreme to the other. The towns in themselves were small, but the country surrounding them was well populated. The generous preparations by the people for the occasions were on a prodigal scale; prominent men at every town took conspicuous parts as committeemen, marshals, and entertainers. At Beardstown, when Douglas spoke, it appeared that, as if by magic, more people were brought together than resided near enough to be present, so incredible was their number. The procession was almost endless, led by thirty-six young ladies on horseback, each carrying a banner with the name of the State she represented. Then followed innumerable banners with mottoes of all kinds: "S. A. Douglas, the Champion of Right," "The Constitution," "The Union as it is, and Fidelity to Correct Principles," and many others. A delegation from Chandlerville carried a banner illustrating Lincoln's expression: "A living dog is better than a dead lion." Mr. Lincoln had referred to Douglas as a caged, toothless lion, and himself a living dog. On the banner was a picture of a lion full of strength with a dog lying down marked "Spot." "The lion is alive, the dog is dead," was written beneath. There were many other pictures representing the prominent features of the campaign. At Havana the crowd was also very large. Douglas spoke there one day and Lincoln the next. Lincoln began his speech by saying he had borrowed a clean shirt in which to appear, as he had filled his carpet-bag with documents, more important than clean clothes.

August 21 was an eventful day in Illinois as the opening of the memorable joint discussion between Douglas and Lincoln at Ottawa, one of the oldest towns in the State and then the home of many distinguished people. From daylight till three o'clock the people came in every conceivable conveyance. Badges, banners, streamers, and flags were seen everywhere; even the horses they rode or drove were gayly bedecked with the national colors. Douglas came into town in a carriage escorted by hundreds on horseback—Mr. Lincoln coming by train from the neighboring town of Morris. They had both been speaking much of the time since the 10th of July, and the contest was then at fever heat. Douglas was introduced first by Colonel W. H. Cushman, in an eloquent speech going over all the issues of the campaign. Mr. Lincoln's speech followed, in which he came back at Douglas with his conclusions, charges, and explanations. Douglas again replied. The vast audiences were electrified by the remarkable speeches of both Douglas and Lincoln. Mr. Lincoln was ill and should not have spoken. His effort completely exhausted him, and he had to be lifted from the stand and supported by his friends to the carriage.

Caricatures, processions, and campaign methods have ever been much the same. We remember that at Bloomington, on the 4th of August, when Mr. Lincoln spoke, they had in the procession a coffin, covered with black and hauled on a dray, which was labelled in large letters: "The Remains of the Democratic Party." Mr. Lincoln was the guest of his life-long friend, Hon. David Davis, and both enjoyed the mournful spectacle, as well as many other comic features of the procession. There was not the slightest abatement in the public interest until the close of the very last debate at Alton, on October 15. The result of the election in November showed a revolution in public sentiment and aroused a great admiration in the public mind for Mr. Lincoln, which culminated, as the world knows, in his nomination to the Presidency in 1860, notwithstanding his failure of election to the Senate in 1858.

John A. Logan was then a young man of thirty-two years. All of his associations, affiliations, and teachings had been under Democratic influence. He was a strong partisan and an ardent admirer of Mr. Douglas. He accompanied Mr. Douglas almost everywhere, and indulged me to the extent of taking me with him. Young as I was, I was a close observer of everything that occurred. The masterful speeches of these intellectual giants was a revelation in matters political.

Mr. Logan's faith in the doctrines of the Democratic party began to waver. He became convinced by Mr. Lincoln's declaration that the Union could not be perpetuated with "one half free and one half slave," and also began to doubt many of the theories advocated by Mr. Douglas. He was deeply concerned over the situation of affairs, and talked to me much about the madness of the Southern leaders of his party. He remained loyal to Mr. Douglas and the party until the firing upon Sumter, which he considered the death-knell to all hope of a compromise that would avert the calamity of a civil war. His whole nature recoiled at thought of a disruption of the Union and treason against the government. In the light of the firing upon the flag, he felt there was no longer any middle ground, and declared a man must be either for or against his country. He therefore resigned his seat in Congress and entered the army for the preservation of the Union.

Notwithstanding the fact that all these things are familiar to the survivors of my generation, I write them for those of the present and future generations who have, and will inherit. the inestimable blessings of a redeemed republic.

# CHAPTER IV

MR. LOGAN ELECTED TO THE THIRTY-SEVENTH CONGRESS — THE JOURNEY TO WASHINGTON — RAILWAY TRAVEL IN 1859 — INSTALLED AT BROWN'S HOTEL — THE CAPITAL DOMINATED BY SLAVEHOLDERS — A CAB ADVENTURE — PRESIDENT BUCHANAN AND MISS LANE AT THE WHITE HOUSE — RECEPTION AT SENATOR DOUGLAS'S — RE-ELECTION OF DOUGLAS TO THE SENATE — HIS LOYALTY TO LINCOLN — ARRIVAL OF LINCOLN IN WASHINGTON — THE INAUGURATION — THE CRISIS AND CURRENT CONDITIONS — OUR FIRST STATE DINNER — GENERAL SOCIAL FESTIVITIES ON THE VERGE OF WAR — THE THEATRES — FIRING ON SUMTER — PUBLIC OPINION AT HOME — LOGAN'S STAND FOR THE UNION — HIS SPEECH AT MARION — ENLISTS "FOR THE WAR" AND RAISES A REGIMENT

As soon as the election returns were in and Mr. Logan was declared elected to represent the Ninth Congressional District in the Thirty-seventh Congress, he began to arrange his affairs to go on to Washington to be sworn in March 4, 1859. We went to Marion, Williamson County, to spend the Christmas holidays with my father and mother, and to visit Mother Logan who lived twenty-four miles west of Marion, at Murphysboro, Jackson County. On account of the discomfort of travelling in winter, we were afraid to take our little daughter, then but a few months old, on so long a journey in February. My husband therefore went on to Washington without baby and me. He arranged everything for our home, when we should come the following December.

I spent the summer arranging our household affairs that I might close our house, and in the far more difficult task of preparing a suitable wardrobe in which to make my début as the wife of a popular Congressman from the West. I spent many sleepless nights designing costumes, hats, and other necessities for a lady's wardrobe. We were too far from Saint Louis or Chicago for me to avail myself of city dressmakers and milliners; consequently, after getting together what I thought would be passable, I waited until I reached Washington to obtain what I should require further.

A few days before Thanksgiving we bade good-by to the numerous friends and neighbors and started, via the Illinois Central and the Ohio and Mississippi Railroad, to Cincinnati; thence, via the Baltimore and Ohio Railroad, to the national capital.

Going to Washington in those days was a very different affair from that of the present. The crude railroading, the uncomfortable, barren, low-berthed sleeping-cars can never be forgotten. The road-beds were rough, and the rolling-stock worse. This, together with the zigzag track of the Baltimore and Ohio Railroad through the Alleghany Mountains, made travelling a question of physical endurance; getting over ground more rapidly than by the primitive stagecoach was at the cost of many an aching bone and dizzy head. The untidy condition of the best sleeping-cars was intolerable. I had never before crossed the Alleghany Mountains, and remember vividly the struggle between the desire to sit up and feast my eyes upon the grand scenery of the mountains and the Cheat River Valley, with that enchanting river appearing and disappearing from view as the train sped on through tunnels and around the craggy points of the range through which the river flows, and the tremendous effort it required to keep from yielding to the desperate car-sickness and fatigue incident to travelling under circumstances then inevitable. All trains were late, overcrowded, and uncomfortable. We had to change frequently. At Bellaire the cars were transported across the river on a boat; the mountains at some places were crossed by the switchback system. From the time one embarked till dropped at the old Baltimore and Ohio Depot in Washington one suffered incessantly either with fatigue, terror on account of the tortuous heights and crooked track, or suffocation from the tunnels and vile air of the cars. Eating-stations were few and far between, and the improvident, who had no luncheon provided, had to endure the pangs of hunger; and when children were of the number their cries added additional annoyance to passengers. We had, among others, as travelling companions, the Hon. and Mrs. S. S. Cox. Mr. Cox was then a member of Congress from Ohio, and was full of life and good stories, which he told so well that he made everybody cheerful and enabled many to forget their discomfort. Others included the eloquent Dick Barrett, of Saint Louis; Colonel Ross and J. C. Robinson, members of Congress from Illinois; Mr. and Mrs. Oscar Turner, of Louisville, Kentucky; Mr. and Mrs. Stillwell, of Indiana.

The Relay House was then the last stopping-place for meals before reaching Washington. Hungry and weary, we all responded with avidity to the supper-call, entering the typical Southern dining-room of the hotel, to be served with a delicious Southern supper of fried chicken, corn bread, baked sweet potatoes, fresh biscuit, butter, honey, tea, and coffee. As the door swung open between the kitchen and dining-room, while the waiters went in and out serving the supper, the old black cook with her bandanna turban could be seen busy with implements of her profession, dishing toothsome fruits of her cunning in the art of the cuisine, and could be heard at the same time delivering lectures to the audacious Sambos and Cuffys for the want of manners they displayed while filling the orders of the guests. Before realizing that twenty minutes had expired, the conductor's cry of "all aboard" made us drop the biscuit and honey and hurry to the train.

Reaching Washington in the early evening, we had scarcely descended from the cars before the rush of burly hackmen crying: "This way for Brown's Hotel!" "This way for the National!" "This way for—" this and that hotel and lodging-house, almost deafened and completely terrified me. Unsophisticated as I then was, I felt I was to be the victim of a mob; but under the guidance of Mr. Logan, to whom the whole proceeding was not a novelty, we were soon ensconced in Brown's Hotel omnibus and driven to that hotel, and to my dying day I shall remember the kindly greeting of Mr. and Mrs. Brown (parents of Mrs. Richard Wallach), the worthy proprietors. Their son-in-law, Mayor Wallach, was a friend of Mr. Logan, and through him they had been advised of our coming, and right royally did they receive us.

I felt that in Mrs. Brown I had a refuge in all the dilemmas that awaited the timid young wife of a Western Congressman. This city was then dominated by the aristocratic slaveholders of the South, who looked upon the North and West as "mud-sills and drudges," quite unworthy of much consideration; and far too often a swaggering manner and a retinue of colored slaves gave a man a prestige over others of scholarly attainments, simple habits, and no attendants. The hotel was quite full of the most pronounced of the aristocratic type who were then threatening disunion. Among them were Wigfall, of Texas; Keit, of South Carolina; Mason and Harris, of Virginia; Benjamin, of Louisiana; Slidell and Barksdale, of Mississippi; and a legion of others who were subsequently leaders in the Confederacy, and who have since paid the debt that all must pay sooner or later. Daily, during the dinner-hour, discussions were heated and often quite boisterous. Sometimes it seemed that a collision was imminent at the table, ladies frequently appearing with secession cockades, which gave encouragement to the advocates of secession. At first I used to listen to these discussions in mortal terror, and sometimes was almost persuaded that the boasted prowess of the Southern men was a reality. I often wondered upon what they fed that they should be so boastful; my heart, meanwhile, praying that, should the conflict ever come, Heaven might protect the Union and give to its defenders strength to save it from dismemberment.

Impatient to secure a presentable wardrobe, and disliking to take up my husband's time, or that of Mrs. Brown, to accompany me on a shopping tour, one morning I started out alone. It was easy enough to wander down Pennsylvania Avenue to Perry's and John T. Mitchell's dry-goods stores, and to find all I dared purchase with my limited purse. Feeling that I had achieved wonders, I started to return to the hotel; but, after walking quite a distance and looking about carefully for landmarks and failing to find one, I went to the corner of Seventh and C Streets, the old carriage stand, got into one of the vehicles and told the driver to take me to Brown's Hotel. Turning around the corner he halted at the ladies' entrance half a block from where I had entered the carriage. He charged me a dollar which I paid without demurring, and hurried to my room. Subsequently, I discovered that I had gone down C Street in the rear of the hotel, forgetting, when I attempted to return, the oblique direction of the avenue. I waited many months before telling my experience to my husband, who enjoyed repeating the story at my expense for the amusement of his friends, and it was a long time before I heard the last of my first shopping expedition in Washington.

To visit the Capitol and public buildings and familiarize myself with the objects of interest which the city contained kept me busy for some time. Congress had adjourned for the holidays before we felt prepared to make our début, and begin the rounds of calls obligatory upon the wife of a new member, if she expects to hold any place in the social world at the capital. New Year's, 1860, I first witnessed the ceremonies of that day. Going to the White House, upon invitation of Mr. Buchanan, we watched with admiration the President, with all the dignity natural to him, and Miss Lane, with graciousness unsurpassed by any of her predecessors or successors, receive the official calls. The Diplomatic Corps, Cabinet, Supreme Court, Congress, and the whole list of officials then, as now, paid their respects to the President on that day. The music of the Marine Band, under the direction of Professor Scala; the gay uniforms and decorations of the foreigners, our army and navy, and the beautiful toilets of the ladies made an impression upon me that can never be effaced. My ideas of democratic simplicity fled precipitately, and I stood aghast fancying no imperial court could rival our republican government in ostentatious display. While Washington was not the city it is to-day in population and improvement, there were aristocratic and pretentious people who made the most of such occasions, and allowed no opportunity to pass without availing themselves of it to display their gorgeous resources.

Senator and Mrs. Douglas had invited me to come and assist them in receiving their friends. This was my first experience in participating as an assistant to a hostess on such an occasion. Senator and Mrs. Douglas lived on I Street in the house more recently occupied by the late Justice Bradley. Their home was one of the most ambitious in the city, with its lovely picture gallery, spacious drawing-rooms, fine library, and luxurious surroundings. Adjoining was the home of Senator Rice, of Minnesota; that of Senator Breckenridge, of Kentucky, adjoined Rice's. All day the callers came and went. Mrs. Douglas, one of the most diplomatic women of her time, received her guests with matchless grace and cordiality, presenting them to her assistants in such a way as to put them at ease and banish their shyness. Most elaborate refreshments, including egg-nog and wines of all kinds, were served in the dining-room; while Senator Douglas, with his wonderful charm of manner, entertained in the library those who lingered as long as politeness would permit. It was long before we slept that night: the excitement of the day, the glittering panorama of the reception, the novelty of meeting so many people, the enjoyment of hearing the bright sallies and conversation of the distinguished callers had enchanted me, but through it all forebodings of the impending "crisis" stirred my soul. The ambition of reckless spirits, who had for so long ruled the land, the arrogance of the slaveholders in their possessions, all tended to keep the political excitement at fever heat. Events occurring in the Capitol were reflected in society. The absorbing topics under discussion could not be dropped even in the drawing-room. Participants in the debates in the halls of Congress could not forget the subject when they met for social intercourse. The very sight of each other suggested continuation of their discussions. Illinois was then represented in the United States Senate by William A. Richardson and Stephen A. Douglas. Douglas's time was to expire on the 4th of March following. In the House of Representatives there were elected in November, 1858, from the First Congressional District, Hon. E. B. Washburne; Second, John F. Farnsworth; Third, Owen Lovejoy; Fourth, William Kellogg; Fifth, I. N. Morris; Sixth, John A. McClernand; Seventh, James C. Robinson; Eighth, P. B. Foulke; Ninth, John A. Logan—forming a galaxy of as strong men as the State has ever had in Congress; and it was not surprising that such representatives were destined to be conspicuous in the thrilling events that took place in the decade following. While the legislature was Democratic, Mr. Lincoln having carried the State by the popular vote the fear that Mr. Douglas would not be returned to the Senate was greatly augmented. When the legislature convened, there assembled at Springfield a great number of persons from all over the State who desired to influence its action. It was evident to the most stupid observer that Mr. Lincoln had made a national reputation during the campaign, and especially in the joint discussions, and that in his questions put to Douglas on the subject of slavery in the Territories he had set many men to questioning whether or not the policy of Mr. Douglas was a safe one for the best interests of the country north of the Mason and Dixon line; whether it was not true that the country could no longer exist "half slave and half free," and whether or not, also, the slaveholders were determined to extend slavery or dissolve the Union. Every man in the legislature was watched with jealous eyes lest he might falter in his allegiance to his party, and thereby defeat party supremacy. The contest was long and bitter, until, finally, Douglas was re-elected to the Senate, but, as was predicted at the time, at the expense of his Presidential hopes and prospects, as beyond all doubt the fame acquired by Mr. Lincoln as the nominee of the Republican party for the Senate in the celebrated campaign of 1858 and the division of Democratic sentiment as to Douglas gave Lincoln the nomination for the Presidency in 1860.

But one issue was before the people, and that was the question of slavery and its extension in the Territories. The proslavery party would listen to nothing but an espousal of their cause absolutely; and the antislavery party would listen to no uncertain sound on that question—nothing but the prohibition of slavery in the Territories would satisfy their demands. Hence there was little chance for a compromise man to accomplish much. The two wings of the Democratic party were just as much at variance as were the Republican and Democratic parties, and when the conventions met the rupture came with full force, so that the result of the campaign of 1860 was not a surprise to Mr. Douglas and his adherents. But, with his hopeful spirit, he thought something might still be done, and we remember well how, during the whole winter preceding the firing on Sumter, day after day he pleaded with leaders for a compromise, and with what anxiety he watched the gathering storm and longed to avert the "irrepressible conflict." I remember, too, how eagerly he joined the venerable John J. Crittenden in his "compromise" proposition, and how, night after night, the young men of his party met at his house and counselled with him as to what should be done, and how his great soul recoiled at the thought of a dismemberment of the Union! I remember his likening himself to a shuttle, going from side to side, between the warp and the woof of party threads, trying to weave a harmonious fabric, but often entangled in the meshes of the political web. He was loyal to the core, and yet his affiliations had all been with the South. His first wife was a Southern lady, and his sons were then with their kindred in North Carolina. At times he felt most keenly his impotency to accomplish anything on the peace commission, even to postpone the evil hour. I remember once when it was discovered that the conspirators had been holding secret meetings in the room of the Senate military committee, of which Jefferson Davis was chairman, Douglas came to our rooms manifesting the greatest possible distress. They had been arranging for secession and even for the resistance of Mr. Lincoln's inauguration. As Douglas talked the matter over with Mr. Logan (then a member of the House) great tears stood in his earnest eyes, and he said: "It is no use. If you gave these men a blank sheet of paper and asked them to write down terms of compromise under which they would agree to remain in the Union, they would not write them." He added: "I, for one, can not be a party to the destruction of the Government, if every man in the Democratic party is with them." He said he would do all in his power to give Mr. Lincoln a hearty welcome to Washington and insure his inauguration; that he was elected by the people, and should be inaugurated at all hazards." As a senator from Illinois, he was most active on the committee of arrangements for the inaugural ceremonies, going with the Illinois delegation to pay their respects to Mr. Lincoln as soon as he arrived. He shared the deep solicitude felt by the friends of Mr. Lincoln lest some madman or rampant secessionists might do him violence before his inauguration. I saw much of Mr. Douglas during those anxious days, and know that he suffered acutely all the time over the condition of affairs, and more over the approaching storm of rebellion than over his own disappointment and waning political power.

Matters had reached such a climax that the most indifferent realized that the nation's weal was paramount to any individual consideration. Men of affairs moved about with grave countenances, absorbed with the awful thought that a civil war was inevitable. We remember perfectly the arrival of Mr. Lincoln in Washington, and the relief it was to know that nothing had befallen him *en route*, and with what intense anxiety many watched every move of the most violent secessionists all Inauguration Day. With bated breath I stood on the balcony of the Metropolitan Hotel (then called Brown's) and watched the procession wending its way down Pennsylvania Avenue to the Capitol. I can remember exactly how Mr. Lincoln looked as he sat beside Senator John P. Hale, of New Hampshire (father of Mrs. W. E. Chandler), so calm and so apparently unaware of the imminent danger that his dearest friends apprehended. I saw them returning after the ceremonies, and was deeply impressed by the change in spirit and manner of the multitudes that followed. *En route* for the inauguration ceremonies anxiety and apprehension were depicted on every face. Returning, they followed the carriage of the new President, shouting: "Long live the President!" But when nightfall was gathering over the city, again the timid began to quake lest some evil soul might improve his opportunity to commit some violent deed under the cover of darkness. For days hope and fear, security and doubt, succeeded each other in the public and private mind. Nominations for the Cabinet were sent in and were, of course, considered firebrands to the South, whose representatives one by one departed from the city and began their work all over the South for the establishment of the Confederacy. Each day some prominent member or senator failed to answer the roll-call. Mr. Lincoln's assurances that he knew "no North, no South, no East, no West," made no impression, and were considered unreliable by the leaders of the secession movement. First one State and then another passed secession resolutions. Then came echoes of the fatal firing on Sumter and all the fearful consequences that followed. Mr. Lincoln, with the deepest anxiety depicted on his face, was tireless in his efforts to restrain the madmen who were precipitating the nation into a civil war. He remained almost incessantly in his office or closeted with some leading spirit through whom he hoped to work a change and heal the breach. His most loyal adherents were untried men. He was ignorant of their abilities and doubted their discretion. The executive departments were completely demoralized. The Treasury and arsenals were empty. General Winfield Scott, the general of the army, was old and decrepit. The army was at its lowest ebb in numbers, and was scattered all over the vast extent of the country, with the most meagre and inefficient communications or means of transportation. The Indians were more numerous and savage than to-day. Our frail naval fleet, insignificant in the number of ships and efficiency of the officers and men, was for the most part on foreign seas, the rest in Southern waters. Fearing the Supreme Court to be in sympathy with secession, apparently a great republic was tottering to its fall. Was a President-elect ever so circumstanced? Upon him alone rested the responsibility of so directing affairs as to save the Union from dismemberment. Yet he was without absolute authority, and wholly dependent upon the legislative branch of the government and the loyalty of the people, albeit there were sounds of disloyalty everywhere, even north of the Mason and Dixon line.

Fortunately, the electric shock of the firing on Sumter startled the whole country, awakened the latent patriotism of the nation, and brought to Mr. Lincoln the much-needed assurance that there was in the hearts of the people an indomitable love of country that would sustain him in all re-

spects and enable him to fulfil the mission for which, in the
retrospect, he seems to have been especially called. I have
often thought that persons who to-day criticise the manner
in which things were done then—particularly the tardiness
which characterized the organization and movements of the
army and the preparations which were necessary to prosecute
the war, seem not to remember the difference between the
situation then and now or the wonderful progress that has
been made for the transportation and mobilization of an
army.

Notwithstanding the undercurrent of political excitement,
social gayety at the capital was attempted, and, like all nov-
ices, I was entranced by the brilliancy of the receptions, balls,
dinners, and other entertainments which my husband and
myself attended. At times I felt timid and so unsophisticated that I feared my embarrassment would provoke many
a smile from the experienced women who chaperoned me on
occasions of great importance. No more courtly President
has ever been in the White House than James Buchanan,
whose innate refinement and dignified manners had been
greatly enhanced by his experience at the court of Saint
James. His charming niece, Miss Harriet Lane, who presided as mistress of the White House, was so queenly and gracious always that she has had no superior as the first lady of
the land. I shall ever bless them for the cordial greeting
extended to Mr. Logan and myself in the executive mansion.

Our first state dinner was an event of so much importance
to me that the picture of the table will be in my mind evermore. It was an elegant affair, notwithstanding the fact that
the decorations of that time were very unlike the richer dis-
plays of the present day. I remember at each end of the
Van Buren mirror, with its filigree railing of gold bronze,
that formerly adorned the centre of the table on all state
occasions, there were two tall gilt baskets in which were

arranged plaster-of-Paris fruits painted in very unnaturally bright colors. The variety included oranges, apples, peaches, grapes, etc., with artificial leaves here and there among the mimic fruits. I remember, too, the historic china, with the red band and coat of arms of the United States in the centre. The gold-plated spoons, solid-silver service, and cut glass, though familiar to me since from frequent dinings at the executive mansion, have never looked half so gorgeous.

Though delighted over the invitation, for days before the affair I was wholly engrossed by the momentous questions of what I should wear; what I should do when I got there; and how I should ever command ideas enough to carry me safely through a long state dinner and not become a bore to my escort—that was the rub. Who that unfortunate individual was to be it was impossible to find out. Was he to be a personage of agreeable manners, or arrogant, pedantic, and probably patronizing? Any of these latter characteristics would make me so unhappy that I should be unable to appear to any advantage. Then if he betrayed in the slightest degree that he was bored or really endured me because there was no escape I should have suffered intensely. I was proud of my husband, whose handsome face and brilliant conversation would charm all about him, but for myself I had many misgivings and visions of hours of agony.

However, the desire to see the pomp and display of a state dinner and to hear the conversation of the distinguished guests I expected to meet at such a ceremonious affair overcame every scruple. Stephen A. Douglas and his universally admired wife, Mr. and Mrs. John C. Breckenridge, Senator and Mrs. Jefferson Davis, Senator and Mrs. Yulee, Senator and Mrs. Mason, of Virginia, Senator and Mrs. Gwyn, of California, Judah P. Benjamin, Senator and Mrs. John J. Crittenden, Colonel Syms, of Kentucky, the Cabinet, and many others to the number of forty sat down to that stately dinner. My escort was Stephen A. Douglas, and of course I was supremely happy, because I had known him from girlhood and had looked up to him as a great leader and most charming man in conversation. He was the personal and political friend of my father and my husband, and was anxious to treat me with every consideration for their sakes. Under his tactful and fascinating conversation I soon forgot my misgivings, and, through the inspiration of the resplendent surroundings, felt never so proud and happy, although now and then in the sallies of the leading spirits in the conversation that went round the table, ominous expressions were made that caused one to tremble and ask one's self: "Is it possible that there is one of this distinguished company who would raise a hand against the flag of the Union or break the bonds that hold the grand constellation of States together?" I little thought that one of the number would in a brief time be the leader and President of the Confederacy, directing deadly blows against a government that had bestowed on him many high honors.

Senator and Mrs. Gwyn, of California, entertained very handsomely, their grand balls being among the finest given in Washington. For years their hospitable home had been the attraction for the most distinguished at the capital. People were still talking of their famous masquerade ball, given the winter before, in which the President appeared in the court dress he had worn at Saint James's. Members of the Cabinet, both houses of Congress, the diplomatic corps, army, navy, and citizens entered into its spirit with enthusiasm, and, all in fancy costumes, represented royalty, dramatic characters, historic personages, great warriors, celebrated admirals, men and women of literary distinction, artists, and many others.

Among those who took part in the occasion was Mrs. William E. Chandler, then young Miss Hale, daughter of Senator Hale, of New Hampshire, who appeared as Sunrise, and of whom Major John De Havilland, who described the affair in verse, wrote:

> "I marvel not, O sun, that unto thee
> In adoration men should bow the knee."

Mrs. Stephen A. Douglas, subsequently Mrs. Williams, then one of the most brilliant and beautiful women at the capital, representing Aurora, inspired the poet to the following description:

> "The bright Aurora in our senses gleams,
> Nor yields to that fair daughter of the morn,
> Whom Guido saw on car triumphant borne."

She was, indeed, "*la belle au bal.*" Mr. and Mrs. Coyle, Mrs. Madison Cutts, Mrs. Emery, wife of General Emery, and Brady the artist were there, though not in masquerade. Nothing of later days has excelled the stateliness of the occasion in all its appointments or the illustrious characters taking part.

Mayor and Mrs. Wallach gave many grand dinners and receptions and one ball so resplendent as to rival anything, save a fancy-dress affair. We recall the venerable John J. Crittenden and his charming wife, whose dignified bearing and genial face were ever pleasing to see; Lord Napier; the French minister; Hon. Anson Burlingame; Mr. and Mrs. C. C. Clay, of Alabama; Mrs. Greenough, wife of the sculptor; Hon. Horatio King; Hon. Daniel E. Sickles, still surviving; Mr. Bouligny, of Louisiana, and his fascinating wife, *née* Miss Parker; the Livingstons; Minister Bodisco and his charming wife; Cochrane, of New York; Banks, of Alabama; General Magruder; Mr. Clingman; Mr. and Mrs. Vance; Mr. Harris, of Virginia; John C. Breckenridge; Senator Rice, of Minnesota; Chief Justice Taney; Barkesdale, member of Congress from Mississippi, who was later killed in the Confederate Army during the Civil War; Stephen A. Douglas; Hon. William Kellogg, of Illinois; Mr. and Mrs. Roger A. Pryor; Doctor Garnett; Senator Judah P. Benjamin; General and Mrs. McClernand; Miss Dunlap, sister of Mrs. McClernand, who married General McClernand after her sister's death in the early sixties; Mr. and Mrs. Foulke, of Illinois; Senator Edward Baker, killed at Ball's Bluff in 1862; Colonel and Mrs. Robert E. Lee; and a host of others—were familiar faces at social entertainments.

On all occasions wine flowed freely, egg-nog being on every table on New Year's Day. Terrapin was as common as the simple bouillon of to-day, the colored cook who presided in every kitchen knowing better how to prepare terrapin than our most skilful chef.

At evening entertainments the guests arrived early and remained until the "wee sma' hours." The Inauguration Ball, March 4, 1861, was a grand affair, but not participated in by many of the opposition or residents of Washington whose sympathies were with the South, many flattering themselves to the very last that there would be some resistance to Mr. Lincoln's inauguration. Fortunately, the theory of bowing to the will of the majority was then a cardinal principle in the decalogue of American politics. It is a melancholy revery for one to think upon those momentous days, and to take up, one by one, the names of men and women who figured in the social and political drama then being enacted. Death has claimed nearly all, as more than half a century has rolled away, not a few having met sudden deaths in the real tragedies in which they took part; while others of the brilliant coterie played important parts in the Civil War that burst upon the country with such violence in 1861 as to stop completely their dalliance with pastimes and pleasures at the national capital, and precipitate the whole nation into its realities. Instead of making merry and dancing to the music of "stringed instruments" in the ball and drawing rooms, they hastened to the field of carnage to the thrilling notes of martial music, changing the light steps of the dancers to the tramp of the warriors' march. Before Ash Wednesday had stopped the festivities, rumors of the coming conflict, the defiant threatenings of seizing Sumter, and the seceding of States from the Union effectually stopped all gayety, and made serious and thoughtful the most giddy devotee of society.

Almost every one was so restless that he must needs be on the go all the time. Even the theatres were packed every night. The actors and actresses of that time were very fine. Forrest, Sothern, Joe Jefferson, Booth the elder, Charlotte Cushman, and other celebrated men and women were on the boards, "Lord Dundreary" furnishing recreation and amusement for the weary, "Rip Van Winkle" bringing tears from the sympathetic, while Charlotte Cushman's "Queen Catherine" and "Meg Merrilies" awakened the wildest enthusiasm for her great power in the rendition of such rôles. In February she came to Washington to play for five nights: the first night giving "Queen Catherine," supported by J. B. Studley, a fine actor; the second night in "Meg Merrilies." When she delivered the curse upon poor Bertram, her figure seemed to rise to the stature of a giantess before her trembling, cringing victim. On this occasion she was brought before the curtain again and again, the whole audience, from orchestra to the top gallery, rising to their feet and cheering wildly. In imagination I can to this day see her majestic figure as she appeared to acknowledge the encores.

She followed the next night (her benefit) with Mrs. Haller, in Kotzebue's play, "The Stranger," and as *Mrs. Simpson* in "Simpson & Company," to a superb audience of appreciative admirers. "Lady Macbeth," "Cardinal Wolsey," and "Nancy Sykes" were also given at the earnest request of a large number of distinguished people, who signed a petition to her to gratify them by prolonging the engagement seven nights. Each night the house was as full as the managers dared to allow. One never tired of seeing her. She was the personification of power and grace, and so forceful that one was impressed by her peerless physical and mental strength, and yet she seemed as gentle as a child. Few women have left a deeper impress upon the age in which they lived.

On the reassembling of Congress after Mr. Lincoln's inauguration the excitement grew greater and greater, reaching a higher pitch when the sound of the firing upon Sumter was flashed across the country. The seizure of the forts in Charleston Harbor and the firing on the flag aroused the whole nation. The people were completely demoralized between the conflicting impulses of their generous natures toward kindred in the South and duty to their country. At first they could do nothing. The hammer lay idle by the anvil; the bellows unused; the fires were out in engines and furnaces; the wheels of machinery still. The plough stood in the furrow, and men wandered about asking for news, and stood in groups for hours talking; crowded around every new arrival in the little town, or gathered about the fortunate possessor of a newspaper, while he read aloud to the anxious listeners every line of news or comment upon the situation of affairs. Wives, mothers, and sweethearts went about their household duties with melancholy faces, and often with tears rolling down their cheeks, as their loving hearts ached with ominous forebodings of what was coming, and what might happen to their loved ones in the near future. Unaccustomed to the suspense and anxiety of war, and the absence of loved ones whom they knew would enlist if war should be declared, they were wretched beyond expression.

Having no alternative, Mr. Lincoln made the call for seventy-five thousand men, and money to protect life and property and uphold the authority of the Government. To our peaceful citizens this seemed an innumerable army, but the response from every loyal State, that their quota would be supplied as rapidly as possible, according to their respective facilities of enlisting and organizing troops, inspired the President with hope and confidence.

To a nation that had only known the annual "Militia Day" in those States which had militia organizations—numbering only a few in the whole country—and whose idea of the militia rose scarcely above the standard of a parade by five companies, the announcement, over the signature of the Chief Magistrate, that the Union was in danger and needed defence at the hands of all loyal citizens, aroused the patriotism of the people. The small, regular army, then scattered to the farthermost borders of this vast country, could not furnish a sufficient number of drill-sergeants or commissioned officers to drill the hastily recruited volunteers.

The few veterans of the Mexican War then surviving north of the Mason and Dixon line had well-nigh forgotten the obsolete manual of arms, which they had learned during the brief war with Mexico; and yet long-neglected tactics were taken down from the dusty shelves and eagerly read. Rusty swords that had done occasional duty on Militia Day since '48 were hunted up and buckled on over citizen dress; old fifes that had not known the touch of human lips for many years were soon responding to the inspiring notes of martial airs; old drummers regained their cunning, and beat an accompaniment calling men to arms. The few industrial establishments that had been kept in operation by a small number of faithful men for the furtherance of private enterprises were immediately converted into busy hives for the manufacture of implements of war, volunteers stepping into line until every place was filled. Those not needed in the field joined the busy army of workers who were occupied with the preparations for clothing, feeding, arming, and supporting the soldiers at the front.

Returning to our home in southern Illinois, we found that the proximity of that section to the slaveholding States and the close ties by nature of a majority of the people to those of the South had caused the most intense excitement. Almost every household was divided in sentiment. The theory of States' rights had so impregnated the minds of the people that they were unable to divest themselves of the feeling that the people of the South really owed their first duty to their States, and not to the Government of the United States. In the heat of discussions of the political campaign they had concluded that the South had a grievance in the election of an antislavery man and the supremacy of the Republican party. At heart they were loyal to their country, and in sympathizing with their kindred of the South it never occurred to them that they were guilty of disloyalty, or that they were aiding and abetting treason. They had an idea that concessions might be made which would in no wise compromise the dignity and power of the Government, and through which the Southern States might be induced to remain in the Union.

We had taken advantage of the interim between the adjournment and the reassembling of Congress under the President's call to go home, I to remain to do what I could to prepare the people for the step Mr. Logan had decided he must take at an early day or be guilty of treason to his country. He felt that he must be for or against the Government, and that his duty demanded that he should enter the army and take with him as many men of his constituency as he could. Therefore he did not want them to continue their excitement, lest they might rashly commit themselves to secession. Mr. Logan, however, returned to Washington to take part in the proceedings of Congress at the extra session to provide ways and means for supporting, arming, and equipping the troops.

Arriving at Marion, Williamson County, Illinois, where we then resided, we were not prepared for the state of public mind that greeted us. Constituents hitherto full of enthusiasm and cordial greeting met us with restraint, expressing eagerness to know what was going to be done; finding fault with this, that, and the other action that had and had not been taken; insisting especially that there had not been given to the South enough guarantees that their institutions would in no wise be interfered with. They were reluctant to believe that everything had been offered and refused. At the same time they blamed the South for the attack on Fort Sumter. Many of them had kindred in the South whom they dearly loved, and still they could not leave their homes in the North and sacrifice everything to go to their friends whom they knew must, sooner or later, lose their all in the cause of the rebellion in which they were embarking. It was touching to see them. They looked to Mr. Logan, then their representative in Congress, to tell them what to do, and they knew instinctively that his advice would be hard to follow. Either horn of the dilemma was painful for them to contemplate.

A few reckless spirits had already departed for the Southern Confederacy, and had thus brought suspicion and opprobrium upon the section of the State south of the Ohio and Mississippi Railroad.

The authorities at the capital of the State and in the office of the United States marshal were watching the movements of every man. Their only hope of restraining the sympathizers was through Mr. Logan, whose influence had been very great. Appreciating the grave responsibility resting upon him, he had occasion for much vigilance and solicitude, lest he should fail in saving the people from getting into trouble through rash acts until their own good judgment and sense should bring them to see whither they were drifting, and the inevitable results of rebellion. Many were the hours he paced the floor revolving in his mind how he should hold them to their duty by enlisting them in the service of the Government, thus preventing their taking steps that would involve them in ruin. He dared not tell them that he should enter the army himself. They would have spurned him and accused him of treachery to his party and to them, and of selling himself to the administration. The time had not arrived for them, with their former political teachings and affiliations, to think of the rebellion as treason against the general Government, and as a confederation for the destruction of the Federal Union. So, without intimating what he should do, he talked to them as though they were children, arguing in the line of patriotism and duty to one's country, warned them of the fate of traitors, the horrors of civil war, and the consequences of aiding and abetting revolution. He then departed for Washington, promising them his faithful devotion to their best interests and the perpetuity of the Union, assuring them that party ties should not be strong enough to drag any man into treason against his country. He tried to prepare them for what was coming—the severing of party allegiance and enlistment in the army.

To remain at home and be surrounded by all these people, to answer all their questions, to satisfy their curiosity and fault-finding with what was being done in Washington, to interpret the meaning of every move North and South, to keep them as nearly as I could in the channel in which Mr. Logan had adroitly drawn them, was an appalling task. Beset by fears lest I might make a mistake, and the awful foreboding that harm might come to Mr. Logan through the hate of some adventurous spirit whose sympathies were with the South, and the knowledge, too, that my husband would soon join the army and embark in all the hazardous movements and dangerous enterprises of a soldier's life in a fratricidal war made me the most unhappy of women.

My eldest brother, then a young man of twenty, at school at Lebanon, Illinois, suddenly returned home, and before we could prevent him left us to join the Confederate army. He was only two years my junior; we had always been together in our childhood and partners in all the joys and sorrows of life. After my marriage he had been much with us, and loved

Mr. Logan devotedly, but in a mad moment he had ruthlessly placed himself in the attitude of an enemy.  He was a
dashing, thoughtless spirit, and had yielded to an impulse to
follow the fate of his college chums who lived South and had
gone to their homes at the mandate of their families in different States which had seceded.  This brought to my already
overburdened heart another overwhelming sorrow.  To see
the blanched faces and tearful eyes of my dear father and
mother as they went about fretting over the impending conflict, with my husband (whom they idolized) and their eldest
son in opposing armies, was almost more than I could endure.
Time flew rapidly, and Mr. Logan wrote me by every mail
(then triweekly) of the progress of events, directing me to
prepare the few we could trust for his return and to apprise
them of his purpose to raise a regiment immediately upon his
arrival.

In the South the seeming restless tide of secession was
sweeping everything before it; in the North the timid and
doubtful were wavering under the impress always made by
success.  What would be the result? no one could foretell;
all felt the feverish state of the public mind.  The spring had
come and gone, the summer's heat was on, half the crops had
not been planted, and those that had been were not properly
cultivated.  Wherever one went naught but the din of discussion was heard; every person seemed suspicious of every
one else; friction and impatience were rife.  The battle of
Manassas, or first Bull Run, with its unsatisfactory result had
discouraged and disheartened the not over-sanguine, and had
made it harder than ever to convince the sympathizers that
there was no foundation for the boasted prowess of the Southern soldiers, and that their claim that one Southern man was
worth five Northern men was baseless.

Events of the most thrilling character occurred daily, and
kept every one in a state of excitement and apprehension.
The very thought of civil war carried with it a heart-sicken-

ing terror, and completely demoralized the people. Senator Douglas had died very suddenly in Washington, and Mr. Logan was left almost alone to face the excited, reckless people of southern Illinois.

Finally the day arrived upon which Mr. Logan was to reach home. J. H. White, later lieutenant-colonel of the 31st Infantry, which Mr. Logan raised; Mr. Swindell, sheriff of Williamson County; one or two others; and myself had canvassed the county on horseback. Going to the houses of the coolest-headed and most reliable men, we asked them to come to the town of Marion on that day that they might hear Mr. Logan, who was advertised to speak to the people in the public square; also asking them to be ready to protect him or to quell any disturbance should mob violence be attempted if he failed to impress them favorably.

It was one of those hot, dusty days in that semitropical climate when man and beast panted for breath. At an early hour the people began to arrive, and before noon—the hour at which Mr. Logan was due—a surging throng of human beings filled the public square, impatiently watching the road over which he was to drive into town.

Getting into a buggy early that morning, I drove out on the road leading to Carbondale, a station on the Illinois Central Railroad, to meet my husband, who was to come to Marion in a carriage that had been sent to bring him from the train. It was a distance of twenty miles from Marion to Carbondale. I kept driving but did not meet him. Fearing something was wrong, I continued my journey to Carbondale, to learn that the Eastern train on the Ohio and Mississippi Railroad, and the Illinois Central Railroad upon which he was to come had missed connection at the crossing at Odin. There was no possible chance for him to get down until two o'clock the following morning; hence he could not speak until the following day. Appreciating the disappointment it would be to the people of Marion, knowing their inflammable natures, and that many men among them had probably been drinking and were desperate by that time, I knew it was no time to trust a messenger with the simple message that my husband had been detained, but would come the following day, at which time they should return to hear what he had to say. I also wished to consult with the trusted friends we had as to the temper of the people when such numbers were together. I therefore took a fresh horse and drove back to Marion. Many eyes were still peering down the long road, and the moment they spied me coming alone they could hardly wait for me to reach the centre of the square when they gathered around the buggy, stopped the horse, and eagerly cried out: "Where is Logan?" "What is the matter?" "What does this mean?" "We have got to know all about this business," and many such questions and threats.

Heartsick, frightened, weary with the forty-mile drive, and choking with anxiety and discouragement over the seeming madness of the men, I could only beg them to be quiet; to call Mr. Swindell, the sheriff, that I might explain to him, and that he should stand up in the buggy and tell them all. I saw that many were drunk and muttering vengeance on somebody, and that they did not know what they were doing, and I was almost in despair. Very soon Mr. Swindell, a tall, distinguished-looking man, with a fine face, blue eyes as gentle as any woman's, and at the same time full of moral courage and coolness, came to me and I briefly told him the facts: that it was purely an accident occasioned by a delay on the then badly managed road. He stood up on the seat of the buggy and addressed the surging multitude, appealing to their manhood, their sense of right and propriety. He besought them to go home and go to sleep; to quiet down, and to come back by two o'clock on the following day when Logan, their leader and best friend, would be there and would tell them everything. He told them that, as they valued their liberty, their homes, and their country, it behooved them to follow him wherever he should go; that he had more at stake than they had; that all that he or they held dear was in the balance against anarchy and rebellion; that they and their posterity would reap the consequences of their sowing; that they knew that his all was at stake with them, and that he, personally, was ready to join Logan with all he had in whatever move Logan said would bring peace to the distracted country, without which they could expect nothing for themselves or their children. Many were deeply affected and did as he suggested, departing for their homes; others manifested an ugly spirit and continued their wrangling and dissipation, making threats, and in many ways causing me great solicitude.

When the crowd had dispersed I drove to my father's home, and, after consulting with our friends, I decided to take another horse and drive back to Carbondale to meet my husband, so that I could have a chance to tell him everything— the exact position of every man in the town, and of many who were in the country; to be able to give him the benefit of what we had done; and suggest to him what we considered the safest line in which he could move. It was a bright moonlight night, and, as it was before the day of tramps, I was not afraid to go alone, although I should not arrive in Carbondale before midnight. In those days the produce was freighted across the country to the railroad in large wagons, forming sometimes quite a train of ten or a dozen together. The drivers camped at the side of the road, parking their teams, sleeping in their wagons, building fires to cook their food and make their coffee—the men sometimes sitting up late, playing cards and telling stories. If one was alone on the highway and had to pass one of these camps, they presented rather a weird appearance, and in times of such excitement it was quite enough to startle the nerves of a weak woman. Driving along the road with a dense forest on either side, and seeing that at the sound of the approaching vehicle some of the men walked out toward the road as if they intended to stop the horse, or at least to know who was passing at so late an hour; fearing that they might not recognize me, and greatly frightened, my heart fluttered like a leaf in a gale of wind. Fortunately they knew me and also my horse, and they called out: "Where are you going—has anything happened?" I halted long enough to tell them, and they expressed regret that I had undertaken so lonely a journey and that none of them could leave their teams, as they were then returning to Marion with valuable freight, or they would not let me continue alone. I bade them good night and hurried on, congratulating myself upon my good fortune. I reached Carbondale two hours before Mr. Logan arrived. It was two o'clock A. M. before his train halted at the Illinois Central depot.

We were both weary and half-sick from fatigue, anxiety, and loss of sleep. We went to the hotel, and, as quickly as he could get away from the many who had been waiting for him, we retired to our room to rest till seven in the morning, when we must go to Marion to meet the crowd that would be waiting impatiently for him. There was no sleep for either of us, so anxious were we both. Events of such grave character had happened since we parted early in April, that it seemed ages since we had been together. The unknown was before us. A more or less reckless people surrounded us, all of them unreasonable in their expectation of what Mr. Logan could do; some going so far as to aver that he could have secured the adoption of the Crittenden compromise if he had tried, forgetting that Crittenden, Douglas, Caleb Cushing, and the oldest and ablest men in the nation had been unable to get anything done in the way of compromise. His former closest friends were the worst secessionists. Our families were much divided, and we felt that we could trust only each other. He had resolved to enter the army for the war with no alternative but to leave me to do the best I could; and, at the same time, to try to sustain my father and mother (my eldest brother, as before stated, having joined the Confederate army) and those who might be left alone should their husbands, fathers, or brothers volunteer to go with him. Not knowing what fate awaited us, we drove over the familiar road with sad hearts, feeling it was our only opportunity to be alone, or to talk over the plans for the present or the future.

As we approached Marion the people began to gather about the buggy, cheering and shouting their welcome to General Logan; crowding so near to grasp his hand that it was almost impossible for the horse we were driving to move. He assured them he would speak to them at two o'clock. It was then almost noon, and he had to go home long enough to remove the dust of travel from his clothing and to get his dinner. The very crowd was enough to alarm one; they were so excited—seemingly on the verge of violent demonstration. When the hour arrived, he came to me and begged me on no account to go into the street. He felt that there might be trouble, and assured me he should be unnerved if he thought I was in the crowd, should mob violence seize the half-crazed people. I gave my promise, with a mental reservation not to keep it; as I determined to be near him whatever happened, thinking by a disguise in dress and keeping behind him (as he was to speak standing in a wagon in the public square) that I could watch the actions of one or two persons who had made threats of a personal assault upon him should he declare for war or attempt to raise a regiment. I felt sure I could at least scream should they move toward him with evil intent.

I waited until he was gone and soon followed, keeping out of his sight, but where I could see him and every movement made toward him. I trembled in every limb, my head swam, and I dared not speak to any one, though surrounded by acquaintances who once were friends. He mounted the wagon, and, after waving salutation to the throng who surrounded him, he began to speak in a voice so clear and with such volume that every person, even those farthest from him on the outside of the crowd, could hear him distinctly.   In a few moments a deathlike stillness prevailed; the most turbulent spirit in the crowd was as quiet as the dead.   You could hear only his sonorous voice as he with great deliberation pictured the situation of affairs, the inevitable consequences of rebellion against the Government should the theory of secession prevail; telling them at what cost of blood and treasure the republic had been established, and how certainly liberty would be forfeited and anarchy reign were the Union once dissolved. Step by step he led them on for nearly two hours, intensity and earnestness depicted in every lineament of his face, his bright black eyes gleaming with emotion, every gesture emphasizing the truthfulness of his remarks, and his earnestness carrying conviction.   The effect upon his hearers was magical. They were swayed by his eloquence until they fairly re-echoed his utterances.   Toward the close he said: "The time has come when a man must be for or against his country, not for or against his State.   How long could one State stand up against another, or two or three States against others? The Union once dissolved, we should have innumerable confederacies and rebellions.   I, for one, shall stand or fall for this Union, and shall this day enroll for the war.   I want as many of you as will to come with me.   If you say 'No,' and see your best interests and the welfare of your homes and your children in another direction, may God protect you."

There was an old fifer, six feet four inches tall, and very large in proportion, in the crowd.   He had been a fifer in the same regiment with Mr. Logan in the Mexican War.   We had seen him previously, and he had promised to come and bring his fife, and at a signal from J. H. White was to go up to Mr. Logan, give him his hand as a volunteer, and then was to play a patriotic air on his fife, whereat Mr. White and a few others were to step in line and start the volunteering. Mr. Logan did not know that Sanders, the fifer, was to be there, or that he was to lead off in that way, and when he saw the herculean figure of his old comrade striding through the crowd, making for him, he lost control of his feelings and wept like a child. It is needless to add that through my own tears I witnessed the most affecting scene that had ever occurred in that or any other town. At the sound of Sanders's fife and the beating of an old drum of Gabriel Cox, who was a member of the drum corps of the same regiment in which Mr. Logan served in the Mexican War, and whom Mr. White and Captain Looney, who was elected captain of the company, and other friends had hunted up, Mr. Logan jumped down from the wagon, stepped into the line that was speedily filling up, one after another "falling in" (my friend the teamster who had frightened me so two nights before being among the very first), gave the command, "Forward, march!" and started around the square, followed by one hundred and ten men, as good and true as ever carried musket. All were enrolled for "three years, or during the war." There was scarcely a dry eye in the whole crowd. The ugly spirits who a few hours before were boasting and threatening all sorts of bloody deeds had hied themselves to safer quarters till the volunteers were out of town. The company enlisted on that day, the 19th of August, 1861, afterward became Company A of the gallant 31st, which Colonel Logan recruited and commanded till after the battle of Fort Donelson, where he won his star.

Those were trying times when the knowledge that one's husband had enlisted for the war and a hundred others had joined him brought to the heart a feeling of relief and respite from fear lest he might be the victim of an assassin or a mob. That one should construe such a *dernier ressort* as a guarantee for the preservation of life and the protection of homes seems an anomaly, but such was the condition of things that from that hour we hoped for the best, and felt relieved from cruel suspense and agonizing forebodings.

Colonel Logan was so absorbed with the details of raising his regiment, and so sure that southern Illinois would be true to the Union, that he seemed almost happy, keeping me busy driving back and forth between Carbondale, the telegraph station on the Illinois Central Railroad, and other points where he went to recruit the ten companies of which his regiment was composed. He would not trust any one else to send or receive the despatches he was constantly sending and receiving from the governor and adjutant-general of the State, who was at Springfield, the capital of the State, and the Secretary of War, at Washington, D. C. Consequently and fortunately, I had but little time to think of the future and all that it might hold for me.

# CHAPTER V

THE vast territory lying to the south, southwest, and southeast of Cairo, Illinois, prior to the Rebellion, depended upon the Mississippi River as almost the only channel through which could be conveyed to the markets the cotton, molasses, and sugar. Through the same source they passed the larger supplies of grain, flour, and other commodities. The Mississippi River and its principal tributaries bounded the shores of several States that had cast in their lot with secession. The lands of these States were owned by the few wealthy slaveholders who had colonies of slaves but very few neighbors beyond the kindred and families of the same estate.

"King Cotton," as they were wont to style their chief product, brought them a rich harvest of money when shipped to distant marts, but could not be consumed or utilized within their own State borders, destitute as they were of manufactories. Hence many thousand bales of cotton, hogsheads of tobacco, and barrels of molasses and sugar found their way to the North on the steamers plying between the Northern cities of Cincinnati, Louisville, Saint Louis, Cairo, and Memphis, Vicksburg, Natchez, and New Orleans, of the lower South.

Coming up the Mississippi River, the steamers touched at Cairo before going on to Saint Louis, or to Louisville and Cincinnati on the Ohio. Here they dropped that which was intended for the extreme North and East, whither it was taken by rail. It was a weird sight to see the black stevedores, clad only in turbans and trousers, rolling these bales and barrels on to the levee at Cairo by the light of pine torches planted on the shore, all the while chanting some plantation song, as they pulled and tugged at the heavy burdens, as if to lighten their loads by their own strange melodies. As soon as all was off and the steamer again "pulled out" and went puffing on her way, one could hear the boatmen still singing their plantation melodies as they lay on the piles of freight on the deck, resting from their labors.

Cairo was in those days little better than the doleful picture of it given in "Martin Chuzzlewit" under the fictitious name of "Eden." It was as unlike one's idea of the Eden of Paradise as possible. Often it was deluged by overflows, whose waters stagnated in every depression and were soon covered by a green scum, almost cutting it off from the highlands by that dismal swamp which extended nearly across the State a few miles north of Cairo. There seemed little hope that a city of any importance could ever be built in that locality. Ague and other diseases from miasmatic influences frightened away many who came to make their homes and fortunes there. Wooden structures, standing pools of stagnant water, bilious and listless white people, shiftless and wretched negroes, were about all there was of Cairo prior to 1861, save the few enterprising men who are found everywhere.

Geographically so well situated, the "great captains" saw that from Cairo there could be moved armies that would sweep the Mississippi Valley to the Gulf, southwestward, and

John A. Logan in 1861, as colonel of the Thirty-first
Illinois Regiment.

through Kentucky, Tennessee, and the Carolinas, to the Atlantic Ocean. Driving before them the best fighting elements of the Southern Confederacy, when once on the soil of these States, they could gather subsistence from the country over which they passed. They foresaw that the cotton-fields must soon be given up, and corn and grain for their own armies and people would take the place of cotton. It was not for the "great captains" to consider the inconvenience, difficulties, and discomforts attending the mobilizing and organizing of these armies, but to conceive and issue orders, and leave it to the patriotic volunteer officers and soldiers to execute their plans. The small regular army was in the East and on the frontier.

Hence Cairo was designated as the place of rendezvous for the brigade which it was proposed should be recruited from southern Illinois. The Confederate troops occupied Columbus, Kentucky, and Belmont, Missouri, a point on the opposite side of the Mississippi River. Price's army was being recruited, terrorizing and controlling all of southwest Missouri. The city of Cairo, occupying the peninsula point of the State at the junction of the Ohio and Mississippi Rivers, was subject to overflows, the levees encircling the city being its only protection from inundation. The very streets were impassable at times. These facts made the occupation of Cairo by troops almost impracticable, but commanding, as it did, the Ohio and Mississippi Rivers, it was imperative that it should be fortified and manned by troops to defend the approach to the north up the Mississippi River. The fathomless mud was not the only unpleasant feature of Cairo at that time. The sudden concentration of thousands of men in the little city, with its half-dozen small hotels and overflowed surroundings, rendered existence as much a problem as that of the occupancy recently of the Canal Zone. Transportation was inadequate to the great number struggling to reach the point from which the great army was eventually to move. Habitations of houses or tents were not obtainable for all these civilians and soldiers congregating there. Quartermasters and commissaries were inefficient, and without any conception of the requirements of a great army and its followers. One single-track railroad with insufficient rolling-stock was to carry all the men, all the supplies, all the horses, all the ordnance and freight necessary for the immediate organization and equipment of the Army of the Mississippi.

The river steamers were of the most primitive character, and, though busy night and day, were unequal to the prodigious emergency. A majority of the men and supplies came from the North under difficulties indescribable. The Illinois Central Railroad was almost the only means of conveying everything to the base of operations. The continuous trains going and coming kept the people along the line of the road in a state of feverish excitement, and impressed them with the stupendous nature of the preparations for the conflict.

The most extravagant imagination had never thought that the little city of wooden houses sitting behind the levees which line the shores of the Ohio and Mississippi Rivers at their junction, could ever be of so much importance in the nation's weal. One could hardly realize that it was the key to the valley of the Mississippi, or that the army rendezvoused and equipped within its small limits was destined to "hew its way to the gulf." The men of the West would not believe that the South would ever establish a blockade or fire upon the "flag of the free." Finally the shot was heard, and the wide-mouthed cannon mounted on the river-bank at Columbus, turned toward the north, announced the establishment of the barrier. Fired by indignation and patriotism, the people rallied to their country's call like the hosts of Roderick Dhu. Accustomed to pioneering and "roughing it," they were equal to the exigencies of the times.

The spirits that controlled in the South and Southwest

were so daring and so reckless that they would have undertaken any venture, no matter how mad, had they not learned of the preparations to prevent them from coming up the river. The volunteers waited not for the regulation appointments, but, with earnestness that meant success, began at once to acquire the profession of the soldier. The old Belgian muskets, with which they were first armed, served every purpose for mastering the manual of arms; many officers, studying the manual of arms themselves, practised by drilling their commands for hours each day. Cheerfulness, and a willingness to learn to do whatever was to be done, were invariably evinced by the men notwithstanding the revolting feelings that sometimes came over them before they became accustomed to receiving and cooking their own rations, and doing the police duty necessary in camp. As fast therefore as the troops were recruited at different points, they were hurried to Cairo. There they were mustered in regiments ready for organization into brigades. The 18th, 27th, 30th, and 31st—and later the 25th Infantry Volunteers, known as the Lead Mine Regiment from Galena—Swartz's and Taylor's Batteries, and some cavalry were to compose the First Brigade.

Very few of the men or officers of these regiments knew anything whatever of the art of war, except a man here and there who had served in the Mexican War. For the most part they were young men just entering manhood, who had never been away from their homes for any length of time, many of them never having been out of the State. They knew nothing of the hardships that awaited them or the full meaning of enlistment in their country's service. When the time came for them to say good-by to mothers, sisters, wives, and sweethearts, it was most pathetic. I remember once watching the face of a sentinel as he paced his beat and looked with intense disgust at the unloading with iron shovels of the loaves of bread out of a wagon-bed in front of the tent where it was to be issued to the companies. This young man had left a home of comfort and plenty, where his fond and fastidious mother presided. Visions of her delicious cookery, snowy table linen, and transparent china made the loaves, thrown from the shovels to a not over-clean board table, anything but tempting. A few months afterward the forbidding loaves would have been hailed with delight in place of the "hardtack" that had not been softened or rendered more palatable by being carried in a haversack for days.

Doing guard and police duty with a lowering sky above them, and mud and water beneath their feet, made many a soldier sick at heart, and caused his courage to drop in the scale of heroism, when first learning the duties of a son of Mars. The discipline of walking to and fro with a gun on his shoulder in the wee small hours of a stormy night was a different thing from marching away on a gala-day to the tune of "Yankee Doodle," or with the drums and fifes beating and whistling "The Girl I Left Behind Me."

I witnessed the departure of many of the men of the old 31st from cottages and more pretentious homes. At the sound of the roll-call could be seen great, manly fellows, folding their loved ones in a last fond embrace, and then, with the tears streaming down their blanched cheeks, rushing out of the door, and down the street to step into line and answer "Here," while their telltale faces betrayed the emotions of their brave hearts. The tearful eyes, pale faces, quivering lips, and sobs of those they were leaving behind; the anguish of the non-combatants who were to guard the hearthstones, care for the dependents, and send cheer to the loved ones gone to the front, told the sad story of what it cost those who volunteered and those who stayed at home.

After marching out of the towns, they found farm wagons and all kinds of vehicles drawn up in a line beside the roads. Into these the "boys" climbed, to be taken to the railroad, because they were destined to have enough of marching on Southern soil. The troops were not allowed to walk when there was no necessity for their doing so. Arriving at the depot they were transferred to the cars, when the last good-bys must be said to those who had accompanied them thus far on their long journey. Reaching Cairo they were deposited on the levee, which, like a great sea-wall, then encircled the city.

Gathering together their little all, they were soon marching to camp to be assigned to tents and begin their duties as soldiers for three years, or during the war, unless sooner discharged by reason of disability. That first night in camp can never be forgotten by a soldier enlisted in time of war: the confusion of being assigned; getting accustomed to the meagre accommodations of tent life; the building of fires; hanging the camp kettle; making the coffee, drinking it out of tin cups; and cooking the rations, eating them from tin plates, without knives, forks, or spoons. To those who had left comfortable homes, presided over by loving mothers and wives, it was a trying initiation into the life they were to lead. The posting of the guard who, in reliefs, were to pace their beats through the weary hours of night, broken only by the dismal call of the hours: "— o'clock, and all is well!" continuing through rain or shine of the morrow, and of each succeeding day and night was a great trial to men accustomed to following the Franklin maxim of "Early to bed and early to rise." Police and guard duty, drilling in the falling rain or broiling sun, kept them busy all the time. There was no going where they pleased or declining to obey disagreeable orders; they had to become accustomed to the confinement of staying within the lines; master the manual of arms; keep their clothes and accoutrements clean; appear at dress parade at five o'clock daily; cook their meals, report for drill and guard duty; and observe other details without questioning the reason why. To men who had known no discipline or superior authority, this was very hard and left little opportunity for aught save the homesickness that every soldier experienced.

In the 31st Regiment there were many men whom both Colonel Logan and I had known for years. They were splendid men, but absolutely ignorant of military discipline or the proper deference due superior officers. It took them some time to learn to address an officer by the title of his rank. They had always called Colonel Logan "John," and me "Mary," and often greeted us both affectionately by our names without realizing there was any impropriety in the familiarity. One day a soldier whom we shall call "Sol," a fine specimen of man—a robust, tall, active, cheerful, willing soldier—came to the colonel's tent looking much depressed. He gave awkwardly the military salute. Colonel Logan inquired what was the matter. He said: "John, I have got to go home, but I swear I will be back in three days." Colonel Logan replied: "What has happened?" "Sol" took out of his pocket a much-blurred and tear-stained letter and said: "Just read that, and you will not refuse to let me go." This was the letter from his wife:

MY DEAR SOL:
For God sake do come home.  I am sick.  There is nothing in the house to live on.  I can't do a dam thing with the children. The cows got in, and ate up the garden, and everything has gone to the devil and you jist have to come.
Your loving wife,<br>AMANDA.

Across the span of fifty years memory brings to mind the amused expression on Colonel Logan's face, as he read this graphic letter. After getting control of himself, he said: "Now, Sol, you know I can not grant you a leave. You know that the reasons your wife gives for wanting you to come would look badly if I sent them up to headquarters. Besides, we are likely to be ordered to the front any day, and you would hate to have it said you were absent from the regiment." Sol replied: "Now, John, do you really think there is any chance for a fight?" Colonel Logan replied: "Yes." "Then no furlough for me," said Sol. The proximity of their homes, the frequent communications with friends, and many other features made the volunteer service at the beginning of the war almost ludicrous.

Day after day they came, till almost every spot of dry ground around the city was covered with the white tents of the boys in blue. The novelty of camp life soon vanished; attacks of illness, unavoidable with so many together in an inhospitable climate, and the discomforts that beset them, brought on an irresistible longing to return to home and friends. But furloughs were not to be thought of with all they had to learn and to do. No law, however, could prevent friends from coming to them, and ere they had been encamped two months, a new army made its appearance. Fathers, mothers, brothers, sisters, wives, and sweethearts came sweeping down in caravans of carriages, wagons, and every conceivable vehicle, and in every imaginable manner, pitching their tents and building their brush houses as near the regiment in which they were interested as the commanding officers would permit. Every moment off duty one could see company officers and men wending their way to the camps outside the lines, where devoted ones were waiting to greet them. Many delicacies and "treats" brought from home were enjoyed during the brief hours of a pass outside the lines.

To add to the discomfort of camp life in muddy Cairo, the measles broke out and spread rapidly. Five hundred of the 31st Regiment (Colonel Logan's) were ill with measles at one time. Medical purveyors were as little skilled as many of the officers in other branches of the service, and knew, if possible, less about providing for the sick. The exigencies of the war at that time had not driven them to a disregard of rights of property-holders in the interest of the army, and property-holders were not anxious to furnish supplies in exchange for the little slips of paper called vouchers, which they feared were of doubtful value. Surgeons and medical purveyors, and, indeed, all the regimental officers, were at a loss to know what to do. Beyond the power to seize and condemn a building for hospital purposes, they could do but little. The supplies in that department had been as heavily drawn upon as any other. Requisitions remained unfilled for days, weeks, and even months. The West was so far from the seat of war that they were the last to receive consideration. Houses large enough for hospital use were hard to get, and in many instances not to be found. There were scarcely enough tents for the troops and none for hospital purposes, and there was no provision for the care of the rapidly increasing number of sick.

Deeply sympathetic, Colonel Logan, of the 31st, could not bear to see the men lying on the damp ground in their tents, so he caused a small hotel, known as the City Hotel, and owned by a Mr. Yocum, to be seized for hospital purposes. The proprietor vacated at once, but as there was no authority to take the hotel furniture for hospital use, there was nothing save the empty rooms and bare floors when the men were brought there. The purveyor's supplies had been exhausted in the establishment of the brigade hospital. The helpless regimental surgeons were in a quandary. Hundreds of the sick were lying rolled up in their blankets, and with nothing but their knapsacks under their heads. Two or three had died, and Colonel Logan was in great distress; something had to be done to render the condition of the men more comfortable.

Despairing of immediate relief through the purveyor's office, I assured Colonel Logan that I could get on the train and go to Carbondale and Marion, sixty miles north of Cairo, and, by appealing to the friends I knew, in thirty-six hours I could secure supplies enough to furnish the hospital with the best of everything, and stock the larder with all the delicacies necessary to the sick. He was so anxious for relief for his men that he decided to let me carry out my suggestion. I was to leave on the first train, which left Cairo at two A. M. The city was under martial law; the provost marshal was Major Kuykendall, of Logan's regiment. At six o'clock P. M. he closed the provost office and returned to the regimental headquarters. Colonel Logan was to get me a pass and send it to me by Captain Edwin S. McCook, who was to take me to the two A. M. train. When we reached the depot and I asked the captain for the pass, he said: "By George, I forgot to get it!" The headquarters were at least two miles away, and there was no time to get a pass. The captain was greatly excited as to how to get me on the train without one. Seeing an old friend come into the depot, who was evidently going on the train, the captain went to him and told him of the dilemma. He said: "Oh, that is all right. I have one for myself and wife, and my wife was ill this morning, and could not accompany me. I will take Mrs. Logan." They came over and told me of the scheme. I said: "Oh, no, good friends as we are, I could not think of travelling with you as Mrs. Wilson. I am sure I can get on the train without a pass, if you two men will stand on the depot platform and see me try to pass the train guard. If I fail, Captain McCook can take me back to my hotel, and I will wait until to-morrow." In those days I knew almost every one south of the Ohio and Mississippi Railroad. As soon as the train pulled in I went down to the car, and seeing young Donahue standing on the platform as guard, I said: "Donahue, I want to get into that car before the crowd; will you let me in?" He replied: "Yes, you bet I will, Mrs. Logan, but where are you going by yourself these times?" I told him that I was going to Carbondale, our home at that time, and passed into the car. As soon as I was seated, seeing the captain standing on the depot platform, I knocked on the window, and nodded to him that I was all right. Mr. Wilson came into the car soon afterward, and we had a good laugh over the episode. McCook hurried back to camp to tell

Colonel Logan the whole story. Later the colonel expressed to me his gratification at my discretion, and told me never to allow myself to be placed in a position that might be misconstrued and bring me many regrets.

Arriving at Carbondale, it required but little time to enlist many volunteers to collect the much-needed comforts. In less than thirty-six hours I had succeeded, by the help of loyal men and women whose friends were in the regiments stationed at Cairo, in collecting car-loads of home-made blankets, pillows, homespun bed linen, jellies, marmalades, wines, fruits, and everything necessary, and more, for the hospital of Colonel Logan's regiment. These blankets were made in bright colors, not unlike the famous "Roman stripes," and were so showy and comfortable, and attracted so much attention, that the hospital was known during its existence as "The Striped Hospital of the 31st Regiment." Pavilion and hospital tents were afterward invented and used, but in the early days of the war there was nothing of the kind in use in the West. It never occurred to the surgeons to decline anything tendered for the sick and disabled soldiers. The brigade and regimental surgeons were only too glad to accept the generosity of patriotic people, and avail themselves of everything that tended to reduce the mortality to a minimum. We were far enough away to disregard the dilatory action of "red tape" methods, which have been many times responsible for the increased death-rate among sick and wounded men. Regimental surgeons were held responsible for the sick of their respective regiments, and no other class of officers had more trying experiences on account of the inefficiency of the surgeon-general's department during the early part of the Civil War. Had the present system of brigade division and corps hospitals been then established, thousands would have died who were saved through the vigilance of regimental surgeons who knew, and had a personal interest in, every man in the regiment to which he belonged. Many monuments should now mark the spot where noble, self-sacrificing army surgeons sleep that "sleep which knows no waking" until they are called to their reward in a better world.

The generals and colonels swore they would never be able to discipline the troops. They longed to move to the front, or to have the power to order the civilian army to their homes. It was no use; there they stayed till the storms and blasts of approaching winter forced them to say a last good-by and retreat. In many cases, it was literally the last farewell, for the fate of war bore many of the officers and men to that unknown land from which there is no returning.

So time moved on. One day word came that a company stationed at "Big Muddy Bridge" had completed their three months' service and declined to renew their enlistment. Governor Yates urged them to re-enlist, but to no avail. A special train was ordered, and General John A. McClernand, who was in command of the First Brigade, composed of the 22d, 27th, 30th, and 31st Regiments, was directed to go up there and to take Colonel John A. Logan and see if they could not persuade the men to remain in the service. One bright morning our party set out. Arriving at the bridge sixty miles above Cairo, on the Illinois Central Railroad, we got off the train and wandered about the camp of a few tents which the men had occupied while protecting the bridge from the torch of the Southern sympathizers who lived in the vicinity, and who had hoped, by burning it, to delay transportation of troops en route for Cairo, over the Illinois Central Railroad. Mounting a box, General McClernand spoke feelingly to the men, and urged them to "stand by the flag." Still no signs came from them as to what they should do. Colonel Logan followed McClernand with an appeal to "Come on, boys, fear not death, but dishonor." Every man shouted: "We will go," and before the hour had arrived for the train to take the party back to Cairo, one by one the men had re-enlisted and taken the oath to serve for three years, unless sooner discharged by reason of disability or peace.

For weeks regiment after regiment arrived at Cairo, and were assigned the most available spots where tents could possibly be pitched. Every one felt that extensive movements must be contemplated to have occasioned such gigantic preparations. Officers and men were impatient at the routine duties of camp life, and longed for marching orders. At last they were gratified. Orders came that rations were to be cooked, ammunition to be issued, and everything to be made ready for a march—whither they knew not and cared but little, so they were on the move. When the hour for starting arrived they filed out of camp. Marching by companies, they were soon drawn up in a position on the levee, ready to take the transports. The boats came steaming round the point, and rounding to the wharfs all were embarked, as the soldiers imagined, for eventful fields. However, before they had settled down or taken in the situation, the boats put into the Mississippi shore, and they were landed and formed in marching order to push forward across the country.

All was expectancy, as they supposed the enemy was not far distant. They found, however, that it was foraging and not fighting that was before them. Jeff Thompson had collected together large quantities of corn, hay, bacon, etc., for his command of freebooters, which was duly reported to headquarters, and General Grant determined to send over there and press the farmers into hauling to the river all they could bring away in boats, and to destroy the rest. It was amusing to hear the soldiers talking about the expedition. Their idea then of war was that all engagements between contending forces must occur upon a field, where each army would be drawn up in a line in strict accordance with military tactics.

They freely canvassed the question of ability to keep their "courage up," or to prevent their legs from carrying them in the opposite direction when commanded to charge bayonets. Hitherto the enemy had not materialized; but as soldiering in camp had proved more real than the holiday training-day of militia service, they began to fear the enchantment of distance between them and the enemy was so rapidly shortening that they must soon face the foe, or play the coward; and while impatience had characterized their conversation, they did not exactly relish the prospect of an engagement.

When, however, they found it was nothing more serious than attacking corn-cribs and haymows, their daring impatience returned, and expressions of disgust were heard from every direction. For many days they continued the monotonous duties of camp life, with continuous rain and mud to contend with, till November 6, when again orders came for cooked rations and everything to be put in readiness for a bona-fide expedition in pursuit of the enemy. The troops were quietly informed that this time they would be initiated into the mysteries of real war. All was bustle and confusion till each regiment was in line on the levee in the order in which they were to embark. Hurrying on board the transports, they waved a good-by to the multitude of men, women, and children who had flocked to the levees for a last adieu to fathers, husbands, brothers, or sweethearts. As they sailed away the band played "We are Coming, Father Abraham," and other patriotic airs.

All the next day, the 7th of November, 1861, the sound of cannonading told sadly and painfully that the battle of Belmont was on. The streets and levees of Cairo were thronged with anxious people trembling for the morrow, knowing only that some loved one was in the fight. Silently we trod the levees, trying to look beyond the "river bend," hoping to catch a glimpse of the returning transports. They knew from the direction of the sound of the firing that the troops were on the Missouri side, and that the gaping guns stationed on the shore at Columbus would prevent the frail wooden crafts, or even the gunboats, from going below that point. They were sure the boats would return. Hour after hour rolled slowly away, and still no tidings save the continuous knell of the cannon's roar. Darkness cut off every hope of seeing anything save the lights on the vessels, should they appear. Nothing daunted, still we lingered and watched. Finally, toward the early dawn a light like a meteor was seen to dart round the bend, another and still another came, until at last the outline of the fleet could be seen. The nearer they approached, the more intense the agony of the anxious watchers on shore. Slowly rounding in, the vessels soon touched the wharf, and the weary and depleted regiments solemnly disembarked and marched to the tented quarters they had quitted thirty-six hours before.

Eagerly the anxious people, myself among them, gazed at every officer and man as he walked the gangway from the boat to the wharf, each looking for some friend. Exclamations of joy rang out as they were recognized among the safe and sound as they passed. Again, cries of distress were heard as first one and then another was missed from their places in the lines. Then came the first prisoners of war I ever saw, and they were so forlorn, so thinly clad, so pitiful-looking, as they stood shivering on the hurricane deck, that my heart went out to them in the deepest sympathy. After the prisoners were all off, the civilians who failed to see their friends in the lines were allowed to go on board the boats, to find them among the wounded, dying, or dead, as they lay stretched in the cabins and on the decks of the vessels.

With tear-dimmed eyes, blanched faces, and quivering lips the friends moved cautiously from one to another in search of some loved one among the unfortunate. All the pomp and circumstance of chivalry and military display had vanished; naught but the agony of pain and terror of death remained.

Tenderly covering the faces of the dead with anything we

could get, and trying to soothe the suffering of the wounded, brave men and women worked unceasingly until ambulances and wagons came and took the unfortunate ones away to the hospitals which had been hastily prepared for the sick and disabled so suddenly assigned to them. Hotels and private houses had been seized, and the inefficient purveyors and quartermasters had put them in as good condition as the meagre and ill-assorted supplies would permit. For days and weeks physicians, surgeons, and volunteer nurses kept their constant vigil, trying to save as many as possible from the roll of the dead. After the battle of Belmont the wounded were brought to the "Striped Hospital," and the casualties of their first battle were evident in the wounded, who were destined to submit to amputations of arms and legs, Illinois soldiers beginning their painful experiences in real war before they left Cairo. It was a sad sight to see strong men pleading with tears in their eyes for a foot or an arm that must be taken off. Many flinched not under fire on the field, but when told they must part with a member of their bodies by the surgeon's knife and saw they wept like children, more than one refusing to lose a limb, preferring, as many expressed it, to lose their lives and be "buried all at once." Inexperienced surgeons were too hasty in making amputations, and needlessly sacrificed limbs which might have been saved. The men were all so cheerful after the battle, and tried so hard to encourage each other, that it was a pleasure to minister to their wants as volunteer nurses.

Captain Looney, of Company A of the 31st, Colonel Logan's regiment, was taken to our rooms in a private house, he having been severely wounded in the shoulder. After weeks of suffering he was sent to his home, where for many months he hovered between life and death; though he lived many years afterward, he was never again fit for duty, the service thereby losing one of the most gallant of men.

One day, in the brigade hospital, I saw a captain of an

Iowa regiment who had been wounded through the left breast sitting up on his cot writing to his wife. He was as bright and happy as could be. Mother Bickerdike, a volunteer nurse who followed the Army of the West from Cairo to the grand review, came in with a bowl of broth for him, which he took and drank with relish, after which I assisted him in getting into a comfortable position to resume his writing on a pad. He suddenly turned very pale and we laid him on his pillow. He looked up with a smile on his face and breathed his last. We were horrified and ran for the surgeon, who came, but too late; all was over with the brave man. Upon examination the surgeon found the minié ball had lodged just above the lung, and in moving it had dropped in such a way as to produce instant death. Other pathetic scenes of those days can never be erased from my memory.

Fortunately the ludicrous and the melancholy go hand in hand or we should not be able to endure the sadness of life. It was very hard for many of the young men to brook the restraint and the monotony of camp life and a soldier's duty, so they used to invent all sorts of excuses to get down into the city of Cairo. One evening I was sitting in Colonel Logan's tent when a young soldier whom we had known before his enlistment came to the door and said that his sister was coming to Cairo on a night train, and as she was unaccustomed to travelling he wished to go down to the city to await her arrival and desired permission for himself and comrade to go. It was an unusual request and should have been made through his captain. Colonel Logan was suspicious that it was not quite a straight story, but he ordered a pass to be given them. He then sent his adjutant to the soldier's captain with a request that he send Colonel Logan a corporal and a soldier. These he ordered to follow the first two, see where they went, and what they did, and if found in any improper place to arrest and bring the soldiers back to the guardhouse of the camp, and leave them there till ten o'clock on

General Logan's camp near Cairo, Illinois, in September, 1861.

the following morning. It was discovered that they were not expecting friends on the train and that they were in for a "high old time," as the corporal reported. The corporal waited until they were both quite drunk, then he arrested them and brought them to the guard-house as ordered. The next morning, when they were marched to the colonel's tent, they were the worst-looking culprits that could be imagined, and when Colonel Logan, with a serious face, inquired if the sister had arrived, where she was, and such questions, the poor fellow looked as if he were under sentence of death. He acknowledged the fraud he had practised and said he was willing to suffer any punishment the colonel might inflict; that he had forfeited all respect by lying and had nothing to say in extenuation of his conduct. The colonel looked at him sternly, administered a lecture on lying and his detestation of liars, and then ordered that the offenders should dig up by the roots an enormous stump which was in the rear of his tent, where he could see them while they worked. They saluted and were marched off to obtain the tools to begin their work, which it took them some days to finish. They said they did not mind the work, but to be obliged to do it under the eye of the colonel whom they had deceived was a bitter trial, but a lesson that served them through the war, and both were as gallant men as ever faced a cannon. They used often to laugh over this escapade after having won their shoulder-straps for gallantry on the field.

Before another expedition was to be undertaken a new commander was ordered to Cairo. The new commander flew from regiment to regiment. He had relieved General Oglesby and put him in command of Bird's Point on the opposite side of the river. He was no other than the hitherto unknown General U. S. Grant. It was announced that he would at once inspect every regiment in and around Cairo, to inform himself of their efficiency and the full strength of his forces. Hurriedly, company and regimental officers began preparing for his visit. Soldiers polished up their muskets and accoutrements, brushed their shoddy uniforms, and were speedily ready to be "ordered out." Expecting every moment that General Grant and staff would appear in full uniform and much military display, they waited impatiently. Imagine their surprise when informed that the unpretending, sturdy gentleman in citizen's dress who had just ridden by on a very ordinary clay-bank horse, attended by one officer and one or two of the officers on duty at general headquarters, was General Grant. Going directly to the colonel's headquarters, he introduced himself, and signified his desire to go through the quarters of the regiment and see the men of his command. Leaving their horses at each colonel's tent, and accompanied by that officer, they walked through the company aisles and personally inspected everything and every man in camp. By this businesslike procedure, void of all display and pageantry, General Grant won the confidence and admiration of officers and men. He afterward said that they were as fine a body of men as he had ever seen; that he would trust them anywhere to meet any equal number in any engagement.

Almost continual drilling and manœuvring filled up every hour for many days subsequent. The soldiers had little time for "larks" or homesickness. The malarious climate, however, began to tell upon the troops, and many became seriously sick.

# CHAPTER VI

AFTER the battle of Belmont, many more troops were
ordered to rendezvous at Cairo, Illinois. General Grant
was designated to organize an expedition up the Tennessee
and Cumberland Rivers. During the months of December
and January, in the worst weather ever experienced in that
climate, the troops in great numbers were mobilized in and
around inhospitable Cairo. Munitions of war and commissary stores were accumulated in great quantity. The troops,
while ignorant of their destination, knew instinctively that
some important movement was soon to be inaugurated. Brief
as was their engagement at Belmont, they began to realize
fully that Sherman's definition, "War is hell," was correct.

Finally the transports began to come into the port at Cairo.
Orders were issued for the troops to be ready to embark on

the 5th of February. From the moment of the receipt of this order the camps were all excitement with the preparations. Camp equipments were to be packed, and personal belongings reduced to the smallest possible compact parcel; business affairs had to be arranged by writing; letters, wills, and farewells had to be written, and everything prepared for a speedy departure to an unknown destination and fate.

The transports set sail in a pitiless storm of snow and sleet. Going as far as they could up the river, the troops were landed and proceeded to surround Fort Henry, which was to be attacked by our gunboats. The whole country adjacent was submerged by water; the land was heavily timbered, and it was almost impassable for the quartermaster and ordnance wagons, while it was with great difficulty that the artillery could be moved at all; but so dauntless were the troops of Grant's command that Fort Henry soon succumbed.

As soon as the fall of Fort Henry was assured, General Grant pushed forward with redoubled vigor, the assault by the gunboats having already begun upon Fort Donelson. The storms of the winter of 1861-2 were unprecedented, being especially wild during the month of February. Everything was covered with ice and snow; night and day a raw, cold wind blew such bitter blasts that men and animals could scarcely stand against its force. They had to move about or freeze to death. More than one of the brave men in the siege died from the exposure they experienced. Their clothing was frozen on them. Officers and men fared alike during the entire siege of Fort Donelson, and there was little respite for either. Colonel Logan was in the saddle almost continuously, taking only brief rests by lying down on the ground with his saddle under his head, and over him his saddle-blanket, which was frozen when he rose to mount his horse again. From this exposure he contracted rheumatism from which he never recovered, and which finally cost him his life. So near the fortifications were they that they did not dare to build fires by which to warm themselves or cook anything to eat.

Colonel Ransom, with the 11th, and Colonel John A. Logan, with the 31st Illinois Infantry, had gone into the siege side by side. Finding the ammunition short, these gallant men made an agreement to stand or fall together. They were to alternate in holding their places in the besieging line and thereby make the ammunition last as long as possible. They supported each other until the victory was won, but at a terrible cost to themselves and the gallant regiments they commanded, every man of whom was ready to follow either leader into the very jaws of death, as attested by the number who fell before the capitulation of Fort Donelson.

The *Telegraph* announced that Fort Donelson had fallen February 15, 1862, and also gave a list of the killed and wounded; in the list of killed appeared the names of Colonel John A. Logan, Lieutenant-Colonel John H. White, four captains of the 31st Regiment, of Illinois, and a great number of the men, all of whom I knew personally. There were many Illinois troops in General Grant's command, and consequently the State lost heavily of her officers and soldiers in the expedition against Forts Henry and Donelson.

On receipt of the overwhelming news of my husband's death, I started at once for Cairo, Illinois, determined, if it were possible, to go to Fort Donelson at all hazards. Transportation was very limited, and hundreds of people flocked to Cairo, anxious to go up the Tennessee and Cumberland Rivers in pursuit of friends who had been killed or wounded. Orders were issued from the War Department to allow no one on board the few transports then at the command of the army. General Grant was to be reinforced at once so that he could continue the march to Pittsburg Landing and on to Corinth. On my arrival at Cairo I learned that Colonel Logan was not killed, but was severely wounded, news which made me all the more anxious to join him. Going to army headquarters at

Cairo, I applied for permission to go up the river. The colonel commanding assumed an imperious air, informing me with much emphasis that military necessity compelled him to refuse me a pass. My heart was almost broken; I could hardly stand on my feet while I addressed this high and mighty personage; hence I could only reply that I trusted, "if the exigencies of the service should ever send him to the front, and he should be so unfortunate as to suffer any of the fatalities of war, a military necessity would not prevent Mrs. Graham from going to him." He answered savagely: "Thank you, madam, there is no Mrs. Graham." And I retorted: "If there was one intended, I hope she died in her infancy." With fast-falling tears I left headquarters, fully intending to go to Fort Donelson if I had to go in a rowboat, or cross the river and drive overland. When I reached the hotel I found that Governor Yates, of Illinois, and Governor Morton, of Indiana, had both arrived, and were going to charter steamers to go and bring the wounded and the remains of those who had been killed home to their respective States. I hastened to call on them and was assured I could go with either of them. Dear old Colonel Dunlap, of Jacksonville, Illinois, brigade quartermaster of McClernand's brigade was present, and as I passed out of the room he followed me into the hall and whispered to me the name of the steamer which was going first and which was then being loaded at the wharf. He said: "Slip down to the boat, tell them you are a member of my family, and that you are to wait for me until I come to the boat a few hours later. After you are on board, hide in one of the staterooms, and you will not be disturbed, as, in the mean while, I will give such instructions as will protect you." I lost no time in getting to the boat and, to my delight, found Captain Arter in command. Colonel Logan had a few years before defended and cleared him of a charge of manslaughter. He was an old river captain and had gotten into trouble with a roustabout employed on his boat. He welcomed me most cordially, and understood without asking that I had no pass. He said: "Come on board, and you shall see Logan." He conducted me up a veritable winding stairs to a stateroom on the hurricane-deck, and I did not stir abroad until we were under way and the stars were shining. Captain Arter came and knocked on my door, calling out: "The coast is clear. Come down to supper."

As we sailed up the river it seemed like a shoreless sheet of water and ice, as the waters were so high they extended over acres of ground far outside the banks. Mammoth trees rose out of the water like islands in the sea, and but for long experience the pilot could not have kept in the channel. The long, gray moss which hung like mystic veils from all the trees invested everything with a weird appearance and made one feel he was penetrating into a mysterious land. We arrived at an early hour in the morning, and as we approached we saw the stars and stripes flying over the ramparts of Fort Donelson. As we neared the landing our boat almost touched the guards of the decks of the steamer *Uncle Sam* upon which were General Grant's headquarters. Recognizing me, a number of the officers who came out on the deck hailed me, telling me to come on board, General Grant having had both Colonel Ransom and Colonel Logan carried to his headquarters after the surrender. In a briefer time than it has taken to write this story, I was ascending the companionway of the *Uncle Sam*, to find my husband lying on a cot with his left arm strapped to his body, it having been wounded near the point of the shoulder, the rifle-ball passing through the shoulder-joint. Another ball struck the pistol he carried in his belt, and nearly broke his ribs, from which he suffered almost as much as from the wound in the arm and shoulder. Colonel Ransom and Colonel Logan lay on cots side by side on the *Uncle Sam*, where General Grant had done the very best he could for them.

From the severe weather and exposure hundreds had come

down with pneumonia and typhoid fever. Transportation
was so limited that General Grant could not send the sick
and wounded North as rapidly as he desired. He therefore
took possession of the many vacant houses and tried to establish hospitals, to make the sufferers as comfortable as possible, with the thermometer below zero and the meagre supplies attainable. As soon as possible, therefore, I made my
two patients, Colonels Ransom and Logan, much happier than
they had been, as I had not been so improvident as to go to
Colonel Logan empty-handed, but had hastily laid in clothing, delicacies, and many necessities for the relief of the sick
and wounded. As I was the eldest of a family of thirteen,
my education in caring for the sick and preparing the proper
diet for invalids had not been neglected, and so I lost no
time in finding the stewards and their kitchens. Only those
who have had like experience can appreciate what a sponge-
bath of alcohol and hot water, clean clothes, and nourishing
food meant to those brave men after the long, weary hours of
suffering and discomfort that they had endured from the
hour they had fallen on the bloody field.

After ministering to their relief and when they were sleeping
quietly, I went with some friends to look after those whom
we knew who were either sick or wounded and had been
carried to improvised hospitals. We also attended the burial
service which was held over the brave men of the 11th and
31st Illinois Regiments that had fought so bravely. While
life lasts I shall never forget the sight upon which I looked
through tears on the battle-field. The long trenches had
been dug by their weary comrades. The heroic dead had
been brought and laid side by side in them. Their overcoats
and blankets were wrapped about their lifeless forms. Tents
were ripped so as to make tarpaulins with which to cover them
over. Chaplains standing close to the centre, with uncovered
heads, prayed fervently for peace to the souls of the gallant
dead about to be laid to rest in mother earth, where they

would sleep their last sleep till the trump of the resurrection should call them to glory in that land where wars can never come. After the bugler's long, sad note I turned away with unspeakable sadness from this, the first interment on a battlefield I had ever witnessed, appreciating more keenly than I had ever done before the melancholy significance of the words: "Buried on the field where they had fallen," and realizing that it was barely possible, after sanguinary engagements, to pay as much tribute to the dead as had been done in this one of the early battles in the West during the Civil War.

For many days I continued my constant vigil over Colonels Ransom and Logan, as serious complications in both cases set in, and it required the surgeon's best skill to save them.

Meanwhile General Grant was steadily pushing his preparations for the continuation of the expedition to Pittsburg Landing (know also as Shiloh) en route to Corinth, Mississippi, then the headquarters of Beauregard's army. Transportation was finally secured for Colonel Ransom to take him North to his friends. The surgeons succeeded in finding quarters to which Colonel Logan was removed, as the *Uncle Sam* had to proceed up the river with General Grant and his staff.

It would seem hopeless now to care for an invalid with the scant supplies, crude utensils, and appliances we could then command; but, thanks to untiring surgeons and devoted friends, who were constantly coming from the North with sanitary stores and most generous commissaries, our larder was kept quite full. Tin pans gradually gave way to real saucepans; broilers succeeded the long forked stick which had been used for broiling everything; coffee and tea pots took the place of tin cans; and wooden johnny-cake boards were supplanted by iron skillets with iron lids. Donations of glass, queensware, cutlery, blankets, bed and table linen increased our stores, until at the end of three weeks we were living in affluence and were able to provide for many more who were wounded or ill in other parts of the building.

I look back upon that experience now with infinite satisfaction, as I was able to nurse my husband back to health and strength and he was spared to me and to his country for a quarter of a century longer.

The surgeons and physicians deciding that Colonel Logan was able to be moved, he was taken on board a transport, and by exercising great care we reached our home, which was then at Murphysboro, Jackson County, Illinois. We had scarcely recovered from the fatigue of the journey when the news of the approaching battle of Shiloh was received. Like an impatient steed, Colonel (now Brigadier-General) Logan sniffed the battle from afar, and though unable to put his arm in his coat-sleeve, he insisted upon rejoining his command in time, if possible, to participate in the expected battle. The stars he had won at Donelson would necessitate his assuming graver duties, and he was most anxious to have his old regiment assigned to his brigade. Ignoring appeals to remain until his wound was healed, he set out for Shiloh, arriving there late in the afternoon of the last day of that memorable engagement, disgusted with the delays of transportation that had prevented him from participating in that mighty struggle, when fortune apparently wavered from the Union to the Confederate army, and then back to the army of the Union.

Scarcely halting long enough to gather up the sick and wounded and to bury the dead, General Grant moved forward, hoping to capture Beauregard and his army. General Logan was placed in command of the First Brigade, Third Division, Seventeenth Army Corps. He was proud of his command, and would have been happy but for the fateful effect of the attacks of scandal-mongers upon General Grant, charging him with intemperance and incapacity to command the dauntless army, which was subsequently a part of the invincible Army of the Tennessee. The authorities at Washing-

General Logan and his staff, at the time of the capture of Fort Donelson.

ton were so impressed by these reports, supposed to come from loyal, honest persons, that, wishing to protect the army which had scored the first victories for the Union, they placed General Halleck in command, and designated General Grant as second in command, a designation never before or since made in the American army. General Grant felt the indignity deeply, but, true soldier that he was, he pushed his plans for the capture of Corinth with unremitting vigor, though handicapped at every turn by Halleck's dilatory, technical methods.

Grant and Logan were on the most intimate terms, and, being aggressive soldiers, they became restive under Halleck's over-cautious tactics. General Logan's command was placed astride the Mobile and Ohio Railroad which ran into Corinth. In this brigade there were a number of men formerly in the employ of railroads and who understood sounds conveyed by the rails. General Logan learned from the telegraphy of these sounds that empty trains were being taken into Corinth and that they were loaded when they were run out. Convinced that the Confederates were evacuating Corinth, and that if they escaped it would mean another long and weary chase which would cost many lives and great hardship to the army, he went to Grant and begged him to let him feel the enemy and attack them if he proved that he was right about their movements.

Grant believed Logan and wanted to let him try, but Halleck condemned the whole suggestion and intimated that if Logan repeated his impertinence by such reports he would put him under arrest and relieve him of his command. General Grant in his memoirs says: "May 28th, 1862, Gen. Logan informed me that the enemy had been evacuating for several days, and that, if allowed, he could go into Corinth with his brigade." Beauregard had begun to evacuate on the 25th of May, but General Halleck would have no suggestions from Grant or Logan, and waited his own time to find,

when he issued his celebrated order of attack of May 30, no
enemy on his front.  Soon after Halleck was called to Washington and Grant, untrammelled by a martinet, began his
campaign in pursuit of the wily enemy.  Our gallant army
continued the chase, stopping ever and anon to fight a battle
and scale fortifications, or rout the enemy.

After Corinth came the trying and tedious march through
the enemy's country to Jackson, Lagrange, and Memphis,
Tennessee.

In the fall and winter of 1862–3 General Logan's command
was encamped at Memphis, Tennessee.  The general had
been almost constantly in the saddle from the time he reached
Shiloh and joined his command in the movement against Corinth.  The weather was inclement and the condition of the
roads dreadful, the streets of the city being well-nigh impassable.

On hearing that General Logan had reached Memphis, I
applied for transportation to join him, and succeeded in getting it—a most difficult thing to accomplish in those days,
with the meagre facilities at the command of the army.  General Logan and his staff were staying at the Gayoso House,
as were also General McPherson and his staff.  When I arrived I found that our friends Mr. and Mrs. Sanger and their
daughter, Miss Harriet, now the widow of George M. Pullman, were guests of the hotel.  Miss Harriet Sanger was
one of the most beautiful and captivating girls in the
West.  General McPherson admired her extravagantly.  She
had also a devotee in the person of Colonel F. A. Starring, of the 72d Illinois Infantry Regiment.  The 72d was
from Chicago and its vicinity and had an unusually fine
band.  One night Colonel Starring arranged for his band
to serenade Miss Sanger.  He had called for Miss Sanger,
who came down to the parlor to receive him, and while they
were listening to the music they heard cheering.  Colonel
Starring stepped out on the balcony and found General Mc-

Pherson on another balcony a few feet away acknowledging the serenade. One of his staff had supposed, of course, that the serenade was for General McPherson, and ordered refreshments in the hotel dining-room for the band men. This naturally inspired the band to play vociferously after the repast. Miss Sanger induced Colonel Starring not to say anything about the serenade having been intended for her, so that General McPherson might enjoy the compliment ignorant of the fact that the serenade had not been intended for him. It was too good a joke, however, to be kept a secret. Somebody told General McPherson, who was much chagrined over the affair. He tried to treat the occurrence jocularly, but was unable to conceal his annoyance.

General McPherson was, without exception, the most unassuming and agreeable man I ever knew. His soldierly qualities were of the highest order. True nobility characterized his conduct as a man and a gentleman. His orders were military in every sense of the word, but without a note of the martinet running through them. The attachment between him and General Logan was very strong, and found expression in General Logan's heroic action after McPherson fell, July 22, 1864.

A few days after the episode related above General Logan's headquarters were established in the grounds surrounding the magnificent Lanier place on the outskirts of the city. General Logan and I were given rooms in the stately mansion. As soon as possible thereafter General Logan began to get his division ready to be reviewed. General McPherson reviewed the whole command, doing us the honor to dine with us in the Lanier mansion after the review was over.

The troops had been paid a day or two before, and naturally many of them went on a grand spree, and it was with great difficulty that the officers could get their troops sufficiently straightened out for the review. Colonel John D. Stephenson commanded a Missouri regiment, one of the bravest, most brilliant, and best of men.  His regiment was made up of men from the docks of Saint Louis, and they were a pretty hard tribe.  They had been fighting among themselves, and almost all of them appeared in line for the review with black eyes and otherwise "bummed up."  The morning of the review Colonel Stephenson started to go into the sutler's tent.  There was a piece of timber standing near by which fell and struck the colonel on the side of the head causing great discoloration of his cheeks and under his eyes. General McPherson was full of fun, and, on returning to Colonel Stephenson's tent after reviewing his regiment, he said: "Colonel, I am surprised to see that you have a black-eyed regiment," a facetious remark which we all enjoyed.

The day of the review was the last time that General Logan was really able to leave his bed.  After his long exposure and hard work I acted as amanuensis and messenger for him, taking his orders to the headquarters tent on the grounds of the Lanier place.  One day he wanted from his adjutant-general a particular paper which he was to use, and I told him that I could go over and get it as well as not.  I started over, and as I passed Colonel Stolbrand's tent I saw his clerk was tied to a tree which stood almost in front of it. Poor Crutchfield looked so unhappy, having just recovered from a debauch, that he touched my heart, and I ran into the cook's tent, got a butcher knife, and cut the ropes to free him. I told Crutchfield to go to his tent and hide himself as soon as possible.  Colonel Stolbrand was on duty somewhere and did not know who had cut the ropes to free Crutchfield. Colonel Stolbrand was a fine specimen of a Swedish officer, with his ruddy complexion and sandy hair.  He wore the red of the artillery, and altogether was rather a flaming specimen when he came rushing into General Logan's room in a towering rage, reporting to the general that somebody had freed Crutchfield, whom he had tied to discipline and sober up, insisting that he could not find out that it was

The Lanier mansion at Memphis, Tennessee, General Logan's headquarters before the expedition against Vicksburg.

anybody in the army. If it was they had got to be punished, and if it was an outsider he must be driven from the
camp immediately. I had said nothing to the general about
what I had done, and enjoyed very much Stolbrand's indignation.

A few days before, Colonel Stolbrand had been telegraphed
to meet his wife, who was trying to join him at some station
above Memphis. The general was not inclined to let him
go. Colonel Stolbrand happened to ask permission in my
presence, and I said to the general: "Oh, let him go, he will
be back all right." After my pleading the general did let
him go, and Colonel Stolbrand was very grateful to me. He
went, and, of course, got back all right.

The incident involving Crutchfield occurred a day or two
after Colonel Stolbrand's return. I listened quietly to what
he was saying to the general, and when he had finished I said:
"Now, colonel, suppose it turns out that the person who cut
that rope does not belong to the army, and nobody has any
authority to drive them out of the camp, what would you
do?" He said: "I would drive them away from the camp
at the point of my sword." I said: "I believe there was a
man who wanted to join his wife a few days ago, and his
commanding officer would not consent to let him go. Somebody interfered and the man finally got permission." This
remark gave the stolid Swede an idea that I might have done
this, and so he said: "Ah, Mrs. Logan, my dear lady, I have
great reverence for you, but you must not do that thing
again, or I shall be obliged to make charges against you."
The general saw at once that I was the guilty party, and
kept up the joke with Stolbrand by saying that if any such
thing ever occurred again he would have the culprit driven
beyond the lines by a drum corps, which put Colonel Stolbrand in a good humor. I was not willing to let it go at
that, so I said to Colonel Stolbrand, "Colonel, Crutchfield
has sworn to me that he will never touch another drop of

liquor while he is in your command, and you know that he
is a very valuable clerk, and I am sure you do not wish to
part with him. Now promise me that you will inflict a very
light punishment on him for this misdemeanor and that you
will give him a chance to keep his oath of total abstinence
in the future." I saw no more of poor Crutchfield for many
years, but I was on a Mississippi River steamer going up the
river one day, when somebody called me by name from the
shore, and, standing on the deck, I responded. He then
called: "Mrs. Logan, this is Crutchfield, and I am sober yet."

Colonel Stolbrand won his star for his gallant and soldierly
conduct, and continued to remain on the general's staff to the
close of the war. He was subsequently elected to Congress
from a district in South Carolina, and died in the South a
good many years ago.

The troops remained in Memphis many weeks, and I stayed
with the general until they were ready to march. He was
very ill for some time with a fever, and worried all the time
as to what to do to keep the soldiers from deserting. Hearing
that they were going to serenade him, he concluded that when
he made his speech on the balcony he would have an order
ready to issue appealing to them not to disgrace themselves
by yielding to the influence of letters from home, which had
created so much dissatisfaction among the troops. We had
a great time preparing this address and this order, because
the general was almost too weak to get them into the shape
in which he wished to have them. It seemed as though almost the entire Seventeenth Corps assembled on the grounds
of the Lanier place on the night that they tendered him the
serenade. Colonel Stephenson was to make a little speech
to the general, pledging the devotion and fidelity of the troops
to him and their hope that he would soon be able to be on
duty again. We stood on the balcony in front of the mansion
during and after the serenade. Colonel Stephenson then
made his address, to which General Logan replied, read-

ing a copy of the order urging them to stand by their colors until they were planted on the ramparts of Vicksburg and New Orleans. He said he knew they could do it if they determined to, and that he would never order them to do anything in which he was not willing to take the lead. He fulfilled that promise to them literally, as he and his command were ever in the van until the fall of Vicksburg and the lifting of the blockade from the Mississippi.

The general had a very delightful staff: Colonel Townes, Colonel Hotaling, Colonel Yorke, Colonel Lloyd Wheaton, now retired major-general of the regular army and on whose escutcheon there is not a blot after his many years of service. Major Whitehead, Major J. H. Hoover, Major Holcomb, and others were also on the staff, and were untiring in the discharge of their duties and in trying to make everything agreeable. They treated me always with the most distinguished consideration. General Logan had some cousins in his old regiment which was encamped quite a distance from where we were staying. Major Hoover wanted me to go and see them very much. I was very anxious to do so, and General Logan desired me to go and look after them and to visit the headquarters of the regiments under his command. Major Hoover had a very fine saddle-horse which he wanted me to ride when we made these visits. There was staying in the Lanier house the wife of Colonel Sloane, of the 24th Illinois. She was one of those women who are always interfering with and crossing the members of her husband's regiment. She came very near at one time breaking up the regiment altogether, and was only prevented by her husband's sending her home. She found out that Colonel Hoover was taking me around to make these visits, and was determined to go too. She asked the general if he did not think she ought to accompany us, and the general, always full of fun and liking to play practical jokes, insisted that she should join us. He ordered Hoover to get her a horse and saddle somewhere. Hoover did not want to do it, as he disliked her excessively. "I'll give her a John Gilpin ride if she insists upon going." The mud and water was something terrible on the morning on which we set out on this expedition, Mrs. Sloane mounted on an unreliable horse. Hoover, knowing that I could ride like a Comanche in those days, had trained the horses to follow a whistle which he gave. Away we went until we were perfectly covered with mud and water. Mrs. Sloane could not ride very well, and it was not long before she was landed in a bank of mud on the side of the road, as her horse would keep up with the others and she could not stay on. Hoover said he knew she could not get hurt, but would be covered with mud, and he would have his revenge. We had to stop and I had to take her horse and give her mine, which was a very gentle animal, and return home, as we were not presentable afterward. The general suspected that Hoover had played this trick because he had not wanted Mrs. Sloane to go. Hoover said it was not his fault. She could not ride, and he could not help it, but got the best horse he could for her. For a long time afterward the staff were regaled with Hoover's description of Mrs. Sloane's ride, hat off, hair hanging down, and clothing all awry.

Such diversions were all we had to break the monotony and anxiety ever hanging over the army. The day dawned all too soon when camp was broken, and the march was begun to Lake Providence. I returned to my home to spend the next few months in unspeakable anxiety, knowing that the army was destined to invest Vicksburg.

Crossing the Mississippi River, the Army of the West began its worst experiences during the war. It was proposed to invest Vicksburg, Mississippi, then supposed to be impregnable, by transferring the army by way of Lake Providence to a position below Vicksburg, recross the river, and besiege the city from above, below, and rear. The swamps and shallow lakes of that region were fearful for men to pass through. They tried to convert them into canals, hoping they might be able to navigate some kind of a craft through them by which they could transfer the troops to Port Gibson, the point chosen to try to land below Vicksburg. After weeks of struggling with mud and water, with little success, General Logan, after conferring with General Grant, called for volunteers from his command to run the blockade on transports, protected by cotton-bales from the frowning guns that guarded the river. More men responded than they could use. Selecting from the number those whom they thought best fitted for the hazardous undertaking, they were ready in a brief time. They waited for the darkest of nights, which finally came, and then the wooden steamers with their walls of cotton cast their moorings. Not a light was visible on any of the boats, not a sound could be heard. Like the weird craft with silent crew on the River Styx, they floated on the placid river, past the mammoth guns of the forts on the river front, on to the port of their destination before the sleeping sentinel knew anything of the daring enterprise. Once below Vicksburg, the transports carried the troops with rapidity from the western to the eastern shore of the river. At Port Gibson the Confederates made their first resistance to the invading army of the Mississippi, but they were completely routed. The bayous, swamps, and impenetrable forests of that whole valley of the Mississippi made it terrible for an army to move after they had landed safely; but the tireless and undaunted troops of the West were equal to that herculean task. The battles of the Big Black, Champion Hills—one of the most brilliant of the whole war—Raymond, 22d of May, 1863, and other engagements around the beleaguered city, proved the indomitable courage and military skill of the officers and men of the Western army. General Grant, acting upon what he supposed was reliable information from Major-General John A. McClernand, one of his corps commanders, that he had captured a section of the outer works, ordered an assault May 22, 1863. General Logan disagreed with General Grant about the wisdom of this assault, doubting the truth of the information which had been given General Grant, but as General Logan never faltered or hesitated to execute his orders, the First Brigade, Third Division of the Seventeenth Army Corps, with General Logan leading, started up the rugged sides of the hills surrounding Vicksburg. Again and again they charged, losing many gallant men in each ineffectual assault. Finally General Grant found he had been misinformed and that the whole force inside the walls had been concentrated against the Seventeenth Army Corps. He hastily ordered them to retire, and as speedily relieved the officer who had so prematurely announced a victory which he had hoped to win but which had not been accomplished.

General Logan considered May 22 one of the most disastrous and fearful undertakings of any siege during his service. The almost perpendicular side of the bluffs surrounding the well-fortified city of Vicksburg, the immense advantage of the besieged over the besiegers, and the almost hopeless task of accomplishing anything made it a most unsatisfactory and ill-advised attack. For six or eight weeks the siege was continued, every day adding to the casualties of the besiegers and the discomfort and certain doom of the besieged.

General Logan felt quite sure of success through the mining and sapping of Fort Hill, which was one of the strongest points in the cordon of fortifications that encircled the natural stronghold of the Confederacy. After a thorough investigation of the proposition, General Grant allowed General Logan to undertake the scheme in which he had so much confidence. His command had led the van from Lake Providence. Officers and men were anxious to continue in the lead, and were impatient to begin the work, which was to result in the explosion of Fort Hill and the making of a breach in the walls through which they might be the first to enter the city. No finer piece of engineering was ever performed. The experience of the veteran volunteers made them expert miners and sappers, and with incredible rapidity they achieved the prodigious feat of undermining and exploding Fort Hill. General Logan's old regiment, the 31st Illinois, waited impatiently to rush into the crater for a hand-to-hand engagement with the brave men who had gallantly defended their breastworks. The conflict was of short duration, but many heroic men fell in this last sally of the Union army upon the breastworks surrounding Vicksburg. With General Logan leading the van, they marched into Vicksburg on the morning of the 4th of of July, 1863. All parts of the besieging line had been unflinchingly sustained, and no braver troops ever encompassed a fortified city than the dauntless Union soldiers who besieged and captured Vicksburg. General Logan and his command had been in the front from the beginning of the expedition; they had furnished the blockade-runners, the assaulting party on May 22, and they made the break in the fortifications by blowing up Fort Hill; consequently, General Grant felt it their due to be the first to occupy the captured city.

With the fall of Vicksburg the Mississippi River was open to the Gulf of Mexico, and from that hour the fate of the Confederacy was sealed.

The booming of the cannon announced the glorious victory on Independence Day, and the deafening shouts of the triumphant Union army were the death-knells of secession. General Logan was appointed commander of the post at Vicksburg, and immediately began the adjustment of affairs between the conquered and conquerors, desiring in every way in his power, consistent with fidelity to his country, to ameliorate the condition of the unfortunate people who had lived inside the walls of the besieged city. Many had lived in caves during the siege, their homes being uninhabitable because they were within the range of the guns of the Union army. They had been reduced to the last extremity, and had lived on food never before eaten by Americans. He listened to their woes, ordered relief for thousands, and was so magnanimous in his administration as to win their admiration and gratitude.

As I stood in the crater of Fort Hill, from which point I could see Grant's, Sherman's, and Logan's headquarters, and looked across the chasms made by nature between the ridges which were occupied by the contending armies at Vicksburg, I marvelled more than ever at the military genius of our great commanders, and the fearless intrepidity of the Union troops, who captured that seemingly impregnable city, justly called the Gibraltar of the Mississippi, fortified by nature and by the most skilful engineering of any age, and defended by the bravest of the brave.

It is a source of infinite gratification that the great State of Illinois has built a Temple of Fame in the National Cemetery at Vicksburg, in the crater of Fort Hill, at a cost of a quarter of a million dollars, for the preservation of the names and fame of the officers and men of the seventy-five regiments who were engaged in that matchless siege and victory.

The siege had lasted without cessation from early in May until July 4, 1863. Officers and men were well-nigh exhausted by the intense heat, burning sun, hot rains, and the long strain of the constant vigilance and the heavy burdens they had borne. It was deemed advisable to furlough as many as possible both of officers and men. Hastening to their homes in the North and West, they found the welcome due returning soldiers who have been valiant in their country's services. Their presence among the people soon dissipated the sentimental sympathies with the South which had been aroused over the Emancipation Proclamation. The descriptions the returning officers and soldiers gave of the dangers through which they had passed, the hardships they had endured, the sufferings they had experienced, the sacrifices they had made and witnessed as they saw their comrades fall on many bloody fields, not knowing what might be their own fate ere the conflict ceased, caused a renewed spirit of patriotism to spread rapidly. When, therefore, at the expiration of the leave the officers and men had enjoyed, they returned to their respective commands, they knew there would be no more lukewarm support of the army in the field by the people at home.

General Logan was wanted to help win victories for the party in the local elections, which were in great doubt because of the effect of the issuance of the Emancipation Proclamation. As soon, therefore, as General Logan could get in shape the complex affairs existing after the bitter contest for possession of the Gibraltar of the Mississippi, he caused the appointment of General John Maltby, of the 45th Illinois Infantry Regiment from Galena, Illinois, as commander of the post at Vicksburg. As the city was under martial law, General Maltby would have the assistance of a competent provost marshal, and, being himself a brave and discreet man, General Logan felt that the people would soon be glad that they were once more under the protection of the Stars and Stripes. With his staff General Logan embarked upon the Mississippi River steamboat, and after a tedious journey reached home for a brief leave of absence. Southern Illinois having furnished a large quota of the troops which had been in every engagement from Forts Henry and Donelson to the surrender of Vicksburg, a great many of them had been furloughed and had arrived at their homes before General Logan. The whole population had been fired with the wildest patriotic enthusiasm by their graphic description of their experiences on the march, in camp, in hospital, and in battle from the time they left Cairo, February, 1862, till Vicksburg fell, July 4, 1863; consequently, by the time General Logan landed at Cairo his heroism, magnanimity, kindness to his men, and his military genius had been so often told by his faithful followers that he found multitudes waiting to do him honor. The citizens had told the soldiers of the reign of terror which the

Knights of the Golden Circle had exercised over the non-combatants who had been left at home. The soldiers insisted upon guarding General Logan wherever he went, following him in citizens' clothing, in much the same way as the President is guarded from assassination in these days. The welcome accorded General Logan was so spontaneous and flattering that he scouted the idea of any one doing him harm; all the same the soldiers continued their self-appointed guardianship, relieving each other from time to time as their leaves expired and they had to return to their respective commands.

The local elections grew more exciting as the campaign proceeded. General Logan spoke almost daily to vast assemblages. The themes he dwelt most upon were the Emancipation Proclamation and its necessity, and the guarantee of final triumph of the Government through victories the Union army, especially the Western army, had achieved. At heart loyal to their country, they were easily won away from their temporary disaffection.

Colonel R. P. Townes, Major Hotaling, Major Lloyd Wheaton, Major Hoover, and other members of my husband's staff were with us in our home in Carbondale, Jackson County, Illinois, almost all the time during General Logan's leave of absence. Dinners, excursions, picnics, balls, parties of all kinds, to which were added political demonstrations, kept all of us busy. Carbondale had an unusual number of pretty girls and the very best society south of Springfield, the capital of the State. They were all very patriotic, and had devoted much time to the soldiers, their families, and the refugees. From nearly every family some one had gone into the army or navy; hence they could not do enough for the soldiers and officers to make their brief visit delightful, and were ever ready to join in anything proposed for their entertainment and diversion. A round of pleasure was inaugurated and kept up till the very last moment of the stay of General Logan and his staff.

When the time came for their departure it was noticed that one or two of the young ladies wore engagement rings on the third finger of the left hand, and that the gallant officers said good-by to the girls they were leaving behind them with tears in their eyes and very sad faces. Their fiancées came often to me afterward to be comforted while waiting for the "cruel war" to be over.

The double stars of a major-general, which General Logan had won by his distinguished service and desperate daring in the Vicksburg campaign, would, I knew, require his transfer to the command of a corps, and, knowing that an expedition against Chickamauga was being organized, General Logan was impatient for his orders. They came, all too soon for me, assigning him to the Fifteenth Army Corps, Army of the Tennessee, then under General J. B. McPherson. General Logan was delighted to serve under McPherson but sorry to leave the veterans of the Seventeenth Corps, especially his old regiment, to whose valor he felt he owed his promotion. General Frank Blair was given the Seventeenth Corps, in which were almost all the regiments that had composed the brigade and division which General Logan had commanded after his promotion to a brigadier-generalship; but as the Fifteenth and Seventeenth were both to be in the Army of the Tennessee, he felt he should be near them. General Logan always regretted that he could not have reached Chickamauga in time to have had a greater share in the battle among the clouds of Lookout Mountain. Another anxiety was his knowledge of the fact that an undercurrent of disloyalty still existed among the people on account of their Southern proclivities.

The few days intervening between the receipt of his orders and his proceeding to Chattanooga to assume command of the Fifteenth Army Corps General Logan spent in making speeches for the local candidates of the Republican party and in final appeals to the people to defend the Emancipation Proclamation which Mr. Lincoln had issued in the name of humanity and freedom for all men. Many times when he was speaking he would be interrupted by bullies who were foolish enough to imagine they could neutralize his influence over the masses by asking questions, uttering insults, and indulging in braggadocio. These disturbers of the peace were always worsted by General Logan's replies. On one occasion he threw the glass tumbler on the stand before him squarely into the face of a bully whose insults he would not brook. The coward had to retreat to a near-by drug-store and submit to a surgeon's skill to save his face from disfigurement. It silenced all others, and enabled General Logan to do valuable service for his party as well as his country before leaving home to return to duty in the field.

The continued disaffection of the troops on the question of the Emancipation Proclamation, through the influence of sympathizers with the South, and the great number of desertions, assumed a most serious aspect. In every community these deserters were hiding and adding to the feverish excitement of the public mind. The recreant soldiers found that by their act of desertion they were delighting the disloyal and rapidly undoing what they had done for the Union cause; also, that they themselves were in great trouble, as they were liable to suffer the consequences of the violation of the articles of war, so severe upon deserters.

Something had to be done to secure their return to duty and at the same time avoid the expense of long trials and loss to the service of the men should they be condemned to penal servitude in the military prisons. Hence the ablest men in the country appealed to Mr. Lincoln to issue another proclamation pardoning all deserters who would return to duty on or before a given date.

As can readily be imagined, the regiments and companies were speedily reinforced by great numbers who were glad to escape the consequences of their rash act in impulsively yield-

ing to their sympathy with Southern institutions born of prejudice and association. Victories along the lines heightened
the prospects everywhere till the proposition to enlist negroes
as soldiers was mooted. Again the ever-present prejudice
against the negro which existed in the West and Southwest
was rife, and mutterings were heard in every direction, soldiers swearing they would not serve with "niggers."

Some officers exhibited a spirit of insubordination, and but
for the fact that the army was constantly on the move it
would have suffered another shock of disaffection from political influence. In southern Illinois the situation was especially critical. As the majority of loyal, able-bodied men, old
and young, were by this time in the army, the disgruntled
sympathizers were left in full possession of every field—business, politics, and everything else. These malcontents grew
more and more bitter, and, while powerless to do anything
but annoy, they indulged in all sorts of persecutions of furloughed Union soldiers and the families of the soldiers who
were at the front.

Mr. William Bandy, father of two or three Union soldiers,
was taken out, tied to a tree, and whipped unmercifully for
his radical sentiments. The home of an officer whose family
lived in the country was entered and the household effects
broken and destroyed. The animals of the Union people
were butchered; the hamstrings of the horses were cut so that
the poor brutes could not work the crops but had to be shot.

Family feuds were increasing, murder was perpetrated, and
all the horrors of civil war and its consequences, added to the
never-ending solicitude for the fate of friends in the field,
made life one continuous routine of anxiety and suspense,
especially for those in the West whose fathers, sons, husbands,
and friends were in the army.

Lookout Mountain and Atlanta, in the mountain fastness,
were considered almost impregnable, and the thought that
the troops in the expedition were so indomitable that they

would all die in the attempt or capture these points gave
occasion for constant anguish.   The approach of winter and
the thought of the mountainous country through which the
expedition was to be made added another cause for deep concern.   In addition, many of the families of the soldiers had to
be provided for at home, and the refugee contrabands were
becoming so numerous and such a burden to the people of the
border States that it was a question of the gravest nature
what to do with them.   They were unfitted, physically, to
take the places of the troops in industrial fields.   They had
already suffered much from exposure.   Among the most pathetic scenes of the war was the sight of the poor, helpless
creatures, black and white, who were dumped under the wood-
sheds on the line of the Illinois Central and Ohio and Mississippi Railroads with nothing but a few clothes and little bundles of bedding and articles of household belongings.   Sick,
destitute, homeless, friendless, and among strangers, in an inhospitable climate, their condition was unutterably sad.

In company with noble women, who worked all the time
for charity or the soldiers, we visited these people to try to
alleviate their sufferings, and were deeply affected to see
them, in their absolutely helpless situation, sitting or lying
on the ground with folded hands, perfect pictures of despair.

One white family of eight I remember were, without exception, the most cheerless and forlorn we had ever seen.   The
mother and six daughters were lying on the floor of an old
freight depot with nothing but their scanty clothing to cover
them, the old man sitting shivering with the cold.   The bleak
winds of November were whistling through the cracks, and
they had not a morsel to eat.   Our aid society had very little
money, but we hoped to relieve their extreme wants, and
asked the poor mother what she desired most.   Imagine our
consternation when, with bated breath, she said, in true
Southern vernacular: "A little terbacker, if you please."
Some of the ladies declared we ought to let her die, but char-

General John A. Logan in 1862.

From a photograph in the Meserve Collection.

ity prevailed, and she was given the much-desired weed. The doctors attended all these poor people faithfully, furnishing medicines for their prescriptions gratuitously. Food and raiment were given them, and after being braced up by the invigorating Northern climate they went to work and made useful citizens.

The poor blacks were, if possible, more pitiful on account of their timidity and extreme destitution; the climate was worse on them than on the whites, and they died as if suffering from a contagion. After a while they began to feel that they were safe from their persecutors and that they were free. Many an old man sang "Old Shady" with enthusiasm:

"Good-by, hard work, and nebber any pay,
I'm going up North, where de white folks stay,
White wheat bread and a dollar a day.

### Chorus

"Away den, away, for I can't stay any longer,
Hurrah, boys, hurrah,
For I am going home."

The poor creatures providentially supplied the places of the men who were in the army. In my own case I blessed the day when they came to southern Illinois, because before that I had been, with the assistance of my companion and friend, Miss Mary E. Tuthill, obliged to play the part of man and maid of all work, feeding, currying, and caring for the animals in the barn-yard, harnessing and driving the horses, washing the buggies and carriages, and performing every species of manual labor necessary to be done, at the same time trying to help others more dependent and timid. Besides this we had to protect ourselves from annoying persecutions inflicted by the senseless sympathizers with the rebellion who were too cowardly to go South and cast their lot with the people for whom they professed so much sympathy.

One day as Miss Tuthill and I were driving we passed a

colored man who sat under a tree beside the road wondering where he should go for a home, food, and clothing. Our "copperhead" rulers of the community had forbidden negroes to stop in that part of the country. I was unable to secure the services of a man servant, and was about as desperate as poor "Albert" as he sat there, an exile and a wanderer. I stopped the horse I was driving and asked the poor fellow what he was doing there and where he was going. He timidly replied: "I ain't doin' nuffin', Miss, and God knows I doesn't know whar to go. Bless de Lord, I would be glad to get sumfin' to do, an' be 'lowed to stay sumwhar."

I told him that I wished to hire a man to work for me, and if he would come with me I would build him a little house in my yard; that if he would work and obey me, taking care of my cattle, horses, and garden, I would pay him fifteen dollars a month and give him his board.

The poor creature bowed his head to the ground almost, and said: "Bless you, Missus, I would be glad to mind you and do anything in the world dat you telled me to, but I'se afeard dat the big white bosses around here won't 'low me to stay here nohow."

I told him I would undertake to protect him if he knew how to shoot. He should have a good gun and plenty of ammunition in his house to protect himself with if anybody should molest him at night; that I was not afraid of their coming on the place in the daytime; that for a while he would have to sleep in the barn till I could put up a little house for him. He said: "Well, Miss, I leaves it all in your hands and hope de Lord will take keer of us bofe."

I directed him how to go to my house to wait for me till I should come. When I reached home he sat on the wood-pile waiting for me, his face shining like the setting sun. He had taken a survey of the premises and was highly delighted, declaring to me he "nebber expected to reach de promised land so soon." I ordered him to carry a wash-tub out to the barn and to take a bath. I bought him a new suit of cottonade at a neighboring store, and when he presented himself at the back door soon afterward for food and orders he looked like a black prince. He was six feet tall and was a fine specimen of his race, his honest face beaming with happiness. He was more efficient in the arts of hostlery and horticulture than my friend Miss Mary Tuthill—afterward Mrs. R. N. Pearson, wife of General R. N. Pearson, of Chicago—and myself, and the poor dumb brutes and the garden soon presented an improved appearance.

Not long after it was noised about that "John Logan's wife has hired a nigger to work for her, and he is on the place to stay." They resolved that he should not do so, and that "if she did not send him away, they would go there, and send him off in a jiffy, and if she interfered to protect him, they would thrash her too."

A member of the secret organization known as the Knights of the Golden Circle, who kept up their warfare and made so much trouble for every Unionist, had been raised with me, and while he was intensely disloyal to his country he was the soul of honor and loyalty to his friends. He knew I would try to protect the colored man when they should attack him, and he could not bear the thought of any harm coming to me. So he came to me, begging that I send the "darky" away, warning me there would be trouble if I persisted in keeping him, because they were "not going to let the country be filled up with niggers." I thought of the matter long and seriously. It seemed so outrageous that men in a free land would undertake, by mob violence, to decide who should and who should not live in the country that I was inclined to test the question and see whether or not these men, avowed enemies of the nation, should dictate to loyal people what they should or should not do. The colored man had in no wise interfered with any one. He was respectful to everybody, was sober, industrious, and was entitled to life, liberty, and the pursuit of happiness both by the Declaration of Independence and President Lincoln's proclamation.

So I told my friend James Durham that, while I appreciated beyond expression his friendship and warning, I must be frank enough to tell him I intended to keep the man and protect him to the best of my ability. It might be selfishness that prompted this decision, because I did need Albert's services, and as he wanted to stay I should certainly keep him; that if Durham would trust me still further by telling me who was going to take part in the dastardly deed of maltreating an inoffensive creature who had never even seen them I would under no circumstances betray him, but that I would make them afraid to come on my premises or to harm the negro. After some hesitancy he told me the names of the men who proposed to do the work for the society. He went away feeling much distressed and quite sure that I would have a serious experience.

I waited patiently that day for one of the men, whom I knew must pass my house going into and out of the town. As soon as I spied him coming down the road on his way to town I walked out to my front gate and called to him, asking him if he would not come in a moment as I desired to see him on a matter of business. He was much embarrassed, but came in. I at once told him that I had been informed by a member of the "Circle" all about their proposed attack upon the colored man in my employ; that I was sorry to hear he was one of the most active parties in the matter; that I had a vivid recollection of having accommodated him in many ways by loaning him my horses, farming-utensils, wagons, etc.; that I should be sorry to cause his arrest and imprisonment, but I had made up my mind to single him out as the one person whom I should hold responsible for the welfare of the colored man. I told him if the colored man was molested in any way I should cause his arrest, and I thought I could prove that he had made threats of violence, not only to the

man, but to me personally if I tried to protect Albert; that
Miss Tuthill, the colored man, and myself were splendid shots;
that we practised daily the use of firearms; that we had a
sort of arsenal for our protection; and that the slightest intru-
sion on the premises would be greeted with a volley from the
house and from the darky's quarters near by.  The frequent
change of color in his face betrayed his guilt in the matter,
but of course he protested innocence of any knowledge of
anything of the kind and avowed his willingness to protect
the "nigger" for me.  I assured him it was all right as long
as he was willing to be that kind of a hostage for Albert's
safety; that I should only have to ask the governor for protection and the provost marshal would be ordered to arrest any
one against whom I might make accusation; that all I wanted
was for them to be law-abiding citizens and attend to their
own affairs; that I had no desire to inform against them, but
I intended to keep the colored man and defend him as long
as he behaved and did the work I desired him to do.  The
miserable wretch was glad when the interview was over, and
beat a hasty retreat after telling me not to worry—it would
be all right.

My friend reported to me afterward that at the next meeting of the "Circle" the fellow told them it would never do
to trouble that "nigger" at John Logan's house, because he
had found out that Mrs. Logan had heard about what they had
talked of doing; that all their names were now in the hands
of officers; that if anything was to happen to the "nigger"
he was certain they would all be arrested and soldiers would
be stationed there to protect Logan's family; therefore, they
had better let the "nigger" alone.  They did, and we kept the
man long after General Logan's return home after the war,
till Albert desired to go South to hunt up his family.  When
we paid him off he had three or four hundred dollars as the
result of his labors and a partnership which he and I had
had in a little cotton crop we had raised together.  As he

drove away from the door on the town express, with a big trunk full of clothes, well dressed himself, and his money in his pocket, he felt as happy as if he had been a millionaire. I confess I too felt glad that I had saved at least one poor creature from being maltreated. We had taught him to read and write and trained him to be a good and useful citizen, of whom we have often heard good reports.

General Logan was delayed so long in reaching Chattanooga from Vicksburg that he did not arrive there till after the battle, greatly to his disappointment, as he desired to take part in what he felt was to be a brilliant victory.

After assuming command of the Fifteenth Corps, Army of the Tennessee, they were some time in moving to Huntsville, that being the objective point, but with his command stretched out about "seventy miles" he had a hard time getting them thoroughly organized and ready for the siege of Atlanta.

They were much exhausted and almost destitute of good shoes and clothing for the approaching winter, which proved to be a very cold one. The supplies were slow in reaching them because of the meagre transportation. For days the troops were moving slowly, for the most part subsisting on the country. General Logan's headquarters were for some time at Bridgeport, where they had a trying experience from the inclement weather and the hardships of soldiering in the enemy's country. Finally, they reached Huntsville, Alabama, where they were more comfortable, and where all their preparations for the Atlanta campaign and siege were perfected.

I had come to look upon the horrors of war with something akin to terror. During the sieges of Forts Henry and Donelson, Shiloh, Nashville, Corinth, and all the battles from Memphis to Vicksburg, and during the capture of that stronghold, so many brave men had fallen and so many widows and orphans were all around us, constantly appealing to our sympathies, that we had no respite. That "Hope long deferred maketh the heart sick" was experienced daily. It took

moral courage to face the facts of the situation, and I sometimes think a special Providence must have sustained both
the people and the soldiers through these trying times. The
women of the country, both North and South, bore no small
part of the burden of the war, and I have vivid recollections
of seeing them display moral courage of the highest order.

Trained nurses and undertakers were unknown in southern Illinois. These important offices were performed by the
neighbors and friends with the loving-kindness and faithfulness
that can not be purchased at any price. Though quite young,
it was often my melancholy duty to bear a part in these sad
services.

One dreary November evening, just as the sun was setting,
two ladies and myself went with a poor old stricken grandfather to bury his little grandchild, the daughter of a soldier who
was away at the front, and whose mother was lying ill. When
we reached the cemetery there was no one near to assist him
in lowering the little body into the grave. We took hold of
the ropes, two standing opposite each other and one opposite
the old man, and gently lowered the coffin. We then alter-
nated in helping him to fill the grave and fashion the mound
over the remains of the soldier's child. Returning with the
aged grandfather, we found the poor mother rapidly sinking
into the same sleep that had taken her little one out of all
suffering. After a long vigil she, too, slept well, when, changing from sexton to undertaker, we prepared her poor body for
the casket and remained with the family till stronger arms
could be found to lay her beside her child.

We never knew a woman to falter or to be found wanting
no matter how trying a duty she had to perform in the field
or at home, where sometimes she had to face trials greater
than those on a battle-field. North and South, the women
of this great nation demonstrated the heroism and devotion
to their loved ones and to the ties that bound them to their
homes and families.

# CHAPTER VII

BATTLES OF RESACA AND DALLAS — GENERAL LOGAN WOUNDED
AGAIN — KENESAW MOUNTAIN — DEATH OF McPHERSON —
LOGAN IN COMMAND — WINS THE BATTLE OF ATLANTA —
PASSED OVER BY SHERMAN FOR CONTINUANCE IN COMMAND OF
ARMY OF THE TENNESSEE — GENERAL HOWARD SUCCEEDS —
SUBSEQUENT RECONCILIATION OF SHERMAN AND LOGAN — THE
CORKHILL BANQUET — POLITICAL CAMPAIGN OF 1864 — LOGAN
TAKES THE STUMP AT LINCOLN'S REQUEST — HIS POWERFUL
INFLUENCE — RE–ELECTION OF LINCOLN — ORDERED TO RE-
PORT TO GRANT AT CITY POINT

APPRECIATING as I did the prodigious undertakings that
were planned for Sherman's army, I spent many midnight
hours in sleepless anxiety. During the day we had plenty to
do to help care for the families of the refugees and soldiers,
who were subject to all the ills to which human flesh is heir.
Playing nurse, comforter, providing ways and means, and
soliciting and dispensing relief kept my friends and myself
very busy. Meanwhile we watched and waited impatiently
for the meagre tidings that came irregularly from the advan-
cing army.

All the winter of 1863 and the spring of 1864 Sherman was
preparing for the campaign and siege of Atlanta. His old
friend and associate, Johnston, was in command of the forces
in and about Atlanta. Sherman had the most exalted opinion of Johnston's military abilities and courage; he was,
therefore, very careful that every precaution should be observed.

The almost impregnable mountain barriers encircling the
well-fortified city of Atlanta added much to the advantage of
the enemy. With an army of less courage and experience,

Sherman would have had reason for solicitude. Vicksburg, Lookout Mountain, and Chattanooga were ours. General Grant and the Army of the East had scored many victories; the enemy were dispirited and rapidly reaching the point of desperation; therefore, the Union troops had reason to expect intrepid resistance to their advance. This, however, in no wise deterred them, and they were only impatient for active operations, growing quite restive under the delays incident to the mobilization of such an army.

May 1, 1864, they started breaking up the headquarters at Huntsville, Alabama, from which date until the 1st of September they were constantly on the move, fighting their way over almost every foot of territory to the frowning breastworks surrounding Atlanta.

At Resaca they first drove the enemy from their works and pursued them in their retreat to Adairsville. General Logan desired to follow up this victory and capture the flower of Johnston's army, but was not permitted to do so. Subsequently it was proved that General Logan was correct in his military judgment, and that his proposition could have been successfully executed. From Adairsville the Union forces marched to Kingston and Dallas, where, in a severe engagement against Hardee's veteran corps, General Logan was shot through the arm about half-way between the elbow and the shoulder. They seemed determined to deprive him of his left arm, as he had been shot through that arm at the point of the shoulder at Fort Donelson. He paid little attention to the wound received at Dallas, feeling that there was no time to be off duty for a single hour. General Logan always claimed that Dallas, for the length of time and number of troops engaged, was one of the most hotly contested battles of the war. The attack of the Fifteenth Corps on Kenesaw Mountain, up its perpendicular sides, was one of the most daring and tragic in history. It was made in obedience to orders against the advice of General Logan, who con-

sidered the impossible feat little short of madness, an opinion
in which General McPherson coincided, but both were subordinate to the general commanding the movements around
Atlanta.

Yet the gallant leader of the Fifteenth Corps never hesitated to obey an order, even though it would lead to dire
disaster. His brave followers tried to go wherever he led;
so, at eight o'clock on the morning of June 27, 1864, they
went bravely forward over two lines of works, driving the
enemy still higher on the precipitous sides of the mountain,
to be mowed down like grass by the enemy intrenched above.
Huge stones, a torrent of iron hail, and canister were hurled
down upon them like the avalanches of the Rocky Mountains.
To proceed further or remain where they were was impossible.
Besides the hundreds of dauntless men, such grand heroes as
Generals Harker and McCook were killed. Finally, the advice of General Logan to flank the position was adopted, but
not until the scaling experiment had cost many valuable lives.
Johnston, seeing that his rear was threatened by the flank
movement, fell back toward Atlanta from Kenesaw.

General Logan commanded the Fifteenth Corps, General
Dodge the Sixteenth Corps, General Blair the Seventeenth
Corps, of the Army of the Tennessee. Between these officers
and General McPherson there existed the most perfect
harmony. General Logan and General McPherson were
thoroughly impressed with the fact that in front of the
Fifteenth Corps there was massed a large force of the enemy
after the fighting that had taken place around Decatur. General Sherman believed the Confederates were evacuating Atlanta, and were retreating toward East Point; therefore he
ordered General McPherson to pursue them with the Army
of the Tennessee, and, if possible, cut off a portion of them.

McPherson felt this to be a terrible mistake, but he was
too good a soldier to hesitate long over an order. So, early
in the morning of the 22d of July, he rode over to General

Map of a road near Atlanta, drawn by Captain H. B. Cunningham.

Logan's headquarters to confer with him, and at the same time order General Logan to put the troops in position to carry out General Sherman's orders, "while I will ride over to Sherman's headquarters, and try to convince him of his error," he said.    General Logan has often, with tears in his eyes, related the thrilling circumstances, and how he proceeded at once to obey McPherson, feeling that they were to be met by an opposing army greatly in excess of their commands.

Scarcely had the sound of the clatter of McPherson's horse's hoofs died away, as he galloped off in the direction of General Sherman's headquarters, when an orderly came on a flying steed to General Logan to announce that McPherson had been killed by Claiborne's Cavalry, which was rapidly swinging around to the rear of the Union army.

Thus, in a twinkling, upon General Logan was thrust the awful responsibility of extricating the troops from the direful position in which they were placed—almost cut off, the enemy in the rear, the Union cavalry sent off to burn a bridge at Covington, and with the command as nearly as possible under the orders given by General Sherman to McPherson, and carried by him in person to General Logan, as mentioned above, in the early morning of July 22, 1864.

The order read as follows:

Three miles and a half east of Atlanta, Ga.,
MAJOR–GENERAL JOHN A. LOGAN,
    *Commanding Fifteenth Army Corps.*
The enemy having evacuated their works in front of our lines, the supposition of Major-General Sherman is that they have given up Atlanta without entering the town.   You will take a route to the left of that taken by the enemy, and try to cut off a portion of them, while they are pressed in the rear and on the right by Generals Schofield and Thomas.

Major-General Sherman desires and expects a vigorous pursuit.

Very respectfully your obedient servant,
JAMES B. McPHERSON,
*Major-General.*

It was proved afterward to have been wholly impracticable.

With the sounds of the guns of the attacking enemy coming from every direction, General Logan, as the ranking officer, and with only the orders which he received from McPherson a few minutes before he was killed, assumed command. General Logan rode with magic swiftness from one end of the line to the other, rallying the troops with the tragic cry of "McPherson and revenge!" and appealing to officers and men to do or die. Hand to hand was the order of the day—victory wavering from one side to the other from early morning until the day was far spent. The irresistible force and intrepid valor of the Union army, led by a dauntless leader, compelled the enemy to fall back. The day was ours, and McPherson was revenged, solely through General Logan's matchless genius, indomitable courage, and leadership of men—men who would have followed him to the jaws of death. He fought the battle without orders, winning a victory when the tide of battle was almost overwhelmingly against him.

I can not resist quoting, from General Logan's address on the occasion of the unveiling of McPherson's monument in McPherson Square in Washington in 1876, his graphic description of McPherson's death:

The news of his death spread with lightning-speed along the lines, sending a pang of deepest sorrow to every heart as it reached the ear; but, especially terrible was the effect on the Army of the Tennessee. It seemed as though a burning, fiery dart had pierced each breast, tearing asunder the flood-gates of grief, but, at the same time, heaving to their very depths the fountains of revenge. The clenched hands seemed to sink into the weapons they held, and from the eyes gleamed forth flashes terrible as lightning. The cry "McPherson, McPherson!" and "McPherson and revenge!" rose above the din of battle, and, as it rang along the lines, swelled in power, until the roll of musketry and booming of cannon seemed drowned by its echoes.

McPherson again seemed to lead his troops—and where McPherson leads victory is sure. Each officer and soldier, from the succeeding commander to the lowest private, beheld, as it were, the form of their bleeding chief leading them on to the battle. "McPherson!" and "Onward to victory!" were their only thoughts; bitter, terrible revenge their only aim.

There was no such thought that day as stopping short of victory or death. The firm, spontaneous resolve was to win the day or perish with their slain leader on the bloody field. Fearfully was his death avenged. His army, maddened by his death and utterly reckless of life, rushed with savage delight into the fiercest onslaughts, and fearlessly plunged into the very jaws of destruction. As wave after wave of Hood's daring troops dashed with terrible fury upon our lines, they were hurled back with a fearful shock, breaking their columns into fragments, as the granite headland breaks into foam the ocean billows that strike against it. Across the narrow line of works raged the fierce storm of battle, the hissing shot and shell raining death on every hand. Seven times Hood's, Hardee's, and Wheeler's commands charged and were as many times repulsed. Once they broke the Union lines and captured De Grass's battery, and he, with tears streaming down his brave cheeks, rode as fast as his horse could carry him to General Logan, begging him to send a brigade of the invincible Fifteenth Army Corps to recover his beloved guns. Fired by the gallant De Grass's heroism, General Logan appealed to the men who had never failed him. Off they went, crying: "The guns! the guns! we will have them or die!" Logan led the way, the very incarnation of desperate daring, and in a brief time the battery was recaptured.

Over dead and dying, friends and foes, rushed the swaying host, the shouts of rebels confident of victory, only drowned by the cry of "McPherson and revenge!" which went up from the Army of the Tennessee. Twelve thousand gallant men bit the dust ere the night closed in, and the defeated and baffled enemy, after failing in repeated and desperate assaults upon our lines, was compelled to give up the hopeless contest. Notwithstanding the fact that our troops had to fight front and rear, victory crowned our arms.

That night, after the battle, General Logan received orders commanding him to report to General Sherman's headquarters, which he reached at the midnight hour, to be congratulated and praised without stint for the work he had done that day. Continuance of the command of the Army of the Tennessee was promised him again and again, as he in detail reported to General Sherman the events of the battle. No intimation was given of his unfitness for the command or of his lacks in the profession of a soldier. His military sense was considered of the highest order; if he was a soldier from civilian ranks, he had never been defeated in any engagement, which can not be said of all the professional soldiers of the Civil War. He felt, as he returned to his headquarters that night, that all was propitious, that he had done his duty well, and that merit would receive its just reward. He was anxious to fulfil every requirement of so responsible a position, so, when orders came that the army under his command should withdraw from their intrenchments and move seven miles to the right under the cover of darkness, that the enemy might not discover the movement, General Logan personally superintended the execution of the command. He ordered the wheels of the wagon-trains and artillery to be muffled with hay and straw, and was so explicit in his directions to the officers in command of the various corps and divisions that, in the stillness of the night they quietly gathered up all their belongings, and all the paraphernalia of war, and were in their new position in the early morning, an unparalleled piece of strategy, and not excelled by any like movement by the greatest warriors of any age.

Imagine the feelings of a man, weary from midnight vigils, marching and personally superintending such gigantic movements as General Logan had directed for days preceding, and in a position to begin another big battle, to be confronted with an order to surrender the command to General O. O. Howard, not before conspicuously connected with the great Army of the Tennessee which Logan had led to victory after McPherson's death! The Army of the Tennessee had never known defeat under him and, to a man, they would have followed Logan through blood and carnage to the very abyss of death. A man of less noble mind and courage would have rebelled, and encouraged the just indignation expressed by the whole command; but he, with his great heart beating with patriotism and soldierly appreciation of the effect of his resentment, quietly returned to his old corps, and led the van in the heroic deeds of the 28th of July, 1864, at Ezra Chapel, the most sanguinary battle of the whole campaign, where the Fifteenth Army Corps captured many prisoners, arms, and battle-flags.

The victory was so complete that the enemy fled from the field, leaving their dead and wounded behind them. General Howard, General Logan's successor in command of the Army of the Tennessee, made special mention of the conduct of General Logan and his corps, attributing the success of the day as much to General Logan, personally, as to any one man. After frequent less important engagements the army reached Jonesboro, where the last great battle before the evacuation of Atlanta occurred.

General Logan did not reach Jonesboro until midnight of August 30. Realizing that they were likely to be assaulted by the corps of Hardee and Lee at any moment, he ordered intrenchments to be made to protect his lines and his men from needless exposure. This was done without orders from either of his superior officers, but from the promptings of his own military genius and wisdom.

At three o'clock the expected assault was made, but, protected by their trenches, the Union forces were able to repel the attacks of the enemy. The artillery were so well posted that they could rake the foe mercilessly. The day resulted in the fall of Atlanta, which had been doomed since the bloody battle of July 22.

General Sherman, in his report of the Atlanta campaign, heaped encomiums upon General Logan, and said no one could possibly have done better than he after the death of McPherson, but admitted that he had recommended General O. O. Howard to supersede General Logan.

It is needless to recapitulate, but General Logan's noble conduct in the most trying experience of his life is beyond exaggeration. I need not dwell upon his matchless achievements after he returned to the command of the Fifteenth Army Corps, who, to a man, would have died for him. Logan never swerved one iota from his loyalty to his commanders, or in the least lessened his energies or his heroism till Atlanta had fallen. After the battle of Ezra Chapel, on August 28, 1864, which was won by the daring of the Fifteenth Army Corps with Logan at its head, General O. O. Howard issued an order congratulating the army, and mentioning General Logan in laudatory terms. General Logan was incapable of inciting or allowing a mutinous spirit to prevail, but he was not able to prevent the army from feeling resentment at the appointment of General O. O. Howard. Had not General Logan gone North at the solicitation of President Lincoln to take part in the Presidential campaign of 1864—after the fall of Atlanta—and had not the army started on its holiday march to the sea, the incident might not have ended as it did. Suffice it to say, that the authorities at Washington deemed it expedient to transfer Major-General O. O. Howard to the command of the Freedman's Bureau, in Washington, and restore General Logan to the command of the Army of the Tennessee. Major-General Logan, therefore, rode at the head of that invincible army at the grand review. The Army of the Tennessee manifested their gratification at his return to the command in every possible way. General O. O. Howard was naturally chagrined,

Letter of General Joseph Hooker to General Logan informing him of General Hooker's resignation because of the appointment of General Howard to the command of the Army of the Tennessee.

and a few years ago, in a public way, tried to explain that the restoration of Major-General Logan to the command of the Army of the Tennessee was brought about by political influence. It was at least strange that this explanation was not given while General Logan and General Sherman were living. Ever since the war closed, and the patriotic societies were organized, on every occasion of their meetings, or rather reunions, General Logan was hailed with enthusiasm as the great commander of the Army of the Tennessee.

It may not be inappropriate for me on this occasion to say that whatever of misunderstanding and estrangement there may have existed at one time between the two great commanders of the Army of the Tennessee, Sherman and Logan, it was wholly obliterated by General Logan's tribute to General Sherman at a notable banquet given by Colonel Corkhill to General Sherman on his retirement as general of the army, in which Logan said, in replying to the toast "The Volunteer Soldier":

There were no questions of numbers or time, and, for General Sherman, I will say there was not a soldier who bore the American flag, or followed it, not a soldier who carried a musket, or drew a sabre, who did not respect him as his commander. There was not one, sir, but would have drawn his sword at any time to have preserved his life. There is not one to-day, no matter what may have been said, that would dim in the slightest degree the lustre of that bright name, achieved by ability, by integrity, and by true bravery as an officer. And in conclusion let me say this: While that army, when it was disbanded, was absorbed in the community like rain-drops in the sand, all citizens in the twinkling of an eye, and back to their professions and their business, there is not one of these men, scattered as they are from ocean to ocean, who does not honor the name of the man who led them in triumph through the enemy's land. Wherever he may go, wherever he may be, whatever may be his condition in life, there is not one who would not stretch out a helping hand to that brave commander who led them to glory. Speaking for that army, if I may be permitted to speak for it, I have to say: May the choicest blessings that God showers upon the head of man go with him along down through his life, is the prayer of every soldier who served under Sherman.

When General Logan finished, General Sherman arose, went around to General Logan, put his arm around Logan's neck, and shook his hand cordially, while the tears ran down his cheeks. His emotions were too great for words.

It was on a Saturday night, and, notwithstanding the approach of the wee sma' hours before the tearful parting of the distinguished guests, General Sherman went home and wrote the following most manly and feeling letter to General Logan, explaining his reasons for certain actions touching General Logan and expressing his gratitude for General Logan's tribute to him.

WASHINGTON, D. C., *Sunday, February* 11, 1883.
GENERAL JOHN A. LOGAN,
*U. S. Senate, Washington, D. C.*
*Dear General:—*
This is a rainy Sunday, a good day to clear up old scores, and I hope you will receive what I propose to write in the same friendly spirit in which I offer it.

I was very much touched by the kind and most complimentary terms in which you spoke of me personally at the recent Corkhill banquet, on the anniversary of my sixty-third birthday, and have since learned that you still feel a wish that I should somewhat qualify the language I used in my Memoirs, column 2, pages 85 and 86, giving the reasons why General O. O. Howard was recommended by me to succeed McPherson in the command of the Army of the Tennessee, when, by the ordinary rules of the service, the choice should have fallen to you. I confess frankly that my ardent wish is to retire from the command of the army with the kind and respectful feelings of all men, especially of those who were with me in the days of the Civil War, which must give to me and to my family a chief claim on the gratitude of the people of the United States.

I confess that I have tortured and twisted the words used on the pages referred to, so as to contain my meaning better without offending you, but so far without success. I honestly believe that no man to-day holds in higher honor than myself the conduct and action of John A. Logan, from that hour when he realized that the South meant war. Prior to the war, all men had doubts, but the moment Fort Sumter was fired on from batteries in Charleston, these doubts dissipated as a fog, and from the hour thenceforth your course was manly, patriotic, sublime. Throughout the war, I know of no single man's career more complete than yours.

Now, as to the specific matter of this letter. I left Vicksburg in the fall of 1863, by order of General Grant in person, with three divisions of my own corps (15th) and one of McPherson's (16th) to hasten to the assistance of the Army of the Cumberland (General Rosecrans commanding) which, according to the then belief, had been worsted at Chickamauga. Blair was with us, you were not. We marched through mud and water four hundred miles from Memphis, and you joined me on the march, with an order to succeed me in command of the Fifteenth Corps, a Presidential appointment which Blair had exercised temporarily. Blair was at that time a member of Congress, and was afterward named to command the 17th Corps, and actually remained so long in Washington that we had got to Big Shanty before he overtook us. Again, after the battles of Missionary Ridge and Knoxville, when Howard served with me, I went back to Vicksburg and Meridian, leaving you in command of the Fifteenth Corps along the railroad from Stevenson to Decatur. I was gone three months, and, when I got back, you complained to me bitterly against George H. Thomas, that he claimed for the Army of the Cumberland everything, and almost denied the Army of the Tennessee any use of the railroads. I sustained you, and put all army and corps commanders on an equal footing, making their orders and requisitions of equal force on the depot officers and railroad officials in Nashville. Thomas was extremely sensitive on that point, and, as you well know, had much feeling against you personally, which he did not conceal. You also went to Illinois more than once to make speeches, and were so absent after the capture of Atlanta, at the time we started for Savannah, and did not join us until we had reached Savannah.

Now, I have never questioned the right or propriety of you and Blair holding fast to your constituents by the usual methods; it was natural and right, but it did trouble me to have my corps commanders serving two distinct causes, one military and the other civil or political; and this did influence me when I was forced to make choice of an army commander to succeed McPherson. This is all I record in my Memoirs. It was so, and I can not amend them. Never in speech, writing, or record, surely not in the Memoirs, do I recall applying to you and Blair, for I always speak of you together, the term of "political general." If there be such an expression, I can not find it now, nor can I recall its use. The only place wherein the word "politics" occurs is in the pages which I have referred to, and wherein I explain my own motive and reason for nominating Howard over you and Blair for the vacant post.

My reason may have been bad, nevertheless it was the reason which decided me then and, as a man of honor, I was bound to record it. At this time, 1883, Thomas being dead, I can not say more than is in the text, viz.: that he took strong ground against you, and I was naturally strongly influenced by his outspoken opinion. Still, I will not throw off on him, but will state to you frankly that I then believed that the advice I gave Mr. Lincoln was the best practicable. General Howard had been with me up to Knoxville, and had displayed a zeal and ability which then elicited my hearty approbation, and, as I trusted in a measure to skilful manœuvres rather than to downright hard fighting, I recommended him. My Memoirs were designed to give the impressions of the hour, and not to pass judgment on the qualities as exemplified in after life.

If you will point out to me a page or line where I can better portray your fighting qualities, your personal courage, and magnificent example in actual combat, I will be most happy to add to or correct the Memoirs, but when I attempt to explain my own motives or reasons, you surely will be the first man to see that outside influence will fail.

My course is run, and for better or worse I can not amend it, but if ever in your future you want a witness to your intense zeal and patriotism, your heroic personal qualities, you may safely call on me as long as I live. I surely have watched with pride and interest your career in the United States Senate, and will be your advocate if you aim at higher honors. I assert with emphasis that I never styled you or Blair "political generals" and if I used the word "politics" in an offensive sense, it was to explain my own motives for action and not as descriptive.

Wishing you all honor and happiness on this earth, I am, as always, your friend,

W. T. SHERMAN.

This letter General Logan acknowledged promptly, responding cordially to the sentiments of regard expressed by his beloved commander.

UNITED STATES SENATE,
WASHINGTON, D. C.,
*Sunday, Feb. 18, 1883.*

GENERAL W. T. SHERMAN,
*My dear Sir:—*

I have delayed acknowledging your letter of the 11th inst. up to this time for the reason that I have been so much engaged every moment of the time that I could not sooner do so; for your expression of kindly feelings toward me I tender my grateful acknowledgments.

I am inclined, however, my dear general, to the opinion that, had you fully understood the situation in which I was placed at the times mentioned by you, that I returned North from the army for the purpose of taking part in the political contests then going on, that perhaps your criticisms on my (then) course would not have been made. I did not do it for the purpose of "keeping a hold on my people." I refused a nomination in my own State for a very high position for the reason that I would not have anything to do with parties while the war should last. In 1863, when I went home to canvass in Illinois, and to help in Ohio, General Grant was fully advised, and knows that although I had to make application for leave of absence, I did not do it of my own volition, but at the request of those high in authority. So, when I left on leave after the Atlanta campaign, to canvass for Mr. Lincoln, I did it at the special and private request of the then President. This I kept to myself, and have never made it public, nor do I propose to do so now, but feel that I may in confidence say this to you, that you may see what prompted my action in the premises. I have borne for this reason whatever I may have suffered by way of criticism, rather than turn criticism on the dead.

So far as General Thomas having feeling in the matter you mention, I presume he entertained the same feeling that seemed to be general, that no one without a military education was to be trusted to command an army; this, I think, was the feeling then, is now, and will ever be. I find no fault with it; this as a rule is probably correct, but the experience of the world has occasionally found exceptions to this rule. I certainly never gave General Thomas any occasion to have strong feelings against me. I did complain that I was not on an equality with him while I commanded between Decatur and Stevenson; that my passes on the roads were not recognized, and I have General Thomas's letter afterward, admitting the fact, and apologizing to me for the conduct of his officers in this matter. I at all times co-operated with him cordially and promptly during my stay at Huntsville and at all other times subsequent. Certainly I did for him afterward what few men would have done. When ordered to Nashville, with a view of superseding him, at Louisville, when I found the situation of matters, I wrote and telegraphed to Grant that he, Thomas, was doing all he could, and asked to be ordered back to my own command, which was done. This I say to show my kind feeling for him, and to say that if I ever did anything to cause him to complain of me I was not aware of it.

One thing, my dear general, that I feel conscious of, and that is that no man ever obeyed your orders more promptly, and but few ever did you more faithful service in carrying out your plans and military movements than myself.

I may have done yourself and myself an injustice by not disclosing to you the cause of my returning to the North at the time I did, but you have my reasons for it. I felt in honor that I could rest.

This letter is intended only for full explanation, and for yourself only. I do not feel aggrieved as you think, but will ever remain your friend,

Yours truly,<br>John A. Logan.

The few brief years that intervened before General Logan preceded General Sherman to that land of eternal bliss they saw much of each other, forgetting, in the happy circumstance of reunited friendship, the unfavorable winds that had temporarily estranged them. The Corkhill banquet was probably one of the most impressive dinners ever given in Washington, including the names of the most illustrious men of that time. Nearly every one of that distinguished company have joined the mighty throng in the great beyond.

The correspondence between Sherman and himself General

Logan regarded as confidential, and therefore he would not discuss the matter or give it to the public. Amicable relations having been restored between himself and his revered commander, to whom he was sincerely attached, he was willing the matter should be dropped, as it was impossible for General Logan, with his generous and big-hearted nature, to long bear malice or be indefinitely estranged from any one to whom he had once been attached.

Prior to the dinner above mentioned General Sherman had at various times and in many ways tried to explain why he was so inconsistent as to recommend General O. O. Howard to the authorities at Washington as successor to General McPherson in command of the Army of the Tennessee, after he had acknowledged that General Logan had rescued that army from defeat and won one of the most signal victories of the war. It was not until Sherman's retirement, as explained by the correspondence between General Sherman and General Logan, and published after General Logan's death, that General Sherman gave to the public the true reason for the injustice done General Logan in returning him to his corps, and in taking General O. O. Howard from another army and giving him command of the Army of the Tennessee. It will be seen that one among others of Sherman's reasons for this action was that General Logan was a volunteer, and not a professional soldier graduated from West Point, notwithstanding the fact that Logan's record showed he had never made a mistake in handling an army, though the same is not claimed for General Sherman and other West Point graduates.

In connection with this matter, there has come into my possession recently a copy of a most valuable record made at the time by that dauntless, efficient, and incomparable officer, Major-General Granville M. Dodge. General Dodge commanded the Sixteenth Army Corps of Sherman's army during the eventful Atlanta campaign. The intimacy which grew up between General Dodge and General Logan while they were engaged in the prodigious work which each performed in that campaign continued through life, and I deem this report so important that I can not resist the temptation to insert it here. It will be remembered that General Dodge's great services to his country did not end with the close of the war, for it was through his indomitable energy and great skill as a civil engineer that the Union Pacific Railroad was completed. He has been president of the Society of the Army of the Tennessee since the death of General Sherman. General Dodge's report reads as follows:

On July 27th General O. O. Howard was assigned to the command of the Army of the Tennessee, which was a great disappointment to that army. They felt that an army which had followed Grant, Sherman, McPherson, and Logan, who had taken it successfully through its last battle, after the death of McPherson, had material enough in it to command it. On the movement from the extreme left to the right, I pulled out first and as I was moving to the rear of General Thomas's army, I saw General Logan sitting on the porch of a log building. I went up to speak to him and found that General Sherman was inside. After speaking a few words to General Logan, I went in and had a talk with General Sherman, inquiring about the change of commanders and expressing my wish that General Logan had been assigned to the command. He answered me by saying it was all right; that he would tell me the reasons sometime. When I came out, General Logan was still sitting on the porch and, as the door was open, I have no doubt he heard what I had to say to General Sherman, for there were tears in his eyes. I spoke to him very cordially and said to him that I was greatly disappointed at the change, but hoped it would end all right. He, like a good soldier, said it would, but he said it was pretty hard on him. Nothing more then was said about it. Years after, I had correspondence in relation to this matter with General Sherman, when the friends of Logan and myself were endeavoring to bring them together. For a long time after the war General Logan never forgot Sherman's treatment of him and at times felt it keenly, but one day, on the floor of the U. S. Senate, General Logan made a speech in defense of Sherman and in praise of him, which finally brought them together and their old troubles were forgotten. Some time after the war, I forget the place but I think it was when we were together at one of the reunions of the Army of the Tennessee, General Sherman made a full explanation to me of the matter and at the time I made full notes of it in my diary, and I quote here what he said:

" Sherman said that in the winter of 1863, after the battle of Missionary Ridge on his trip to Meridian, he left Logan in command at Huntsville with the 15th Corps, and Dodge in command on line of railroad from Nashville to Decatur with the 16th Corps, both in General Thomas's Department. On his return, he found Logan much dissatisfied with Thomas and complained of his treatment of him. He could not send an officer or soldier to Nashville until he got his orders or passes approved by Thomas's provost marshal or some local commander. Sherman, when he saw Thomas, told him he should not have treated Logan in that way; that he was a corps commander and was entitled to better treatment. Thomas complained of Logan in several matters and said he was hard to get along with and that he had had no trouble with Dodge. Sherman said he had tried to smooth the matter over, but he discovered an unfriendly feeling that continued through the Atlanta campaign.

" When McPherson fell, on the 22nd of July, in front of Atlanta, Logan by seniority of rank assumed command by his direction and handled the army well. After the battle Thomas came to Sherman and they discussed the question of a commander for the Army of the Tennessee. Sherman told Thomas that Logan was entitled to the command, was competent for it and he desired to place him in it. Thomas answered with much feeling that he was sorry to hear him say so, for, if Logan was assigned to the command of the Army of the Tennessee, he should consider it his duty to resign his command. Sherman answered General Thomas: 'You certainly would not do that and leave me here in that condition.' Thomas hesitated and finally said: 'No, I don't know as I would go so far as that,' but protested that Logan should not be assigned to the command. Sherman said: 'I don't see how I can pass him by; I don't want to do anything that will seem to reflect on Logan.' Thomas answered: 'Well, let the President or Secretary of War select a commander.' Sherman said: 'No. I do not want them to send a commander here that is outside of this army.' Sherman said: 'In other words you don't feel that with Logan in command you and he could act cordially and harmoniously together?' Thomas said: 'Yes, that's it, and I think, to insure success, that there should be not only harmony but entire cordiality between the army commanders.' Sherman's answer was that he could not afford to put Logan in command under such circumstances.

" Finally they sat down and discussed the merits of the different generals and settled upon Howard. 'I have,' said Sherman, 'always been a friend to Logan in a great many different ways. He was a good soldier. He handled the army splendidly on the 22d, and in his movement to the right. But you see I had a great responsibility and had to do the best I could under the circumstances. I consider Logan the representative volunteer general of the war.' "

While I never knew the exact facts in the matter, I know the Army of the Tennessee wanted Logan and was greatly disappointed when Sherman went outside of it for a commander. The officers and men felt that the little army that had had for its commanders Grant, Sherman, McPherson, and Logan had filled every post of responsibility to which it had been assigned, and that there was material left in it to command it; but I think no one in it knew of this complication and it is well they did not.

Sherman showed himself a master when he took the responsibility and made no explanation, and thus preserved the good feeling throughout the great command. I heard the news of the appointment of Howard in place of Logan as we were marching from the left to right. I did not know Howard personally.

While these events were occurring at the front, the political excitement was waxing hot all over the North, and the old feeling between the war and anti-war parties in the North was growing more and more intense. Many Democrats, General Logan among them, had gone into the army to save the Union. Many others failed to see that the Emancipation Proclamation was the legitimate sequence of secession; the disasters in the East were seized upon as an excuse for declaring the war a failure. McClellan, the first general of the army, was nominated for the Presidency by the Democratic party; many War Democrats flocked to his standard, and it was supposed that all of them would do so. It was thought that the disaffection thus created would result in the defeat of Mr. Lincoln, and thereby the transfer of the Government and all its interests to Democratic hands. For weeks all communication with the army engaged in the siege of Atlanta had been cut off. The conventions had been held, and the candidates were regularly in the field. The deepest solicitude was felt all over the country as to which of the parties and candidates would receive the moral support of the army.

Illinois, as the home of Mr. Lincoln, was watched with great anxiety. General Logan had refused all political preferment after he entered the army in 1861. This election of 1864 was the first Presidential election since the war began, and his old-time friends thought to win him to the support of McClellan. Mr. Lincoln realized that Illinois was so important to the Republican party that he was anxious to have General Logan's support. Hence, the moment that General Sherman decided that the army should not continue the pursuit of Hood's army until they had rested after their superhuman labors in the siege and capture of Atlanta, and it was evident that there would be no movement requiring General Logan's presence, Mr. Lincoln requested him to come home and take part in the civil campaign, which was fraught with quite as much importance as the military one just closed so gloriously.

After the army had entered Atlanta and all were to have a respite, General Logan came home. The plaudits of the people followed him everywhere, and I shall remember as long as I live the eagerness with which they surrounded him and plied him with questions as to his future political course. To all of them he said: "Wait till the arrival of the date when I am to speak to you." He had been advertised to speak in the grove near Carbondale, Illinois, our home at that time. The grove was a most beautiful place, a natural amphitheatre shaded by grand old oak-trees, where outdoor public meetings were held. On this occasion, fully twenty thousand people assembled there, all breathless to hear what General Logan had to say. A large majority of the residents of that section were War Democrats, and inclined to the support of McClellan, a brother-in-law of mine among the number. My relative was so enthusiastic that he declared over and over again, while communication was cut off during the siege of Atlanta, that he knew General Logan, as a War Democrat, would espouse McClellan's cause, greatly to the vexation of General Logan's friends, who were devoted to Mr. Lincoln. One day, in the presence of a number of persons, he became so sanguine that he offered to bet a fine span of mules he owned against five hundred dollars that Logan would support McClellan. Seeing the annoyance and unhappiness his statement produced upon the friends, though not given to such practices, I said: "All right, Mr. Campbell, I will take your bet, since you are so confident." A half-dozen hands were instantly thrust into plethoric pockets, and the money was proffered to be put up to pay if I lost, and to be sure that I would have the mules if I won.

I heard nothing from General Logan for many weeks, and knew as little as any of them as to his position on political questions, except from intuition, and an appreciation of the situation and his well-known devotion to his country.

At last the day arrived on which General Logan was to speak. He was much worn and looked haggard and weary from his ceaseless labors in the Atlanta campaign which had lasted from May till September. He was so sunburnt that he looked like an Indian. The scenes through which he had passed had furrowed his brow, but the flashing light of his eyes was still there, and the return to home and his family made him happy. We soon told him all that had transpired during the thirteen months since we had last seen him; especially about the political situation, and the claims of both

Letter of President Lincoln to General Logan in 1864.

parties for his support and influence. When told that I had committed him to the extent of actually betting that he would not support McClellan and the platform upon which he was nominated, he was greatly amused, and I soon saw I had his approval, ever a requisite to my happiness. The incident had been telegraphed everywhere, and much comment indulged in, so, when General Logan mounted the beautifully decorated stand from which he was to speak, he was greeted by wild cheers and yells from the vast crowd: "Now he will win the mules." He spoke for some time, telling them the duty of all loyal men, of the cost of blood and treasure at which the victories of the Union had been won, and closed with a glowing appeal for Mr. Lincoln's re-election, that the war might speedily be brought to an end.

Scarcely a dry eye was to be seen among the thousands upturned to him, their idolized leader in civil as well as military campaigns. At the conclusion they made a rush for my brother-in-law's barn, and soon returned with the mules hitched to a carriage in which they insisted upon taking General Logan, and driving him around the town to our home. For weeks he travelled over the country in a carriage drawn by the mules, canvassing the State in the interest of the Republican nominees, and did as much as any other one man for the re-election of Mr. Lincoln.

After the lapse of so many years, and through the veil of oblivion that has obscured the circumstances then existing, it is hardly possible to fittingly portray the importance of General Logan's presence in the campaign for the re-election of Mr. Lincoln. It was the first Presidential election after the issuance of the Emancipation Proclamation; our victories had been won by great sacrifice. The platform upon which General McClellan was nominated had declared the war a failure, and was in favor of an armistice and renewal of fruitless peace negotiations, thereby betraying a want of sympathy with the policy of the Government on the part of the party nominating him. Had the Government changed hands at this critical juncture, no one could have answered for the consequences. Mr. Lincoln felt this most deeply. His own perpetuation in office occupied little of his thoughts, but the vigorous prosecution of the war and the preservation of the Union were of infinite importance; hence he was as anxious for the success of his party in the civil campaign as he was for the army in the field.

General McClellan's acceptance of the nomination inspired the Democracy with much courage. They thought the element known as "War Democrats" in and out of the army would rally round their leader. The most prominent journalists and party leaders were untiring in their efforts. General Logan was known as a War Democrat, and they expected he would support McClellan. They wrote him earnest letters, and appealed to him, the moment Atlanta had fallen, in such communications as the following, which was from one of the ablest journalists ever in Illinois, and a devoted friend and mentor of Senator Stephen A. Douglas during his eventful life:

OFFICE OF THE CHICAGO POST,
93 Washington Street,

CHICAGO, *August* 31, 1864.
DEAR GENERAL:—

I enclose you a copy of the platform adopted by the convention. I want you, as a Democrat, to write a letter indorsing your fellow soldier, patriot, and Democrat. You never failed yet to meet any demand that the Democratic party or your country ever made upon your talents, or even your life. Will you refuse both when they jointly ask your voice in the election? In God's name, dear Logan, by all your hopes for your country and yourself, let not the Democracy ask your arm and be refused. You and I persistently refused to join any party, refused to accept the title of "War Democrats" as distinguished from the old Democratic party of our early love, and, now that that party gives a rational and a national platform, will you refuse to give your voice in be-

half of our own soldier, patriot, Democrat, and statesman—Mc-
Clellan? Give us one of your characteristic letters indorsing platform, nominee, and all, and from the very hearts of the party will
go up a shout of thanks to you.

Yours truly,<br>J. W. SHEAHAN.

Equally earnest letters were written from every quarter,
not only to General Logan but to other officers of Democratic
antecedents at the front, and to their friends at home, urging
upon them the importance of winning the Presidential campaign with "Little Mac" as the leader.

Mr. Lincoln's anxiety to have General Logan enter the
canvass being under discussion in a correspondence years
later between General Sherman and General Logan, General
Sherman wrote:

HEADQUARTERS, ARMY OF THE UNITED STATES,<br>WASHINGTON, D. C., Feb. 20th, 1883.

GENERAL JOHN A. LOGAN,
U. S. Senate.

DEAR GENERAL:—

I beg to acknowledge receipt of your good letter of February
18th, and recall well the fact that about September 20th, 1864, I
received at Atlanta a telegram from some one in authority, I think
Mr. Lincoln himself, to the effect that your presence in Illinois
was important to the National cause. You probably know that
all my records were transferred to Lt. General Sheridan at the
time he succeeded me in command of the Military Division of the
Mississippi, and were burned up in the great Chicago fire. I only
retained the blotters from which the official records were made
up. In one of them I find my letter to Gen. Howard, commanding Army of the Tennessee, East Point:

"I consent that you give Gen. Logan a leave. I have not yet
heard from Gen. Grant, but in case of necessity, we can in Gen.
Logan's absence, take care of the 15th Corps. There seems to be
a special reason why he should go home at once."

This fully confirms what you write me, and looking back from
the distance of time, I doubt not you were able to give material

help in the election of Mr. Lincoln, which was the greatest consideration of that day.

                    With great respect,
                            Your friend,
                                    W. T. Sherman.


Colonel D. L. Phillips was bearer of Mr. Lincoln's note to General Logan, expressing his fears, and desiring Logan's services, which Mr. Lincoln believed would be potential on account of General Logan's affiliation with the Democratic party before the war. I regret extremely that Lincoln's request to General Logan was mislaid by a historian years ago, and could never be recovered. General Logan often spoke of it to me, and of the pleasure it gave him to think that Mr. Lincoln had such implicit faith in his power to influence the people to stand firmly at that vital period.

As soon as General Logan's speech after his arrival home from Atlanta was telegraphed over the country, he was deluged with telegrams from every part of the State, urging him to speak in the more prominent places, declaring it was necessary to counteract the efforts that were being made to induce voters of Democratic proclivities at the beginning of the war to support McClellan. Mr. Lincoln's friends realized the jeopardy that would follow a division of the vote of Illinois in the Electoral College, and therefore were determined that no such calamity should occur, if it was possible to prevent it by vigilance and desperate effort.

A list of appointments was made out by General Logan and the committee, which would consume nearly all the time intervening between his arrival home and the election. The list was published and a party made up to accompany him, including ladies and gentlemen who were well known in the State.

We left Carbondale in carriages, General Logan's carriage being drawn by the mules I had won from my brother-in-law.

In this carriage were Colonel Phillips, General Logan, and myself.

When we reached the first town on the list the enthusiastic crowd that greeted General Logan was innumerable. Many soldiers were home on furlough after the fall of Atlanta, and they were important factors in arousing the patriotism of the people. As we neared the towns we were met by throngs who, impatient to see General Logan, had gone out on the roads for miles to intercept him. The nearer we approached the wilder the cheers, until, before the people could be restrained, they had unhitched the mules, and, attaching a long rope to the axle, in a twinkling they were drawing the carriage, while others were following the mules, screaming: "Here's your mules, won by Mrs. Logan on Lincoln's election!" Gay streamers of red, white, and blue ribbons bedecked the dumb brutes that seemingly understood they were attracting attention, and were as docile as lambs, though we expected to see them resent with their heels the familiarity with which they were being handled. The towns were ablaze with bunting; the brass bands filled the air with patriotic music. We sometimes trembled lest the people, in their exuberant spirits and manifestations of cordiality and admiration, might permanently disable General Logan. He had to manage adroitly to seize their hands before they could get hold of his, so that he could drop theirs and save his from being crushed by their vigorous shaking. As it was, he had occasionally to put his hand in a sling. The people seemed unhappy if they could not get hold of him, and if his right hand was bound up they would slap him on the shoulders, embracing him in a way that would make him wince, though he knew their hearts were full of loyalty for him. Sometimes old fathers and mothers, whose sons had gone into the service under General Logan and had fallen in battle or died of disease or wounds in hospitals in the South, would come up to him and, with tears running down their cheeks, would grasp his hands or pat him on the head affectionately.   They could rarely speak for their emotions.   When they could speak they would say: "Logan, can you tell us anything more about our boy?   Was he a good soldier?   Was his face always turned to the foe?   We shall see him no more, but we will stand by the flag and Mr. Lincoln, because our boy gave his life for his country, and Mr. Lincoln is trying to save the Union and our country."   General Logan's great heart was deeply moved by such encounters, and the tears which ran down his cheeks told of his sympathy in stronger language than he could find words in which to express it.

Perhaps the next to push their way to him would be a company of men and women gotten up in grotesque uniforms of red, white, and blue, who were presented by their pseudo-captains, who usually had some amusing design worn as an insignia of the rank they held.   Once, I remember, they carried a splendid live eagle, who sat his perch with becoming dignity while he was presented to General Logan in an elaborate speech which had to be repeated to the end by the voluble orator chosen for the important duty.   General Logan accepted the gift, and assured his friends that he would carry the bird through the campaign; that he should be allowed to scream for the Republican party and its worthy nominees; and that with the eagle and the mules he was sure his canvass would not be in vain.

For six weeks we travelled from place to place, being at last obliged to take the train, and send the mules home, as we went farther North and the distance increased.

The farther North we went the greater the crowds and the wilder the excitement, convincing General Logan long before the election that Illinois could safely be counted for Lincoln and Johnson.   Pathos and comedy followed each other in such quick succession during that memorable trip that we were constantly vibrating between tears and laughter over the grave and comic scenes we witnessed.

We tried to be cheerful and to think that the worst of the war was over, but when the hour came for General Logan to return to the army it was with many forebodings that we bade him good-by.

He was ordered to report to General Grant at City Point, Virginia, as before mentioned. I was advised of the order sending him to relieve Thomas. With intense anxiety I watched the very meagre despatches in the papers, and hailed with delight the news of Thomas's victory and General Logan's return to Washington and New York, en route to Savannah, to join the Fifteenth Army Corps, which had made the holiday march from Atlanta to the sea under General Sherman. I believed then that by the time he could reach his command all the fighting would be over.

It was, however, a long and anxious winter. The troops were marching through swamps, over almost impassable roads, through Georgia and the Carolinas to Washington, stopping now and again to dislodge the Confederates from their final attempts at resistance to the Union troops, who were driving everything before them in their triumphant progress toward ending the bitter struggles for the preservation of the Union and for peace. We could get news from the army far less frequently than we desired. The refugees came in hordes from the South, seeking homes as near the border of the Southland as they could find. Colored and white dreaded the cold of the North, and as a consequence the people of the border States were overwhelmed with the numbers of impecunious creatures who had to leave the South. It was some time before they could adapt themselves to the changed conditions and accept the inevitable. New laws were passed giving the negroes protection on Southern soil, so that they came in very well as a solution of the problem of what to do for laborers with all the able-bodied men at the front. Although both races were insufferably slow, they could do something. If you tactfully kept away from them when they were engaged in any kind of work they would get through eventually, and were a great improvement on having no one to do the indispensable manual labor.

# CHAPTER VIII

AFTER the November election, with its glorious victories, and the triumph all along the line dividing the Union and Confederate armies from the Potomac to the Gulf of Mexico, every one was much encouraged and began to hope for an early cessation of hostilities. The Thanksgiving of that year was observed with fervent thankfulness to Him who holds the destinies of nations in the hollow of His hand. People greeted each other with—"Well, what is the good news of to-day?" "Grant will be in Richmond soon." "Lincoln will be inaugurated as President of a reunited country the 4th of March."

The approach of the holidays was hailed with delight. The old-time Christmas festivities were looked forward to with anticipations of much pleasure. Homes that had been shrouded in gloom for four long years began their wonted preparations for celebrating the happy season. The church societies which had been absorbed in the work for the sanitary commission and soldiers' families began to talk of a Christmas tree for the old and young of the whole town. In Carbondale, Illinois, where I lived, it would have been con-

sidered heartless and treasonable to have suggested such a
thing during the holidays of '61, '62, '63; but every one was
full of enthusiasm for the tree of Christmas, 1864. For weeks
before many men and women were busy making presents for
everybody, especially the children in the town, including those
who only went to Sunday-school during the holidays. Mit-
tens, caps, comforts, socks, stockings, pinafores, handkerchiefs,
collars, ribbons, sleds, toys, candies, cakes, fruit, nuts, and all
kinds of gifts were prepared to gladden old and young.

Two large cedars were secured and brought into the Methodist church, it being the largest in town. Willing and skilful
hands were found to decorate the whole church in living
green, with branches of evergreens, artificial flowers, and flags
profusely interspersed. The tree was festooned with yards
of pop-corn strung on a cord by passing a needle through
the snow-white kernels. Oranges were hung on the boughs,
while tiny flags and glass balls of every color of the rainbow
were hung on almost every branch. The tinner kindly do-
nated little tin saucers with wires so arranged through the
centre that they would hold the little candles and at the
same time fasten them to the limbs of the tree. These were
for the illumination. In the afternoon of Christmas Eve the
presents were all brought to the church done up in packages
and labelled with the name of the person for whom they were
intended. They had to be tied on the strong limbs near the
body of the trees. When completed and the mounds at the
base had been covered over with mats made of green woollen
ravellings to imitate grass, they looked majestic—no grander
ever graced a royal palace or brought greater joy to hearts
of imperial households. The ceremonies began at seven-
thirty. The programme consisted of music, songs, recitations, and addresses by guests. It was a union of all denominations in the town to celebrate the Holy Nativity. Brief
speeches from the pastors of the different churches followed.
After this Santa Claus appeared in a long fur coat and cap,

his white beard reaching nearly to his waist. He was hailed by a chorus of childish voices and the clapping of many hands. When it was found that his generosity extended to every one present, and that on all were bestowed the very things they wanted, exclamations of delight filled the church. No such sight as the merry children running from one to the other, comparing and exhibiting their treasures, had been witnessed since the sound of booming cannon had broken the spell of sweet peace of the nation. A cloud of anxiety and suspense had always overshadowed every entertainment during the years of the war. After singing with a zest the Christmas carols, and an eloquent benediction, the joyous people wended their way to their homes with hearts full of happiness, feeling that Christmas-tide was bringing the glad tidings of peace on earth and good will toward men.

The political triumphs emphasized by the military victories seemed to bring hope and gladness to the people who fancied through it all they could see the dawn of peace. Everywhere there was less of the spirit of revolution and disloyalty; grumblers and evil prognosticators were fewer; anxiety and solicitude were no longer in every face. As soon as the election was over and Mr. Lincoln was declared elected, General Logan asked for orders to return to his command. Much dissatisfaction still existed throughout the Army of the Tennessee because General Logan had not been restored to the command of that army. General Grant, therefore, bade him come to Washington, where he arrived on the 23d of December, 1864, and stopped at Brown's—now the Metropolitan —Hotel, where he spent Christmas Day, the most agreeable one to him since 1860. He was satisfied that it was only a question of a brief time before the war would be over, and he was consequently very happy. His corps had made the jolly march through Georgia without even a skirmish since he left them to take part in the Presidential campaign after the fall of Atlanta. His corps was then at Savannah and impatient to begin the march through the Carolinas en route to Richmond. He was equally impatient to lead them, but General Grant had other plans for him.

After the fall of Atlanta Grant was anxious that Sherman should start out upon his march to the sea, which he and Sherman had considered the most effective movement that could be made at that time to bring the war to a close. In order to make this expedition and avoid a catastrophe, Grant was most anxious that General Thomas, then in command of the troops about Nashville, should drive Hood out of Tennessee. The history of this General Grant gives in his "Memoirs," * including copies of orders which he had issued to General Thomas urging him to attack Hood, but which Thomas had ignored because he took it upon himself to decide as to the wisdom of these orders, steadily delaying to make the attack until he had succeeded in getting his army in the position he desired it should be before carrying out his orders. In the light of the glorious victories won by Thomas, one forgets what might have been the consequence of his disobedience to orders if defeat instead of victory had characterized these sanguinary engagements.

This was the situation when General Logan reached Washington, December 3, 1864, en route to join the Fifteenth Corps at Savannah by water. He reported to General Grant at City Point, Virginia. He found General Grant much exasperated at General Thomas's delay. Grant says in his "Memoirs": "Knowing General Logan to be a prompt, gallant and efficient officer, I gave him an order to proceed to Nashville and relieve Thomas." General Logan disliked extremely to obey General Grant's order implicitly, because he felt quite sure that Thomas would consider that he had taken advantage of an opportunity to displace him and thereby be revenged for General Thomas's personal injustice to General Logan in urging that General Howard supersede General

* Vol. II, pp. 357–386.

**Head-Quarters, Armies of the United States,**

City Point, Va. Dec. 13th 1864

Special Orders,
No. 140 } Extract

I, Maj. Gen'l John A. Logan, will proceed immediately to Nashville Tenn., reporting by telegraph to the Lieutenant General Commanding, his arrival at Louisville Ky. and also his arrival at Nashville, Tenn.

By command of Lieut. Genl. Grant.

T. S. Bowers

A.A. A'djt. General

Logan in the command of the Army of the Tennessee after General McPherson was killed. However, he reluctantly departed promptly for Louisville, Kentucky, from which place he was to communicate with Thomas and advise him of the orders he had received. General Logan, however, stopped at Cincinnati and sent one of his staff-officers on a confidential mission to General Thomas, at Nashville, with a copy of the order he held to relieve him, instructing the officer to try to induce Thomas to make the attack which General Grant had ordered him over and over again to do, and to impress upon Thomas General Logan's disinclination to take advantage of the orders he held. General Logan felt that Thomas's further persistency in delay, notwithstanding the fearful weather and almost impassable roads which had been his excuse, might result most unfortunately for the Union army by allowing the enemy to amass such a large force. Therefore General Logan wished to use his influence to have Thomas obey Grant's orders at once and thereby relieve him of the necessity of superseding General Thomas. General Thomas, being convinced that longer delay would cause him to forfeit his command, and that he would be superseded by General Logan, made the attack December 15, 1864.

General Logan, receiving at Louisville the news of the battle of Nashville, at once sent to General Grant the following telegram:

LOUISVILLE, *Dec.* 17, 1864.

LIEUT. GEN'L. U. S. GRANT, City Point, Va.

Have just arrived, weather bad, is raining since yesterday morning. People here all jubilant over Gen'l. Thomas's success. Confidence seems to be restored.

I will remain here to hear from you. All things going right, it would seem best that I return soon to join my command with Sherman.

JOHN A. LOGAN, *Maj. Gen'l.*

Thus it will be seen that General Logan made the suggestion to return to his command after Thomas's victory, ignoring the opportunity which had been given him to be revenged upon one who had done him so much injustice. He was not moved by any other consideration than that of doing unto others as he would that they should do unto him, albeit he felt that Thomas's long delay was inexcusable, and that he could have won even a more glorious victory weeks before if he had not been of so "slow" or deliberate a temperament. General Logan often said that, had he been in Thomas's place, he would have made the attack much sooner than Thomas did, and believed that he would have had a victory as brilliant as that of Thomas's on the 15th of December.

I often heard General Grant and General Logan discuss Thomas and his heroism as a soldier, but they expressed regret that his temperament was so obstinate and that he shrank from responsibility. General Logan always insisted that he was not deterred from obeying orders to relieve Thomas on any other ground than that he would not be guilty of snatching laurels which he knew Thomas could win if he would only obey orders to attack Hood promptly. Of course, whether it was General Logan's appeal to Thomas to save himself and fight the battle or because Thomas had finally succeeded in making the preparations which he had spent so much time perfecting, no one will ever know, as General Thomas was of a peculiar disposition, and was so set in his opinion as to the wisdom of his conception of a situation that he would never give utterance to an appreciation of indulgence extended to him or of gratitude to those who had done him great service.

Again General Logan telegraphed General Grant requesting that he be allowed to return to the Fifteenth Army Corps, then near Savannah, Georgia. His request was granted, and he accordingly repaired to Washington, thence to New York, and by sea to Savannah, and was soon with his much-loved and devoted corps, with whom he was destined to continue in their march through the Carolinas to Washington.

From incessant rains the whole country was inundated,

Louisville
Dec 17. 1864

Lieut Genl U. S. Grant.
        City Point Va.

                        have just
arrived, weather bad, is raining since
yesterday morning, people here all
jubilant over Gen Thomas success,
Confidence seems to be restored,
    I will remain here to hear from you,
all things going right, it would seem
best that I return soon to join my
Command with Sherman

                        John A. Logan
                        Maj Genl

every stream swollen beyond the confines of its banks, roads were almost impassable, and the entire command destitute of shoes or warm clothes, but happy as lords and eager to continue the march toward Richmond. A less practical commander or less courageous men would have faltered before the almost impassable barriers of mud, ice, and water which surrounded them on every hand, but Sherman's "bummers" and General Logan's gallant men, among whom was the 31st Illinois, his old regiment, knew no discouragement. Captain A. M. Jenkins, a cousin, frequently gallantly commanded the squads which waded waist deep in mud and water to build the corduroys across the swamp. They could build pontoons, fell trees, and make corduroy roads, and march over them dragging ordnance after them, and subsist on the country while they did it.

From Savannah they went to Beaufort, thence to Columbia, Fayetteville, Goldsboro, Raleigh, and on to Richmond—not as they marched from Atlanta to the sea, but driving an intrepid army who fell back fighting. Reaching the Salkehatchie River, they found the enemy had determined to make another stand and had again intrenched themselves, thinking the swollen streams would serve like the moat of olden-time fortifications. But the Fifteenth Army Corps knew nothing of the tardiness of ancient warfare, so, dashing through the sluggish stream, they assaulted the enemy with such fury that they were soon in possession of their intrenchments, and, pushing along the railroad, arrived at North Edisto by the 12th of February, where, in an engagement, General Logan captured many prisoners. When they reached Columbia, South Carolina, they found the retreating Confederates had set a lot of cotton bales and other stores on fire, from which a general conflagration ensued. I have often heard General Logan tell, with tears in his eyes, of the horrors of the night his troops entered that burning city and of the wreck that the desperate and intoxicated enemy left behind them. Barrels of whiskey and wine were here and there and everywhere;

the desperate troops had been drinking their fill, and those arriving were not behind them in bacchanalian propensities. Life and property were of little consequence to either the Union or the Confederate. Total destruction seemed inevitable, and but for General Logan's perfect command over his men and his herculean efforts there would not have been left one stone upon another of the houses, or a single soul of the inhabitants to tell the tale of the awful holocaust. People were flying to and fro in the streets, wild with excitement and fear, while the flames were consuming everything before them. There were poor facilities for extinguishing fires under most favorable circumstances, and with no one of the city authorities at his post, and the triumphant general and his army just entering the city, it seems incredible, even now, that they saved anything; but through wise management and superhuman efforts many houses were wrested from the devouring flames and order restored.

Lynch Creek, Lumber, Cape Fear, South and Neuse Rivers, with the bottomless swamps between presented the most formidable and trying obstacles every mile of the march to Goldsboro. The weary men had scarcely finished building roads, bridges, and causeways, and succeeded in dragging the wagons and artillery over them, when they would strike another seemingly impassable lagoon or swamp. The swamps were thickly timbered, fortunately for the army, for the men could wade into the water and fell the trees to form corduroy roads and build bridges. When it is remembered that this was done with a stubborn enemy in front of them, ready to take every advantage, it must be acknowledged that this march has no parallel in difficulty. The country about Goldsboro was almost devastated, and subsistence was difficult; but the invincible army pushed on, feeling sure that they were nearing the end of hardship and warfare. At Bentonville the Fifteenth Army Corps met the enemy and again repulsed them, after which Johnston retreated, burning the

(Cifer)

## South-Western Telegraph Company.

THE PUBLIC are notified, that in order to guard against mistakes in the transmission of messages, every message of importance ought to be repeated by being sent back from the station at which it is to be received to the station from which it is originally sent. Half the usual price for transmission will be charged for repeating the message, and while this Company will, as heretofore, use every precaution to ensure correctness, it will not be responsible for mistakes or delays in the transmission or delivery of repeated messages beyond an amount exceeding two hundred times the amount paid for sending the message; nor will it be responsible for mistakes or delays in the transmission of unrepeated messages from whatever cause they may arise, nor for delays arising from interruptions in the working of its Telegraphs, nor for any mistake or omission of any other Company over whose lines a message is to be sent to reach the place of destination.

All messages will hereafter be received by this Company for transmission subject to the above conditions.

SAM. BRUCH. Supt., Louisville, Ky.

Dec 17 186_4_

By Telegraph from Burlington N J 186_
7 30 P m

To Maj Genl J A Logan

The news from Genl
Thomas so far is in the
highest degree gratifying
You need not go further
before starting to join
Sherman report in
Washington

U S Grant
Lt Genl

(Cifer)

bridges behind him. Halting at Goldsboro to recuperate, they heard that Petersburg had fallen and that Richmond was in the hands of General Grant, and the attempted Confederacy was no more. Going into camp at Raleigh, North Carolina, they waited for the whole army to come up, and with the conclusion of negotiations between Sherman and Johnston Richmond was ours, and now they had nothing to do but to push on to Washington and behold a united country.

While rejoicing over this happy thought, they were startled by the overwhelming news of the assassination of Mr. Lincoln, which so exasperated the soldiery that, with the fury of madmen, they swore vengeance on every inhabitant of the South, and but for their devotion to General Logan they would have destroyed the city of Raleigh, North Carolina, and every soul within its precincts. Hearing of the wild grief and intense indignation of the men, General Logan mounted his well-known horse, Black Jack, and flew from one command to another, calling on the men to be worthy of their own heroic deeds and innocent of the blood of guiltless people, to remember that he who had been sacrificed would not that they should thus avenge his death, but let the laws they had upheld take charge of the guilty. Weeping like children, these brave men went to their quarters. A perfect pall hung over the whole army, which the good news of so soon being mustered out of the service was not able to dispel. Thinking men could not divine where the conspiracy was to end or to what extent the military would be obliged to act. They were ready for anything, and would not have hesitated to seize any suspected persons; but seeing the magnanimity of Mr. Lincoln so ruthlessly betrayed, and such madness and desperation indulged in by the reckless spirits who sympathized with the rebellion, they feared the worst. In Washington no such gloom had ever been known. Such a tragedy as the assassination of the President and the attempted assassination of the cabinet officers, following the triumph of the Government, made the most indifferent feel that they were standing over a volcano that was likely to burst forth in fury at the most unexpected moment; that the lives of the executives were insecure, and that after all the sacrifices of human life and the nation's treasury, there was no peace or security of life; that the republic was a failure, and that, like Mexico and South America, we were destined to experience continuous revolutions. Nothing but the inherent wisdom that had guided us through the whirlpool of rebellion saved us from anarchy. Our people never dreamed that the methods which had characterized monarchies would ever be attempted in our republic, and it required time for them to rally from such a shock. But, as before, the deliberate judgment of cool heads soon regained the mastery, and order was maintained. In the country the people were overwhelmed with grief, and with folded hands presented sad pictures of despair, the strongest not ashamed of their tears. They even suspected Mr. Johnson, who was born on Southern soil. Their faith was only firm in the army and its great commanders. General Grant could have made himself dictator had his ambition prompted him to such daring. His timely support of Johnson and his assurance that the will of the President should be obeyed by the army did much toward quieting the excitement. In the mean time the army was gradually nearing the capital for the grand review and disbandment.

Every day after the assassination of President Lincoln the news which came to the army was of a succession of disasters to the Confederacy and its faithful adherents, till the last armed foe had to surrender. Even those remote from the armies were eager to hear of the final capitulation. Feeling that peace was near at hand, they were impatient for the return of loved ones who had now been away for more than four years. The crops and business had been neglected, because at the beginning of the war the people did little else but go to the station and to the telegraph office to hear everything possible. Finally Lee's surrender was telegraphed all over the country, and the Army of the Tennessee was ordered to Alexandria, Virginia. All the country around Washington was occupied by troops. The Army of the Potomac, having finished its work in Virginia, on the James, at Gettysburg, and all along the Chesapeake, had retraced its steps, and was again encamped around the capital it had hastened to defend in 1861. The armies from the Southwest who had been from Cairo to New Orleans, on the coast from New York to Saint Augustine, from Vicksburg to Lookout Mountain, from Atlanta to the sea, were all ordered to report to headquarters in Washington. The men of the Army of the Tennessee, ragged and worn by their long marches and desperate fighting, but with a glorious record for heroism and endurance, were delighted that they were to have an opportunity to see the Capitol, the White House, where Mr. Lincoln had lived, and the theatre where he had been so cruelly murdered.

Reaching Alexandria May 12, 1865, they were encamped in and around that degenerate city, where brave young Ellsworth, the first martyr of the war, lost his life in hauling down a Confederate flag that had been hoisted over the Jackson Hotel, almost under the shadow of the dome of the Capitol. General Howard was ordered to take charge of the Freedmen's Bureau, and General Logan was reinstated, as he should have been before, in command of the Army of the Tennessee. He was received by the soldiers with cheer after cheer, and was made happy by the feeling that justice, though tardy, had at last been awarded him.

When the negotiations of peace had all been signed, and were unchangeable, the President and cabinet and some wise counsellors said: "Now the war is over we shall never again see such an armed force in this country. We must have a grand review in Washington and allow the survivors of the gigantic rebellion to march up Pennsylvania Avenue with the commander of each army and his staff at its head." When

Napoleon returned from Italy, the whole army of France and its allies passed in review down the Champs Elysées and were marshalled on the Champ de Mars; the trophies of arms, flags, and captured cannon that were arranged artistically on that broad plain inspired the whole of France with implicit faith in Napoleon. The spectacle of the victorious legions marching to the music of the Marseillaise on that great occasion so impressed the people that it was possible for the great conqueror to lead them, as he did, to the very jaws of death.

Our republic had been saved by our invincible army, and in order to confirm the faith of the nation in them, it was a wise suggestion to have the review; hence it was arranged for the 23d and 24th of May. No fairer days ever dawned. To the bright sunshine were added the magnificent accessories of military and spectacular scenery. General Logan once described the day as follows: "It looked as if the great Republic was on dress parade; the house-tops, the windows, the doors and balconies and all available space around, below and above was packed with men, women, and children. They were well clothed; the Nation had put on its best. Tens of thousands of bouquets made settings for the picture and were subsequently thrown to the officers and troops as they passed in review. Cannons boomed, engines whistled, flags fluttered in the breeze, innumerable brass bands and drum-corps filled the air with patriotic music. Every conceivable demonstration manifesting the enthusiastic welcome of a grateful people to their heroic defenders characterized the day."

For many hours of each day before, every soldier, to the most untidy and reckless in the ranks, was busy polishing his arms and accoutrements, repairing well-worn uniforms and soleless shoes. Artillery guns and caissons had not been so polished before, mountings and housings were never so bright, while bayonets were polished till they glittered like Damascus blades.

General Sherman, accompanied by his formidable staff, to which he added Major-General O. O. Howard and other general officers, preceded the almost endless columns from the Capitol west on Pennsylvania Avenue. First came the Army of the Potomac, trim and neat, marching like regulars on parade; then the Army of the Tennessee, composed of the Fifteenth, Sixteenth, Seventeenth, Twentieth, and Fourteenth Corps, with well-worn uniforms and almost shoeless feet, followed their dauntless and idolized leader, General John A. Logan, who sat his steed like a statue. On horseback he was majestic, as erect and graceful as an Indian, his long black hair and mustache, flashing eyes, olive complexion, and broad-brimmed army hat giving him the air of a cavalier. On that day he was the recipient of such ringing cheers that he was very happy. Bouquets and wreaths of flowers were showered on him. The enthusiastic men in the street, rushing up to his horse, put the wreaths over the proud animal's head down on to the creature's neck until it was covered. When division after division was hailed with such deafening shouts, General Logan's heart beat high with pride and gratification. He cared little that they were called "Sherman's bummers," or that scarcely a uniform of officers or men in the whole army would have passed a regulation inspection. In the glory of that day Logan's men forgot the fathomless mud of Cairo, the sleet, mud, and water around Forts Henry and Donelson, the heat and long siege of Vicksburg, the rugged mountains of Kenesaw, the siege of Atlanta, the swamps and corduroys of Georgia and the Carolinas, the burning suns, and pitiless storms of winter, the marches, the battles, the suffering and carnage of the long four years intervening between April, 1861, and May, 1865. General Logan forgot that he had been relieved unjustly of the command of the Army of the Tennessee after his great victory at Atlanta and speedy avenging of the death of McPherson, July 22, 1864. All were going home soon and only thought and dreamed of bliss, like

Campbell's soldier. Even in the dead of the night "sweet visions" they saw, "and thrice ere the morning" they dreamed them again.

From morning till night, for two days, these victorious cohorts were marching through Pennsylvania Avenue, past the President, and back to their quarters. Banners were flying; battered flags were borne by proud color-bearers; the bands played the familiar airs that had inspired many a faltering heart in battle, while the glittering bayonets of the infantry and bright plumes of the cavalry and artillery presented a picture never to be effaced, and aroused the patriotism of every American heart. Decimated ranks and riderless horses told the story of what the final triumph had cost, and was the one cloud over the matchless pageant that can never be repeated on American soil.

Immediately following the review were orders for the mustering out of the service of the Union army those whose heroic work had been so gloriously accomplished. General Logan and the Army of the Tennessee were ordered to Louisville, Kentucky, where they were to be honorably disbanded, the men to be allowed to go whithersoever they listed. It was most pathetic to see them anxious for a leave of absence to visit their loved ones, but loath to leave the army and their idolized commander; many of them pledged themselves to return speedily upon a call from him for service anywhere in the world. Time nor distance can ever break the bonds cemented by the experience of soldiers who have marched, suffered, and bivouacked together. Before disbanding, General Logan issued the following order, which very feebly expressed his feelings toward them and their gallant service:

HEADQUARTERS ARMY OF THE TENNESSEE,
LOUISVILLE, KY., *July* 13, 1865.
OFFICERS AND SOLDIERS OF THE ARMY OF THE TENNESSEE:
The profound gratification I feel in being authorized to release you from the onerous obligations of the camp, and return you,

laden with laurels, to homes where warm hearts wait to welcome you, is somewhat imbittered by the painful reflection that I am sundering the ties that trials have made true, time made tender, sufferings made sacred, perils made proud, heroism made honorable, and fame made forever fearless of the future. It is no common occasion that demands the disbandment of a military organization before the resistless power of which mountains bristling with bayonets have bowed, cities have surrendered, and millions of brave men have been conquered. Although I have been but a short period your commander, we are not strangers; affections have sprung up between us during the long years of doubt, gloom, and carnage which we have passed through together, nurtured by common perils, sufferings, and sacrifices, and riveted by the memories of gallant comrades whose bones repose beneath the sod of an hundred battle-fields, which neither time nor distance will weaken or efface. The many marches that you have made, the dangers you have despised, the haughtiness you have humbled, the duties you have discharged, the glory you have gained, the destiny you have discovered for the country for whose cause you have conquered, all recur at this moment in all the vividness that marked the scenes through which we have just passed. From the pens of the ablest historians of the land daily are drifting out upon the current of time, page upon page, volume upon volume of your heroic deeds, which, floating down to future generations, will inspire the student of history with admiration, the patriotic American with veneration for his ancestors, and the lover of republican liberty with gratitude to those who, in a fresh baptism of blood, reconsecrated the powers and energies of the Republic to the cause of constitutional freedom.

Long may it be the happy fortune of each and every one of you to live in the full fruition of the boundless blessings you have secured to the human race. Only he whose heart has been thrilled with admiration for your impetuous and unyielding valor in the thickest of the fight, can appreciate with what pride I recount the brilliant achievements which immortalize you, and enrich the pages of our national history. Passing by the earlier but not less signal triumphs of the war in which most of you participated and inscribed upon your banners such victories as Donelson and Shiloh, I recur to your campaigns, sieges, and victories that challenge the admiration of the world and elicit the unwilling applause of all Europe. Turning your backs upon the blood-bathed heights of

Vicksburg, you launched into a region swarming with enemies, fighting your way and marching, without adequate supplies, to answer the cry for succor that came to you from the noble but beleaguered Army of Chattanooga. Your steel next flashed among the mountains of Tennessee, and your weary limbs found rest before the embattled heights of Missionary Ridge, and there with dauntless courage you breasted again the enemy's destructive fire, and shared with your comrades of the Army of the Cumberland the glories of a victory than which no soldier can boast a prouder. In that unexampled campaign of vigilant and vigorous warfare from Chattanooga to Atlanta you freshened your laurels at Resaca, grappling with the enemy behind his works, hurling him back dismayed and broken. Pursuing him from thence, marking your path by the graves of fallen comrades, you again triumphed over superior numbers at Dallas, fighting your way from there to Kenesaw Mountain and under the murderous artillery that frowned from its rugged heights; with a tenacity and constancy that finds few parallels you labored, fought, and suffered through the boiling rays of a southern midsummer sun, until at last you planted your colors upon its topmost heights. Again, on the 22d of July, 1864, rendered memorable through all time for the terrible struggle you so heroically maintained under discouraging disasters and that saddest of all reflections, the loss of that exemplary soldier and popular leader, the lamented McPherson, your matchless courage turned defeat into a glorious victory. Ezra Chapel and Jonesboro added new lustre to a radiant record, the latter unbarring to you the proud Gate City of the South. The daring of a desperate foe in thrusting his legion northward exposed the country in your front, and, though rivers, swamps, and enemies opposed, you boldly surmounted every obstacle, beat down all opposition, and marched onward to the sea. Without any act to dim the brightness of your historic page, the world rang plaudits where your labors and struggles culminated at Savannah, and the old "Starry Banner" waved once more over the wall of one of our proudest cities of the seaboard. Scarce a breathing spell had passed when your colors faded from the coast, and your columns plunged into the swamps of the Carolinas. The suffering you endured, the labors you performed, and the successes you achieved in those morasses, deemed impassable, form a creditable episode in the history of the war. Pocataligo, Salkahatchie, Edisto, Branchville, Orangeburgh, Columbia, Bentonville, Charleston, and

Raleigh are names that will ever be suggestive of the resistless sweep of your columns through the territory that cradled and nurtured, and from whence was sent forth on its mission of crime, misery, and blood, the disturbing and disorganizing spirits of secession and rebellion.

The work for which you pledged your brave hearts and brawny arms to the Government of your fathers you have nobly performed. You are seen in the past, gathering through the gloom that enveloped the land, rallying as the guardian of man's proudest heritage, forgetting the thread unwoven in the loom, quitting the anvil, abandoning the workshops, to vindicate the supremacy of the laws and the authority of the Constitution. Four years have you struggled in the bloodiest and most destructive war that ever drenched the earth with human gore; step by step you have borne our standard, until to-day, over every fortress and arsenal that rebellion wrenched from us, and over city, town, and hamlet, from the lakes to the gulf, and from ocean to ocean, proudly floats the "Starry Emblem" of our national unity and strength. Your rewards, my comrades, are the welcoming plaudits of a grateful people, the consciousness that, in saving the Republic, you have won for your country renewed respect and power at home and abroad; that, in the exampled era of growth and prosperity that dawns with peace, there attaches mightier wealth of pride and glory than ever before to that loved boast, "I am an American citizen." In relinquishing the implements of war for those of peace, let your conduct, which was that of warriors in time of war, be that of peaceful citizens in time of peace. Let not the lustre of that brighter name you have won as soldiers be dimmed by any improper acts as citizens, but as time rolls on let your record grow brighter and brighter still.

JOHN A. LOGAN, *Major-General.*

When the last good-bys had to be said, heroes of many battles wept like children, feeling that they would probably meet no more in this world. Alas! if the muster-roll of the Army of the Tennessee of 1865 were called to-day, tears would dim the eyes of the few survivors who would answer "Here!"

Like patriots they took their several ways and in a few brief weeks the thousands who had followed the life of soldiers laid aside the accoutrements of war and took up the implements of peace, dissolving into citizens as rapidly as they had become soldiers.

At home, from the day of Lee's surrender there was continual rejoicing until the shock of Mr. Lincoln's assassination changed it to mourning. Then there was vibration between the emotions of joy over peace and grief over the sacrifice of his great life. Finally, the news came that the regiments raised in the vicinity of Carbondale, Illinois, would arrive within a few days of each other. Then all was activity and bustle to make suitable preparations for welcoming them home again. No building in the town was half large enough to hold the people or spacious enough for tables upon which to spread the bounteous repast they determined to lay before the returning soldiers, so the lovely grove heretofore mentioned was selected. Every twig or branch that had fallen, every dead leaf and unsightly bit of rubbish was cleaned away and the grass swept, leaving a lovely green sward beneath the spreading boughs of the majestic oaks. A grand stand was erected on one side, from which welcoming speeches were to be made by the hosts. The most prominent of the returning heroes were expected to tell some of their experiences and give expression to their joy that peace had at last brought them home. Canopies of red, white, and blue were thrown over the speakers and the band-stands, and the columns that supported them were wound with garlands, the whole being beautiful and effective. On the other side there were long tables spread with spotless linen, china, silver, glass, a profusion of flowers, and everything that a prolific country and an abundant harvest could produce. After the music and speeches every soldier was seated at these tables for such a feast as he had not known for many a weary day. Every man and woman in the town, no matter how proud their position, was ready to wait upon them, each one turning into as skilful a waiter as ever served at Delmonico's. With smiles for those who were there and tears for those who were not, they made their return as pleasant as possible, repeating the same welcome for the various commands as they arrived.

When it is remembered that everything that was cooked, the decorations and all the work done was accomplished by loving hands, it can be imagined that there was little necessity for gymnasiums, Swedish movements, or other exercises of which we hear in these modern days. The benevolent had plenty to do to look after the widows, orphans, and unfortunates, and ere long affairs had assumed their wonted routine, each drifting into the channels he had followed before volunteering.

General Logan reached home on the 28th of July, 1865, accompanied by two members of his staff. He brought his horses, camp equipage, and two colored men and a boy about sixteen years old, who were with him when they struck the tents in Louisville for the last time. He did not have the heart to turn these freedmen adrift without employment, with no home and away from the haunts of their childhood, so he brought them home, providing for them until he could secure them something to do and a chance to be self-supporting. "Boston," the boy, was as black as ebony. He had been the valet, jockey, and petted servant of a sporting-master who was killed in battle. He was a daring, mischievous, wiry little scamp, with many monkey instincts and antics, and required constant watching. He was a born gambler and would slip out and gamble with the dissolute men about the town. He pretended to have been converted, and joined the colored Baptist church, and together with a number of colored men and women was to be immersed in a large pond in a field near the town. Boston wanted us to attend; it was a cold, lowering Sunday afternoon in March. We drove out and sat in the carriage near the shore on the opposite side of the pond from where they had tents erected, one for the women and one for the men. One minister went to the tent-door and escorted the candidates for baptism down to the steps which had been placed at the edge of the water, while another minister led them one by one quite a distance toward the centre of the pond. When the water was waist-deep, the minister crossed their hands, took hold of the belt around their waist with one hand while with the other he caught them by the back of the neck and dipped them into the water. All their heads were tied up with white handkerchiefs, and as they rose out of the water they were so frightened it was with difficulty that they could walk to the steps. One thin little colored girl preceded our Boston. She was frightfully nervous and screeched as loud as she could the moment she was led into the water, and as the minister took hold of her she jerked away from him, and went plunging through the water across the pond. Boston bolted after her, and in a twinkling the impressive ceremony changed into the most ludicrous performance one could have imagined. Boston grabbed her around the waist, lifted her up in his arms, and bore her triumphantly to the women's tent, then darted to the men's tent, tore the white handkerchief from his head, the belt from around his waist, dressed himself, and fled precipitately from the place, the girl following on behind. The wild singing and shouting of the clergy and the members of the church was not sufficient to drown the laughter and jeering of the curious crowd.

That night, when Boston reported for his duties, General Logan began to scold him for his unseemly behavior. He replied: "General, I saw they was gwine to drown that girl, and I is her sweetheart and I was not gwine to let 'em. You wouldn't yourself stand still and see 'em drown the Missus. I was done clean 'gusted with that old parson, so I just lit out."

After a hopeless struggle with him for months, he ran away, and the last we heard of him he was engaged as a jockey in Saint Louis. The men remained with us for some months, but returned to their Southern homes and were both conspicuous in the conflicts between the colored and white races in the early days of the reconstruction.

On the 30th of July, 1865, occurred the grand welcoming of the returning volunteers at Carbondale, Jackson County, Illinois. For weeks our home was a hostelry for the accommodation of constantly arriving visitors who were not satisfied until they had greeted General Logan in person. Carbondale was a small town without markets, catering establishments, comfortable hotels or competent servants, and under such circumstances, it was not an easy matter to entertain unexpected guests who came by the score. In my happiness over the declaration of peace and General Logan's safe return I murmured not, and, with the assistance of friends who insisted upon aiding me as a labor of love, we so managed that it was around well-laid, bountifully supplied tables, that we listened to stories of the trying and amusing experiences of the four years of the Civil War.

Another source of rejoicing in our home added much to our happiness: our son, John A. Logan, Jr., was born July 24, 1865, and was from the very hour of his birth so bright and handsome as to attract the attention of every one, and to us evermore a blessing beyond compare.

Early in September, having been notified by the departments in Washington that his accounts were all audited and that there was nothing against him on the records, General Logan tendered his resignation, as he was unwilling to continue on the pay-rolls without rendering active service. He had been importuned to remain in the service, having been offered a brigadier-general's commission in the regular army, a proffered honor which he highly appreciated; but knowing so well his restive disposition, he feared he would be unhappy in time of peace to be confined to the regulations in his coming and going, and declined the generous offer. About that time there was an apprehension that we might have trouble in Mexico. Every one looked with suspicion upon the appearance of Maximilian in the city of Mexico. General Logan was requested to hold himself in readiness to go there as United States minister, should it be necessary to send him, and but for the discomfiture and the melancholy taking off of that ill-fated and deluded sovereign, Maximilian, General Logan would probably have entered the diplomatic service. He had no taste for it, however, when there was little probability of eventful times. Soon after he was requested to accept the mission to Japan, but having no desire to become isolated from his own country, he also declined that position, expecting to again return to the profession of the law.

During the winter he was called to Washington to attend to some business affairs of his own and of some friends. He went thither, therefore, and while waiting for the settlement of these matters with the government he became much interested in the reconstruction and readjustment of national questions then under discussion. At the State convention held in May, 1866, he was nominated by acclamation for Congressman-at-large, the State being entitled to an additional member who was chosen at large until the legislature assembled to redistrict the State. He could not well refuse to accept, notwithstanding the fact that he had not intended to again enter politics. His majority was overwhelming. March 4, 1867, he again took his seat as a member of Congress, after an absence of six years, having resigned his seat to enter the army in August, 1861. Bringing to the position so much renown, he was immediately assigned to the most important committees of the House, and made chairman of the military committee which had before it the difficult task of providing for the reduction of the army to a peace basis. With his impetuous disposition and intense nature, it was impossible for General Logan to be an indifferent or passive member; hence he plunged into all the vexing details of the most knotty questions, working day and night that he might understand them thoroughly and be able to do that which would result in the greatest good to the greatest number. Every day, during the discussion of the problems of reconstruction, he was confronted by questions which he felt were vital to the perpetuity of the government. He appreciated the fact that if mistakes were made by the party in power, they would recoil in the future or spring up like Banquo's ghost to torment posterity.

We took up our residence in the old Willard Hotel, which had been the leading hotel of Washington during the war. It was of fearful and wonderful construction, the Fourteenth Street side having been built on to some buildings fronting on Pennsylvania Avenue. The floors of the Fourteenth Street addition of each story were three or four feet higher than those of the Pennsylvania Avenue buildings; the ceilings were low, the halls dismal, and the dining-room cheerless. From long occupancy and unsanitary sewerage it was anything but an agreeable abode. The house was, however, full of guests. Among them were General Francis E. Spinner, United States treasurer, whose autograph on the greenbacks was so famous all over the world, and his interesting family; Senator Simon Cameron, of Pennsylvania, who was Mr. Lincoln's Secretary of War, and his wife and daughter; Senator Harris and his family; the eccentric bachelor, Senator Salisbury, and others.

A number of members of Congress and their families were also in the house. Mr. and Mrs. James G. Blaine with their four children had a suite near ours. When Mrs. Blaine and I were out making calls, Emmons, Alice, and little J. G. Blaine, Jr., and Dollie and baby John A. Logan, Jr., had fine times impersonating different distinguished men and women of whom they had heard their elders talk. Frequently we returned home to find confusion reigning supreme in our rooms, the children having amused themselves by dressing up in their parents' clothes, playing grown-up people. Impromptu parties were organized, and the other children in the house invited to partake of the banquets they served through the indulgence of Hughes, the head waiter, who was so devoted to General Logan and Mr. Blaine that their children could have whatever they wanted. Emmons presided over their affairs with much suavity of manner inherited from his knightly father.

There were frequent exciting discussions at the dinner-table. The members and senators and prominent people assembling at that hour could not resist the temptation to continue their controversies.

Mr. Blaine's election as speaker, his appointment of the chairman and members of important committees, were matters of as much importance as they are to-day, and probably greater because of the momentous questions that had to be settled after the close of the Civil War.

With all of his diplomacy and fascinating manners, Mr Blaine did not escape bitter criticism on the announcement of the chairmanships. Personal disappointments were many and not concealed by aspirants for these important positions. It would have saved speakers of the past much vexation of soul if the present method of shifting the responsibility of selecting the committees and chairmen to a committee of the House, as is done in these progressive times, had then been in vogue.

After the departure of General Logan for the rendezvous of the troops at Cairo, Illinois, in 1861, we had decided that I had better reside in Carbondale, Jackson County, Illinois, on the Illinois Central Railroad, where I could be in communication by telegraph with the then Colonel Logan, of the 31st Illinois, or join him, if necessary, by rail. We had formerly lived twenty-two miles east of the railroad and, in consequence, suffered great inconvenience on account of the overland travel necessary to reach a railroad. The uncertainty of the movement of the troops would have kept me anxious for my husband's welfare, and besides this the families of the members of his regiment depended upon me for information in regard to their soldier husbands, sons, and fathers.

The present generation is perfectly ignorant of the lack of facilities for communication and rapid transportation to and from the army in 1861 and 1862. We received the mail, part of the time, once a day. The newspapers were triweekly, and they contained very meagre reports of the direful things that were going on between the Union and Confederate armies. The telegraphic reports were censored so closely by the authorities that they did not dare to give out anything like full accounts of battle engagements and casualties of the war. Consequently, we did little else except to wait impatiently for news. Our daughter, now Mrs. Mary Logan Tucker, was in her second year, and was my constant companion. I was afraid to leave her with any one, and therefore took her with me wherever I went, whether on an errand of mercy to the unfortunate families of the soldiers at the front, or to attend to the business affairs which my husband had left in my care when he dropped everything and went into the army. The citizens of that part of the country were so divided in their sympathies between the North and the South that it caused many unpleasant situations and embarrassing meetings. Those whose friends were in the army of the Union were naturally sensitive and could not bear to hear their husbands, fathers, and sons accused of being Lincoln hirelings, negro-lovers, and many other opprobrious names which were applied to them, while those in sympathy with the South were just as resentful over being called rebels, traitors, and numerous other names. Mr. Lincoln was held directly responsible for all the calamities of the war, the secessionists and their friends insisting that he caused the conflict of armies by his demand for the abolition of slavery. After three long years I knew nothing but that we were solicitous for the unfortunate by whom we were surrounded.

When peace was declared there was universal rejoicing

and excitement. We knew then that the soldiers and sailors would soon be returning to their homes and their friends, as they would be disbanded as soon as possible after the surrender of Lee's army. General Logan was in command of the Army of the Tennessee which, after the grand review, was mustered out of the service at Louisville, Kentucky. The families of the returning volunteers were overjoyed at the thought of having their loved ones with them again.

There was a class, however, who pretended to be very much troubled for fear the troops would prove a disturbing element as soon as they had recovered from the excitement of meeting those they had left behind them. Some went so far as to say they feared that they would form marauding parties who would be a terror in the vicinity where they resided, and would go about and take possession of whatever they wanted without regard to law, order, or the rights of others. This was an unfounded fear, because there never could have been a more orderly return to peaceful pursuits. To a man, the soldiers and sailors seemed to realize that they had been engaged in a war for the preservation of the Union, and when that had been accomplished they had nothing to do but to return to their homes and resume their various vocations which they had laid down when they volunteered. They soon became law-abiding, industrious citizens of the Union they had saved. There was no such thing as violation of the law, visits of vengeance, or any species of unlawful, riotous conduct on the part of any of these men. In thirty days from the time they were discharged, many of them had begun their work for the support of themselves and their families. Legions of them engaged in all kinds of industrial, commercial, professional, and other pursuits necessary for the preservation of life and liberty. In a most exciting political campaign there were few personal conflicts or settlements of old scores on account of unjust and outrageous acts perpetrated during the warfare between the North and the South. Veterans met veterans and extended the right hand of fellowship to each other. There were reunions, reconciliations, and happy meetings between the bitterest of foes.

Naturally they differed much in political affiliations, some being most ardent Republicans, while others returned to the Democratic party, to which they had belonged before they entered the service. Before going into the army General Logan had acted with the Democratic party, and left it when he had to choose between his party and his country. On account of the change of principles of that party during the war, he felt he had no desire to again become an advocate of the principles of Democracy, but would continue his adherence to the Republican party, whose platform advocated the principles for which he and thousands of others had stood during over four years of blood and strife.

He did not intend to enter politics again, desiring to resume the practice of law, but this was not to be. In the very first campaign after his return home from Louisville, Kentucky, where he mustered out the entire Army of the Tennessee, our home was crowded with men from all over the country, insisting that he accept from the Republican party nominations for political positions. There were hordes and hordes of ex-Union soldiers from almost every State north of the Mason and Dixon line, who were untiring in their efforts to secure the adherence of the most distinguished men of the army. The assassination of Mr. Lincoln had left such a deep spirit of resentment that Republicans were busy in securing the support and advocacy of the ablest men who had been in the army, to fit elective official positions.

We kept open house and entertained legions of people, which was no small thing to do at that day and time, with the inconveniences of poor markets and independent employees upon whom we were obliged to depend. It would be an incredible story were I to describe graphically the chase for chickens, fresh meats, fish, and edibles considered fit to be placed before these numerous guests. It was the old, old story of choicest fruits, vegetables, poultry, and other good things being shipped to the higher-priced markets, and the cities and residences in the rural districts having a great scramble to get anything worth being put upon the table. As I look back upon it now, I think we performed miracles in the line of satisfying hungry men and women who joined in the petitions to General Logan to accept the various nominations for official positions. Illinois had been represented since the census of 1860 by a Congressman-at-large, as they had not redistricted the State. Hon. S. W. Molton, a most estimable man, was a candidate for re-election as a member of Congress in 1866, but, the soldiers being in the majority in the Republican party, they demanded that General Logan should succeed Mr. Molton in Congress because they anticipated serious trouble over the various questions that should follow the close of the war and the assassination of Mr. Lincoln. General Logan talked to me very seriously on the subject, and I felt intensely interested in what he might do, as he had sent his resignation to Washington as soon as he got his affairs properly adjusted, but had not yet embarked in the legal profession, which it was his intention and ambition to do. Mr. Molton was a loyal friend of General Logan's and insisted that he would withdraw in favor of the general if the general would consent to allow his name to be used. Without waiting for his answer, the State convention convened and General Logan was nominated by acclamation on receipt of his reply. But for the fact that they insisted it was necessary for the success of the Republican party for him to make the race, he would not have done so. As soon as the convention was over and he had signified his acceptance, then began an indescribable scramble for him to make promises to almost every county in the State to speak in the interest of the State ticket.

The months of June and July we had spent in our headquarters in Saint Paul, Minnesota. Our party consisted of Eliza Logan Wood, the great tragedian, Katie Logan, who was subsequently our adopted daughter, General Logan, myself, our daughter Dollie, and baby son, John A. Logan, Jr. We made Saint Paul our headquarters and went to all the important lakes in Minnesota, having a very delightful time fishing. The general had had no such respite from constant care and anxiety since he entered the army in 1861. He entered into all our plans for recreation and rest with the enthusiasm of a boy. When we visited the lakes we had our boats and went out in the morning, returning in the afternoon with boats laden with beautiful fish, all of us having participated in the catch. It can be said to have been one of the most delightful summers of our lives.

Upon the announcement of the general's nomination for Congress, we returned to Chicago and the general immediately entered upon the campaign. I remained at Joliet, Illinois, to visit cousins of General Logan, Mr. and Mrs. Henry Fish, Mrs. Fish being a daughter of Joel Manning, many years auditor of the Illinois Canal, and one of the most splendid men of his time. In the midst of enjoying their hospitality I received a telegram telling me of the death of my mother at Marion, Illinois. A young man by the name of Henry Hopper, of that town, having gone to a Democratic convention at Cairo, Illinois, was exposed to and attacked by cholera. He arrived home at noon and was dead at night. His wife followed him a few hours later; her mother, with whom they lived, was seized and having no one to aid her she sent for my mother, who went to her and remained until after her death, after which she secured some one to take charge of the body. Returning home, she was not at all alarmed about herself, as she was fearless of danger or disease and only very glad that she had been able to perform the last offices of nurse and physician for the poor woman. Before the dawn of another morning, August 24, 1866, she herself was a corpse.

My father, in great grief and bewilderment, had directed that telegrams be sent to the Republican headquarters at the old Tremont House in Chicago. They arrived after we had left the city, and were laid on a table in the committee-room where they stayed until some one came in who felt that they should be opened. Finding the contents so sad, they tried to find General Logan, who immediately thereafter telegraphed me the overwhelming news. It was, up to that time, the greatest sorrow of my life, as my mother and I had been companions from my childhood. I appreciated her great mentality and remarkable executive ability. I knew that my father in his wonted dependence upon her was perfectly undone, so I lost no time in joining him, and to my dying day shall I remember his anguish and the desolation of our beloved old home. There were five children of the thirteen brothers and sisters at home, and my dear father to whom I had to give my immediate attention. Consequently, the remainder of the year was a very busy one for me, as I felt my first duty was to my husband, and, of course, there were many occasions when he needed me to accompany him. I made it a point to look after him carefully, for after he made long speeches in the open air he was always completely exhausted. I was ever glad to be with him to give him my personal attention and to receive his friends and guests while he took a few hours' rest.

Travelling and canvassing in those days were a very different proposition from the present day. There were not so many railroads in any State as there are to-day, and various points had to be reached by driving overland, and not always upon the best of roads. This necessitated the spending of much time in covering the distance from point to point, and as these campaigns are always conducted in the heat of summer and the inclemency of fall rains, great fatigue and exposure were inevitable. The result of the campaign was most flattering to General Logan, as he received practically the largest number of votes that had ever been cast up to that date for any candidate.

Early in December General Logan went to Washington to attend to some matters before the departments and to settle the accounts of a number of officers under his command who had not been able to get a complete settlement with the Government when the troops were mustered out of the field. My father's family and my own two children requiring my attention, we decided that I had better remain at our home in Carbondale, Illinois, until the general should take his seat in Congress, March 4, 1867.

The people were so relieved by the close of the war and the prospects of great prosperity that, although I was in mourning myself, I found it far less depressing than it had been the preceding winter when the end of the war was so uncertain. It was interesting to see the activity of the men who had been in the service, who were so anxious to take up some sort of peaceful pursuit which promised success for them. The elections having resulted in such stupendous majorities for the Republican party, no one doubted that in a few brief months all the vexatious problems arising from the war would be settled, and that this country would enter upon an era of progress and prosperity.

# CHAPTER IX

A WONDERFUL movement was started early in 1866 to carry out the organization of the Grand Army of the Republic, the history of which is as follows:

To an Illinoisan belongs the credit of conceiving the grandest organization ever thought out by man for the perpetuation of "Fraternity, Charity, and Loyalty." Reverend William J. Rutledge, while chaplain of the 14th Illinois Infantry, was the tent-mate of Major B. F. Stephenson, the surgeon of the regiment, to whom he was devotedly attached. In the weary hours of their marching and bivouac, Chaplain Rutledge had many conferences with Major Stephenson. Among the topics which they discussed was the future of the million and more of men who would soon lay down their arms and be scattered all over the Union, the chaplain insisting that they would naturally desire some form of association by which they could perpetuate their experiences as soldiers of the Union, and at the same time cultivate such a spirit of loyalty that a rebellion would be impossible in this country in the future.

Major Stephenson was deeply impressed by this suggestion, and appreciated the fact that an organization that would include all honorably discharged soldiers and sailors and the gallant officers who commanded them, whose fundamental principles were fraternity, loyalty, and charity, would be far-reaching in its benefits, the important point being to formulate a ritual that would serve the high and noble purposes they had in mind for such an organization. After a long correspondence Chaplain Rutledge went to Springfield to consult with Major Stephenson and to read the rough draught that Major Stephenson had prepared. In March, 1866, a conference was held in that city. To this conference, under bonds of secrecy, they invited Colonel J. M. Snyder, Doctor James Hamilton, Major Robert M. Woods, Major Robert Allen, Colonel Martin Flood, Colonel Daniel Grass, Colonel Edward Prince, Captain John S. Phelps, Captain John A. Lightfoot, Colonel B. F. Smith, Major A. A. North, Captain Henry F. Howe, and Lieutenant B. F. Hawkes (since colonel).

Captain John S. Phelps was so enthusiastic over the proposition that he worked untiringly with Major Stephenson in perfecting the ritual, charter, and by-laws for the order. It is possible that the name was suggested by an organization that bore the name of "The Grand Army of Progress" which was then in existence. The printing of the ritual was guarded so sacredly that the committee took it to Decatur, Illinois, so that they might put it into the hands of reliable friends whom they knew would join them, and who would not allow the matter to get out until they were ready to urge the formation of posts. Seeing the magnificent future of the order, the friends in Decatur determined to apply to Major Stephenson for a charter, and through him to organize the first post in that city. The 6th of April, 1866, Major Stephenson, by virtue of his authority as departmental commander of Illinois, having been so elected at the first meeting in Springfield, went to Decatur and, assisted by Captain

Phelps, organized the first post of the Grand Army of the Republic, the charter members being Captain M. F. Kana, Major G. R. Steele, Captain George H. Cunning, General Isaac C. Pugh, Major John H. Hale, Captain J. T. Bishop, Captain Christian Riebsame, Doctor J. W. Routh, Doctor B. F. Sibley, Isaac N. Coltrin, Sergeant J. M. Prior, and Lieutenant Aquilla Toland, all of whom had been in the service of their country and were keenly alive to the importance of the order as is shown by the Declaration of Principles expressed in the constitution of the Grand Army of the Republic, in the following heroic language:

## DECLARATION OF PRINCIPLES

*Article I.* Section 1. The soldiers of the Volunteer Army of the United States during the Rebellion of 1861–5, actuated by the impulses and convictions of patriotism and of eternal right, and combined in the strong bands of fellowship and unity by the toils, the dangers, and the victories of a long and vigorously waged war, feel themselves called upon to declare in definite form of words and in determined co-operative action those principles and rules which should guide the earnest patriot, the enlightened freedman, and the Christian citizen in his course of action, and to agree upon those plans and laws which should govern them in a united and systematic working method with which, in some measure, shall be effected the preservation of the grand results of the war, the fruits of their labor and toil, so as to benefit the deserving and worthy.

Section 2. The results which are designed to be accomplished by this organization are as follows:

1st. The preservation of those kind and fraternal feelings which have bound together, with the strong chords of love and affection, the comrades in arms of many battles, sieges, and marches.

2d. To make these ties available in works and ties of kindness, of favor and material aid to those in need of assistance.

3d. To make provision where it is not already done for the support, care, and education of soldiers' orphans, and for the maintenance of the widows of deceased soldiers.

4th. For the protection and assistance of disabled soldiers, whether disabled by wounds, sickness, old age, or misfortune.

5th. For the establishment and defence of the late soldiery of the United States, morally, socially, and politically, with a view to inculcate a proper appreciation of their services to the country, and to a recognition of such services and claims by the American people.

At a subsequent national encampment, an additional section to Article I was added:

Section 6. The maintenance of true allegiance to the United States of America based upon paramount respect for and fidelity to the national Constitution and laws manifested by the discountenancing of whatever may tend to weaken loyalty, incite to insurrection, treason, or rebellion, or in any manner impair the efficiency and permanency of our free institutions, together with a defence of universal liberty, equal right, and justice to all men.

Following the organization of the posts at Decatur and Springfield, a call was made for a grand convention at Springfield for the launching of the Grand Army of the Republic. It was held July 12, 1866, and was largely attended by ex-Union officers and soldiers. This convention gave its unqualified indorsement to the plans formulated by Major Stephenson and his coworkers. They provided for the first national encampment, which was held at Indianapolis, November 20, 1866. General S. A. Hurlbut was elected commander-in-chief. The senior and junior vice-commanders, subordinate officers, and a council of administration were elected, and the order formally launched in its great work.

For some reason the national encampment was not called in 1867, but met in Philadelphia January 15, 1868, when General John A. Logan was elected commander-in-chief. As was his wont, he threw his whole soul into the work and, after a conference with the officers then elected and the council of administration, proceeded to encourage the extending of the order and increasing its good works. He established national headquarters in Washington, and drew around him an able staff.

General Logan was thrice elected commander-in-chief, and no service of his whole life was more satisfactory than that given in behalf of his comrades at arms. The destinies of the Grand Army have been presided over by the truest and the best. From its very inception the Grand Army of the Republic was destined to a great and noble work and to supply a place in the desires of patriotic men that no other had been able to do. The provision eschewing politics and religion and providing for the banding together under the most sacred secret obligations to work together for the defence of their country, for the alleviation of each other's woes, for the uplifting and betterment of each other and those dependent upon them, touched a responsive chord in the heart of every soldier, who knew by experience that every man who signed such an obligation would be true to it. The plan for the organization of posts in every hamlet, town, and city, and to unite them in departments in every State, and once a year to meet in a grand national encampment, would insure the perpetuity of their comradeship. The post would supply the place of the soldier's regiment; the convention of the department of the State his corps; and the national encampment that of the army to which he belonged. At the camp-fires of these meetings he could live over again scenes which were burned into his memory by the heat of battle. He would have a resource in every dilemma that might overtake him through life, and friends to succor him in sickness and misfortune and who would follow him to the grave when he was finally mustered out. The ritual appealed so strongly to the men that to-day, nearly fifty years after the war, the Grand Army of the Republic is many thousands strong. It has borne upon its rolls more than 300,000 ex-Union soldiers. It has expended thousands of dollars in charity for its members and their families. To the Grand Army of the Republic more than to any other order do the unfortunate look for aid. If a comrade is sick, he sends to his post for sympathy and help. If he seeks employment, he can rely upon his comrades to vouch for him. He knows that when the end comes he will be laid to rest by the members of his post, and that a stone will mark his last resting-place, and that it will never be reared in a potter's field. He knows that each recurring 30th of May flowers will be strewn above the low green mounds where sleep the loyal dead.

It is a curious fact that the genius who was the author of so magnificent an organization should have been in his last days one of the very unfortunates for whom he was so solicitous in his days of prosperity. Overtaken by misfortune and an ill-starred fate, Major Stephenson, after years of discouragement, died and was buried at Rock Creek, Menard County, Illinois, August 30, 1871, though scarcely at the zenith of his manhood. August 29, 1882, Estill Post 71, Grand Army of the Republic, Department of Illinois, removed Major Stephenson's remains to Petersburgh, Illinois, and reinterred them among the soldiers of Rose Hill Cemetery with impressive ceremonies, thus rescuing him from the oblivion of an unmarked grave. A few years ago the national organization of the Grand Army of the Republic erected a monument to his memory in Washington.

In their stupendous work of succoring the suffering, comforting the living, caring for the dying and the dead, the Grand Army of the Republic has far exceeded the work of any other organization of the same age the world has ever known. In the cultivation of a spirit of patriotism it has accomplished more than has been done by any other methods ever adopted. The rush to enlist for the Spanish-American War and for service in the Philippines attests the patriotism of all American citizens from whatever section or nationality they may have sprung. This influence in the retrospect doubtless inspired the organization of the Sons and Daughters of the American Revolution and other kindred societies. It is probably not too much to say that had there been a

Grand Army of the Republic at the close of the War of the Revolution, there never would have been any War of the Rebellion. Fraternal ties in the interest of patriotism would have prevented the growth of sectionalism.

Realizing that a time would come when the last ex-Union soldier would lie down to peaceful slumber, a wise provision has been made for the perpetuation of the spirit and principles of the Grand Army of the Republic by the formation of the Society of Sons of Veterans, who are pledged:

To keep green the memories of our fathers, and their services for the maintenance of the Union. To aid the members of the Grand Army of the Republic in caring for their helpless and disabled veterans. To extend aid and protection to the widows and orphans. To perpetuate the memory in history of their heroic deeds and the proper observance of Memorial Day. To inculcate patriotism and love of country, not only among our membership, but among all the people of the land, and to spread and sustain the doctrines of equal rights, universal liberty, and justice to all.

Thus we see another result of the inculcation of the principles of patriotic devotion to the land of our nativity or adoption, and can rest secure for the eternal preservation of a government that guarantees to its people the protection of life, liberty, and the pursuit of happiness. In executing their deeds of local charity the Grand Army of the Republic found they must call to their assistance the good and loyal women. There were innumerable cases where only a woman could minister to the unfortunate; hence almost every post has auxiliaries in the persons of noble women who do as much as the members of the posts for the helpless and indigent. In 1883, at the national encampment of the Grand Army, held at Denver, Colorado, such glorious women as Florence Barker, of Massachusetts; Kate B. Sherwood, of Ohio; Annie Wittenmyer, of Pennsylvania; Mrs. L. A. Turner, of Massachusetts; Clara Barton; and a score of others organized the

Woman's Relief Corps as auxiliary to the Grand Army of the Republic. Since the time of the organization of this corps, the parent society has had to look well to its honors, as these noble women have raised and distributed their hundreds of thousands of dollars; built homes for the indigent widows, mothers, and daughters of ex-soldiers, and in all respects have performed heroic benevolent service. They have borne upon their rolls the names of gifted and famous women, and perhaps have had the largest membership of any benevolent society ever organized.

Their management of the enormous sums of money coming into the treasuries of the national and local corps has commanded the highest encomiums from the ablest financiers of the country, assuring the continuation of this great society of patriotic women, who in turn will be succeeded by the Daughters of Veterans, their worthy auxiliary.

Soon after Vice-President Johnson had assumed the reins of government murmurings were heard from every quarter of his disaffection toward the reconstruction plans of the party in power. It was feared by many that, upon the principle that "blood is thicker than water," Mr. Johnson would allow his Southern blood to influence him to such an extent that he would surrender everything that had been won to the parties late in rebellion, and for whom, notwithstanding their persecution of himself and family during the war, he had suddenly conceived the most intense infatuation.

I have vivid recollections of the stirring events which occurred during the session of Congress which convened December, 1867, at which time there were grave apprehensions over reconstruction. The political rivalries of the summer had intensified the partisan feeling. States lately in rebellion, seeing their advantage in the sympathy of the administration, were clamorous for rehabilitation in all their forfeited rights. The domination of the ignorant colored people, and their unfitness for a proper use of hitherto unknown priv-

ileges; their pliancy, in many instances, in the hands of unscrupulous men; the resentment and ugly spirit of the native
Southerners toward all who came among them to make their
homes in the Southern States; the absence of slaves to do
their bidding, and the galling necessity that they must work
like the hated "Northern mudsills," made the situation deplorable.   It was a serious problem how these seemingly irrec-
oncilable elements were to be harmonized and made to dwell
in peace together, until Congress should pass a general law
under which the seceded States could again take part in the
Government.

Disagreement waxed hotter and hotter between the Republican party and President Johnson over the policy adopted
by Mr. Johnson, and a serious conflict ensued.   Congress, then
Republican by a large majority, preferred articles of impeachment against Johnson, and spent much time in an unsuccessful
effort to convict him.   During these long, eventful months
Mr. Johnson, in a spirit of resentment, as much as of clemency
toward the criminals, pardoned a great many who had been
convicted of various treasonable offences, reaching a climax
during the last few days of his administration by the pardoning of Spangler and Arnold, conspirators in the assassination of Mr. Lincoln, who were then confined on the Dry
Tortugas.   The remains of Henry Wirz, the keeper of Ander-
sonville prison, were surrendered to his friend Louis Schade,
who caused them to be interred at Mount Olivet Cemetery,
in the District of Columbia, the 3d of March, 1869.   They
were exhumed from the ground floor of Warehouse No. 2 of
the arsenal.

About the same date the family of John Wilkes Booth secured an order from President Johnson for the surrender of
Booth's body through his brother Edwin Booth, another
famous tragedian of this illustrious family of actors.   John
T. Ford, owner of Ford's Theatre, who had suffered much on
account of his supposed complicity in the assassination of

Mr. Lincoln, but had succeeded in vindicating himself without any break in his friendship with the Booths, aided materially in bringing about the interview between Edwin Booth and President Johnson which resulted in the President making the order that the remains should be given to Edwin Booth's representatives. Mr. Booth was then playing an engagement in Baltimore, and, while he had never visited Washington, nor could be induced to play at any of the theatres at the capital after his brother's mad act, came quickly to carry out his desire of recovering his brother's body and to inter it in the burial lot of the Booth family, in Greenmount Cemetery, Baltimore, Maryland. On what was to him a melancholy day he waited in the front room of the undertaking establishment of Harvey & Marr, then on F Street in the city of Washington, while a Baltimore undertaker, who had performed the service of undertaker for the Booths many times previously, Mr. Jacob H. Weaver, and R. F. Harvey went to the arsenal, armed with the President's order for the body. The officer in charge promptly obeyed, causing a detail of soldiers to assist in exhuming and transporting the body to the wagon provided by Mr. Harvey, to whose establishment it was taken, where it was identified by Edwin Booth, and subsequently taken to Baltimore and buried privately beside his kindred. So carefully was the transfer made, and so discreet was every one who had to be intrusted with the matter, that even the alert newspaper reporters failed to get a hint of the disinterment and removal of the body of the assassin until some time afterward. That these are the facts there is no doubt, though there is no record of the matter, unless Mr. Weaver or his descendants have one, but up to this time none has ever been made public. Mr. Harvey died some years ago, but unfortunately the records of his business could never be found by his son, his successor. Public feeling at that time was so strong against every one connected with the conspiracy and the assassination that Mr. Johnson was execrated for these acts. Had it been known at the time, there might have been violent opposition to the execution of his orders for the surrendering of Booth's body. Fortunately time has softened the bitterness and cooled the passions of the people, and to-day there would be no opposition to the surrendering of the lifeless body of so great a criminal as John Wilkes Booth to those dear to him by the ties of nature after he had paid the penalty of his crime. There is probably not a single survivor of that appalling conspiracy, or any one living who participated in the capture, trial, conviction, and punishment of the conspirators, or the restoration of their bodies to their relatives and friends.

Mr. Johnson conceived the idea that Mr. Stanton, Secretary of War under Lincoln, was inimical to the consummation of his designs, and decided that he would remove Stanton from his position. The party resented this step indignantly, and insisted on Mr. Stanton remaining. The President as vigorously demanded that he should vacate his office, until the matter became so serious that the President threatened forcible ejectment. At the request of his party Mr. Stanton remained continuously in the War Department, having a bed placed in his private office and his meals served there also, lest, during his absence after office hours, the President should install General Lorenzo Thomas as Secretary of War, as he threatened to do. General Grant, then General of the Army, was consulted as to calling out the troops, but, happily, he advised against such a step. At that time General Logan was commander-in-chief of the Grand Army of the Republic, and, realizing the delicacy of the situation, he called the members of the organization together secretly, there being many ex-Union officers and soldiers employed in the departments in Washington at that time. He formed battalions and placed them under the command of efficient officers. Sentinels in citizens' dress were on duty every hour of the day and night, especially in the vicinity of the White House and the old War Department building. Countersigns were given and signals agreed upon for an emergency, should it be necessary to protect Mr. Stanton. General Logan occupied a cot beside Secretary Stanton in the War Department, so that he could summon the Grand Army at a moment's notice.

During the imbroglio between Mr. Johnson and Congress, the greatest excitement since the assassination of President Lincoln prevailed. Every day startling announcements were made of the President's overt acts, and of the resentment of Congress. The climax was reached when Brevet Brigadier-General Lorenzo Thomas was arrested on the charge of attempted usurpation of authority that did not belong to him as adjutant-general of the War Department. He was released on a bond of five thousand dollars, signed by a Mr. George R. Hall and Elias A. Eliason. President Johnson irritated Congress further by sending in the name of General Lorenzo Thomas for Lieutenant-General. He was not confirmed.

The warfare continued until articles of impeachment of President Johnson were prepared and presented in the House of Representatives. General Logan being chosen one of the managers on the part of the House, he was wholly engrossed with the case for many weeks, scarcely leaving our rooms except to attend the sessions of the House, and, although they were unsuccessful, General Logan demonstrated his great ability as lawyer and statesman, and has left on record an unanswerable argument for the prosecution. I was deeply interested in everything transpiring, and spent many hours of the day and night hunting up authorities, marking paragraphs in law-reports and the newspapers which had any bearing on impeachment cases. This work, in addition to the care of my two children, receiving calls, returning visits, accepting and declining invitations kept me busy. I was, however, very happy, as I enjoyed the interesting people who came as visitors and those who were temporary or permanent residents of the capital.

During the winter and spring the political excitement that invariably precedes a Presidential campaign grew to a white heat, the Republican party almost unanimously desiring General Grant as the nominee for the Presidency. The assembling of the national convention, the presenting of General Grant's name by General Logan, and Grant's unanimous nomination by the convention, with Schuyler Colfax as Vice-President, were brief affairs. With the overwhelming majority of the Republican party north of the Mason and Dixon line at that time, it would be superfluous to add that they were both elected at the November election of 1868.

Socially the winter of 1867 and 1868 was as brilliant as possible under the circumstances. Mr. Johnson's family were much out of health, and, though his charming daughters, Mrs. Stover and Mrs. Patterson, did all in their power, they were unable to dispel the gloom that ever overhangs a discordant administration. With the executive out of harmony with his party, it made it doubly hard for the cabinet to keep up social good feeling, notwithstanding the fact that Secretaries Seward, McCulloch, Browning, Randall, Welles, and General Grant, as General of the Army, gave the regulation receptions and dinners. They were magnificent affairs, and under serene political skies would have been happy events. Many of the private entertainments were on a grand scale.

Senator and Mrs. Pomeroy, of Kansas, gave delightful parties, dinners, and receptions, as did also General and Mrs. Butler. One magnificent party given by General and Mrs. Butler in their home on the corner of I and Fifteenth Streets on the occasion of the début of their daughter, Miss Blanche, has scarcely been rivalled by the superb affairs of later years. The house was decorated profusely with the rarest flowers of the season. The soulless, scentless camellias were then the fad. Thousands of these flowers, whose petals will not bear the slightest touch, were arranged in every conceivable shape, while ferns and palms made the whole house a bower. Everybody of any distinction was there, and was loath to leave when the wee sma' hours announced the near approach of the dawn of another day.

Mr. Sumner gave many of his superb dinners where delicate viands lost their flavor in comparison with the "feast of reason and flow of soul" all enjoyed who sat at his board. It is a melancholy thought that the march of time necessitates the removal of these historic houses. The dumb walls have not rehearsed for preservation the many occasions when, around Mr. Sumner's table, the most distinguished and cultured men and women of this and other lands have discussed the absorbing questions of the day. Under a recent arrangement by capitalists to erect a magnificent hotel on the grounds where once stood the Arlington, a conglomerate combination of the historic houses once the homes of Sumner, Reverdy Johnson, and Hon. James A. Harlan, who was Mr. Lincoln's Secretary of the Interior and later senator from Iowa, these houses have been torn down and very soon these edifices and their illustrious occupants will be known no more.

Mr. Hooper, of Massachusetts, who lived in a house on the corner of H and Fifteenth Streets, which has been supplanted by the Hotel Shoreham, also gave many delightful dinners, his inseparable friend, Mr. Sumner, usually being one of the guests. I remember once, at a dinner given by General and Mrs. Butler, to have had the honor of Mr. Sumner's escort to the table, and shall ever recall it as one of the most delightful dinners of my life, though I have long since forgotten all about what we had to eat. So charming was Mr. Sumner in conversation that the three hours we sat at the table in those days slipped by all too quickly.

February 1, 1868, Dickens came to Washington to give readings from his own inimitable writings. There was not a suitable auditorium in the city at that time, and Mr. Dolby, agent for Dickens, could only secure old Carroll Hall, which was formerly on F Street, between Ninth and Tenth Streets. Mr. Quimby, of Detroit, Michigan, a devoted friend of General Logan, invited the general and myself to accompany him for the series. They were a rare treat. Notwithstanding Mr. Dickens's monotonous style of reading, the innate drollery of the man, manifested in his intonations and gestures, made his readings very interesting. Beginning February 6 with "Doctor Marigold," and the trial scene from "Pickwick," he also read extracts from "Nicholas Nickleby," "Old Curiosity Shop," "Martin Chuzzlewit," "Dombey and Son" and "The Christmas Carol," using precisely the same intonations for every character, whether pathetic or comic.

During his stay he was entertained by Charles Sumner and many other distinguished people, enjoying particularly walking about the city at night with Captain Kelly, Charles Sumner, and Mr. Stanton. He was the guest of Sir Edward Thornton, the English minister, who had succeeded Sir Frederick Bruce on the death of that illustrious diplomat. Dickens carried away, as a result of his readings in America, thirteen thousand dollars, then considered a fabulous sum. At the time of his first visit, 1847, he had given much offence to the people of this country by his criticisms of America and Americans, and by his drastic description in "Martin Chuzzlewit" of Cairo, Illinois, and the swamps of that section, which, he declared, caused even the frogs to shake with the ague.

It is a curious coincidence that his son should have come to the United States so lately to deliver lectures, and that he should have been invited to Cairo, Illinois, in order to counteract, even at this late date, the impression which "Martin Chuzzlewit" had created of Cairo. He was royally entertained in that city, and subsequently addressed a letter to the mayor that did him great credit. Unfortunately, the brilliant son of a brilliant father died in New York at the close of his tour.

It is not too much to say that the prima donnas, actresses, and actors of that time were greater artistes than those of to-day. The operas were finer, and the plays which came under the head of legitimate drama were of a higher order than those presented in these latter days. Washington was favored by the engagements of Adelina Patti, Brignoli, Ritter, Cellini, Boetti, and Herr Hermanus. Ole Bull gave two concerts during the winter. Parepa Rosa, cantatrice, gave two grand concerts in Metezrott Hall during January. Mrs. Scott Siddons, granddaughter of the great Siddons, appeared at the National with a fine company in Shakespeare's plays. Kate Bateman, John Owen, Sothern, and many other celebrated actors and actresses made the amusements for the winter delightful, the theatres being crowded every night.

General and Mrs. Grant were the recipients of much attention; you met them everywhere. General John A. Rawlins, General Dent, Mrs. Grant's brother, General Badeau—later General Grant's biographer—General Comstock, General Horace Porter, General O. E. Babcock, all members of General Grant's staff, often accompanied the general. General Grant's friends had presented to him the house on I Street, owned and occupied by the late Matthew Emery. The large parlors of that palatial mansion were inadequate to accommodate the numbers who were eager to pay their respects at every recurrent reception day of Mrs. Grant. All their children were at home then and the survivors of that time remember the charming household. With General and Mrs. Grant in the centre, Fred, the eldest son and the most like his illustrious father, Ulysses, Jr., Nellie, with her sweet face, her long hair hanging down her back, and her beautiful eyes as gentle as those of a gazelle, and Jesse, the youngest, they are immortalized in the painting by Cogswell, known as "Grant and His Family."

In the Grant home on I Street, I witnessed one historic gathering which will ever be most vivid in my mind. After the nomination of Grant and Colfax at Chicago, the committee appointed to wait upon them and notify them of their nomination was composed of J. R. Hawley of Connecticut, Lewis Barker of Maine, C. N. Riottet of Texas, Willard Warner of Alabama, J. M. Hedrik of Iowa, John Evans of Colorado, S. M. Cullom of Illinois, R. T. Van Horn of Missouri, J. K. Dubois of Illinois, T. L. Tullock of Virginia, J. W. Holden of North Carolina, T. F. Lee of North Carolina, W. C. Goodloe of Kentucky, Valentine Dill of Arkansas, J. H. Harris of North Carolina, A. McDonald of Arkansas, B. F. Rice of Arkansas, H. A. Pierce of Virginia, and others. They came to Washington, and it was arranged that Mr. Colfax should go to General Grant's house, and that the committee should call upon them there. Mrs. Grant kindly advised a few special friends, inviting them to be present. General Logan and I were among the fortunate number. We reached the Grant home about eight o'clock, or a little after. Mr. Colfax, his distinguished mother, Mrs. Matthews, and his half-sister, Miss Matthews, arrived soon after, followed by Mr. E. B. Washburn, Mr. Halsey, of New Jersey, and General Grant's staff—Generals Rawlins, Babcock, Dent, Badeau, and Colonel Comstock.

After exchanging greetings and pleasantries, General Grant was informed that the committee had arrived. He and Mr. Colfax moved to the rear of the parlor, and stood side by side while the committee was presented. Mrs. Grant and her venerable father, Mr. Dent, and Mrs. and Miss Matthews were not far from them. After the presentation, Governor Hawley, with all the power of his eloquence in his palmy days, made the speech on behalf of the committee, informing General Grant and Mr. Colfax that they had been chosen the standard-bearers of the Republican party for the campaign. General Grant had the same unpretentious bearing, so characteristic of him under all circumstances. His reply was very brief, and that with much embarrassment, leaving Mr. Colfax, a fine speaker, to make the speech of acceptance for the nominees of the Republican party. The guests who were present stood about the group with rapt attention, feeling it a great privilege to have been present at such a ceremony. After it was over the party was invited into the dining-room where refreshments were served, and the company dispersed. Mrs. Grant was so cordial and unassuming, and received her guests with such simplicity of manner that she won all hearts. Every one went away quite as ready to be her champion as that of her husband, their chieftain.

While writing the names of the committee and the guests present that I remember, I am overwhelmed with the melancholy thought that so few remain of the conspicuous figures of that occasion.

The campaign of 1868 was probably the most enthusiastic of any since 1860. The ex-Union soldiers were everywhere wild with delight over the nomination of General Grant as the leader of the party. Every political demonstration was participated in by them. Flags, banners, patriotic music rendered by glee clubs and brass bands were the order of the day. The well-worn uniforms of the soldiers were donned for all such occasions, and it was not surprising that the November election witnessed the largest majorities ever polled by a party, nor that General Grant and Schuyler Colfax were elected overwhelmingly.

When Congress assembled December 1, 1868, there was general rejoicing, because it was thought there would be little trouble over reconstruction and other vexatious problems. The South felt that so magnanimous a conqueror as General Grant had shown himself would be their friend under the severe trials through which they must pass before they could again become a part and parcel of the compact they had tried to dissolve. You heard no mutterings from any quarter.

Congress felt sure that, now the die was cast, Mr. Johnson would not attempt further arbitrary action, but would probably finish his term in a quiet way. He gratified himself and vented his spleen on Congress for their attempted impeachment by pardoning every one he could, especially those who had been debarred from political rights because of participation in the rebellion. His proclamation covered such cases as those of Jefferson Davis, Slidell, Mason, Mann, and other exiles who hastened to return to the United States after having sought refuge across the seas.

He closed his career with a "Farewell Address," in which he arraigned all who opposed him, and lauded himself in a most remarkable manner. After Congress reassembled, the Tenure of Office bill was repealed in time for Grant to make such changes as he thought important.

Reconstructive legislation continued, many of the States wishing to come back into the Union that they might reassume their relations to the Government, and have representatives in both Houses of Congress; so, while they deemed Mr. Johnson powerless for harm, they pressed the work, well knowing that the new Congress, who would take their seats after the 4th of March, 1869, would be so largely of one party that there might be delay in adjusting these questions. The opposition, recognizing this fact, in most cases acquiesced. At no time in the history of the Government have there been abler men in Congress than there were then. Among the senators were Sumner, Wade, Chandler, Morton, Fessenden, Conkling, Morgan, Sherman, Morrill, Voorhees, Trumbull, Anthony, and Wilson. In the House were Garfield, Colfax, Butler, Brooks, Bingham, Blaine, Shellabarger, Wilson, Allison, Cullom, Logan, Ames, Hooper, Washburne, Boutwell, Randall, and Voorhees. Such men were earnest, thoughtful, patriotic and keenly alive to the interests of the country. They allowed nothing to pass that was in any sense questionable.

February 10, 1869, was a memorable day. It was gloomy

and disagreeable, but that had no influence on the multitude that gathered at the Capitol to witness the counting of the electoral vote which was to declare Grant and Colfax President and Vice-President of the United States. Senator Wade, of Ohio, vice-president of the Senate, and Mr. Colfax, then speaker of the House, were to preside over the joint session of the two Houses, which was to assemble in the House of Representatives. Tickets were necessary to procure admission to the galleries. By ten o'clock every available space was taken. The diplomatic gallery was occupied by the foreign representatives, including Sir Edward Thornton, Baron Gerolt, Blacque Bey, Mr. DeBille, and other distinguished foreigners who were much engrossed with American affairs. In the reserved galleries were Mrs. Grant, Mrs. Dent, Mrs. Sharp, members of General Grant's staff, Mrs. Matthews, Schuyler Colfax's mother, and his sister, wives and ladies of the Supreme Court, senators and members, and also many distinguished visitors in the city. On the motion of some member, permission was given to admit ladies on the floor in the rear of the members' seats. In a brief time every available spot was occupied. At twelve o'clock the House was called to order, and the opening prayer was followed by some minor motions incident to the morning hours. The hour-hand pointed to one o'clock; the sergeant-at-arms, General Ordway, announced the presence of the Senate and their desire to be admitted. Preceded by Colonel Brown, sergeant-at-arms of the Senate, the whole body filed in and took the seats provided for them. The imperturbable Ben Wade, ascending the speaker's platform, took the presiding officer's chair with Mr. Colfax on his right. As soon as all were seated Mr. Wade took up the gavel and called the joint House to order. The clerk then proceeded to call the roll of States. As soon as the first contested State was reached, a discussion arose and the Senate withdrew to discuss the question separately.

After an hour and a half the Senate returned to continue the count. During the absence of the Senate, the members of the House discussed also the question of rights of States to cast their votes where an irregularity was charged, some of the members exhibiting much feeling. They had not gone far when they again got into a wrangle over the State of Georgia, General Butler leading in the attack upon Mr. Wade, who, in the generosity of his heart, had recognized the gentleman from Massachusetts, not anticipating the muddle to which it would lead. A second withdrawal of the Senate was necessary, and while they were out they determined that such proceedings should not continue, as it looked at one time as if the time prescribed by the Constitution might elapse before they could finish their work, from which untold complications might arise. Consequently, upon the renewal of the motions by General Butler, a number of members arose to the defence of Mr. Wade and Mr. Colfax seized the gavel and restored order, declaring that the sergeant-at-arms would be called to his assistance if the disorder continued. After some further discussion the count was finished, and the joint assembly adjourned.

General Logan was much excited over what he termed discourtesy to the revered Mr. Wade. It seemed to him outrageous that any member of that body should embarrass and confuse the venerable statesman in the closing hours of his long and faithful career. General Logan's castigation of Butler in as strong terms as parliamentary rules would allow elicited prolonged applause and contributed much to restoring order, securing for Mr. Wade the respect and consideration due to him. On adjournment it was most interesting to see the groups of men discussing the proceedings of the day, and to hear their denunciatory remarks on those who had attempted to delay the count and annoy Mr. Wade.

We were then living at Willard's Hotel. That evening about eight o'clock there was a knock on our parlor door, and in answer to the command to enter Mr. Wade walked in, and, extending his hand to General Logan, he said: "Logan, God bless you; I have come here to thank you for coming to my rescue to-day when they attempted to crucify and mortify me. My blunder was in recognizing any one, after which I could do nothing but bull it through." He had his umbrella in his hands, and emphasized every word by striking it on the floor. In all respects he was a quaint figure, but so earnest and enthusiastic that he commanded the admiration of every one who came in contact with him. We prevailed on him to sit down, and the memory of that visit will abide with me forever. He spoke with much emotion of his long service for the cause of human liberty. He said he retired to private life to spend the remnant of his days contentedly in the consciousness of having performed his duty to the best of his ability. He spoke most affectionately of Mr. Lincoln, and was grateful his lines had been cast in the same epoch, and that he had been able to do something to further the cause for which Mr. Lincoln had been martyred.

We heard much that winter of *Alabama* claims, the great methods of arbitration in international affairs and other questions, signifying that we were entering upon a wonderful era in human affairs; that, with the close of our rebellion, came a new order of things which was to mark the greatest progress in republicanism.

Congress met the first Monday in December, 1868. The gloom following the assassination of Mr. Lincoln by a madman, immediately upon the dawn of peace after four long years of fratricidal war, still hung like a pall over Washington. To this melancholy event was added the personal sorrow of very many who wore the habiliments of mourning for loved ones lost during the war. Mr. Johnson was naturally a serious man, and was so overwhelmed by the grave responsibilities resting upon him in the trying position in which he was placed that it seemed as if the pall would never lift. Mrs.

Johnson was an invalid and could do nothing to brighten the home of the President. Fortunately their daughters, Mrs. Stover and Mrs. Patterson, were typical Southern ladies with rare accomplishments, fascinating manners, and fine conversational powers. They appreciated keenly their social rank, and were anxious to do everything possible to make the White House attractive and to have every one feel that it was the people's house, which they occupied temporarily. Therefore they extended a very cordial welcome to all who were entitled to be received.

In both houses of Congress there were many of the most distinguished men of the nation. In the Senate Hamlin, Sumner, Conkling, Fenton, Fessenden, Frelinghuysen, Booth, McDougall, Simon Cameron, Chandler, Howard, Kellogg, Morrill of Vermont, Morrill of Maine, Wilson, Boutwell, Bayard, Morton, Williams of Oregon, Yates, Trumbull, and others, made it one of the ablest bodies that ever convened in any country. In the House there were Washburn, Logan, Cullom, Judd, Arnold, Singleton, Wentworth, Henderson, Farnsworth, Cook, Sherman, Schenck, Garfield, Grow, Shellabarger, Bingham, Archer, Thaddeus Stevens, Clymer, Williams, Colfax, Voorhees, Davis, Banks, Butler, Wheeler, Wood, Slocum, Brooks, Frye, Blaine, Hale, Boutwell, Allison, Wilson of Iowa, and a score of others who were leaders of men and statesmen in every sense of the word.

Before the Christmas holidays the breach between the President and Congress had widened so seriously that it was evident that the last days of Mr. Johnson's administration were to be full of friction and unpleasantness between himself and his party. As if in sympathy with the political situation, January 1, 1869, was one of the gloomiest of days; a cold rain fell all the night before and continued during New Year's Day. Every preparation, however, had been made for the reception at the White House.

The Marine Band, under the leadership of the well-remembered Professor Scala, was in its accustomed place. The President, his daughters, Mrs. Stover and Mrs. Patterson, and Miss Cohen, of Tennessee, assisted by one or two of the ladies of the cabinet, received the callers. Secretary Seward presented the Diplomatic Corps and their ladies, all of whom appeared in regal costume; the gentlemen were in full court dress, wearing all their orders. Stately Sir Edward Thornton and gracious Lady Thornton led the column in which followed M. Bethemy, the French minister; M. Blacque Bey, the Turkish minister; Baron Gerolt, of Prussia, and his lovely wife and beautiful daughters; Mr. DeBille, the Danish minister, and his charming wife; Don José Antonio Garcia, of Peru; and the whole list of the distinguished diplomats then in Washington. This was Mr. Seward's last appearance at a New Year's reception, and, as many looked upon him as the last of Mr. Lincoln's cabinet, they felt a pang of regret that in so brief a time every representative of that administration should have gone out forever. The diplomatic corps was followed by the Supreme Court, headed by Chief Justice Chase, Associate Justices Nelson, Clifford, Davis, Miller, Strong, Swayne—all now gone to another world, with the majority of the throng that surged through the White House that dreary day.

The cabinet was well represented, Secretary Stanton alone being absent. Secretaries Welles, McCulloch, Browning, Stanberry, P. M. G. Randall were there, each contributing his best efforts to the pleasure of every one. Very few of the Senate and House appeared—Senators Sprague, Dixon, Doolittle, Grimes, Trumbull, Ross, and a few others attended; of the House there were even fewer who paid their respects.

The army, led by General Grant and a long list of military officers, presented an imposing appearance, as also the officers of the navy, following Admirals Farragut and Porter. There were then a number of officers of both branches of the service in Washington who had but recently been relieved from active duty.   The bureau officers, different organizations, and privileged persons had scarcely passed the President when a fearful crowd from the streets pushed their way in, their feet muddy and their clothing dripping with the rain in which they had been standing outside.   The President encouraged their coming, and very soon the reception became a motley surging crowd, to the disgust of dignified people.

Mr. Johnson's cabinet, Mr. Seward, Mr. McCulloch, Mr. Stanton, Mr. Welles, Mr. Browning, Mr. Randall, and Mr. Stanberry, were all men of national reputation.   Their families were, without exception, charming people who enjoyed conforming to all the social requirements of their positions. They gave dinners, luncheon parties, afternoon and evening receptions, and made their guests feel they were pleased to see them.

No one ever heard the wives of those officials say they were "bored to death by callers" or that they "despised society." Their entertainments were beautiful and on a scale of magnificence equal to those of the moneyed kings of to-day, who claim to rival Belshazzar's feasts in their extravagant entertainments, which are, as a rule, ordered from caterers and decorators and have few personal touches displaying the taste of the hosts or anything that betrays the delightful hospitality of a real home.

The most refined people came to Washington every winter, because of the opportunity to meet celebrities.   It was a pleasure to take these visitors to pay their respects to officials and their families, of whom all loyal Americans were justly proud.   Every one was assured of a cordial welcome, the recipients appreciating the honor conferred upon them by those calls.   No one was made to feel he was an intruder; neither did any one presume upon the courtesy extended to him.   If the cabinet ladies felt their duties irksome, they were too well bred or too diplomatic to betray their feelings.

Chief Justice Chase, in his then considered palatial home

on the corner of Fifth and F Streets, gave royal dinners and parties. His daughters, Mrs. Kate Chase Sprague and Miss Nettie Chase, both fascinating and brilliant women, presided over the home of the chief justice, and made it one of the most attractive in the city. Here eminent statesmen and learned men and women of the time were dined and entertained with lavish hospitality. Justices Miller, Strong, and Swayne, and their attractive families gave many social functions in their spacious homes, where one met persons who were interesting and celebrated on account of their achievements.

It may be imaginary, but when one recalls the resplendent social affairs given by Sir Edward and Lady Thornton, the French minister, the German minister Baron Gerolt, Mr. De Bille, the Danish minister, Mr. Zamacona, the Mexican minister, the Garcias, of Peru, and others of the Diplomatic Corps, one feels that diplomatic hospitality was more brilliant and frequent than it is in these days of boundless prosperity and greater cordiality between all nations and the United States.

Many of the senators and members of Congress were men of wealth for that epoch, who entertained lavishly in their own homes. It was rare that their dinners were cooked by caterers. They lived well every day, and a dinner was to them merely a question of what guests they desired to invite. Mr. Sumner's dinners, as I have already said, were famous. The most delicious viands lost their flavor when compared with the intellectual feast that all enjoyed who sat at his board. Mr. Hooper, his most intimate friend, vied with Mr. Sumner in dinner-giving and in the choosing of brilliant people. The Frelinghuysens, with three lovely young ladies in the house, General and Mrs. Butler with their charming daughter Blanche, afterward Mrs. Ames, were delightful hosts who enjoyed having their friends. General and Mrs. Grant, Admiral and Mrs. Porter, and very many more gave superb dinners and receptions that were no less resplendent than those given every winter since. There was a charm about the dinners given in those days which, it must be admitted, does not characterize such gatherings now. They were less formal but there was more sincere cordiality than is manifested in latter-day social functions.

On account of the political imbroglios which Mr. Johnson was unfortunate enough to precipitate, the state dinners, though given punctiliously, were not especially enjoyable. With the President out of harmony with his party, no amount of feminine tact could keep the sparks from flying, especially when the poles were in such close proximity as a dinner-table necessitates.

However, President Johnson's daughters, with consummate tact, decided to give a brilliant and memorable social function in the White House which would not be clouded by any political collisions or awkward coupling of guests. The grandchildren of President Johnson, Frank Johnson, Andrew Stover, Sallie and Lillie Stover, were all very attractive. Mrs. Stover, a most charming woman, conceived the idea of converting the staid old mansion into fairy-land and filling it with the fairies that inhabit every city, in this way hoping to avoid the unpleasant meeting of political rivals. Invitations of the most formal character were issued two weeks or more before the affair was to occur. Every child honored by one was in a great state of excitement lest his costume should not be gorgeous enough for such a grand occasion. Indulgent mammas exhausted every resource in designing and providing the bewildering fairylike garments, which were often provided with wings, that the children might have the true resemblance to elves. The decorators made the corridors, east room, and parlors bowers of vines and flowers, that the little creatures might disport themselves in a veritable fairy-land.

Professors Marini and Bates prepared the grand promenade,

fairy dances, and music for the occasion. "Mammas" and
"papas" were invited to accompany the children, so that the
company was very large. The children of the White House
received their guests in the blue room, thence passing into
the green room, the doors of which were closed, so that none
might enter the east room before the procession. The hours
were from six to eleven. It was nearly seven o'clock when
Frank Johnson and Sally Stover headed the procession, keeping time to the lovely music. After them came the numerous couples who had assembled in the blue and green
rooms, and who were to take part in the dance in the east
room.

A more enchanting scene was never witnessed in the White
House. Nellie, Ulysses, and Jesse Grant, the Barneses and
McCullochs, the Wallachs, the Blairs, children of the Diplomatic Corps, and many others from the families of officials
and citizens made a bright picture, with their gay dresses and
pretty faces, while their merry laughter rang out above the
strains of delightful music. At the proper time President
Johnson, surrounded by fairy queens, led the way to the
state dining-room, where the long table, spread with every
delicacy, refreshed them after they had danced and prom-
enaded to their hearts' content. The Italian minister, Chev-
alier Cerruti, although a bachelor, had given a charming
children's party previously, he himself crowning Nellie Grant
queen of the evening. Thus the little people had that winter
two wonderfully pretty parties.

The winter was so full of stirring events that it passed
quickly, and yet every one was impatient for the 4th of
March and the inauguration of General Grant and Schuyler
Colfax as President and Vice-President. Mr. Johnson, his
family, and cabinet longed to be released from the continual
bickerings and warfare between the President and Congress
that had reached and passed the pitch of an "impeachment
trial" of the President by Congress. The trial only failed

by one vote to result in conviction, but to all intents and purposes convicted the President of bad faith to his party, and placed him in a humiliating position before the nation, causing him and his family to long for the seclusion of his home in Tennessee.

General Logan had made an engagement for both himself and me to accompany Colonel Charles L. Wilson, of Chicago, editor of the *Journal* of that city, to visit the battle-fields of Virginia and the city of Richmond in March, 1868. Colonel Wilson came on, accompanied by his niece Miss Anna Wilson, and the young lady to whom he was engaged, Miss Farrar, of Boston. However, it so happened that there were such important matters before Congress that General Logan could not go. The colonel, however, insisted that I, with my two children, our daughter Dollie and baby son John A. Logan, Jr., should carry out the plan of our visit.

We arrived in Richmond on a cold bleak day in March, to find the hotel in a very wretched condition. As it was so soon after the war, we were prepared to find evidences of the rebellion everywhere. The colonel had great difficulty in finding an equipage to drive over the battle-fields around Richmond. He particularly wanted to go to Libby Prison, and to inspect the fortifications that had afforded defence for the capital of the Confederacy for so many long months. I shall never forget the poor horses, the well-worn carriage, and the miserable-looking white man, accompanied by a boy about thirteen years of age, who sat on the box. We had, fortunately, brought lap-robes, cloaks, and warm robes, expecting the weather to be disagreeable. Driving about over the battle-field, we saw the colored people picking up the bullets and pieces of shell which afforded them quite a livelihood immediately after the war. Foundry men had established agencies around all these fortified cities to buy up exploded shrapnel-shells, broken cannon and Minie balls, and every species of old iron that was so abundant on these bat-

tle-fields. Driving about from place to place, we were greatly
interested, and realized more than we ever could have, had
we not visited the city immediately after the war, the horrors
through which the people of the Confederacy had passed. I
remember hearing the poor little boy, who was so thinly clad
that he had little to protect him from the inclemency of the
weather, call out to the driver: "Well, it isn't so miserably
hot to-day, is it?" At the same time his teeth were chatter-
ing in his head with the cold from which he was suffering.
We were not long in finding that we could do without one
of the lap-robes, which we insisted that the poor child should
wrap around his shivering body.

During this trip we visited the churchyards and cemeteries
at Richmond, Petersburg, and other points made historic by
the struggle which had taken place in and around these cities.
In the churchyard near Petersburg we saw hundreds of the
graves of Confederate soldiers. These graves had upon them
small bleached Confederate flags and faded flowers and wreaths
that had been laid upon them by loving hands on the occasion
of their Decoration Day.

Upon our return General Logan was much interested in
our account of what we had seen and I remarked to him that
I had never been so touched as I was by seeing the little flags
and the withered flowers that had been laid on these graves.
At this General Logan said that it was a beautiful revival of
the custom of the ancients in thus preserving the memory of
the dead, and that he, as commander-in-chief of the Grand
Army of the Republic, would issue an order for the decoration of the graves of Union soldiers. Colonel Wilson, heartily
approving of the plan, said that he would be glad to exploit
it in his paper in Chicago. General Logan sent for General
Chipman, then adjutant-general of the Grand Army of the
Republic, and dictated Order No. 11, for the first decoration
of the graves of Union soldiers that ever took place in the
United States, as follows:

HEADQUARTERS GRAND ARMY OF THE REPUBLIC,
Adjutant-General's Office, 446 Fourteenth St.,
WASHINGTON, D. C., *May* 5, 1868.

General Orders ⎱
   No. 11. ⎰

I. The 30th day of May, 1868, is designated for the purpose of strewing with flowers or otherwise decorating the graves of comrades who died in defence of their country during the late rebellion, and whose bodies now lie in almost every city, village, and hamlet churchyard in the land. In this observance no form of ceremony is prescribed, but posts and comrades will in their own way arrange such fitting services and testimonials of respect as circumstances may permit.

We are organized, comrades, as our regulations tell us, for the purpose, among other things, "of preserving and strengthening those kind and fraternal feelings which have bound together the soldiers, sailors, and marines who united to suppress the late rebellion." What can aid more to assure this result than by cherishing tenderly the memory of our heroic dead, who made their breasts a barricade between our country and its foes? Their soldier lives were the reveille of freedom to a race in chains, and their deaths the tattoo of rebellious tyranny in arms. We should guard their graves with sacred vigilance. All that the consecrated wealth and taste of the nation can add to their adornment and security is but a fitting tribute to the memory of her slain defenders. Let no wanton foot tread rudely on such hallowed grounds. Let pleasant paths invite the coming and going of reverent visitors and fond mourners. Let no vandalism or avarice or neglect, no ravages of time, testify to the present or to the coming generations, that we have forgotten as a people the cost of a free and undivided Republic.

If other eyes grow dull, and other hands slack, and other hearts cold in the solemn trust, ours shall keep it well as long as the light and warmth of life remain to us.

Let us, then, at the time appointed, gather around their sacred remains, and garland the passionless mounds above them with the choicest flowers of spring-time; let us raise above them the dear old flag they saved from dishonor; let us in this solemn presence renew our pledges to aid and assist those whom they have left among us, a sacred charge upon a nation's gratitude — the soldier's and sailor's widow and orphan.

II. It is the purpose of the Commander-in-Chief to inaugurate this observance with the hope that it will be kept up from year to year, while a survivor of the war remains to honor the memory of his departed comrades. He earnestly desires the public press to call attention to this order, and lend its friendly aid in bringing it to the notice of comrades in all parts of the country in time for simultaneous compliance therewith.

III. Department Commanders will use every effort to make this order effective.

By order of—

JOHN A. LOGAN,
*Commander-in-Chief*

*Official:*
WM. T. COLLINS, *A. A. G.*

N. P. CHIPMAN,
*Adjutant-General.*

After much discussion and investigation as to the time of the year when flowers would be in their greatest perfection in the different sections of the country, it was decided that May 30 would probably be the most appropriate time when this ceremony should take place. General Logan's anticipations were fully realized by the universal observance of the day in every State in the Union. The exercises were characterized by patriotic addresses, recitations, music, and ceremonious decoration of the soldiers' graves with flowers. Almost all loyal people participated in the observance of the day devoted to the perpetuation of the memory of the heroic dead.

May 30, 1868, was a beautiful day. Most extensive preparations had been made for the decoration of the graves of the soldiers buried at Arlington. There were a great many ex-Union soldiers in and around Washington at that time, and they seemed to vie with each other in their efforts to make the occasion a memorable one. The probabilities are that a greater number of ex-Union officers and soldiers took part in the ceremonies than have since participated. Among those occupying seats on the platform during the ceremonies were General and Mrs. Grant, Mr. Dent, Mrs. Grant's father; Secretaries Fish, Rawlins, Borie, Boutwell, and Cox;

Postmaster-General Creswell; Sir Edward Thornton, the British minister; Senators Nye and Warner; Treasurer Spinner; Mayor Bowen; General Sherman; the venerable Amos Kendall; Hon. Mr. Laflin, of New York; Hon. Sidney Clarke, of Kansas; the Swiss consul-general; Mr. John Hitz, Doctor L. Alcan, of Paris, and others.

General Logan subsequently succeeded in getting an appropriation for the publication of the reports of the ceremonies of Memorial Day, and also in making the 30th of May a national holiday. Since his death there have been many who have claimed for themselves or their friends the authorship of Decoration Day, but the story I tell here contains the true facts as to the origin of Memorial Day. It was conceived by General Logan, his sympathetic nature being deeply touched by what we had told him that we had witnessed in the cemeteries of Virginia. He said that it was strange that a people who were so loyal to their country as had been the Union soldiers and their friends should not have been the first to inaugurate this beautiful ceremony, and that it must be attributed to the fact that they were so engrossed in taking up their vocations in life that they had not had time to indulge in sentiment. He said it was not too late for the Union men of the nation to follow the example of the people of the South in perpetuating the memory of their friends who had died for the cause which they thought just and right. General Logan had infinite satisfaction in the thought that he was the author of Decoration Day.

# CHAPTER X

As the flight of time brought the 4th of March nearer and nearer, committees were formed and the most extensive preparations ever conceived were made for the inauguration of Grant and Colfax. Experts and artists from New York and other large cities were brought to suggest schemes and designs for decorations and the arrangement of the programme.

General Grant being the greatest military hero who had ever been elected President, and there being so many ex-soldiers in Washington at that time from all parts of the country, it was determined that the military display should be greater than it ever had been on previous inaugural occasions. State and local organizations made extensive preparations; everybody in and around the capital city was on the alert for weeks before the 4th of March. The local committees were untiring in their labors. The citizens were most generous in their subscriptions. Consequently, no grander scene could be imagined than was presented, notwithstanding the day was stormy and that it rained very hard at night.

The committee on the part of the Senate was composed of

Hon. Richard Yates, of Illinois; A. H. Cragin, of New Hampshire; and T. C. McCreary, of Kentucky. They attended to the details of the arrangements at the Capitol, while the numerous committees for every part of the ceremony succeeded in having everything perfect. The procession was magnificent. It began with the grand marshal, General Alexander S. Webb, and his efficient staff composed of prominent military officers, members of General Grant's staff and others. Then the carriages with the President and Vice-President elect and the committee. Then the outgoing President and the committees, followed by an unusual quota of distinguished officials—judges, senators, governors, ex-senators, ex-governors, and many other noted visitors. Then the various organizations—military, masonic, and civic to the number of thousands, while the numerous bands played martial airs with much enthusiasm. The whole of the space, including the park east of the Capitol, was literally packed with people. The waving banners of the various organizations here and there made it a gay panorama. The usual ceremonies of swearing in the Vice-President by the Chief Justice took place in the Senate chamber at the constitutional hour of twelve o'clock. The Senate chamber was packed to suffocation. The diplomatic corps, in full court dress, presented an imposing appearance, while the galleries were filled to their utmost capacity. Mrs. Grant, her children, and father Colonel Dent, and Mrs. and Miss Matthews, mother and sister of Mr. Colfax, occupied front seats in the reserved galleries. The diplomatic gallery and that reserved for ladies looked brilliant with their complement of well-dressed beautiful women. Every movement was chronicled by the vigilant reporters, who occupied their accustomed places in the gallery reserved for them.

Vice-President Colfax was as pale as death while taking the oath, and seemed deeply moved in assuming the responsibility of the office of Vice-President, and, as he occupied the chair a few moments his pallor became even greater. After Chief Justice Chase had pronounced the last word which made Mr. Colfax the legal Vice-President of the United States, the Senate arose and, preceded by Chief Justice Chase, the President-elect, Vice-President, and Supreme Court, filed out of the Senate chamber in order according to rank through the corridor to the rotunda, and out through the bronze doorway to the platform always erected before the east front of the Capitol for the ceremony of administering the oath to the President by the Chief Justice, and from which the President delivers his inaugural address. The day was inclement, but, as General Grant's address, like most of his state papers, was very short, the people were not long exposed.

Notwithstanding the multitude of people massed in front of them and on every side, so interested were they that absolute silence prevailed. The deep voice of Chief Justice Chase reached to the very outside of the crowd. General Grant's great diffidence almost overwhelmed him, and he could be heard only a few yards from where he stood. No one could have believed that the shrinking, unpretentious man stammering through the well-prepared address had commanded thousands of men and conquered as many more. After the close of the address, and when all within reach had congratulated and blessed the President many times over, the procession again re-formed and escorted the President to the executive mansion, the bands playing all the triumphant familiar airs they knew. Reaching the White House they were received most formally, without the luncheon and other hospitalities the outgoing President uniformly extends to his successor. General Grant did not remain that night in the White House, but returned to his home on I Street.

The north wing of the Treasury was just nearing completion at that time, so that the committee made arrangements to have the reception and inaugural ball in the new building, occupying all the floors. Immediately over the entrance hall were the reception-rooms of the President, Mrs. Grant, the Vice-President, and the ladies of his family, all communicating, while other rooms furnished ample accommodations for the cloak-room. The magnificent marble or east room was the main dancing-hall. It was furnished and elaborately decorated, as was the whole building. The bronze gallery running round this room made a grand place for the music and spectators. The decorations in this room were the finest of all, the soft tints of the Pyrenees, Siena, Egyptian, Tennessee, and Vermont marbles contrasting exquisitely with the bright colors. The whole effect was superb.

There was a very great crowd, and, but for the solidity of the building and the perfect management it might have been most uncomfortable. About ten o'clock President Grant entered the reception-room assigned him. He was accompanied by Senator Morgan, of New York, and one or two others; Mrs. Grant was escorted by General George H. Thomas. Mr. and Mrs. Colfax came in together. Horace Greeley, Julia Ward Howe, Governors Jewell of Connecticut, Oglesby of Illinois, Curtin of Pennsylvania, Fenton of New York, and innumerable others, including many army and navy heroes were there, among them that illustrious Illinois soldier Major-General James H. Wilson, whose daring as a cavalry-officer placed him in the front rank of officers of that arm of the service. The capture of President Jefferson Davis, as he was fleeing from Richmond, was the crowning glory of his brilliant career. I remember seeing a group of such men as Porter, Farragut, Du Pont, Dahlgren, and Rogers together, while Generals Sherman, Logan, McDowell, Meade, Burnside, Hancock, Thomas, Sickles, and a host of others recalled the stirring events of the war so recently over. Celebrities from every part of the country were among the numbers who were glad to honor General and Mrs. Grant by their presence, making the inauguration ceremonies of 1869 the most notable up to that time in the history of the Government. The 5th of March found the city full of weary people, who felt themselves almost too fatigued to take their departure for home after the procession, ball, and ceaseless tramping about.

The day before the inauguration an event occurred in General Grant's office in the War Department that few knew about, which reflected great credit upon the generosity of some of our patriotic and worthy citizens. The house occupied by General Grant on I Street had been given him by some friends when he was General of the Army. He was about to move into the executive mansion, many thought for a residence of eight years at least. His successor as General of the Army was the next most renowned soldier of the Union army, General W. T. Sherman. A committee composed of A. T. Stewart, Hamilton Fish, B. F. Field, W. H. Aspinwall, Judge Hilton, Solon Humphrey, and William Scott had been chosen by the subscribers to present this house and the furniture to General Sherman. They had negotiated with General Grant, and had arranged that Mr. Hoyt and General Butterfield should take General Sherman to General Grant's office at an appointed hour. When they all met, the committee handed General Grant sixty-five thousand dollars. He, in exchange, gave them the deeds, bills of sale, and documents, making an absolute conveyance to General Sherman of the property on I Street and all thereunto belonging. Then the committee gave General Sherman the subscription list, informing him that a check for the balance of the subscriptions, in all about one hundred thousand dollars, would be sent to him at an early date. General Grant was delighted that General Sherman was so soon to have the house, and Sherman was completely overcome by the unexpected kindness of his friends. When the little group separated each felt supremely happy, the donors knowing they had done a graceful thing and the recipient feeling that his services had been appreciated. General Sherman lived a longer period probably with his family about him in this house than anywhere else, and enjoyed more uninterrupted pleasure here than in any other house he ever occupied.

In a few days after Grant's inauguration the question of the cabinet was settled by the appointments of Hamilton Fish as Secretary of State, vice Mr. Washburne, who was transferred to the French mission, and of Mr. George S. Boutwell as Secretary of the Treasury, vice Mr. A. T. Stewart, resigned. Notwithstanding the fact that Chief Justice Chase decided that the transfer of his business to trustees made Mr. Stewart eligible, many lawyers held it did not. General Grant, desiring to avoid any technical questions on the subject, accepted Mr. Stewart's resignation, which Mr. Stewart enclosed with the opinion of Chief Justice Chase. General John A. Rawlins, long his faithful adjutant-general in the field and after the war, was made Secretary of War. Adolph Borie, of Philadelphia, was appointed Secretary of the Navy, but occupied that position only a few months. General Jacob D. Cox was made Secretary of the Interior, General John A. Creswell Postmaster-General, and Judge E. R. Hoar Attorney-General.

Everybody applauded these appointments, and the political skies seemed clearer than they had been since the assassination of Mr. Lincoln. Few persons knew that Senator J. F. Wilson, of Iowa, then a member of the House, and one of the impeachment committee, was very strongly urged by President Grant to accept the position of Secretary of State. He even consented at one time to consider the matter favorably, but, subsequently learning that Mr. Washburne desired to name a number of the appointees to the diplomatic service, he reconsidered his promise and declined to have any connection with the cabinet, after which Mr. Fish was chosen at the request of Senator Morgan, Mr. Conkling, and other New York friends of President Grant. Had Mr. Wilson accepted this position, who can tell the effect upon the policy of the administration? Cuba might have been one of our strongest allies and a prosperous republic before the expiration of President Grant's second term.

Upon reflection it will be remembered that very early in Grant's administration the Cuban question came up as one of the most important of the time. I recollect that many earnest and prolonged conferences were held as to the duty of the United States in the matter of the various troubles in that unfortunate island. Mr. Fish bitterly opposed any recognition of Cuba by the United States and finally carried his point, notwithstanding the urgent solicitation of many prominent citizens, senators, and members of Congress to the contrary. General Grant entertained a strong desire for negotiations, but was ever handicapped by the fear of the cry of dictator, knowing that the mercurial temperament of the people all over the country was ready to start such a sensation, should they be given the slightest foundation in the line of any desire for the acquisition of territory.

Upon the appointment of four of his staff to clerical duty in the White House there was another spasmodic outburst of clamor against the military. Generals Porter, Babcock, and Badeau and Colonel Dent were looked upon with much suspicion when it was announced that they were to be secretaries to the President. It was considered most unwise that applicants for appointments should be obliged to file their applications through the executives of the respective departments, who in turn sent them to the President through these secretaries. There was especial sensitiveness on the subject of uniforms being worn about the White House. There were then a great number of officers of the army and navy in Washington, some on duty and some on leave of absence. The mutterings of Congress frightened many of them, who, to avoid attracting attention, secured the passage of a resolution permitting officers on duty or leave in Washington to wear citizens' dress. When the Navy and War Departments presented themselves to President Grant at the White House, there was a large number of distinguished officers in the company that assembled in the east room to pay their respects, which must have made Grant feel that he would be ably sustained by friends whom he had trusted in darker days and who had never been found wanting.

The pressure, unfortunately as great as ever, for appointment in the civil service was the one great drawback to his peace of mind. The applicants would not be satisfied, and kept up their importunities in and out of season. Mr. Wade, who would have been President had Andrew Johnson been impeached, called upon President Grant after he had been in the executive mansion some weeks and congratulated him, and the President replied that he was not sure the Presidency was a thing to be desired, on account of the annoyances that hedged about the incumbent as a result of the impossibility of satisfying the demands of all his friends. Mr. Wade advised him to be master of the situation, to please himself, and to let those who were disappointed murmur as they wished. He said, for himself, he was delighted to go into retirement, and, feeling that he had done his duty faithfully, he had no regrets but that of leaving his friends. The parting between these two men, who had both played so conspicuous a part in national affairs, was most touching.

President Grant was unfortunately situated, because of the number of men whom he knew to be eminently qualified for the various positions, and the comparatively few positions to fill. His cabinet were equally embarrassed in the matter of choosing among the multitude, who came favorably indorsed by men who had been with Grant through the war. Many were the heart-burnings, and, as a matter of fact, many mistakes occurred in the selections that had finally to be made. Subsequent troubles brought upon the administration by the action of these appointees caused President Grant great suffering and vexation of spirit, and involved him in difficulties that it required a long time to outlive.

In the reorganization of the Senate, Reverend J. P. Newman, pastor of the Metropolitan Church, was made chaplain; Mr. George Gorman, of California, was made sergeant-at-arms. Mr. Blaine was re-elected speaker of the House, and immediately confronted a galaxy of as able men as were ever in that body. His first duty was to solve a most difficult problem in assigning the chairmanships of the committees, with such men to choose from as Logan, Garfield, Banks, Schenck, Dawes, Allison, Windom, Holman, Brooks of New York, Williams, Orth, Myers, O'Neil, Shellabarger, Wilson of Indiana, Wilson of Iowa, Butler, Lochridge, Bingham, Stoughton, Paine, Wheeler of New York, Ingersoll, Cook, Cullom, Farnsworth, Frye, Hale, Judd, and a legion too numerous to mention. Mr. Blaine was then young and vigorous, and probably the most promising statesman of the nation. His administration of the speakership was, without doubt, the most brilliant in the history of Congress, spanning the most important epoch of the nation. There were then, perhaps, more critical occasions when the great skill, knowledge, and quick perception of the speaker were necessary to avoid serious trouble than during any other period. Mr. Blaine was ever ready for any emergency, at times displaying diplomacy, tact, and a memory that had been unequalled by any other parliamentarian.

I remember once listening to some debate upon postal matters wherein Tucker, of Virginia, was criticising the action of the post-office authorities for throwing out matter deemed unmailable on account of its political character. Mr. Blaine was in the chair. As quick as a flash he beckoned some one to the chair and took his place on the floor. As soon as Tucker had finished, Mr. Blaine addressed the chair, saying: "If the gentleman from Virginia will permit, I should like to ask him a question." Mr. Tucker assented. Mr. Blaine continued: "Were you not attorney-general for the State of Virginia during the administration of Henry A. Wise as governor of Virginia, and did not you decide that a post-office official in the State of Virginia had committed no offence by the destruction of copies of the New York *Tribune?*" This question Mr. Tucker admitted to be quite true, and thereby lost the whole point of his argument in the case then under discussion. That evening we were dining with Mr. Blaine, and as I sat on his right I remarked to him that I was astonished at his memory. He told me that at the time of Tucker's decision he was publishing a paper up in Maine, and remembered writing an editorial on the subject, but that he had quite forgotten the whole thing, and had never thought of Mr. Tucker being the former attorney-general of Virginia until attracted by his utterances. It flashed through his mind that he must be the man, and, seeing his opportunity to disconcert and defeat him, he determined to make the inquiry. Such remarkable instances of his great ability were of frequent occurrence. Before the close of the first session the House of Representatives had reason to be proud of its speaker and to congratulate itself upon having elected James G. Blaine.

Immediately after the inauguration ex-President Johnson returned to his home in Tennessee, where in a speech he repeated his eulogy upon himself and his anathemas against the Republican party. Mr. Seward returned to Auburn, New York, where he spoke in glowing terms of President Grant, prophesying that his administration would be a blessing to the country. The remainder of Mr. Johnson's cabinet went to their respective homes. In a brief time everything was adjusted to the change of administration and the affairs of the nation proceeded as if nothing had occurred.

Among the callers at the White House soon after the occupancy by President Grant and his family was General Robert E. Lee, who came to Washington to visit his wife's kinswoman, Mrs. Kennon, of Tudor Place, Georgetown. Mrs. Kennon was the niece of George Washington Parke Custis, father of Mrs. Lee, and occupied for many years her home in Georgetown.  Her husband was on board the ill-fated *Princeton* at the time of the explosion of the Stockton gun during Tyler's administration, when so many distinguished persons who were members of the excursion party lost their lives.  The greeting between Lee and Grant was very cordial, but General Lee could not have been otherwise than embarrassed; hence he remained but a short time.

One of the first appointments made by President Grant was that of General James Longstreet as surveyor of the port of New Orleans as a recognition of the reconstructed Confederates.  They were warm personal friends, the memory of their happy days at West Point having survived the stormy days of warfare, and President Grant desired to show his magnanimity and good faith in his wish to encourage those lately in rebellion to renew their loyalty to the government. General Longstreet, who had nobly stuck to a bad cause, and more nobly acknowledged his error when defeated, was therefore a fitting representative of his section.   General Longstreet has since occupied other honorable positions and always to the credit of himself and the United States.   I saw not long since in the newspapers a most interesting description of a banquet given in Atlanta, where a meeting between General Sickles and General Longstreet was the initiative of a most enthusiastic and delightful reunion of survivors of the two great armies. The speeches were eloquent, the music fine, and the picture of Sickles and Longstreet clasped in each other arms, with tears trickling down their cheeks, must have touched the sternest hearts.   General Mosby was appointed by President Grant, as also a number of others.   Thus the great conqueror became the great benefactor of those whom he had conquered, and was the first to inaugurate sectional harmony and the rebuilding of the devastated Southern States, culminating recently in the celebration of the fiftieth anniversary of the battle of Gettysburg, July 1, 2, and 3, 1863, by a reunion of the Blue and the Gray, furnishing a spectacle never before witnessed in any other country. The policy of General Grant doubtless opened the way for the reunited country which exists to-day, and it is not too much to say that the nation owes General Grant a debt of gratitude, not only for his brilliant military achievements, but for his widsom and magnanimity which won back to the Union those who were in rebellion against its preservation.

The White House at that time was not what it is to-day. During the Civil War Mr. Lincoln permitted every one who desired to see him, whether through curiosity, friendliness, or on business, to have free access to the executive mansion, and as a result the wear and tear on everything in the house was something frightful. The excitement which attended Mr. Lincoln's assassination brought great throngs, who were not refused admission to pay their respects to the sacred remains of the dead while they lay in state in the east room. When Mr. Johnson and his family succeeded Mr. and Mrs. Lincoln in the staid old mansion they found everything in a shabby condition. Be it said to the credit of Mrs. Patterson, who directed Mr. Johnson's household affairs, that she did the best she could to make the White House habitable without occasioning great expense to the Government. She had the carpets, curtains, and upholstery cleaned, remade, and put in place with as much economy as if she had been paying the bill out of her own purse. The style of furniture, draperies, etc., was out of date, and was never beautiful in either style or color. The dear lady could not accomplish very much with the small appropriation that was made for the repairs in the White House. Congress had at that time a very different idea of the necessities of the home of the President from the one it holds to-day. Americans had not arrived at an appreciation of the gorgeousness of European palaces and the requisites of the home of the ruler of the country. When President and Mrs. Grant moved into the White House, March 5, 1869, they consequently found it in a very deplorable condition, to say nothing of its hideous appearance. I remember well the bright green curtains with gay trimming which used to hang in the state dining-room. Congress was more generous in its appropriation for the repairs necessary at this time than it had been previously. General O. E. Babcock was authorized to negotiate for many changes, refurnishing and redecorating during the summer of 1869.

The relations between General Logan and President Grant were so intimate that we were constantly summoned to the White House for formal and informal dinners, lunches, and receptions. I was very familiar with the economies and efforts of Mrs. Grant to utilize everything that could be retained in the executive mansion, and to make it as attractive with as little expense as possible. General Babcock had exquisite taste, and had a wonderful ability in the line of duty to which he had been assigned. Mrs. Grant was so gentle, so kind, and so gracious to every one, that she doubtless received more people than any of her predecessors. She was the same thoughtful, generous, devoted wife and mother, whose gentleness and loyalty to her family and friends made her equally beloved with her husband by the whole nation. After General Grant's election to the Presidency, and their final establishment in the White House, she was still the unpretentious, sincere friend of the unfortunate. Among the first guests invited to the executive mansion were her old associates whom she had known in her early days of adversity. Nothing she could do for these dear friends, who had been so much to her before fortune had smiled upon them, seemed onerous. Her only grief was that the President could not provide each one of the many with lucrative positions, and thereby improve their conditions in life. Many sought her aid, and were never turned away impatiently. She at least made an appeal for them. Every member of President Grant's cabinet had stories to tell of Mrs. Grant's kind heart. Every Christmas the asylums, hospitals, and charitable institutions in Washington received donations from Mrs. Grant, while the members of her family and her friends and their children were most generously remembered. She was the veritable "Lady Bountiful" in more than one household. Her greatest fault, if she had faults, was her extreme leniency. She could never discipline either her servants or her children, her kind heart always suggesting some excuse for misdemeanors or neglect of duty. She was never so happy as when planning entertainments and indulgences for her children and their multitude of friends. The basement of the White House was reserved for the boisterous games of the boys who were always with "Buck" and Jesse, Fred, the elder, being then at West Point. Nellie, with her companions, had full sway on the upper floor. Scarcely a Saturday passed without a large theatre-party of children from the White House and the homes of the cabinet officers, especially if the amusement column of the newspaper contained anything attractive for children.

President and Mrs. Grant entertained constantly. There were always guests staying in the house, for whom entertainments were given. They were especially fond of having young people with them. They entertained more distinguished people and scions of royalty than any other occupants of the White House. Among them were the Duke of Edinburgh, Earl de Grey, Lord Northcote, and the young Prince Arthur of England, the Grand Duke Alexis of Russia, King Kalakaua of Hawaii, and the first Japanese and Chinese ministers after the signing of the Burlingame treaty. We were present at the state dinners and receptions tendered these celebrities, and have since sat at the table of royalty more than once, and are proud to say that in no wise did the latter surpass in bounty, elegance, and good taste the entertainments of President and Mrs. Grant.

It must be remembered that the Joint High Commission, composed of more distinguished men than had ever served on such a commission, was in session in Washington during that winter. The usual official state dinner was given, of course, but, in addition to that, President and Mrs. Grant gave a reception in honor of Earl de Grey and his associates. Mrs. Grant was assisted by Mrs. Sharpe, Miss Washburne, Miss Pelt, and myself. The appointments of this reception surpassed anything that had previously been given in the White House. Lady Thornton, with her tall, spare figure and dignified dress, accompanied the aristocratic Lady MacDonald, whose brunette complexion and dark hair were in striking contrast with the blond hair and fair complexion of her chaperon, Lady Thornton. In contrast to them was the superb figure of Madame Catacazy, magnificently dressed and crowned with that beautiful head of hair for which she was so generally admired.

The whole Diplomatic Corps, the judges of the Supreme Court, members of the Senate, the House, and many other official dignitaries were in attendance on this rare occasion. The press was represented by Horace Greeley, David A. Wells, Horace White, Samuel Bowles, Charles Nordhoff of the *Herald*, Sands, Minturn, Marshalls, Halstead, Samuel Read, Gobright, Benjamin Perley Poore, and John W. Forney. The usual number of senators and representatives were in attendance, also a large contingent of the army and navy.

A few evenings later Hon. Zachary Chandler, of Michigan, who occupied one of the most beautiful homes in Washington, on H Street between Fourteenth and Fifteenth, gave a very large reception to the commission, many of the persons above enumerated being among the guests who were glad to honor our British friends. Members of the cabinet also gave dinners and receptions in honor of the commission, all of which were brilliant affairs, and must have made a very favorable impression upon the British members, as the son of Lord Northcote subsequently married Miss Edith Fish, daughter of Secretary Fish.

Neither the President nor Mrs. Grant could ever have been considered a fine conversationalist; no one, however, partook of their hospitality who was not charmed by them both, because of their sincere and unpretentious cordiality. President Grant was full of sly fun, and particularly enjoyed a joke at Mrs. Grant's expense, and often perpetrated one himself. Her frankness and pronounced opinions frequently gave him opportunity to turn what might sometimes have proved an embarrassing situation, particularly when her views were in contravention to those of a guest or host, Mrs. Grant never remembering individual characteristics or histories. Her noble nature would never have permitted her to wound any one, but she often failed to remember that Mr. and Mrs. So-and-so had been twice married, were or were not temperance leaders, Protestants, or Catholics, and of such other personal tastes or opinions as to make it dangerous to express oneself too frankly. The President at such times would lead her on to her own undoing, and then chuckle over her embarrassment, as one has seen brothers do when teasing their sisters. The absolute harmony of their domestic lives was ideal. The boasted domestic bliss of our ancestors in the early days of the republic furnishes no history of a happier or more united pair than the General and Mrs. Grant.

From the hour of Grant's entering upon his duties as the President of the United States the political caldron began to boil; and, while the Republican party which had elected him was greatly in the majority, there were the same rivalries among men that have always existed, and the same vexatious problems in regard to national affairs which had to be settled.

Reconstruction of the States late in rebellion was, by no means, the smallest of these problems. Smarting under the whip of adversity and failure, the people of the South naturally resented the advent of Northern men into the Southern States. They resented the tendency of these men to occupy representative positions when the majority of the support of their ambitions was the colored race, so lately the slaves of these same Southerners. The colored men themselves were not without ambitions and were numerically in a majority in many localities, and this majority was greatly increased by the disenfranchisement of those lately in rebellion. Therefore they became candidates for representative positions, as well as places of trust. Conflict between these two elements was inevitable, and waxed hotter and hotter in the States where the negroes were in greatest numbers.

It may have come from prejudice acquired in my youth in regard to the colored race, but I must confess that when I first visited Richmond, and, on going into the Capitol, saw the negro members of the House and Senate of the Virginia legislature occupying the places that were once filled by the great men of Virginia, the spectacle was repulsive to me. I could readily understand that a true Virginian could not do otherwise than resent the conditions that had brought about such a situation. The débris and the desecration that had almost destroyed that beautiful capitol made one heart-sick, and I turned away with unspeakable disgust and the feeling that it would take a much longer time than it really has taken to adjust political affairs in the late Confederate States.

The tragedies of the early days of reconstruction are matters of history, and are not a part of my story. I make this digression to recall the chaos which confronted President Grant, who had had previously no sort of experience in legislative or executive affairs beyond those of a military character. Reports of outrages in almost every State south of the Mason and Dixon line, the evident wrong on both sides, and the responsibility for the protection of human life weighed heavily upon the chief executive. Grant appreciated that he was without power to issue orders as he had done when he was in command of a great army.

All the winter of 1869–70 we were subject to daily startling reports of public scandals, defalcations, and high-handed outrages. The reckless extravagance practised during the war had so demoralized the money-making people of the country that they were ready to organize any sort of scheme out of which they could expect a fortune. In addition to this, many men who had lately been in the service had gone West and were undertaking stupendous enterprises for the development of the then Far West. They were asking subsidies from Congress to build railroads and carry on various projects that would expedite the advancement of the new States and Territories west of the Mississippi River. President Grant was so trustful of his friends that he was oftentimes greatly deceived and placed by charlatans in unenviable positions. Contractors whose occupation was gone had to turn their attention from furnishing supplies for a great army to industrial undertakings which had to be watched to avoid criticism and national scandals.

General Logan was then a member of the House, and having been elected commander-in-chief of the Grand Army of the Republic, and a representative-at-large from the State of Illinois, he had an innumerable constituency who made insatiable demands upon him. It required all of his time and much of my own to attend to his correspondence and to obtain information from the Treasury Department in regard to finances, customs, revenues, and the various branches of the Government that belong to the Treasury Department. From the War Department he had to obtain information about military affairs, the army, and the various military posts throughout the country; from the Navy Department, about the navy, its organization, the position of the various squadrons, and personal information as to the whereabouts and condition of the officers and seamen; from the Department of Justice, the information to answer all sorts of inquiries as to prisoners and the possibility of having them pardoned, and personal inquiries as to the condition of cases being prosecuted by the Government. From the Interior Department he had to find out about back pay and pensions and the various tracts of land subject to entry under the Government; also all about Indian reservations, Indian posts, and other important facts in reference to the various tribes of Indians. From the Department of Agriculture General Logan had to secure information in regard to agriculture and horticulture, the cultivation of our rich farming lands, as well as the distribution of seeds, plants, and agricultural reports; from the Smithsonian Institution, all sorts of information in regard to scientific matters. General Logan was also supposed to obtain for his clients what they wished to know in regard to fish and fisheries and the furnishing of spawn for the planting of the streams with the various fish that would thrive in the waters of certain localities. All this, together with the extensive personal correspondence of his constituents and the members of the Grand Army of the Republic of the whole nation, made a stupendous task which was not lightened in those days by stenography and typewriting. Many of General Logan's correspondents were grossly insulted if it were intimated that any of these letters were written by a clerk. They were supposed to be written by General Logan himself.

To satisfy these unreasonable demands, I cultivated the art of counterfeiting the general's penmanship and signature, so that many thought they were receiving letters from the general which I had written out and signed. In fact, the general had only time to sign the most important ones, and I must not forget to add that a voluminous correspondence was going on all the time in regard to local political affairs. More than once we appreciated that "brevity is the soul of wit," especially when these correspondents were rather long-winded. I remember one letter, which we took the trouble to measure, was written in a very close, fine hand on foolscap paper. When pasted end to end it reached the incredible length of thirty feet by actual measurement.

So intimate were the relations between General Logan and

his constituents and the members of the Grand Army of the
Republic that they thought he could accomplish everything
which they desired.   Not infrequently they had to be disappointed, and to reconcile them at long range to their disappointment and hold their friendship required skilful
diplomacy which often taxed one's strict adherence to the
truth.

We had removed from Willard's Hotel into a large brownstone house which formerly stood near the corner of New
York Avenue and Fourteenth Street.   Thus we were very
near the White House.   General Butler's residence on I Street,
Zachary Chandler's on H Street, Speaker Blaine's in the
row on Fifteenth Street between H and I Streets, General
Garfield's near the corner of I and Thirteenth Streets, made
it convenient for these dignitaries to come to our house, or
have General Logan go to theirs, to consult in regard to many
important measures before Congress.   These consultations
were often held after an informal dinner in one house or
another, and were most delightful affairs.   After dinner the
gentlemen retired to the library or parlor, and there could
indulge in the freest possible expression of views on public
affairs without the fear of interruption or of the omnipresent
newspaper reporter.

It may be imagination, but from knowledge of the way in
which affairs are handled at the present time I believe that public men really gave more time to their public duties then than
they do now.   I further believe that there were fewer instances
when members and senators paired with other members and
senators and went to attend to their personal affairs during
the session of Congress.   I know one thing, that General
Logan was so conscientious in regard to his duties as a representative and senator that he rarely absented himself from
the halls of Congress unless he was confined to our home by
illness.   It was an unusual thing to hear that it was impossible to have a quorum in the House or Senate on account of

absentees who had to be summoned by the sergeant-at-arms before the public business could proceed.

General Butler was then a member of the House. He used frequently to boast of his great friendship for Grant and at the same time insist that he ran the administration. President Grant facetiously said to a friend one day: "I understand that Butler thinks that he runs the administration. He comes up here with a dozen names for some appointment, and I can not see my way clear to give him more than one of the number for which he asks. After explaining all this to him, he goes away very well satisfied. It is a very different thing with Logan. He comes here with a dozen names which he wishes me to appoint to positions, and, after listening to his pleas and demands for some time, I try to provide for at least ten or eleven. Generally, he goes off with ten or eleven appointments, and I hear that he tells his friends he is sorry he has no influence with the Grant administration."

President Grant had as much confidence in General Logan in politics as he had in military affairs, and when he was worried over anything he generally sent for him to come to the White House to talk over issues in Congress which were under consideration.

There were a few men who had been conspicuous in the Confederacy, either in the army or in Mr. Davis's cabinet, who had been elected to represent their people either in the House or Senate. They had not lost any of their Southern fire or prejudice, and occasionally indulged in the most violent criticisms of the Grant administration and of officers in command of posts in the South. Grant knew that he could always depend upon General Logan's coming to the rescue, and more than once General Logan came home in a great state of excitement after having defended the administration or some officer who was in command of a military post in the South.

Mrs. Grant was ably supported on all social occasions by

Mrs. Matthews and Mrs. Colfax, the mother and the wife of Vice-President Colfax. Both Mrs. Matthews and Mrs. Colfax were charming, graceful women who appreciated their position and the obligation they owed to the people who had elevated Mr. Colfax to the second highest position within their gift. They realized that, should anything happen to President Grant, Mr. Colfax, by provision of the Constitution, would slip into the very highest position in the land. They were untiring in their efforts to be agreeable. They not only gave the social functions required of the Vice-President, but many more, because of their extensive acquaintanceship with people from every State in the Union, Mr. Colfax having previously been speaker of the House of Representatives.

The majority of the ladies of the cabinet were eminently fitted to grace their positions as wives of cabinet officers. Mrs. Hamilton Fish, of New York, as the leading lady of the cabinet, was one of the most superb women of her time. In imagination I can see her to-day as she appeared on all occasions, the personification of dignity, graciousness, and cordiality. Her manner put the timid at ease, and restrained the overpresumptuous. Notwithstanding her age, she was so vigorous mentally and physically that every one considered her much younger than she really was. Her style of dress was regal without the slightest suggestion of inappropriateness. She had mastered the manual of etiquette in her youth, and found, when she came to Washington, there was nothing new for her to learn, except the relative rank of officials and the Diplomatic Corps at the national capital. Her experience as a member of the best society and as the wife of Hamilton Fish, in the various positions he had held in the State of New York, fitted her to preside over the home of the Secretary of State. She was ably assisted by her daughters, Mrs. Benjamin and Miss Edith Fish, subsequently Mrs. Northcote, wife of the son of Lord Northcote. Mrs. Fish was punctilious in the observance of all the duties of the wife of the Secretary of State and next in rank to the wife of the Vice-President.

One morning Washington was thrown into a spasm of horror over the stigma brought upon society by the marriage of Senator Christiancy, of Michigan, to an obscure young German girl occupying an insignificant position in one of the departments. The disparagement between their ages and positions being considered appalling, a tremendous hubbub was raised. Senators' wives were indignant and vowed ostracism of the poor, unfortunate girl who dared to enter the sacred social senatorial circle as the wife of a man old enough to be her father, if not her grandfather.

Never a word came from Mrs. Fish, the recognized leader in social affairs. Mrs. Grant's position being fixed by Thomas Jefferson, the author of "Etiquette at the American Court," was not supposed to venture as to what was to be done with the offender against the dignity of the senatorial coterie.

While the excitement was waxing hotter and hotter, Mrs. Fish's carriage stopped at our door one Thursday morning at about ten-thirty o'clock. The footman came to the door, rang the bell, and handed Mrs. Fish's card to our servant, the footman saying: "Mrs. Fish's compliments to Madame Logan, and Mrs. Fish will be obliged if Madame Logan will grant her an interview about an important matter." I directed the servant to have Mrs. Fish shown into the parlor at once, and I came down to greet her, as I was naturally flattered by so early a call from Mrs. Fish, whom I honored and loved. She made quite sure we were alone, and then said: "I have come to talk to you about the Christiancy affair."

I replied: "Dear Mrs. Fish, I shall be delighted to follow you in the matter," her motherly smile assuring me that no ill boded the poor little unsophisticated victim of remorseless criticism and injustice. She then said: "I am glad you will agree to join me in a quiet vindication of the inoffensive girl who has been so mercilessly criticised. I want you to go with me this afternoon (senatorial day) to call on Mrs. Christiancy, and, if she is not too frightened and will see us, we will simply pay her the respect due a senator's wife, saying nothing about the excitement, invite her to call on us, and come away." I said: "I shall be glad to go with you, notwithstanding the fact that it is Mrs. Christiancy's place to call on me first. She probably does not know her duty, and I am sure will be grateful for the recognition."

We went to call about four o'clock and found Mrs. Christiancy in very unpretentious quarters, evidently much embarrassed by the notoriety which had been given her on account of Senator Christiancy's position as United States senator. She was a shrinking, modest young woman, who betrayed the fact that she was as guileless as a child. As soon as she recovered from her shyness, her face brightened up, and with innate grace she expressed her gratitude for the honor done her. After the announcement that Mrs. Fish had called on Mrs. Christiancy, and that Senator and Mrs. Christiancy had dined with Secretary and Mrs. Fish, no further adverse comments were made about the incongruous marriage of the doty senator.

Mrs. and Miss Boutwell, the wife and daughter of the Secretary of the Treasury, were plain, New England women of great refinement and reticence. The Boutwells then lived in a noted boarding-house on Twelfth Street, kept by the no less noted Mrs. Rines, where many of the most distinguished men of the nation and their families lived for years. There were few millionaires in official life in the '60's. Apartment houses were unknown. A majority of officials and their families lived in more or less pretentious boarding-houses and paid quite as extravagant prices for their rooms and board as are paid for the far more comfortable apartments of to-day. They had not the privacy and convenience offered by the furnished housekeeping apartments, now so numerous.

General John A. Rawlins, Secretary of War, lived in a modest house on the corner of M and Twelfth Streets. Mrs. Rawlins, like her husband, had very poor health. They had four children, the care of whom occupied much of Mrs. Rawlins's time.

George M. Robeson, of Trenton, New Jersey, was appointed Secretary of the Navy. He was a widower at the time of his appointment, but afterward married Mrs. Aulick, widow of Commodore Aulick. Mr. Robeson rented a commodious house on K Street, formerly occupied by Secretary Stanton, of Mr. Lincoln's cabinet. Both the Secretary and Mrs. Robeson were fond of society and understood the art of entertaining royally. They had travelled extensively and had always lived handsomely. Mr. Robeson was a veritable *bon vivant*. Soon after the 1st of January they began a series of entertainments which were long remembered by the fortunate guests who were honored by invitations to them. Later on Secretary Robeson built a large house on Sixteenth Street, where they continued their lavish entertainments. While Secretary Robeson was Secretary of the Navy, reverses overtook these hospitable people, and the auctioneer's voice was heard in the drawing-room, library, dining-room, and chambers of this pretentious home, crying: "Who bids?" for this, that, or the other many valuable treasures that the Secretary and Mrs. Robeson had collected. Secretary and Mrs. Robeson, like legions of others who live for a period in Washington society, finally passed on with none of the multitude whom they had entertained following them in their exit, when the clouds of adversity had overshadowed their pathway.

General George Williams, of Oregon, was appointed Attorney-General, greatly to the delight of his beautiful and ambitious wife, whose elevation from obscurity on the frontier to the wife of a United States senator had inspired her with an ambition which was destined to be her undoing. They moved into a large house on Rhode Island Avenue, near Connecticut Avenue, close to where Saint Matthew's church now stands.

In this gorgeously furnished house they lived in great splendor, notices appearing daily in the newspapers describing Mrs. Williams's rich gowns and elaborate social functions. Mrs. Williams became so elated over her sway that she undertook to change the time-honored rules of etiquette at the national capital. She induced Mrs. Grant to call the ladies of the cabinet together in the White House to consider the changes she deemed necessary. At the same time Mrs. Grant insisted that it was foolish and could not be done, but gratified Mrs. Williams's whim by calling the ladies together for a confidential talk about social affairs. The majority, in fact all but Mrs. Williams, agreed with Mrs. Grant that they had no power to change Jefferson's code of official etiquette. Mrs. Williams said she, for one, would not make the first call on the families of senators. She very unwisely so informed many of the senators' wives and insisted they must call first on her, as the wife of the Attorney-General. This provoked the indignation of the senatorial ladies and many of their husbands, among them Senator Matthew H. Carpenter, of Wisconsin.

Chief Justice Salmon P. Chase died, and General Williams's name, on account of his ability as a jurist and man of high character, was sent to the Senate as the proposed successor of Mr. Chase. The moment the Senate went into executive session Senator Carpenter made a violent speech against the confirmation of General Williams's name, making many charges against Mrs. Williams, accusing her of numberless peccadilloes, acceptance of presents without General Williams's knowledge from persons who had cases before the Department of Justice, presumption, and other undesirable qualities in the person of the wife of the Chief Justice. General Williams's confirmation was defeated, the real trouble originating in Mrs. Williams's arrogance toward the wives of senators who joined Carpenter in his determination to humiliate Mrs. Williams. Therefore, notwithstanding General Williams's masterly ability and distinguished statesmanship, they eventually retired under the whips of outrageous criticism.

Mr. Columbus Delano, of Ohio, was made Secretary of the Interior. Mr. and Mrs. Delano were wholesome, ingenuous people. They appreciated the honor which had been conferred upon Mr. Delano by his appointment as a member of President Grant's cabinet. It is possible that Mr. Delano was too honest a man to contend with the insidious cormorants who have ever besieged the Interior Department and, like many of his predecessors and successors, was unable to escape the entanglements of scandals that have ever pursued the Secretary of the Interior. Mrs. Delano was a motherly, unassuming, loyal wife and mother, who made no attempt to introduce changes in the mode of etiquette in Washington. She tried to conform to all the rules laid down for the members of the cabinet and their families. She gave all the entertainments, discharged all the duties supposed to be obligatory upon the ladies of cabinet officers' households, and into them she put real hospitality and pleasure. She extended a hearty welcome to her callers, repaid their visits as soon as she could, and acknowledged every courtesy extended her with a grace born of innate refinement.

The latter-day ungracious manner of receiving calls, and the almost universal custom of returning visits by sending cards through the mail or by footmen, was almost unknown. If the ladies of the cabinet and the wives of other officials felt it a tax upon their strength and time to receive callers once a week, they never made themselves disagreeable by expressing their distaste for their duties.

General Horace Capron, of Illinois, was chosen commissioner of the Agricultural Bureau, then a bureau of the Interior Department. General Capron, in addition to his fitness for the position on account of his knowledge of agriculture, hailing as he did from the great Prairie State with its wonderful agricultural resources, was a most accomplished and patriotic man, who soon elevated the bureau and its important work to a high place on the list of bureaus, and, doubtless by the methods he introduced, paved the way for its becoming a department. Mrs. Capron was a lovely woman. Their house on N Street, near the corner of Twelfth, became worthy of being added to the official list. Their receptions were largely attended, proving their popularity. During the visit of the Japanese embassy at this time it was discovered that the Japanese visitors were really a commission sent to secure teachers and agents from every department of the Government to go to Japan to teach the Japanese Western civilization. The Japanese also desired to learn data connected with every phase of a republican government, as well as finance, agriculture, and various industries.

General Capron accepted an appointment under the Japanese Government, and went to Japan to teach them agriculture. Many other Americans returned with the visitors to engage in initiating these Orientals in American methods of doing things, which probably partly accounts for the rapid advancement of the Japanese.

Hon. John A. Creswell, of Maryland, was appointed Postmaster-General. He was an eminent lawyer, and his administration of the Post-Office Department was the most successful of any up to that time. He was a man of ambitions, and his beautiful house on the corner of Eighteenth and I Streets is still the property of Mrs. Creswell. In this palatial home General and Mrs. Creswell gave superb dinners and receptions, and extended to all of their guests a warm welcome. General Creswell had occupied a prominent position in the State of Maryland; therefore Mrs. Creswell had much experience in the matter of entertaining, and, being a person of unusual amiability and charm, won the admiration of every one.

Every member of the cabinet and his family delighted to carry out all the usual schedule of social affairs, and, as the city was full of visitors from every city in the Union, it was probably as brilliant a winter as ever was passed in Washington. I can not think that it is an imagination when I say that all officials of the Government worked more assiduously than they do to-day. It might have been because of the fact that there were all sorts of matters that had to be attended to promptly. Absenteeism from the cabinet or any other branch of the Government was a very rare thing, and I shall always believe that every one did his part nobly. But for the jealousies and political rivalries, it would have been one of the most delightful winters ever known in Washington.

Admiral and Mrs. Porter were among the hospitable entertainers in the city in their handsome home on H Street. Admiral and Mrs. Dahlgren were for some time at the navy-yard. Mrs. Dahlgren, with her genial disposition, literary taste, and unusual intelligence, made their entertainments among the most popular in the city. The receptions of Professor Henry, of the Smithsonian Institution, and his interesting family were especially charming, as they had something out of the usual to show from the wonderful scientific collections under his supervision. Hon. Alexander and Mrs. Shepherd gave lavish entertainments. I regret that space forbids a more extensive description and enumeration of social affairs which were once so attractive in Washington.

# CHAPTER XI

WHILE affairs socially were moving so smoothly there were many important matters arising in Congress. There was a proposition to remove the capital to Saint Louis, as a more central location for the capital of the United States than that of the District of Columbia. General Logan championed the movement for the removal of the capital, on the ground that the present location was made at a very early time in the history of the Government, and the vast area west of the Alleghanies had not been considered by white men and was only inhabited by the various tribes of Indians and aborigines that were to be found in what subsequently became the States of Illinois, Wisconsin, Michigan, and the great territories that have added many new States to the galaxy of the Union.

While the movement may have been abortive, and from a historic point of view justly failed, it had the effect of arousing a spirit of pride in the citizens of the District of Columbia, and caused them to become active in the introduction of improvements of all kinds, especially in the municipal government. They succeeded in organizing a Territorial government for the District and in appointing a governor and a secretary of state, and in organizing a Board of Public Works, who deserve great credit for the transformation of the city of Washington from a slow-going Southern city of magnificent distances and void of every evidence of beauty and progress into the progressive and beautiful city of to-day. But for the indomitable courage, unfailing energy, and patriotic devotion of such men as Alexander Shepherd, Crosby S. Noyes, J. W. Douglas, A. B. Mullett, Kilburn Claggett, and others, the movement for the removal of the capital to the West might have succeeded, and Washington would never have attained its great beauty and attractiveness. The Board of Public Works employed skilful engineers who levelled the perpendicular hills and filled up the deep chasms that had made Washington unattractive and impracticable. Pennsylvania Avenue being the first street in the city to be paved with modern paving, the completion of the work was an event fraught with so much importance that it was celebrated by a great carnival.

This seemed to be the beginning of the prodigious work of the Board of Public Works and those in authority in the Territorial government. Washington had been fortunate in having secured years before, as superintendent of the botanical gardens, that wonderful genius William Smith, the great Scotch horticulturist. Previously the botanical gardens had done little else than furnish plants, seeds, and floral specimens for the members of Congress. William Smith had become greatly interested in L'Enfant's wonderful plan for the capital of the United States, and had, as far as he could, planted trees along the streets and avenues of the city. The Board of Public Works interested him enthusiastically in their scheme to beautify Washington, and in a few years they had accomplished such wonders as to make a proposition for the removal of the capital seem ridiculous, and again confirmed forever the action of the earlier commissioners in making Washington the immovable capital of this great country.

This question created the most intense interest, and the galleries of Congress were crowded day after day. Be it said to the everlasting shame of the then citizens of Washington, and of many representatives in Congress, that they heaped such ignominy upon Governor Shepherd and his associates that he departed from Washington a heart-broken man, and sought a home in old Mexico, where he lived until his death a few years ago. Others of his associates were accused of limitless graft, and their families have since had a great struggle for existence. Time has vindicated these men, but, alas, too late for them to have had the satisfaction of knowing that their herculean achievements had at last been appreciated.

Another question that was all-absorbing was the reduction of the army to a peace basis. It might have been easy to solve the problem of mustering out regiments and officers down to the peace standard, but to do so without readjusting the salaries of those that were to remain would have created universal resentment. Therefore General Logan, as chairman of the committee on military affairs in the House, had to work very hard and call into conference men interested in the army and its requirements, who were both in and out of Congress. Personally, he had no desire to reduce the salary of the General, Lieutenant-General, and the officers of higher rank, but as it was deemed necessary to reduce the pay of commissioned and non-commissioned officers, it seemed unfair to allow the officers of higher rank to retain the same pay they received during the war. These men, however, had most gallant records, and made many friends who, looking at it from a personal standpoint, were anxious, as far as possible, to keep up these officers' pay to the war standard. This question can be said to have been among the first to bring about a break of friendship between General Logan and General Sherman, who was then General of the Army.

There were quite a number of military men in Congress whose constituents demanded that a reduction of the army should be accompanied by a reduction of the salaries of the higher officers of the army. General Logan felt that the private soldier, non-commissioned and subordinate officers were not receiving too much pay, but that the higher-rank officers' pay was greatly out of proportion when compared to that of the lower-grade officers. Therefore, he began to scale the salaries from the General of the Army down, and reported a bill providing that the General should receive $12,000 instead of $19,000 a year; the Lieutenant-General, $10,000 instead of $14,000; the major-generals, $8,000 instead of $10,000; brigadiers, $5,000 instead of $7,000; colonels, $3,500; lieutenant-colonels, $3,000; majors, $2,500; captains (mounted), $2,000; captains (foot), $1,800; first lieutenants, $1,600; second lieutenants, $1,400; the pay of the non-commissioned officers and privates to remain unchanged.

General Sherman wrote a long letter to the committee, bitterly complaining of the injustice of General Logan's plan, but the schedule was received with so much favor, as being eminently just, that General Logan carried his point, and his bill providing for the reorganization of the army on a peace basis was adopted.

All this meant a great deal of work. At that time I was so occupied with hunting up facts about the armies of every country and the rules which had governed our army from the time of the Revolution that I had little time to do anything else. I really enjoyed making researches for the general, so that he could take up the question when not engaged at the Capitol, and thus I enabled him to get at the very best possible basis upon which to report his bill.

In the midst of the discussion of the army bill reports of scandalous conduct on the part of members of Congress were rife. From time immemorial there have always been delinquents who have, by their improper and dishonest practices, brought harsh criticism down upon public men. Many Northerners had gone South and established homes in the different States lately in rebellion, some investing their all in these homes and business enterprises, which they subsequently were forced to defend with unparalleled heroism. Unfortunately, some of these men were very unworthy, and removed to the South thinking that they would have a greater opportunity for political preferment, and to become conspicuous in public affairs, than they would ever have in the North. They expected to profit by the ignorance of the colored people, and in that way to monopolize the offices— both State and national. There were many of these "carpet-baggers" in Congress, and some of them were a disgrace to that body and to their country. It began to be whispered that some of these gentlemen were selling their appointments to cadetships at West Point and Annapolis, and that one member from North Carolina—one Whittemore, who posed as a Republican and an honest man—had sold a cadetship to West Point for the paltry sum, as I remember it, of three hundred dollars.

Charges were made before the military committee. General Logan investigated the matter thoroughly, summoning before the committee all persons who were supposed to have had something to do with the transaction. He succeeded in bringing before that committee indubitable evidence of the truth of the accusation. Led by General Logan, the committee reported the matter fully to the House with the recommendation that Whittemore be expelled. General Ben Butler was a conspicuous figure at this session. He was very fond of antagonizing men like General Logan, but he did not understand General Logan as well as he thought he did. Whittemore went to Butler and begged Butler to defend him on the floor of the House. I shall never forget the scene, as I sat in the gallery and watched the proceedings the day the Whittemore case came up. Every inch of space on the floor and in the galleries was occupied. General Logan, as chairman of the military committee, soon after the morning hour addressed the speaker to make his report on the case. He had not gone far with his remarks and the reading of the report when General Butler arose in his place and attempted a defence of Whittemore. General Logan had been advised that Butler would probably do this, so he quietly hunted up the statute which forbids a member of Congress to act as attorney for another member in any case before the House. He merely asked Mr. Butler whether he wished to be considered the attorney of Mr. Whittemore. Without hesitation Mr. Butler replied that he did wish to be so considered, whereupon General Logan read the clause of the statute mentioned, which fell like a pall on General Butler and the whole House and galleries. Butler stammered a disclaimer, explaining that it was a matter of sympathy on his part. General Logan followed this up by a scathing rebuke to a man who would undertake to apologize for a criminal who had violated the law, and who, as a member of Congress, had disgraced his State. One of the general's greatest gifts was that of eloquence as a prosecutor, and perhaps no greater arraignment of a criminal has ever been heard in the House of Representatives. His plea for the preservation of the honor and integrity of the members of the House has never been equalled. General Butler withdrew from the floor of the House, but got little sympathy from his friends on account of his downfall in the attempt to defend Whittemore. Whittemore was driven from the House in disgrace as he should have been.

I may be wrong and may overestimate General Logan's keen sense of honor and integrity in representing the people, but I can not help feeling that if those who came after him had been as strong champions of the preservation of the honor of members of the House and Senate as was General Logan, there would not have been the very many scandals that have reflected upon our national and State legislators in these later years.

In the month of April General George H. Thomas died.

He was mourned throughout the whole nation as a gallant soldier. Memorial services were held throughout the country. General Logan, being the commander-in-chief of the Grand Army of the Republic, caused a meeting to be held by the Department of the Potomac in Masonic Hall, which was then the largest auditorium in the city. The hall was profusely decorated with mourning, draped flags, and other evidences of the grief of the nation at the untimely death of this great soldier. General Logan was the orator of the evening, and paid a glowing tribute to the memory of General Thomas, forgetting, in his grief at the nation's loss, the personal differences which had existed between him and the dead soldier, thus giving another illustration of the unusual magnanimity and nobility of his own character.

On April 30 General Logan called the attention of the House to the conspicuous ingratitude with which the memory of General John A. Rawlins, late Secretary of War under Grant's administration, and the faithful adjutant-general of General Grant during the Civil War, had been treated, in that his remains were still lying in a vault in the Congressional cemetery, eight months after his death, and had not had honorable burial. He asked that a suitable place be selected, suggesting that General Rawlins's remains should be taken to Arlington and interred in that cemetery. Others joined in suggesting that a monument also be erected to General Rawlins. General Logan felt very deeply on this subject, as he always recognized in General Rawlins one of the most gifted men in the army and one of the most earnest patriots of the Civil War. As a result of this movement General Rawlins was buried in Arlington and a full-length statue of him was erected on the south side of Pennsylvania Avenue in Market Space, where it still remains.

The session was a very long one, and I remained in Washington until June, before taking the children to our home in Carbondale, Illinois. General Logan was very late in reaching home, but found plenty of work awaiting him. The candidates for the local offices of representative and senator were clamoring for him to come to help them in their campaign for election to the legislature. Political feeling ran high in the State and General Logan was busy canvassing. He was much embarrassed by the continued importunities of men desiring appointment to official positions. They believed Grant would not refuse him anything he might ask for his friends. He realized better than they did that there was a limit, and that there were innumerable petitioners for everything within the gift of the President. He tried, however, to do all he could for every applicant.

General Logan's friends insisted that he should enter the senatorial race before the legislature met on January 1, 1871. Ex-Governor Palmer and General Oglesby were also candidates. A majority of the candidates for both houses were men of high character and, if elected, would know no bosses or any power but the dictates of their own consciences and the maintenance of their principles in the selection of a United States senator. Their choice for United States senator would be based absolutely on their desire to elect the men whom they believed would serve the best interests of the great State of Illinois.

The three most popular candidates had splendid records in the Civil War. Two had occupied, with great credit to themselves and the State, the highest position within the gift of the people of Illinois. General Logan was then in Congress from the State at large, and therefore could be said to be enjoying honorable reward for his services. He was disinclined to accept the nomination of Congressman-at-large, preferring the position of United States senator. He had resigned his seat in Congress to go into the army, and felt that after five years of hazardous service in the army he had earned the position he desired. Therefore he finally agreed to take his chances in the senatorial contest. He went to

Washington December 1 for the beginning of the session. Returning to Illinois for the Christmas holidays, he decided to go at once to Springfield, the capital, to be present when the legislature met, and to enter the contest. We had adopted Miss Kate Logan, a distant relative, one of the talented and beautiful Logan sisters, aunt of Commander George Logan of the United States Navy. She was a fascinating girl with a charming manner and a fine, highly cultivated voice. We begged General Logan to let us go with him to Springfield, and, as it was hard for him to refuse any request from me, he consented. He secured a suite of rooms for us on the second floor of the Leland Hotel, kept by that prince of landlords, Mr. Horace Wiggins, who was untiring in his efforts to make us comfortable. The general had a suite of rooms on the first floor as headquarters, where men congregated to talk politics and discuss their plans.

I consulted Mr. and Mrs. Wiggins and told them I wanted to change the aspect of our rooms to make them as nearly homelike as possible. Our daughter, Dollie, was in school in Cincinnati; Baby John A. Logan, Jr., was with us in the hands of a good nurse, but I wanted him to be in our rooms much of the time. Mr. and Mrs. Wiggins obligingly took a personal interest in everything and very soon we had a large drawing-room with plenty of easy chairs, sofas, a piano, and other appointments found in a home. The citizens of Springfield gave us a warm welcome. Many ladies called and extended invitations for luncheons, dinners, teas, and receptions. We reciprocated by inviting them to spend much time with us in our rooms at the hotel. Kate sang and played by the hour, and our drawing-rooms soon became the rendezvous for a majority of the members and senators and young people of Springfield, who entered with enthusiasm into the spirit of the good time. I wish I could recall some of the good stories that were told or hear again the peals of laughter they provoked. They all enjoyed themselves. Every night it was long past the midnight hour before the happy parties broke up and our guests sought their rooms or homes in the city.

Among the members and senators were some of the ablest men in the State. In those days men who were incorruptible and independent in every sense of the word accepted nominations for the legislature. They had the courage of their convictions and were not subservient to the influences of corporations, trusts, or combinations. The majority were not self-serving, but patriotic, far-seeing men, loyal to their trusts and faithful in the discharge of their public duties. The most solemn among them enjoyed coming to our rooms, sitting in an easy chair listening to good music, stories, and anecdotes, or telling stories themselves. General Logan led them on by his own jocular disposition into forgetfulness of the passing of time. The newspaper correspondents—friends and foes— came and went at their pleasure. There was nothing going on that they were not permitted to know all about; hence they could not in conscience write anything disagreeable or indulge in criticism.

Colonel Clark E. Carr, of Galesburg, Illinois; General T. O. Osborne, of Chicago; General Thomas Scott; General Berry; Colonel William L. Distin; Colonel Beardsley, of Rock Island; Judge R. S. Tuthill; Colonel E. S. McCook; Colonel R. N. Pearson; Colonel Rowett S. D. Phelps; Cadet Taylor; General Shaffer; Captain Isaac Clements; and a host of others were in and out continually, doing far more effective work in influencing voters than if they had adopted the methods that are said to have been in vogue in later years. It was a new feature in politics, and I can not refrain, egotistical as it may seem, from incorporating the report of one of the correspondents in the *Evening Post* of January 6, 1871:

The levees which Mrs. Logan is constantly holding in her parlors in the Leland have not been properly "written up," but their interest is certainly sufficient to justify mention. The *Tribune* has gazed into Parlor No. 26 from the standpoint of a humorist, and the *Times* from the standpoint of a clown; and it is high time that the public is permitted to see it as it is. It may readily be admitted, to begin with, that it is one of the phenomena of this exciting struggle—one of its very pleasantest and most grateful features. Here, directly over the headquarters of the general himself, is a levee always in session presided over by Mrs. Logan herself, who is assisted by her husband's younger brother and his handsome cousin, Miss Logan. In this room all are welcome and all are graciously received, and to this room almost all the members of the first, second, and third houses have beat a retreat at some time during the heat of the contest. It is where they go to escape for a moment from the fetid atmosphere of politics. In Parlor No. 26 politics are not among the refreshments. It is an oasis of peace in a desert of wrangling. It is a retreat, a neutral ground which the combatants of both sides fly to, to get their soured hearts sweetened with music and their bewildered brains cooled by sensible conversation.

Mrs. Logan is a native of Missouri, transplanted to southern Illinois — a small, fragile lady with an attractive mobile face, a mass of turbulent black hair and sharp eyes selected to match it, a wide experience of the social world, a good fund of information, abundant wit, and a ready tongue freighted with complaisance and suavity. She certainly impresses very favorably all who come within her influence. Having accompanied her husband in the field, she is acquainted with camp life in its varied phases. At Belmont and Fort Henry, at Donelson and Vicksburg, she hovered on the edge of battle, and kept her eye fondly on one particular flag. Is it extraordinary that she should follow his fortunes with equal fidelity now? And is it anything less than infamous that her fair name should now be made the subject of insults in the Chicago *Republican*, whose editor, when a correspondent in the field, broke free bread at her table for weeks together and rode her husband's horses and drank gratuitously of the commissary whiskey? Strangers and lifelong enemies are safe from the outrageous calumnies of this young man; it is only those whose guests he has been that he assails.

Mrs. Logan dresses neatly and plainly: a black silk, edged with satin, point laces, a silken knot at the throat, and a gold chain. Her parlor is an exchange of suavities; she never herself introduces the subject of politics, but, if asked, has no hesitation in confessing that she is strongly prejudiced in favor of Logan, and in stating tersely why she thinks he ought to be sent to Washington. She is never aggressive or intrusive on this point, but is fearless and confident and exercises her woman's right of speech with such persuasive tact that there is no doubt whatever that she has made some votes for the coming man. Doubtless a round dozen of gentlemen from the unpaved districts have crossed that charming threshold, confident that they were for Oglesby or "neutral," who have ever since worked steadily for the swarthy little general, and haven't any idea what changed their minds. The fascinations are so thoroughly disguised that even the Oglesby man is disarmed in their presence, but he feels their potency.

This evening, about supper-time, Oglesby and Mrs. Logan, old acquaintances, met in the hall and after an exchange of compliments, a dialogue ensued, somewhat like this:

*Mrs. Logan:* "Ah, general, I fear you are forgetting the old-school politeness that used to become you so well; you have not called on me."

*Oglesby:* "Well, madam, the fact is that I am afraid to subject myself to your blandishments. You are making trouble here; I am afraid I might leave your presence a Logan man."

*Mrs. Logan:* "Now, general, don't joke; I would like to see you sociably; you would meet a good many pleasant people at my rooms; it would do you good."

*Oglesby:* "I am not sure about that. I wish you would leave town, Mrs. Logan. You see I am forgetting my politeness. But I really think it is an unfair advantage."

*Mrs. Logan:* "Not at all. You are suffering one of the disabilities of bachelorhood, as you ought. It seems to me obvious that General Logan should have the senatorship. He has not received any promotion since the year he volunteered for the army, and you have been governor ever so long. Now, general, you see you can be senator next time—or what do you say to Congressman-at-large?"

Mrs. Logan was as gracious as could be, and the fact that she did not mean to be impertinent rendered the last proposal exceedingly cunning, and the old soldier smiled a broad, deep, long, thoughtful, profound, and penetrating smile and withdrew, promising to think about it.

On January 17, 1871, at twelve o'clock, the two houses met in joint session. The vote was as follows: Senate—

Logan, 32; T. J. Turner (Democratic candidate), 18. House—
Logan, 101; Turner, 70; William H. Snyder, 2. Logan was
then declared duly elected United States senator, vice Richard
Yates, for six years from the fourth day of March, 1871.

A committee visited General Logan and announced the
good news to him, when he appeared before the assembly and
addressed them as follows:

*Mr. President, and gentlemen of the Senate and House of Representatives:*

I find myself at a loss for appropriate language to express my
high appreciation of the distinguished honor you do me in conferring upon me the position of United States Senator, and I can
only assure you that my heart wells up with gratitude to you;
and, through you, as their representatives, I desire to convey my
grateful acknowledgments to the people of Illinois. It is very
gratifying to me that I have been chosen with such unanimity by
political friends as to leave no serious wounds to be healed. The
contest has been one marked with a degree of kindness of feeling
among political friends that is very unusual, but highly commendable. The greatest respect has been and is entertained for the
ability, integrity, and generosity of those who sought the same
position at your hands.

To the interests, prosperity, and happiness of the people of
this State I am allied by the closest ties. Born in the midst of
this people, I have passed with them through the storms of adversity and the sunshine of prosperity. Their interest is my interest; their prosperity is my prosperity; their hopes and aspirations
are mine. All I have ever been or will be, I owe to the people of
this State. They have sustained me beyond that which I had a
right to expect. For that I owe to them a debt of gratitude that
I fear I shall never be able to pay. Whether I shall come up to
the standard fixed for me by my friends, or their hopes and anticipations be dashed to the earth, must be left to the future to dis-
close. I shall, however, enter upon my duties, giving whatever
of abilities and energy I may possess to the promotion of the interests of our whole country, but especially shall I devote myself
to the interests of that constituency which I shall immediately
represent; and trusting implicitly in Divine Providence to guide me
in the right direction, I hope to succeed in making you a faithful

senator. Again thanking you, with all the warmth of my heart, for your partiality in conferring upon me this great honor, I, for the present, bid you farewell.

It is a melancholy fact that with all our boasted progress along all lines of civilization the question of the election of a United States senator should have degenerated to its present level, and it is one of the incomprehensible questions why this should be. It would be considered disloyal to suggest that there has been a decadence of patriotism and that men of meaner minds have been destined to represent the people in the legislatures of the various States, that money has taken the place of higher motives, and that a majority are prompted to seek these positions by a desire to advance their pecuniary interest, expecting to receive a reward from wealthy and ambitious men for their support of these parties for the position of United States senator. They ignore altogether the very necessary qualities of patriotism and integrity so essential in all members of the United States Senate.

General Logan took his seat March 4, 1871. He soon found that election to the Senate multiplied instead of decreased his work. He was ambitious to comply with every legitimate request of the people of the State, and to co-operate with senators in their advocacy of measures for the general welfare of the country and nation. His comprehension of all subjects, and his—up to that time—tireless energies enabled him to perform stupendous labors. His personal relations with every member of the Illinois delegation were most cordial, notwithstanding his intense loyalty to his party.

In May, 1871, in connection with the delegation, he secured an appropriation of eighty-five thousand dollars for the improvement of the Illinois River and Hennepin Canal. Every movement for the development of the resources of his State claimed his faithful vigilance and earnest labors.

My own social duties were quadrupled, and I was determined that I should not be found ignorant of, or remiss in, the discharge of them. In addition, hordes of the people from the great State of Illinois, and especially from Chicago, were continually arriving in Washington. A majority of them hastened to find us and to claim our time to assist them in accomplishing the object of their visit, whether it was sight-seeing, seeking appointments, or a glimpse of society. General Logan knew that he could rely on me to assume the rôle of guide and chaperon and to secure the introduction to every sanctum of the capital which they wished to enter. He usually brought me a long list of engagements he had made for me to contribute to the pleasure of his visiting constituents.

Early in May I returned to Carbondale, as the general had concluded, after conferring with many of our friends, that it would be a wise thing for him to remove to Chicago. There existed at that time a sentiment in regard to the geographical location of the homes of senators, and Chicago claimed that it should be the residence of one of the senators from Illinois. General Logan had bought a house in Chicago sometime before, which a friend had been occupy-ing, intending to go to Chicago to practise law, if he had not gone into politics in 1866. We had always lived in southern Illinois, and it was a tremendous wrench to take our goods and gods away from Egypt, and to take up our abode in a great city. After Congress adjourned the general went to Chicago to have our house put in order for us, and I took charge of the packing, making good-by visits, and trying to reconcile these old friends to the change we were about to make. My part of it was no small task, and I had to explain over and over again "the reasons why." Finally, in August, we shipped our goods and bade good-by to friends who were very dear to us.

Our house in Chicago was located on Calumet Avenue, just north of the Twenty-second Street depot of the Lake Shore, about the middle of the block, with detached houses on the north and south sides of us.  The houses fronted west, the rear facing the lake.  We had broad lawns that extended down to the track of the Illinois Central Railroad, with no division fences, and it was a most beautiful location.  Here we spent many happy years during the interim between the sessions of Congress.  I was obliged to dispose of this home after General Logan's death, and have since had the painful experience of seeing it fall before the march of the resistless commercialism of Chicago.

We had not gotten our home settled when that fearful holocaust of October 9, 1871, swallowed all of Chicago north of Twelfth Street to Lincoln Park.  We had friends calling on Sunday evening, when we heard the continuous ringing of the fire-bell and went out on top of the house, where there was an observatory, to try to locate the fire.  In the northwest we saw the heavens lighted up by the flames, which were consuming the wooden houses and lumber in the lumber districts of northwest Chicago.  It seemed many miles away; so, after watching it for hours, we descended to our rooms, our friends departed, and we retired.  In the early morning we were awakened by a great confusion in the street and looked out upon our front lawn to find the whole of the block from Twenty-first to Twenty-second Streets occupied by every conceivable article of merchandise.  Men, women, and children were crying and wringing their hands, having come from the fire district to our locality as a place of safety.  The alleys in the rear of our barn were full of tremendous trucks loaded with goods.  We hastily dressed and came out to open our doors to welcome these frightened and stricken people.  On General Logan's going to the alley to see what he could do there, he found that the goods which J. V. Farwell & Company had rescued from the fire were being piled high in the rear of our barns.  He quickly had the coachman open the doors and, in a twinkling, almost every inch of space in the barn and its loft was occupied by cases of priceless laces and rare imported goods. Our first thought was that all the supplies would be cut off, as the gas-house on the north side had been exploded, and the gas was escaping from every main all over the city. We realized that we should be in total darkness when the sun went down. I hurried over to Twenty-second Street and bought from our grocer and butcher large quantities of supplies, including boxes of candles which we had to use for many days. We had no candlesticks, but in their place found that empty bottles served every purpose.

I shall not attempt to describe the horrors of many days and nights. I joined the army of people residing south of Twelfth Street who were, without exception, gathering together all they could get to take to the churches that were being used for hospitals and for sheltering homeless people. They had gone into old barns, residences, churches, and houses, and every place that furnished a roof for the people that had fled from their homes. General Logan and General Sheridan had had much experience in such catastrophes during the Civil War, and they rendered valuable service by assuming direction of the armies of men who were tearing down houses, and using the fire department as much as they could in breaking the fire line. Almost every one was worn out, and some were so exhausted that there was nothing to do but to lie down wherever they could get shelter. The patriotic and noble State of Illinois responded within a few hours with train-loads of provisions and supplies of all kinds for the immediate relief of the victims of the fire district. The world knows the generous response that came from all over the globe and of the long and tedious months when armies of men, women, and children had no resource but to visit the relief depots and have issued to them their daily supplies. When we look at Chicago to-day, we realize the situation during those unhappy early days of October, 1871. About one hundred persons, and tons of goods of delicate and valuable character were in our house for more than two weeks.

We had to have as many cooks as could be utilized in a private kitchen, and the range was going from early morning until late at night to furnish meals for these friends who had been deprived of their homes and abiding-places. The memory of meeting the survivors of families that had been swept by the flames from their homes through the darkness of that Sunday night will abide with me forevermore. We found men broken and weary, weeping like children because they knew not where their families were. We found women crying for their babes; babes crying for their mothers; wives in tears over the loss of their husbands and their homes. Hand-presses of Chicago and the newspaper presses of the neighboring towns and cities were busy publishing the names and location of persons, hoping in this way that their friends and families might learn of the whereabouts of their loved ones. Hundreds of families were reunited in this way who had not known for days how many of them were alive. The hospitality of the districts not included in the fire, and that of the towns and homes within miles of Chicago was taxed to its utmost. Many died and were borne to their last resting-places unattended by any member of their family, and but for the records that were kept, and the stories that were told before these poor creatures died, their fate would never have been known. Bodies were recovered from the tunnels and in out-of-the-way places where the victims had succumbed in their attempt to escape from the smoke, darkness, and confusion that reigned supreme for the hours between sundown Sunday night and Monday morning.

General Logan was more deeply impressed with the horrors of the Chicago fire than with anything he had ever experienced. His prodigious efforts in Congress as soon as it assembled in December, 1871, told the story of how deeply his great heart was stirred by the misfortune of his beloved city of Chicago. Through his efforts the Government did very much to enable the city to rise from its ashes. Probably Chicago would not be the city it is to-day but for this unutterable calamity which may have been a blessing in disguise. It roused an indomitable spirit in the men of that generation and those that have followed them which has never been exceeded by mankind.

In November, 1871, we returned to Washington and removed to No. 8 Grant Place, to a house occupied by Major and Mrs. Hayden, brother of Professor Hayden of the geological survey. The members of the Hayden family and ourselves being the only occupants of the house, it was more like our own home would have been than anything we had previously had in Washington. The house was new and well appointed, and Mrs. Hayden was a delightful housekeeper; hence we had all the comforts of a home without any of the cares and the indispensable vexations attending housekeeping. Katie Logan was with us, and we had a very delightful time on account of her wonderful musical genius. Every evening our parlors were crowded with friends who came to enjoy her music.

General Logan on his entrance into the Senate was made chairman of the military committee, greatly to the disgust of General Ames, who had been chairman of that committee prior to General Logan. General Logan was also second on the committee on judiciary, second on the committee on appropriations, and second on the committee on privileges and elections. The amount of work which devolved upon him as a member of these important committees was something prodigious. He had very little time for recreation, and constantly devoted himself to his duties. To the labors of the committees was added a voluminous correspondence, as he was commander-in-chief of the Grand Army of the Republic, and had so lately occupied the position of Congressman-at-large from the State of Illinois that his constituents did not relinquish their claim upon him, but desired him to attend to everything in which they were interested. The collection of pensions, back pay, and bounty, and the inquiries which followed the passage of his bill for the establishment of the geological survey also augmented the work of the daily grind very much. Naturally, I could not see my husband working day and night without also doing what I could to share in the burdens of the drudgery attending the detail of proper attention to these various interests.

Among the first things that confronted him was the contested election case of Ransom and Abbott of North Carolina. Abbott was a Republican and had demanded the throwing out of the votes cast for Ransom, which would have given him (Abbott) the majority of the North Carolina legislature, and secured for him a seat in the United States Senate. General Logan, though a steadfast Republican partisan, differed with the committee in his opinion of the case. Upon its submission to him, he asked for a delay of one week before making the report of the committee. He had, in a way, scanned the evidence and thought that to throw out Ransom's votes would be an outrage in view of the facts then existing. There seemed to be no evidence that any fraud had been perpetrated in the election of those members of the North Carolina legislature whose votes Abbott demanded should be thrown out. It further seemed from the evidence that was before the committee that, even if Abbott's demands were acceded to, he was not the choice of a majority of the legislature.

The amount of work that General Logan put on this case was beyond description. He came home one evening telling me that he had asked for the delay in submitting the report, but had previously sent his clerk to the Library of Congress to get such authority as parallel cases afforded, or cases bearing on these contested elections. The mail-wagon brought to our house that evening five bags of books from the Library of the Senate and the Congressional Library. These books were journals and reports of law cases. To read each of the cases and at the same time attend to the duties of

each day would have been impossible. When General Logan
had anything very important that he desired to do and wanted
to be sure he made no mistake about it, he always asked me
to hunt up the information for him, for he insisted that he
could trust me implicitly to give him the facts of a case
without perverting them, as is often done by secretaries who
are more anxious to please their chief than to disappoint him
in not finding material he desires.

Three days and three nights we stayed in the back parlor,
which was the general's office, working on this case, with the
exception of the few hours that General Logan had to go to
the Senate to be present during the session. We had our
meals served in our rooms, and never went to bed during the
three days and nights except for an hour or so in the early
morning. While he was at the Capitol I ran over these various cases, wrote on slips of paper what they were and the
points upon which they bore, and marked for him the paragraphs that were most important. When he came in, as soon
as we had our dinner he would take these volumes and read
only the paragraphs which I had marked for him. Notwithstanding the digest which I had prepared, it was almost impossible to have his report ready for the meeting of the committee at the end of the week. We had no such helps in those
days as stenography and typewriting; all this work had to
be done by writing it out in longhand, and after deciding which
cases had the strongest bearing upon the position he had
taken he wrote out his report, giving the authority, the case,
the page, and the paragraph in support of his decision. When
he asked for the delay in the submitting of the report, it was
to prevent the committee from making a favorable report on
the case and casting out Ransom's votes. When he had
made his argument before the committee he changed the
whole feature of the case, and an adverse report was made
upon the side of Abbott and in favor of Ransom. Naturally
we were pretty well worn out for a week afterward, but we

were young in those days and soon recovered from the over-taxing of our mental and physical strength.

January 1, 1872, President and Mrs. Grant gave the usual New Year's reception. There were most elaborate preparations made for the reception, as there was at that time a greater number of officers of high rank of the army, navy, and marine corps in Washington than have ever been there at one time before or since. The Diplomatic Corps was represented by distinguished men, as Washington had been considered an important post during the long years of the Civil War.

New Year's Day was bright and clear, and at an early hour—as the reception was to begin at ten o'clock in the morning—the streets were full of carriages en route to the White House. Mrs. Grant had invited the ladies of the cabinet and the Supreme Court and the wives of the more prominent members and senators. I was fortunate enough to be included on this list, and I shall never forget the remarkable splendor of the occasion. Every member of the Diplomatic Corps was in full court dress, wearing innumerable decorations. They were accompanied by ladies who, it seems to me now, were very superior in their gracious manners to those whom I have met in later years. The ladies' jewels were quite as dazzling as those of the orders worn by their husbands. Sir Edward and Lady Thornton; Baron and Madame Gerolt—who set the magnanimous example of giving the French fair such articles as she had been unable to use in the German fair for the relief of the wounded and unfortunate of the Franco-Prussian War—accompanied by her beautiful daughter, who subsequently took the veil in the Convent of the Visitation at Washington; the distinguished Spanish minister and his brilliant wife, wearing flame color and yellow, and resplendent diamonds half veiled by her rich Chantilly; Count Marquis de Chambrun, many years an attaché of the French legation, with his charming wife, a descendant of Lafayette; Madame Catacazy, wife of the

Russian minister, with her great beauty heightened by her wealth of golden hair, who created such a sensation by her magnificent dress and diamonds, represented the Diplomatic Corps.

The ladies of the cabinet who were not assisting in the reception accompanied their husbands and sustained themselves admirably as representative American women.

In the throng there were such distinguished persons as Gail Hamilton—Mrs. Blaine's cousin—Sydney Hyde, Mary Clemmer Ames, Miss Foote, John W. Forney, Ben Perley Poore, and many other representatives of literary circles, while Senators Fenton, Conkling, Chandler, Bayard, Morton, Ferry, Howard, Drake, Carpenter, Thurman, Edmunds, Frelinghuysen, Fessenden, William Pitt Kellogg, and hosts of others represented the Senate. Of the House, there was Wilson, of Iowa; Frye and Blaine, of Maine; Hawley, of Connecticut; Pomeroy, of Kansas; Farnsworth and Burchard, of Illinois, and many others whose names are associated with the stirring events of that era.

To this brilliant galaxy were added our army, navy, and marine corps, all in the full-dress uniforms of their respective branches of the service, wearing all the medals and gold lace to which they were entitled. Almost all of them were accompanied by wives or daughters, who, not wishing to be outdone in expressing their appreciation of the occasion, had worn their most beautiful costumes, many carrying magnificent furs.

The mantels of all the reception-rooms, the red, blue, green, and east rooms, were banked with most gorgeous flowers, while palms and pots of flowering plants were distributed in every available spot. The brilliant lights of the crystal chandeliers made it a veritable fairy scene. The well-known Marine Band, led by Professor Scala, with their red coats and blue trousers heavily trimmed with gold lace, played in the corridor and added much to the gayety.

President Grant was most democratic in his manner, and had

given instructions that none who came to pay their respects should be excluded from the White House. Consequently, an hour after the programme had been finished a long line of citizens and visitors, two abreast, passed through the White House, halting only long enough to speak to President Grant. It was after twelve o'clock when the last one had been gratified by a welcome to the White House.

Secretary Fish had the customary breakfast for the Diplomatic Corps, foreign relations committees of both houses, and other distinguished guests, who did full justice to the bounteous buffet feast. It was then the custom for persons receiving on New Year's Day to furnish refreshment, and it has been said that there were barrels of egg-nog used every New Year's Day in Washington. I regret, sometimes, that the good old custom of New Year's receptions with their accompaniment of beautiful ladies, flowers, music, refreshments, and cordial greetings has passed away. It seems that one should be able to make this day a happy one, to renew old acquaintances and make new friends, to start the year as it should be started—with good cheer.

The New Year's reception was the beginning of the social season, and was rapidly followed by state dinners and receptions in the White House, in the homes of the cabinet, in the homes of the Diplomatic Corps, justices of the Supreme Court, members of both houses of Congress, and prominent and wealthy people of Washington. As I remember it, no administration has exceeded that of President and Mrs. Grant's in hospitality. President Grant was very fortunate in choosing members of his cabinet who seemed to realize that they had to make acknowledgment of the honor which had been conferred upon them in some way besides the daily routine of properly discharging their official duties. There were hosts of beautiful women in Washington at that time who had been well-trained for the positions they occupied. Social events seemed less attended by commercial features than they are to-day. Men and women apparently laid aside everything for the purpose of greeting their friends and making them feel that they had time enough to devote to their entertainment.

As if to emphasize their welcome of General Logan and myself to the senatorial circle, we had many invitations for dinner, President and Mrs. Grant inviting us for the first state dinner of the season, notwithstanding the fact that the letter "L" was low down on the alphabetical list. Members of the cabinet and senior senators and their wives included us among their guests for the first dinners after New Year's Day. Those were delightful functions and we enjoyed them to the full.

Mrs. Kate Chase Sprague presided over the home of Chief Justice Chase. There could not possibly have been sisters more unlike each other than were the Chase sisters, not only in personal appearance but in disposition, talents, and characteristics. Nettie, though of a plainer face, was one of the most gentle, modest, retiring, and lovable characters that one could possibly imagine. Their mother had died when they were both quite young. Kate was the elder; hence, when she was in her teens she was mistress of her father's house, and presided over the executive mansion while he was governor of Ohio. Her remarkable beauty attracted much attention. Her famous Titian hair, peach-blow complexion, graceful figure, and bewitching manners seemed to have especially fitted her for the position which she was destined to occupy.

Soon after Mr. Lincoln's inauguration Mr. Chase was chosen Secretary of the Treasury and took up his residence in Washington in a commodious house on the corner of Fifth and E Streets, N. W., which was then considered an eligible part of the city. It was not long before his daughter Kate became the leader in society. Her inborn diplomacy enabled her to harmonize the discordant elements then existing in Washington and to capture the Diplomatic Corps, who were extravagant in their admiration of her brilliant conversational powers and incomparable beauty. Her devotees were innumerable, and no queen ever held a more imperious sway than did Kate Chase. Legions of suitors sought her hand, apparently without touching her heart. Finally Governor Sprague, the multimillionaire merchant of Rhode Island, joined the ranks of suppliants for her favor. After their marriage Mr. and Mrs. Sprague departed for Europe. The newspapers were full of reports of the lavish expenditures of Mrs. Sprague. Her wardrobe was equal to that possessed by crowned heads—priceless jewels and laces were added to her collection, and excesses of all kinds characterized the honeymoon of this ill-mated pair. Before their return home hints were given in the press that the old house of Sprague Brothers was approaching failure. Governor Sprague, however, was elected to the United States Senate. At the beginning of the session they took up their abode with Chief Justice Chase, and Mrs. Sprague resumed her accustomed sway as the wife of a senator.

Late in January, at the height of the season, sorrow came to us through the death of the illustrious Eliza Logan Wood, elder sister of our adopted daughter, Kate Logan. She had been one of the most brilliant actresses of her day. She played all the many rôles in legitimate drama for a female tragedian. She was the daughter of Cornelius Logan, one of the celebrated actors of his time. She was once a great favorite in the South and West, and on her benefit nights she was often the recipient of rare and valuable gifts. On one of these occasions a wealthy Southern planter, residing in the interior of Georgia, travelled many miles on horseback to see Miss Logan act, accompanied only by his faithful negro boy servant. The planter and his servant attended the play. He was enthusiastic over Miss Logan's acting, and was most anxious to convey to her some expression of thanks for the pleasure which she had afforded him. Taking a card from his card-case, he wrote above his address the words: "To Miss Eliza Logan, with the compliments of ———" and, pinning it upon the coat-sleeve of his faithful negro valet (worth at the then market price two thousand dollars), bade him present himself to his new mistress. The slave presented himself at the stage-door, and the management advised Miss Logan of his presence. She was much amazed, and, not knowing what to do with him during her nomadic career, resolved to return him. The following morning Miss Logan returned the slave to his owner, with an autographic letter couched in such terms that the planter was more than satisfied. This is probably the only instance in this country when a human being was ever presented to an artist as a token of esteem.

Miss Logan was so successful that she took care of her mother and sisters and when she was married had a large fortune in her own right. She married Mr. George Wood, retired from the stage, and continued to reside in New York until her death, January 15, 1872.

General W. W. Belknap had succeeded General John A. Rawlins as Secretary of War. He and his bride—for he had not long been married to his second wife—took up their residence on Lafayette Square in a house that was long considered a fatal place of abode on account of the tragic events that had taken place in and near the plain red brick, three-story building that was removed to make place for the present Belasco Theatre. This house had been occupied by Secretary William H. Seward at the time of the assault upon him when Mr. Lincoln was assassinated. Mrs. Belknap's death cast a shadow over the gayeties of the official circles.

In March a great sorrow came into our own household through the death of our adopted daughter, the talented and beautiful Kate Logan. Early in the month she expressed a desire to make a visit to her mother, who resided in Philadelphia. She had been such an assistance and had won so many friends that we were loath to do without her, but we appreciated her loyalty and devotion to her widowed mother, and therefore consented to her going. She had been in Philadelphia only a few days when we received a telegram that she was dangerously ill from peritonitis. I hurried to her bedside, and the moment I saw her I knew that death was near. I telegraphed to General Logan and to Doctor J. M. Woodworth, superintendent of the Marine Hospital Service, to whom she was engaged. They came at once and immediately secured the ablest skill in the profession, and everything that was possible was done to save her life, but all to no avail. She died in my arms, surrounded by her family, among them her brothers, Thomas A. Logan, of Cincinnati, and C. A. Logan, of Leavenworth, Kansas. Her father, Cornelius A. Logan, the distinguished tragedian, and other members of her family, were buried in Cincinnati, at Glenwood Cemetery, and so it was decided that her remains should be taken to that city. It was a long, sad journey, and cast such a shadow over our home, which she had made so bright by her gracious manners and lovely voice, that we could not rally for some time. I withdrew from further participation in social affairs during that session of Congress.

# CHAPTER XII

POLITICALLY excitement was running high.   Rivals of President Grant were busy in the manufacture of all kinds of
charges against and abuse of his administration.   Unfortunately, some of his appointees had not conducted themselves as
they should, and he was held responsible, though totally ignorant of their misdeeds.   James G. Blaine was ambitious to be
nominated for the Presidency, and it was said that he had
used the speakership in every possible way to secure delegates to the national convention which was to nominate the
candidates for President and Vice-President.   There was never
a more bitter campaign than that conducted before the holding of the national convention.   President Grant's friends—
General Logan among them—were so outraged at the methods
that had been used that they allowed themselves no respite
day or night in their defence of the administration.   It is
probable that General Logan's defence of President Grant
against the attacks of Senator John B. Gordon, of Georgia,
and other ex-Confederates who were then in the Senate,
together with those of the Sumner-Schurz coterie, has never

been equalled in fervor and vehemence. To General Logan probably belongs greater credit in rendering service to President Grant in the halls of Congress than to any other man.

At no time in the history of the Government has there been a greater number of able men in Congress than there was in the early seventies. Unhappily, ambition all too often attributes evil to the motives of rivals. Grant was naturally the only barrier in the road to the White House to each of the men ambitious to occupy it. He had reluctantly accepted the nomination for President in 1868, realizing that he had no training for an executive position. The Republican party would not listen to his objections, knowing that his name was a synonym for a victory. He had conscientiously and wisely administered the affairs of the Republic, and had advanced the United States to a high place on the roll of nations. Yet he and his followers were the targets against whom the shafts of the designing were levelled. Grant was held responsible for every act of his appointees—the whiskey-ring scandals, sale of arms to the French, and nepotism. It was said that he might have averted the grasshopper scourge in Kansas had he been equal to the position of President! Charges against the administration by the coterie determined to destroy Grant and able defence of him and his administration were heard daily in Congress. The galleries of both houses were crowded to suffocation with men and women eager to hear the eloquent men of both sides engaged in the discussions. Meanwhile conventions were being held in every district of the country to elect delegates to the national convention to be held at Cincinnati, in June, 1872.

The imbroglio between Charles Sumner and President Grant was especially bitter. Mr. Sumner was one of the most learned men in the Senate. He was commanding in his personal appearance—tall and straight as an arrow. His head was large and covered with heavy hair; his eyes were dark and expressive. He spoke with great earnestness. He had made a national and an international reputation by his opposition to slavery, and had suffered bodily injury at the hands of the slaveholding Brooks of South Carolina, which, together with his unwavering demand for the abolition of slavery made him the idol of the Whigs and Abolitionists.

A person once told Grant that Sumner did not believe in the Bible. Grant replied: "That is because he did not write it himself." Sumner had been elected to the Senate four times, first succeeding Daniel Webster, and had rendered splendid service to his country. All loyal people regretted exceedingly that the controversy between him and President Grant should have arisen. It was apparent to observers that Mr. Sumner's influence and powers were waning. He had brooded over his unfortunate marriage and separation from the widowed daughter-in-law of his old and cherished friend, Mr. Hooper, of Massachusetts, and, in addition, it broke him down to be obliged to endure the daily relentless excoriations of brother senators with whom he had previously been on most intimate terms. He died March 12, 1874, never having regained his wonderful mental and physical vigor.

Carl Schurz supported Mr. Sumner in his attacks upon President Grant and the administration. He was a German revolutionist of 1848 and had had a most remarkable career in the United States. He had been teacher, newspaper correspondent, editor, and, as a reward for his support of Mr. Lincoln in the convention of 1860, was made minister to Spain, a position he soon resigned to enter the service during the Civil War. He was made brigadier-general of volunteers, and was assigned to a command in the army. He was in the battles of Chancellorsville, Gettysburg, and other engagements of the Army of the Potomac. He lived first in New York, then Wisconsin, and from there went to Missouri, from which State he was elected to the United States Senate to succeed General John B. Henderson. He was most intense in the advocacy of any measure of which he approved and in the denunciation of anything which he opposed. He used effectively weapons of sarcasm and ridicule.

But he was no match for Senator Conkling in this line of debate. Schurz had dubbed Senator Conkling "The Powter Pigeon of the Senate," but Conkling was probably the author of the cognomen "Mephistopheles" which had been conferred upon Schurz in virtue of his peculiar physiognomy. It is needless to add that Carl Schurz was not re-elected to the Senate from Missouri, but he was subsequently appointed Secretary of the Interior by Mr. Hayes. He was a very remarkable man, but could never quite get over his revolutionary ideas. He was wont to say that the Roman punch was the life-saving station in Mrs. Hayes's temperance dinners. Mrs. Schurz and her daughters were among the most charming women that have ever been in Washington. I was especially fond of Mrs. Schurz, who was so serious-minded that she had no appreciation whatever of a joke, and was often shocked by the easy manner of the ladies who received at the White House. Propriety and dignity were her chief characteristics. She could not bear to see the line of ladies assisting at a reception in the least irregular, and was constantly calling them to order, greatly to the annoyance of some and the amusement of others. She was a stately German matron whose kindness knew no bounds, and who was so sincere in her profession of friendship that you felt perfectly at ease in her company. The daughters were charming young women, but they left Washington when they were quite young, and I trust have married well, as I am quite sure they were equal to any position they might undertake to fill. Mr. Schurz wrote in his "Memoirs" a voluminous history of his life and times, and died only a few years ago in the city of New York.

Days and weeks were consumed in the debates in both houses over the charges of mistakes and misdoings of the administration. Among other things, there was a great scandal created about the Crédit Mobilier, which meant that Oakes Ames, of Massachusetts, who had organized a company inside of the company which built the Union Pacific Railroad, had sold its stock to members of Congress, many of whom were so afraid that their names would be mentioned in connection with it that they denied having made the purchase or knowing anything about it. Those who admitted having bought the stock as an honest investment of their own money in what promised to be a legitimately profitable venture suffered nothing whatever. General Logan, who had invested in the stock, suffered no discredit, because when he discovered that Congress would be asked to pass additional legislation in the interest of the Union Pacific Railroad he returned his stock to Mr. Ames. The truth is that Mr. Ames was a very much persecuted man. He had patriotically put his fortune into the Union Pacific Railroad to save it from failure, and received for this courageous and noble venture on his part condemnation and almost ostracism. He was only vindicated in after years, when the whole facts in connection with the matter came to light.

In the midst of all this the Japanese embassy arrived. Congress made an appropriation for their entertainment, which sum was to be expended under the direction of General Myers, then quartermaster of the United States army, on duty at Washington. Among the social features of their entertainment a grand reception was given in the Masonic Temple, then the only hall in Washington spacious enough for such affairs. General Logan was on the committee for their entertainment, and was very much interested in all the arrangements. A magnificent banquet was laid in a room adjoining the reception-room of the Masonic Temple. The main hall was used for the reception and had been decorated profusely with flags of all nations, palms, flowers, and colored globes for the gas-burners, as electricity was not known in those days.

The President and Mrs. Grant, all the members of the cabinet, and everybody entitled to be present on state occasions came to welcome this interesting Oriental delegation. Many were disappointed that the ladies of the Japanese party were not present, but at that time they were not permitted by their own people to mingle in society as they do to-day. A commodious house in Georgetown had been secured for their accommodation, where every luxury was provided. The "little yellow men of the East," however, were the keenest observers of everything and lost no time in asking questions and gaining such information as they had been authorized to secure. They engaged the services of many teachers, artisans, agriculturalists, financiers, and political economists and returned to Japan, having recruited quite an army of educators in Western civilization. This was the beginning of the friendly relations between the United States and Japan.

Soon after the visit of the embassy, the first Japanese minister made his appearance—Mr. Mori and his interesting family, who has been succeeded from time to time by other most interesting diplomats. Mr. Yoshida, one of the early ministers from Japan, became so much interested in the United States and its progress that his family adopted many of our customs. When he came to Washington he brought his bride, who had the most gorgeous gowns, made up in true Japanese style. Mrs. Grant was very fond of Madame Yoshida, and insisted upon her attending many of her receptions. Madame Yoshida was a most agreeable, sensitive lady, and was naturally much distressed over the curiosity manifested by ill-bred people in her dress, coiffure, and appearance. One evening, at one of Mrs. Grant's receptions, Madame Yoshida wore one of the gorgeous gowns of her trousseau. Some one had the rudeness to take hold of it to feel the quality of the rich brocade of which the gown was made. She was so much distressed over it that she confided her feelings to her husband. He went to the French dressmaker, Madame Soulé, and told her she was to go up to the legation and see if she could not change Madame Yoshida's gowns into regular court-dress, so that she might appear in European dress at the next reception. Madame Soulé was much elated over the order, and at the next reception Madame Yoshida appeared in one of her rich gowns which had been converted into a regular European court-dress.

The Yoshidas were here many years, making visits to Japan and returning. General Logan and I were dining at their home one night, when Associate Justice Field sat on Madame Yoshida's right and I sat next to Justice Field. The Justice was a very agreeable conversationalist and Madame Yoshida had learned to speak English quite well. Justice Field said: "Madame Yoshida, how many children have you?" She replied: "I have two American and one Japanese children," at which Justice Field smiled. Quickly realizing the fact that she had made a mistake, she said: "Two born in America, and one in Japan. One is named Ulysses Grant, and one other Roscoe Conkling." They were hospitable entertainers, and when you went there to a dinner they had many favors at your plate, which was then the custom. I said to Madame Yoshida at one time: "It will be necessary to have an express to take the beautiful things you have given us to our home." She laughed heartily over it and said she would send them to the house by her servant if I so desired. Fancy boxes, beautiful carved ivories, and all kinds of exquisite and dainty favors, besides the menu-card, were laid at our plates, and you would have committed a grave offence if you had not taken them with you. One felt quite ashamed to leave the dining-room with hands so full of souvenirs of the occasion.

Soon after March 4, 1872, I returned to our home in Chicago for the summer, General Logan going directly from Washington to the convention in Philadelphia, where, after a stormy time, Grant and Wilson were nominated for the Presidency and the Vice-Presidency. The national committee met soon after the adjournment of the convention and made a programme for the conduct of the campaign. General Logan was booked to speak almost every day until the election, having appointments in Indiana, Ohio, Maine, Kansas, Nebraska, and Iowa, in addition to the many made for him in the State of Illinois, a State which he had ever a pride in carrying. Indiana was always a battleground between the Republican and the Democratic parties, and it required much labor to carry it for the Republican party.

After my father's second marriage, he desired to go west. He was appointed an assessor under the Internal Revenue Bureau, and removed to Provo, Utah. Early in August, when the campaign was at its height, I received a telegram from Doctor Taggart, a friend of ours, who was the collector of internal revenue at Salt Lake City. He said that my father was dangerously ill from meningitis and desired that I should come to him. Knowing how dependent he was upon me after my mother's death, and how unhappy he was to be seriously ill so far away from us, I communicated with General Logan at once, to ask his permission to join my father. It was impossible for him to accompany me on account of his duties in the campaign, but I insisted that I could go alone, and hence it was arranged. I set out upon the journey a few hours after receiving the telegram. At that time the arrangements were not as perfect as they are now. Persons travelling over the Union Pacific Railroad were obliged to change cars and get their sleeping-berth at Omaha. Following the directions of the agent in Chicago, I went into the depot at Omaha to find the Pullman office to secure the tickets for the section which I supposed had been assigned to me. There were many passengers in the room in line before the window of the Pullman office. Realizing that I would have no chance to reach the window for some time, I sought one of the officials on duty in the depot. He knew General Logan very well and at once busied himself to secure my tickets. He stood up on a chair and called to the Pullman agent, saying: "What is the number of Mrs. Logan's section in the Salt Lake car?" After some delay the agent responded: "Number twelve." The official then escorted me to this car, and I was soon with all my belongings ensconced in section twelve. The official probably knew more about the matter than I did, because he said to me: "No matter who claims this seat, you sit still. Nobody will dare to take hold of you." I was rather uncomfortable for fear there was something wrong about the seat, but made up my mind to follow his instructions. A little while afterward two Englishmen came into the car and deposited their numerous pieces of "luggage" in number eleven, directly opposite my section. They were muttering to each other and manifesting much displeasure over something that had occurred, but fearing that I might in some way have disconcerted their plans, I looked out of the window steadily for some time. It seemed to me a long time before everybody was assigned to his proper place in the car.

Finally we were off, and, in my great anxiety, I realized that it was to be a long and tedious journey, relieved only by the enjoyment of the magnificent scenery as we reached and crossed the Rocky Mountains. In order to have a better view, I retired to the observation car. There being a vacant seat next to my neighbor, number eleven, I sat down. The gentleman said: "I beg your pardon, are you Mrs. John A. Logan?" I replied in the affirmative. He said: "I speak to you, madam, to apologize for our seeming discourtesy, but you will pardon me if I tell you that you have one of our sections. I am afraid that we manifested much displeasure when we found that we both had to occupy one section, whereas we expected to have two." I told him I was very sorry, but that I was not aware of the fact that I had displaced them. He replied: "Oh! it is all right now, because we have learned of your sad journey, and we wish to apologize for what may have seemed rudeness." They proved to be English officers of the army and navy making a journey around the world. They were delightful gentlemen, and we grew to be very good friends before we reached Salt Lake. I noticed that the naval officer had a copy of "Lucille," which he read very assiduously. Upon my remarking that I was very much attracted by the literature which he seemed to enjoy, he told me all about a very serious love-affair which he had had just before leaving England, and that he was trying to pull himself together a "bit" by this journey. I reminded him that "there are just as good fish in the sea as ever were caught." I shall never forget their great courtesy and attention during that long and weary journey. I invited them to make themselves more comfortable by depositing part of their luggage on one of the seats of my section. They were to stop in Salt Lake to learn something of the wonders of that famous city, and therefore attended me to the hotel.

Doctor Taggart met me soon after my arrival and relieved me by saying that my father was better, but that he was still very ill. He told me that he had made arrangements for me to go to Provo on the stage-coach. The stage line at that time was under the management of Gilmer and Saulsbury, men from Illinois, and, of course, I felt quite sure that I would have every care and attention. The railroad only extended a few miles out of Salt Lake, where we were met by a stage-coach. At the terminus of the railroad there was nothing but an empty freight-car for a depot, and a few tents and cloth houses, where it seemed to me there was nothing but gambling-places and whiskey saloons. Near the car which was used as a depot were a number of barrels upon which were laid some boards. Around them men were gathered playing cards. Imagine my dismay when I descended from the car to go into the stage to see all these men pick up their bottles and cards, put them in their pockets, and get into the stage! I knew no one, but I was obliged to go to my father. I shall never forget the absolute silence that prevailed in that coach. The men were as polite and as considerate as they could possibly be, and spoke never a word until we reached the first station where the horses had to be watered. Doctor Taggart had evidently told the driver who I was and where I was going, for I shall ever remember the gallantry with which he came to the door and asked me if I would have a drink of water. He then said: "I think you would enjoy riding on top of the stage if you would not mind sitting by me." It was a great relief, and I accepted his invitation with much gratitude. He had watered his horses and assisted me up to the box on top of the stage. He had the reins tied to the brake, the passengers were all in, and we were about ready to start, when he darted into the house and returned with an umbrella in his hand. It was a very hot day, and nothing I could do would induce him to surrender that umbrella to me, but he drove his horses and held the umbrella over me all the way to Provo. We went to a dizzy height over mountains, and crawled along the sides of precipices. If he had made the slightest mistake, we might have been dashed hundreds of feet to our death. I was scarcely seated on top of the coach before I could hear the men inside cracking jokes, laughing, and enjoying themselves hugely. It made a deep impression on me, realizing, as I did, that their silence was their way of expressing their profound respect for a lone woman. Rough as they were, they still retained the innate instincts of gallantry of American men toward women.

It was nearly five o'clock when I reached Provo, and was again embraced by my dear old father. He improved rapidly after my arrival, and, after spending ten days with him and seeing him convalescent, I decided to return home. After he had improved and was quite on the road to recovery, he wanted me to meet his Mormon friends of the city of Provo. Among them were many of the highest intelligence and refinement, and I used to enjoy hearing them talk. I remember one Bishop Dusenberry, an Englishman, who was as fine a looking man as I have ever seen. Though a bishop of the church, nothing would induce him to practise polygamy. He had one wife and lived handsomely in a substantial house surrounded by beautiful grounds. Though he was loyal to the tenets of the church, I discovered in conversation that his bank account was kept in England, and I jocularly remarked to him one day: "Bishop, I expect some day to hear that you have renounced Mormonism and gone to England." He laughed quite heartily and replied: "What makes you think so?" I said: "Because I understand the greater part of your fortune is deposited in the Bank of England, in London." He again laughed and replied, "Don't you think that it is in a very safe place?" thus avoiding a direct reply to my remark.

Knowing General Logan's position, the friends of my father lost no time in paying me every respect, bringing me fruits and flowers, and in every way manifesting their great admiration for my husband. I could but admire the courage that had enabled these people with their teams and wagons to cross the great American desert and hew their way over the Rocky Mountains to the great valley of Salt Lake in the Territory of Utah at a time when pioneers had to brave every conceivable danger, including that of hostile Indians. They surely could never have succeeded in making this great valley blossom as a rose and in establishing homes that are as comfortable as those of other sections if they had not been sustained by the fanaticism of their remarkable religious faith. I felt more resigned to my father's living in this part of the country after having seen and known that these people were full of kindness and generosity.

After my return home I frequently accompanied General Logan in the campaign, to look after his health and to entertain his friends so that he might be able to snatch a little rest between his engagements. In this way I met the representative people from every part of the country, and, being anxious to spare General Logan all that I could, I confess to having carefully studied the histories of the different States and as far as possible to have informed myself as to the exact position of every man in politics. I tried to find out all I could about their relations with their own people so as to enable General Logan to put a correct valuation on their services to the party. Naturally, there were many pleasant things in connection with these visits to different towns and cities, and I have no recollection of any disagreeable episode. I came to think in those days that a man's politics were akin to his religion, and that most men were moved by motives of patriotism and an honest desire to serve the best interest of their respective States and the nation at large.

I shall always feel that Henry Wilson added little to the influence of the ticket. He was known to be an honest and faithful New England senator, but he had little knowledge of the people or of the interests of the middle-west, northwest, and western States. He had spent his life in Massachusetts, and, while it was never necessary to defend his reputation, it was hard to arouse enthusiasm for a man of neutral character. The world knows the result of the campaign and of the sad death of Vice-President Wilson.

As an outcome of the savage attacks of Sumner and Schurz on General Grant and the leaders of the regular Republican party, what they called the Liberal Republican party was organized by such ambitious newspaper men as Whitelaw Reid (our late ambassador to England), Horace White, Alexander McClure, Henry Watterson, Samuel Bowles, Murat Halstead, and a number of disgruntled Republicans, who held a convention in Cincinnati, May 1, 1872, and after three or four days' farcical sessions nominated Horace Greeley for President and B. Gratz Brown, ex-Governor of Missouri, for Vice-President. One might be forgiven for saying that this was a cruel attempt on the part of ambitious young men who had nothing to lose and all to gain if they could succeed in electing "Father" Greeley President of the United States. The whole attempt was so abortive and so ludicrous that it gave Thomas Nast, then at the meridian of his power as a cartoonist, an opportunity to inflict the most cruel blows upon Mr. Greeley. One caricature which caused great amusement was a cartoon of Mr. Greeley as the candidate for President, with a placard on the tail of his coat marked "B. Gratz Brown," which was all that was said of Mr. Brown as the Vice-President. How Mr. Greeley and Carl Schurz and men of their great ability could have been so foolish as to express their willingness to participate in this gigantic Falstaffian effort to capture the Presidency I do not profess to know. Mr. Greeley canvassed the country and made a most feeling appeal to the people, who, he thought, ought to support him for the Presidency. Notwithstanding the fact that Mr. Greeley and Mr. Brown were indorsed by the Democratic convention held in Baltimore on July 9, 1872, this indorsement did not at all increase the possibility of their election. Even Mr. Greeley's letter of acceptance of the Democratic nomination and his appeal to the people failed to make any serious impression.

In the midst of the campaign Mr. Greeley was summoned to his home on account of the serious illness of Mrs. Greeley, which proved fatal. This sad event so affected Mr. Greeley, in addition to his great disappointment in not being made President, that his mind gave way and he was sent to a sanitarium, where he died. The whole episode was so pathetic as to touch the heart of the country. President Grant and his entire cabinet, together with many noted men of the North and South, attended the funeral. Mr. Greeley had gone on the bond of Jefferson Davis, that Davis might be released from prison. This act, while it lessened his influence in the North, made many friends for him in the South, where he had previously been hated on account of his advocacy of the freedom of slaves.  He was one of the most remarkable men of his time, and should never have been induced to depart from the position of a great editor for which he was so eminently fitted.  He was earnest, tender, and guileless, and was in no sense a man suited to the handling of the vexatious problems of politics.  As has often been said before, his death may have saved him from a more cruel fate—that of ridicule.

Notwithstanding the bitter warfare that had been waged against General Grant, he was elected by an overwhelming majority, as were also a majority of the nominees of the Republican party for members of Congress.

We returned to our apartments in November, 1872, I to take up the usual routine of looking after my children, acting as secretary to General Logan, receiving and entertaining friends who were daily growing more numerous, and discharging my social duties.  These were not at all distasteful, because, as I recall now, society women, or rather the families in the official homes of the capital, made a great effort to make themselves a reputation for refinement, cordiality, and intelligent appreciation of the positions of their husbands and what was required of themselves to discharge their duties as wives and daughters.  A majority of the senators and members lived in hotels and boarding-houses, for at that time Washington furnished very meagre accommodations for congressional and other official families.  The schools were poor, and those who could possibly arrange for their children to attend boarding-schools away from the city did so.  Almost without exception the ladies felt that they must welcome to Washington visitors who were entitled to consideration.  They felt that they must, on the days assigned to the Supreme Court, the Senate, the House of Representatives, the speaker, the army, and the navy, receive all who did them the honor to call.  These receptions began about two o'clock and were not supposed to end before half-past five.  During these hours hundreds of calls were made, and they were not, as to-day, considered a bore and a drudgery. Most hostesses made every preparation for their afternoons at home, wearing beautiful gowns, inviting their friends to assist them in preparing tables where refreshments were served, and decorating their rooms with flowers. They extended a hospitality that made every one feel that their call was appreciated. There were many bright women, and often before you entered a drawing-room you could hear the peals of laughter and the bright conversation of the happy people within. The hours being early, it was possible to make a great many calls in the afternoon and to reach home in time to welcome my husband after the adjournment of Congress and the official duties of the day were over. Monday was the day for the Supreme Court, Tuesday for the House of Representatives, Wednesday for the cabinet and the speaker, Thursday for the Senate, Friday for the army and the navy, and Saturday afternoon for the White House. The mistress of that mansion always made extensive preparations for her Saturday afternoons. The Marine Band played as at an evening reception, and every room was beautifully decorated with plants and flowers. It gave an opportunity for the wife of the President to extend invitations to some of the wives of members of the Supreme Court, Senate, House of Representatives, army and navy, and citizens and visitors in Washington to assist her at these receptions. The recipients never forgot this compliment, and it helped to make fast friends for the President of the husbands of these women who had had these little attentions.

Latter-day wives of Presidents seem to have forgotten that it is in their province to extend such courtesies, or do anything to acknowledge the honors that have been paid their husbands and themselves by their elevation to the highest position within the gift of the people. It is impossible for any lady in the White House to go through the long list of persons entitled to consideration if she confines herself to the regulation state dinners, the four evening receptions, and the occasional musicale or garden-party. People are so quick to discover whether the invitation is sent through a desire to do one an honor or whether it is a grudging discharge of a disagreeable duty. The only way to account for the difference in treatment accorded guests in the White House latterly and in the olden time is by recognizing the fact that money is now more highly considered as a standard. It has been interesting to contrast the *menus* served in the state dining-room to his guests by President Arthur with the bowls of punch and gingersnaps that have been served in the corridor of the White House by caterers after musicales within the past few years. Not that one accepts these invitations expecting a feast, yet one feels a pride in having whatever is done in the White House either well done or altogether omitted.

Allowing for the Christmas holidays, any session beginning December 1 and closing on the 4th of March is very short, and there is little time for the passage of many bills that must fail altogether if they are left on the calendar March 3 of the last session of a Congress. Therefore, those interested work prodigiously at these last hours. March 3, 1873, was the close of the Forty-second Congress, and, though many of the senators and members had worked heroically, the calendar was far from being exhausted. Work in the departments was also greatly in arrears, as possibly a larger number of bills had been introduced in Congress, and more important matters laid before every department, than had ever before been done in the history of the Government.

March 4, 1873, was probably the most inclement inauguration day within the memory of any American. The thermometer had fallen below zero, a thing previously unknown in this climate. The militia from many States almost perished with the cold while they were en route, and they arrived in Washington to find inhospitable temperature and few preparations for their accommodation. The decorations of the city were frozen stiff and looked dismal with their coats of ice and sleet, which had fallen the night before. The cadets from West Point and Annapolis were nearly frozen in line, many dropping out on account of their inability to stand on their feet, and, though they were taken back to their academies as speedily as possible, they left a number behind in the hospitals of Washington, while others were borne to the hospital on their arrival at West Point and Annapolis, fatal pneumonia claiming several in each corps.

The procession was the poorest display ever seen on such an occasion. Senators Logan, Cragin, and Bayard, were the committee on the part of the Senate, supplemented by a large committee of distinguished men. Governors of many States with their staffs were present. The weather spoiled their splendor, their feathers and gold lace yielding to the frost in the air. Helmbold, of patent-medicine fame, was then in Washington with a famous four-in-hand mouse-colored team of horses which he drove attached to a superb landau with light lining. He insisted that the committee should allow him to use this turnout to convey President Grant and the committee to the Capitol for the inauguration, and back to the White House. The committee accepted his offer, and on inauguration day Grant, together with the Senate committee—Logan, Cragin, and Bayard—drove to the Capitol and thence to the White House in this beautiful equipage. Another though less pretentious outfit conveyed Vice-President Wilson to the Capitol. A commendable but futile effort was made by the shivering throng on either side of Pennsylvania Avenue to cheer the President, Vice-President, and distinguished men whom they recognized in the procession. The crowd assembled in the park on the east side of the Capitol were packed close together in front of the rotunda steps, which were covered over to serve as the platform upon which the President takes the oath of office and delivers his inaugural address. These people were better able to resist the bitter blast that had been wildly blowing for forty-eight hours, beginning the day before the inauguration, than were those who held exposed positions on the avenue. Fortunately, the ceremonies were brief. The Vice-President proceeded to the Senate chamber to adjourn that body to wait for the President's message, while President Grant and the committee resumed their seats in the carriage to return to the White House.

We had in our employ at that time a faithful colored man servant, Louis Davis, who has occupied the position of trusted messenger in the Interior Department almost ever since. He insisted upon taking our little son, John A. Logan, Jr., who was then eight years old, to the inauguration, promising to be very careful of him. He took the child up to the Capitol and stood beside the general who occupied the place of committeeman near Grant. After he had finished the inaugural address, President Grant noticed the boy, and, Jack being a great favorite with him, he said to General Logan: "Bring Jack in the carriage as we return." Louis, overhearing President Grant, preceded them to the carriage. Imagine General Logan's surprise when he saw Louis sitting on the box beside Helmbold with Jack on his knee! The President laughed heartily and insisted upon his being left there. When they arrived at the White House, President Grant took Jack by the hand and led him into the reception-room to be welcomed by Mrs. Grant. When they adjourned to the state dining-room for the luncheon which Mrs. Grant had provided for the large party accompanying the President, he insisted upon taking Jack with him.

It was a red-letter day in the dear boy's life, and he used to tell it to all of his school friends with a good deal of satisfaction. It spoke volumes for the kind heart of General Grant. Jack was always proud of being a favorite with the President and Mrs. Grant, who never forgot him at Christmas, but always sent him some beautiful Christmas gift. He was her champion and made many speeches in eulogy of Mrs. Grant, which were reported to her and caused her to be very strongly attached to him as long as she lived.

The afternoon was spent by everybody in trying to get warm. The inaugural committee had made most extensive preparations for the inaugural ball. They had built a temporary marquee on Judiciary Square. It was magnificently decorated and extensive enough to have accommodated the thousands whom the committee expected would attend the ball. A superb banquet had been provided, and hundreds of waiters secured, and the committee on music had provided many bands. The weather abated not a whit or tittle, and, as night came on, it seemed to grow colder and colder, and yet every one felt they must carry out the inaugural programme.

We had as our guest Miss Nina J. Lunt, of Chicago. Mr. E. B. Wight, representative of the Chicago *Tribune* had invited Miss Lunt and our daughter, then in her teens, to go to the inaugural ball, and, while Dollie was not in society, we thought it might be an event she would like to remember as long as she lived. Therefore we gave our consent to have her go with Mr. Wight. After they had gone, and before we could reach them, we became very anxious indeed, because of the growing intensity of the cold. Mr. Wight was very careful, and through his influence in newspaper circles, was able to get them a most comfortable position, and they suffered no inconvenience or ill-effects from this, our daughter's first experience at an inaugural ball. Like all young people, she was so enthusiastic about all she saw, and the interesting people who were present, that she was unmindful of the cold.

The President and Mrs. Grant and Vice-President Wilson, who was a widower, arrived at about half past eleven o'clock. Mr. and Mrs. Fish, Secretary and Mrs. Boutwell, Secretary and Mrs. Belknap, Secretary Robeson, Postmaster-General and Mrs. Creswell, Attorney-General and Mrs. Williams, Secretary and Mrs. Delano, accompanied by Mr. and Mrs. John Delano, were in the Presidential party, while the Diplomatic Corps, led by the Dean Blacque Bey of Turkey, Sir Edward Thornton, the Marquis de Naoville of France, Mr. and Madame Mori of Japan, and the Peruvian minister, all in full court dress—as on the occasion of all inaugural balls, the ladies wearing their most gorgeous gowns—attended the ball, and the grand promenade was given. The marquee not being heated, it became so cold that one lady was seized with a congestive chill and died in the room. This sad event, in addition to the intensity of the cold, from which everybody was suffering, cut short the ceremonies of the evening. The food on the tables in the banquet hall was congealed, the coffee almost freezing into a *frappé*. Men and women in evening dress sought their heavy wraps to keep from perishing while they waited for their conveyances to take them to their abodes. Drivers of vehicles of all kinds were almost frozen, and great confusion reigned inside and outside the temporary building. Musicians were unable to play their instruments, the mouthpieces of some of the smaller instruments being frozen, and the festivities ended unceremoniously. The great crowd which had come to Washington for the inaugural ceremonies left the city as rapidly as they could get trains to carry them away.

The newspaper men and women then in Washington were among the most brilliant of the guild. All the metropolitan newspapers had bureaus in Washington, presided over by a coterie of men who were the equals, if not the superiors, intellectually of the men at the head of the bureaus of the metropolitan newspapers of to-day. Among them were such men as Whitelaw Reid of the New York *Tribune;* J. B. McCullough of the Saint Louis *Democrat;* Alexander McClure of the Philadelphia *Ledger;* Horace White, Mr. Sheehan, of the Chicago *Times;* Murat Halstead, L. A. Gobright, E. B. Wight,

George A. Townsend, J. Russell Young, subsequently librarian of the Congressional Library, W. Scott Smith, Eli Perkins, Charles Lanman, Don Piatt, Ben Perley Poore, E. V. Smalley, Mark Twain, Frederick Douglass, and a host of correspondents who have made enviable reputations in their calling. Among the women reporters who wielded influential pens as correspondents of important newspapers were Mary Clemmer Ames, Mrs. Lippincott, Mrs. H. M. Barnum, Mrs. Olivia Briggs, Mrs. Coggswell, Mrs. and Miss Snead, and Miss Mary E. Healey.

General Grant soon nominated his cabinet, retaining those who had served during his first term, with the exception of the Secretary of the Treasury. The members of the cabinet were: Hamilton Fish, Secretary of State; William A. Richardson, Secretary of the Treasury; W. W. Belknap, Secretary of War; George M. Robeson, Secretary of the Navy; Columbus Delano, Secretary of the Interior; John A. Creswell, Postmaster-General; George H. Williams, Attorney-General. Congress resumed its treadmill routine, with now and again outbursts of criticism and vituperation heaped upon President Grant.

On March 9 our friend Doctor John P. Taggart, of Salt Lake City, telegraphed General Logan that my father had passed away from a return of the meningitis from which he had suffered the summer previous. There were three of my mother's children with my father in Utah, and we realized at once that there was no alternative but for me to again return to Utah. It was impossible for General Logan to leave his post of duty, and we had no one whom we could send who could attend to matters and who understood affairs as I did. Consequently I made the second long, sad trip to Utah, to bring my father's remains home to be interred beside my mother, in the cemetery at Marion, Williamson County, Illinois, and to assume the care and support of the three children left unprovided for. I do not even now like to recall that melancholy journey, or the multiplied cares which I had to assume, and which could never have been borne but for the unfailing tenderness and encouragement of my devoted husband. He was perfectly willing to share everything we had with my minor brother and sisters, who by my father's death had become double orphans. We had taken a furnished house on Capitol Hill when I returned to Washington, in November previous, for the session of Congress which ended March 4, and as soon as it was possible took the children and returned to our home in Chicago.

# CHAPTER XIII

IT was quite late in the summer before General Logan
reached home, as the extra session of the Senate which convened after the inauguration, March 4, 1873, had been protracted much longer than had been expected. The children
were out of school, and we were all settled in our lovely home,
2119 Calumet Avenue. The rear of our house overlooked
the lake, and, the broad lawns of the block being undivided
by fences, those who lived in this square had the benefit of a
beautiful park in the front and back of their homes. Consequently we found it unnecessary to go away in summer.

General Logan had worked very hard in the campaign,
which was scarcely over when the last session of the Forty-
second Congress began. He had really had no rest from the
day he took his seat in the Senate, in 1871. We had a number of friends in the West who begged us to come to Colorado.
Through the death of my father my cares had multiplied so
greatly that it was impossible for me to leave home. I
urged my husband to go, however, and after much hesitation

he went. While there he joined a party of capitalists, who were making prospecting tours over the mountains and along Cripple Creek, hunting for gold and silver mines. They discovered some "rich indications." General Logan always insisted upon putting up his quota of expenses for these prospecting expeditions, and promptly drew upon the small savings we had in bank. All went merrily while he remained and helped to furnish the "stake," and he was considered one of the partners, on an equal footing with the others. Finally General Logan had to come home on account of urgent affairs. After his return the others frequently drew upon him for funds to continue the prospecting, which was being made by these "true friends," who "were anxious to strike a bonanza on General Logan's account," because he had done so much in securing for them lucrative appointments. Letters came regularly, saying they had not yet struck a "rich vein," but the *indications* were good, and they required only fifty or one or two hundred dollars more, as the case might be, to insure success. General Logan was one of the most trustful men I have ever known. He simply would not believe in the infidelity of a friend until indubitable evidence forced him to see what was plain to every one else. He could ill afford the demands made upon him, but could not bear to disappoint these supposed faithful friends. He became very sensitive over the matter, and did not like to have me inquire "how much fodder the mules needed," when letters came requesting remittances. Finally he became suspicious and declined to send more money. Soon afterward there was great excitement over the discovery of the "Morning Star" mine by the parties with whom he had been associated. They telegraphed him that they were very sorry, but the discovery of the "Morning Star" had not been made until after the funds to which he had contributed had been exhausted, and therefore he was not a partner in the ownership of the great mine. He felt very badly over this treatment by men for whom he had done many acts of kindness, and no one dared mention the matter in his presence. He was subsequently very glad that they had ruled him out in the beginning, as all the world knows of the shocking imposition that was played upon General Grant and of all the scandal and trouble which ensued. These same men were the ones implicated in the swindle that brought so much sorrow to General Grant, and ended in a penitentiary term for at least one of them.

General Logan was very anxious to make money in a legitimate way, and therefore invested in mines in Colorado rather extensively, but the story was always the same. He was too trustful and too honest to gamble in mining-stocks, and, as a consequence, we had enough beautifully engraved certificates of stock in mines, for which he paid cash, to paper a good-sized room, which were, of course, worthless. Everything that General Logan ever had he earned by hard work, and, while he had many successes, he could not be said to have been born under a lucky financial star.

The year 1873 was the beginning of the revolutionary action on the part of strikers. I shall not soon forget that I one day received a letter from General Logan, who was then in Colorado, desiring me to go down to our bank to arrange some matters for him. I was so much afraid that, if I waited for the coachman to get the carriage ready, I should not have the package in time for the mail that I decided to go down on the street-car and forward from the bank the documents he wanted out of the safety-deposit vault. I was not aware of the excitement existing in Chicago at the time, and imagine my consternation when I found the streets full of strikers, with militiamen trying in every way to preserve order. I went into the bank and found the cashier standing at the window with a pistol lying on either side. I inquired what the trouble was, and he said that the strikers had threatened to sack the banks of Chicago; that they were obliged to keep the doors open during banking-hours, and consequently had had to provide themselves with arms to defend their deposits. It was the year in which such fearful destruction of property occurred in Pittsburg, and I have always felt, if those in authority had thought less of the consequences to themselves politically, and had caused the law to be executed and these men in Chicago punished, we should not have had such frequent repetitions of revolutionary action on the part of men nursing imaginary wrongs.

General Logan had assumed the burden of the care of the members of my father's family so cheerfully and willingly that I could not help worrying, greatly to his distress, over the rapidly multiplying expenses to which we were in consequence subjected. Hence I decided that it would be better for me not to try to go to Washington with the general for the meeting of Congress, December 1, 1873. For the first time since the general had re-entered Congress after the close of the war I remained away from the capital until after the holidays, which General Logan was to spend with us in our Chicago home.

Chicago was rapidly regaining her importance as a great city. The world had been so generous that the citizens no longer required the relief which had been extended them from the time of the fire in October, 1871. The Grand Pacific Hotel had been built and was one of the largest which had, up to that date, been erected in Chicago. For a long time it had been the custom of the two noted hotel-managers, Messrs. Gage and Drake, to have in November what they called a game dinner. It was always a wonderful affair, and this fall it was especially notable on account of the unique manner in which it was served in the new Grand Pacific dining-room, which seated five hundred persons. The walls and every part were decorated to represent a forest. On all the tables they had different devices representing the various animals and birds that come under the head of game. I remember one especially fine stag which had been secured from the far west, and stood on a table in the centre of the room. The superb antlers that crowned the head of the animal attracted universal attention, as did a fawn and the head of a great bear, which were also among the decorations. There were specimens of the rabbit, squirrel, and the opossum, while members of the feathered kingdom were interspersed in all their glory in the decoration of every table. The beauty of the arrangement of birds' nests in artistic devices was beyond the description of an ordinary pen. These specimens were, of course, stuffed, while on the menu appeared bear, venison, opossum, rabbit, and squirrel meat, followed by pheasant, turkey, goose, duck, guinea-keat, chicken, plover, quail, and reedbird. An example of every member of the entire feathered kingdom which is used as food was laid before the guests. There were many speeches and songs written for the occasion, and the "wee sma' hours" had approached before the happy party dispersed.

The indomitable spirit of Chicago was just as irresistible then as it has been ever since, and it seemed as if a magician's wand had been employed to cause so many superb buildings and other improvements to spring up in such a short time as had elapsed since the fire of October, 1871. We had just come to Chicago when the fire occurred, and had been away almost ever since. We were very glad therefore to renew the acquaintance of the friends we had known before, and to make new friends. New Year's Day had not been as universally observed in Chicago as was the custom in Washington. Therefore I conceived the idea that, as General Logan would be at home for the holidays, I would celebrate New Year's Day by keeping open house.

January 1, 1874, was an unusually bright day for that climate, and we had the pleasure of receiving our friends continuously from ten o'clock in the morning until that hour at night. I had caused a notice to be given out that we should be glad to see our friends, and many came who were delighted to welcome General Logan and myself as residents of Chicago. I invited quite a number of young ladies to assist me, and some of them sang and played beautifully. To make this essentially a home affair, they furnished the music at intervals during the day instead of introducing hired musicians. We had a bountiful table from which our callers were served with whatever they desired. This was the last New Year's Day we ever had the pleasure of being in Chicago. The population of Chicago increased so rapidly that it became impracticable to observe the general custom of receiving on New Year's Day.

There were many magnificent homes on Wabash, Michigan, Indiana, Prairie, and Calumet Avenues, south of Sixteenth Street, which were not reached by the fire. They were occupied by courageous men who were foremost in the work of rebuilding Chicago. On the corner of Twenty-second Street and Calumet Avenue lived Mr. Daniel Jones and his interesting family. Mr. Jones was one of the pioneers of Chicago—a short, sturdy, active man, who took part in everything that contributed to the prosperity of his beloved city, and by his will many charitable institutions were greatly benefited.

Mr. L. Z. Leiter, the famous merchant, and his family lived directly opposite us. Their children, like our own, were quite small and played together constantly. Mr. Leiter was a great study. He was methodical and indefatigable in his attention to his business. I used to see him go out of his house every morning at seven o'clock, to get into a buggy which stood in front of the door waiting for him. He seemed to return every day at one o'clock to give an hour for his luncheon, and then back to business, not to reach home until six o'clock. Day after day he proceeded in this routine. His family entertained by giving dinners occasionally.

Mr. Aldrich, subsequently a member of Congress, was on the other corner, while on our side of the street, on the corner of Twenty-first and Calumet Avenue, was the residence of the celebrated surgeon Doctor Gunn and his charming family. Mrs. Gunn was a lovely woman, who was very domestic in her tastes. Their sons and daughters received her constant attention, and are now among the worthy citizens of the city of their birth.

Mr. and Mrs. A. B. Meeker, father and mother of Mr. Arthur Meeker, one of the enterprising men of Chicago, lived in our block; Mr. and Mrs. John Markley, Mr. and Mrs. John Alling, of the firm of Alling & Markley, lived in adjoining houses to us and were among our most intimate friends; while that ill-fated public-spirited man John R. Walsh, with his splendid family, also resided within two doors of us. Mr. Walsh was a very tall, rather stooping man, whose keen eyes indicated the restlessness of his disposition. He was in every sense a self-made man, and it is a melancholy thought to recall the combination of circumstances which led to his undoing. If, in an evil hour, he did anything that could be construed as irregular, he paid a penalty too sad to contemplate. One thing is certain—Chicago owes him as much as any other man for its rapid advancement to its present greatness and for his generosity to the charities and philanthropic enterprises of the city. I can never believe Mr. Walsh did anything in his whole career which had not previously been done by others. I am quite sure he had no dishonorable intent in any act of his life.

Ex-Governor Bross, one of the proprietors of the Chicago *Tribune,* was our next-door neighbor on the north. Mrs. Bross was an invalid, hence their intellectual and charming daughter Jessie did the honors of the house. She was interested in music and literature, and in all social matters. She subsequently married Henry D. Lloyd, the noted writer.

Mr. and Mrs. H. O. Stone resided near us. Mr. Stone was one of the earliest successful men of Chicago, and came to the city when it was a wooden hamlet on the great prairie.

He appreciated the possibilities of making Chicago the wonderful city it is to-day, and joined heartily in the various movements to accomplish this end. He had married for his second wife the beautiful Elizabeth Yager, of Saratoga, New York, who made his home very attractive. Mrs. Stone was gifted in the matter of dispensing hospitality and in providing entertainment for her friends. As a result, their house was one where society met most frequently.

Mr. and Mrs. Marshall Field were also near neighbors of ours. Marshall Field was of the Field-Leiter firm, merchant princes of Chicago from the days of the Civil War. In personal appearance Mr. Field was a French marquis, and no one could imagine that back of his suavity of manner there was that rigidly calculating nature which enabled him to change the discouragements and calamities of the fire into means with which to turn the wheels of prosperity and success. The first Mrs. Field was of slight stature, medium height, with dark-brown eyes and hair, and very fair complexion. Her manners were charming; her wit fascinating. She always had about her interesting people. She encouraged every artist who appealed to her for aid, and her natural generosity caused her list of pensioners to be quite long. Unfortunately, the attractions of Paris won her away from her Chicago home and friends, and like the many who become infatuated with the illusion and unreal life of the French capital, she drifted into its current and died an untimely death in France, surrounded by people who had lived on her bounty while they encouraged her estrangement from her native land.

Mr. George M. Pullman was one of the foremost men of that matchless coterie who rehabilitated Chicago and pushed forward the interests of that great city years in advance of what it would have attained in the ordinary course of events. Mr. Pullman was a man of unusually fine appearance—six feet tall, with a well-developed physique, a fine head, and dark-brown eyes which expressed his genial, generous disposition. He married in 1866 Miss Harriet Sanger, one of the most famous beauties of Chicago and the West. As soon as possible after the fire he built his palatial brownstone residence at the corner of Eighteenth Street and Prairie Avenue. In this mansion Mr. and Mrs. Pullman royally entertained the most distinguished visitors who came to Chicago, especially during the World's Columbian Exposition. Both host and hostess had travelled extensively and had legions of friends who were glad to accept their invitations. Artists in every line were sure of a warm reception and encouragement from Mr. and Mrs. Pullman, and more than one has been able to cultivate their special talent through the generosity of these kindly people. No movement in the line of progress, education, or charity was ever started in Chicago without a liberal donation and every encouragement from Mr. and Mrs. Pullman.

Mr. and Mrs. Henry Strong and their family, Mr. and Mrs. Lester, the Armours, Mr. and Mrs. J. W. Doan, Mr. and Mrs. Spalding, Mr. and Mrs. Cobb, Mr. and Mrs. Norman Williams, Mr. and Mrs. John M. Clark, Mr. and Mrs. E. B. Sherman, Mr. and Mrs. Jerome Beecher, Mr. and Mrs. Enos Ayers, Mr. and Mrs. Dunlevy, Mr. and Mrs. Coolbaugh (Douglas's great friends), and Colonel and Mrs. John M. Loomis resided near us. Colonel Loomis attracted universal attention because of his love for riding on horseback with all the paraphernalia of an officer of the army. He could be seen any afternoon, mounted on his beautiful black horse, with all the trappings of a colonel of the army, and his mounted orderly close behind him, riding along the avenues and through the parks of Chicago. Colonel Loomis was a noble and generous man, and had an illustrious record as a volunteer officer during the Civil War. Mrs. Loomis was in all respects a fitting companion for this noted man.

Many others of that remarkable generation were within a few squares of our door. I was glad of an opportunity to come to know them better and, as far as possible, to participate in their many schemes for the betterment of social conditions and the welfare of mankind.

When General Logan went to Washington in December, 1873, he removed from Willard's Hotel, where we had formerly lived, to 1114 G Street, where he found delightful accommodations in a private house. When we returned to Washington after the holidays were over, we went directly to these apartments where we remained for a number of years. Our host, Captain Havard, was a most interesting man. He was a Frenchman, and had served in the French army as a commissioned officer, but came to America at the breaking out of the Civil War. He was an officer in the Union army, and was wounded in one of the battles in Virginia. He was brought to Washington and nursed back to health again by a widowed lady who had removed from Virginia. He was a very scholarly and a most interesting man, and it was a great study to see him and his Virginian wife together, as her chief qualifications were those of a good housewife.

The calendar of the Senate was a long one, and General Logan soon became absorbed in the matters before that body. Among the questions to be decided was the settlement of the *Virginius* massacre, which was conducted so satisfactorily that General Grant received the thanks of the survivors. Congress also passed a resolution asking all foreign powers to take part in the Centennial Exposition which was to be held in Philadelphia in 1876, and made an appropriation of $1,500,000 to aid Philadelphia in carrying out the plans for the exposition.

In the discussion of the Louisiana imbroglio which took place at this time the ablest men in the Senate took a very active part. Matthew Carpenter, of Wisconsin, made his famous review of the situation.

So much criticism had been made of the government of the District of Columbia under the territorial law, and so many charges of fraud and unjust rulings in the administration of its affairs, that Senator Thurman of Ohio introduced, in January, 1874, a resolution asking for the investigation of the affairs of the District of Columbia. Under this resolution Governor Shepherd was furnished with a list of questions as to the affairs of his administration, to which he replied. After a long and tedious discussion of the subject in Congress, the form of government was returned to that of commission, President Grant sending in the names of A. R. Shepherd, A. G. Cattell, and Henry T. Blow for commissioners of the district. These men failed of confirmation, and subsequently J. H. Ketchum of New York, Henry T. Blow of Missouri, and W. Dennison of Ohio, were appointed and confirmed. The commissioners discharged many of the employees who had held positions under the territorial government.

Among the important work of the committees of the Senate was the investigation of General O. O. Howard's administration of the Freedmen's Bureau. The trial culminated in the acquittal of General Howard in July, and he was ordered to take command of the Department of the Columbia, U. S. A., with headquarters in Portland, Oregon. J. S. Creswell, Doctor Purvis, and L. H. Leipold were appointed to take charge of and wind up the affairs of the Freedmen's Bank, which from the first had been a very ill-managed affair and caused lots of trouble to the colored people in whose interest it was supposed to have been organized.

The question of the finishing of the Washington Monument was taken up, and a handsome appropriation made by Congress, which, together with private subscriptions, caused to be completed this matchless shaft to the memory of George Washington, first President of the United States.

It was no small thing at that time to be one of the leaders in the Senate, for that body was made up of men of keen minds and indomitable courage. Anthony of Rhode Island, a ponderous sort of a man, with all the alertness and intuitive grasp of a New Englander, was always on the watch and ready for discussions of every question that might in any way lessen the influence of New England. Roscoe Conkling was probably the handsomest man in the Senate, and was most fastidious in his style of dress and manner. He was ever ready for a debate, and made many enemies by the sneers with which he treated the remarks of brother senators with whom he disagreed. He was so intense in everything he did that he sometimes apparently forgot there was any other person in the Senate besides himself, and seemed to feel that upon him alone rested the responsibility of averting all the evils that threatened the republic. His industry was prodigious, and the great State of New York never had a more able or faithful senator than was Roscoe Conkling. He eschewed all social functions, as his family were rarely with him, and was infrequently seen at receptions, even in the White House. He occasionally accepted invitations to dine with gentlemen, but had few intimates. It was natural for him to be reserved, but no more faithful friend could be found than Roscoe Conkling when he once allowed himself to become attached to a brother senator.

In striking contrast to Senator Conkling was his colleague, Senator Fenton. He had a most genial disposition and agreeable manner. He had not the intellectual power of Conkling, but probably accomplished more through his diplomacy. He had a charming family, consisting of his wife and the Misses Fenton, who were very popular in Washington.

The venerable Hannibal Hamlin of Maine was a tall man, who had become somewhat bent by the weight of years. He was mentally as keen as when in his thirties. He was uncompromising in his Republicanism, and had no patience with colleagues who were ready on the slightest provocation to yield points of advantage to the opposition. He was not especially aggressive, but could be relied upon as one of the most faithful committeemen in the Senate. His spotless reputation as Vice-President while the war was at its height secured for him the respect and admiration of all his associates. Mrs. Hamlin was a typical New England woman. They had two daughters. One of them had married General Batchelder, at one time a splendid soldier. General Batchelder was appointed to some position out in one of the Territories, where he became very much demoralized, and the marriage in consequence turned out badly, and Mrs. Batchelder returned to her father's home. Batchelder finally lost his position, came to Washington, and died friendless in an isolated quarter of the city. Mrs. S. P. Brown, who was a friend of the Hamlins, learned of Batchelder's death, and telegraphed the news to Senator Hamlin. With characteristic promptness the old senator telegraphed back: "Bury him decently, and I will pay the bill with pleasure."

Matthew H. Carpenter of Wisconsin has been described as a short, heavy-set, shaggy man, and that is probably a correct description. He had, however, a phenomenally large head, which was said to be full of brains. His record in the Senate shows that he was one of the most brilliant men in that body. He was relentless in his prodigious and fearless advocacy of the principles of his party.

Another intellectual giant and forceful man was Governor O. P. Morton of Indiana. His physical disabilities did not in any way affect his wonderful mentality. Living as he did in a border State, he was accustomed to being in a controversy all the time, and was ever ready to defend the principles of his party and his own integrity. He had made an imperishable reputation as war governor of Indiana. His people were much divided in their sympathies between the North and South. Thomas A. Hendricks, Daniel H. Voorhees, and other intellectual giants of his State were equally fearless advocates of the principles of the Democratic party, and often defended the acts of the Confederacy in its efforts to destroy the Union. It is remarkable that Senator Morton, as governor of Indiana, was able to protect his State from being overrun by raiders under such men as Morgan, an imaginary line only dividing Indiana from the slaveholding States of Kentucky and Tennessee.

Simon Cameron of Pennsylvania was one of the most remarkable men in the Senate. Born in the last year of the eighteenth century, his experience covered many years of his country's history. As journeyman printer and editor, he worked his way into politics, and was for a long time adjutant-general of the State of Pennsylvania. Reaching the exalted position of United States senator in 1845, he was re-elected in 1857 for the term ending 1863. He took an active part in the nomination and election of Mr. Lincoln in 1860, and in consequence resigned his seat in the Senate to accept the position of Secretary of War under Mr. Lincoln. His reputation as a wonderful organizer led Mr. Lincoln to choose him for the then important matter of organizing the Union army. He was the author of the scheme to enlist the negroes, a movement which contributed much to the numbers and strength of the army. Mr. Cameron, like all successful men, had many critics, and surrendered the war portfolio for the ministership to Russia in 1862. He had amassed a large fortune and could afford to give the United States her proper place among nations by supplementing the meagre salary of a minister to foreign lands with ample means from his private income. Diplomatic life was not congenial to him or his family, and he soon returned to his beloved native land. Notwithstanding the charges which had been made against him, he was elected to the United States Senate in 1867, and again in 1873. His increasing years and great desire to have his son, James Donald Cameron, succeed him in the Senate, caused him, as soon as he had consummated arrangements for his son's election, to resign for the second time his seat in the Senate.

He was an unusually tall, spare man, with sandy hair and clear blue eyes that spoke determination. His energy was indomitable, his astuteness limitless. He was not a fluent speaker, but so positive and immovable when he had taken a position that he almost invariably carried his point. His prejudices were intense, his friendship steadfast, and while he may have failed in his relations with the Diplomatic Corps, the management of the political and national affairs of his own country was an art with him. His power in the Senate in no wise waned with the years.

John Sherman, cold and calculating, who, in rendering great service to his country as representative, senator, Secretary of the Treasury, and Premier, did not neglect to look after his personal interests, was one of the most active and efficient senators in the Forty-third Congress. His colleague, Allen G. Thurman, was one of the ablest men in the Senate. He had been a member of the House, and had served on the bench as a district and Supreme Court judge in his adopted State of Ohio. He was originally a native of Virginia, and was one of the foremost men of the Democratic party. He was ever ready to join the men on that side of the Senate in defence of the measures that had been advocated and the policies adopted by his party.

Rumors of the great wealth of Stewart and Jones of Nevada, had been heralded before they made their appearance in the Senate, and it was not long before they demonstrated that they were men of untiring energy and keen perception of the requirements of the nation during the progressive era that followed the close of the Civil War. They were both steadfast Republicans and devoted friends of President Grant.

Hon. William Pitt Kellogg was a native of Vermont, but removed to the State of Illinois at an early age. From that State he was appointed Chief Justice to the Territory of Nebraska. At the breaking out of the war he returned to Illinois and raised a regiment, the 7th Illinois Cavalry. After the war he was appointed collector to the port of New Orleans. The bitterness toward him was so intense that his life was in jeopardy many times, but he bravely protected the persecuted citizens and upheld the laws while occupying this position. He was subsequently appointed governor of the State of Louisiana from which position he was elected to the United States Senate. No man has ever displayed more indomitable energy, sterling integrity, and dauntless courage in the discharge of the duties attendant upon the positions he held. In the Senate he was a fearless advocate of the supremacy of the law and of the protection of Union men in the States lately in rebellion.

On the other side of the chamber were such men as John B. Gordon, a man of imposing appearance and great ability. He was proud of the part he had taken as a Confederate officer during the rebellion, and was generally the leader in criticising everything that was done by Federal officers in the South. His criticism of General Sheridan's handling of the troops in New Orleans caused an exciting debate between him and General Logan, which friends thought at one time might end in a personal difficulty, as both men were known to be of unflinching courage and intense partisan feeling. There has rarely appeared anything in the record of Congress so caustic as General Logan's arraignment of Senator Gordon. Gordon soon discovered that his policy would not result in anything good for his people or his party, and had the grace to discontinue his personal assaults upon representatives of the Government.

Senator William B. Allison of Iowa had had a very long experience in the House of Representatives. He was a most conscientious and careful man, and soon attained the position of chairman of the appropriations committee because of his great discretion. He had one serious fault that kept him from being a really great man, and that was his disposition to be non-committal on every subject. He was never willing to take the lead in the advocacy of any measure that had not been previously advocated by some other senator. His reputation for being non-committal was so well known that there were a great many stories told at his expense. Senator Ingalls of Kansas once said to him: "Brother Allison, you could walk across the Senate floor in a pair of wooden shoes, and you would not make any more noise than a fly crawling on the ceiling, so non-committal are you on all questions at all times." His State and the nation had implicit confidence in his integrity, his patriotism, and his steadfast adherence to Republican principles, but he was in no sense aggressive, and many times allowed golden opportunities for doing great service to his country to pass because of his timidity. Allison was a large, heavy man with dark hair and brown eyes. He was phlegmatic and conservative in every sense of the term.

Hon. John J. Ingalls was one of the most sensitive, nervous men that was ever in the Senate. His intellect was keen, his mind active, and he manifested his caustic disposition almost every day he appeared in the Senate. He could no more help being sarcastic and critical than he could help the color of his eyes. He was very thin and tall, with dark hair and sharp features. He was a fine lawyer, a forceful writer, and probably no man's utterances in the Senate were couched in more refined language or expressed in better style than those of John J. Ingalls. He was at one time accused of buying his election to the Senate. General Logan was on the committee on privileges and elections. We lived in the same house with Ingalls, and one morning, after the Kansas committee had called on General Logan, Ingalls came into the room and asked the general what the members of the committee had said. The general replied: "I am one of the jurymen, and I can't tell you what they said." I was standing near by, and, seeing Senator Ingalls's intense curiosity in the matter, I said: "Senator, I am not on the committee, and I am going to tell you what they said." He laughed and urged

me to do so. "They say that you bought your election."
"Nonsense," he said. "I hadn't money to buy a single vote,
even if I had been so disposed. The truth is, I couldn't buy
a yawl, if ships were selling at a quarter apiece." At this we
all laughed heartily. He was my *vis-à-vis* for a long time at
the table, and I used to be most uncomfortable at his phi-
lippics. His criticism of persons for whom he had a contempt
was a thing to be dreaded. He was always so very kind to
me, however, that I had great admiration for his ability.
One day, after he had finished a tirade against somebody, I
said: "Senator Ingalls, I want to ask a favor of you." He
very gallantly replied: "Mrs. Logan, you could ask me nothing that I would not promise to grant." "It is this," I said.
"Promise me that you will never speak of me save in kindness,
whether I be living or dead." He got up from his seat, came
round the end of the table where General Logan sat, and took
my hand. "Why do you ask that, when you know that I
could never speak of you except to praise?" he asked. He
was a charming man in his family. Mrs. Ingalls was one of
the loveliest characters I ever knew. Senator Ingalls's deference for her and his affection and kindness were in striking
contrast to his sarcastic treatment of so many others. Kansas
made a great mistake when she discontinued the services of
John J. Ingalls in the Senate. In the house where we boarded
they had a "Travel Club," and many of the senators and representatives who boarded in the house used to give papers
or addresses at the evening sessions of the society. Senator
Ingalls gave a most interesting paper on George Washington's
birthday, which he commenced in this language: "George
Washington, the father of his country, and said to be the
father of Judge Blank, of Indiana, etc." You can imagine
the consternation with which this announcement was received,
but the senator went right on with his beautiful address as if
he had said nothing out of the way.

Zachary Chandler of Michigan was another formidable

man in the Senate. He was ponderous in appearance, with a very large head covered with dark hair. He was so positive in his manner that every word he uttered seemed to come from an unchangeable determination in his mind. He was a big man with a big heart, fierce as a lion as an antagonist but true to his friends, toward whom he was gentle as a lamb. The probabilities are that in all his public life he was never more outraged than over the part which he was deceived into taking in securing Grant's acceptance of Belknap's resignation before people understood the great scandal which was Belknap's undoing. Chandler was so honest a man that he could not conceive of a public official, especially a man with such a record as Belknap had as a soldier, playing the part of which he was accused in the matter of commissions on the sale of post-traderships. He knew no such word as timidity, and was always ready to join in the advocacy of measures supposed to be in the interest of the public welfare. His record as a senator and as Secretary of the Interior is without a stain.

Meanwhile, in a political way, excitement was waxing hotter and hotter, and the most stupendous charges were being made against President Grant and his administration, while the prominent men of the Republican party ably defended them.

On July 1 General John A. Creswell of Maryland, Postmaster-General, and one of the most efficient and distinguished members of any cabinet, resigned. Eugene Hale of Maine was appointed his successor, but for some reason, after considering the matter, declined the post-office portfolio. Marshall Jewell, a prominent Republican of Connecticut, was appointed and confirmed as Postmaster-General.

As soon as Lent was over society began a series of entertainments. Members of the cabinet, senators, and citizens of Washington rivalled each other in magnificence of their luncheons, dinners, and receptions. It was rumored that there was to be one of those unusual events in the White

House in which everybody takes a personal interest. Nellie Grant was to be married to Algernon Sartoris of England. In the early springtime of 1869 Secretary and Mrs. Borie had decided to take a trip to Europe, inviting Nellie Grant to go with them. On board the ship she met the young Englishman, who had been assiduous in his attentions, and, though almost every intimate friend had filed a protest against the marriage, the general and Mrs. Grant felt they could not hold out against Nellie's expressed wish to be allowed to marry the man of her choice.

The President and Mrs. Grant had a bitter trial in yielding to the importunities of Mr. Sartoris, and allowing their daughter and idol to marry and go to England to live without any hope of her ever returning to America. Their daughter's happiness, however, was paramount to all else with them, and, though they did not approve of her choice, when they found that she could not be persuaded out of it they allowed her to have everything as she desired.

Undoubtedly Nellie Grant's was the most elaborate wedding that ever took place in the White House. Social affairs in Washington were never brighter than in the spring of 1874. The city was full of officers who had won distinction in the army and navy during the Civil War. The Diplomatic Corps was composed of representative men. Many of them, as also numberless citizens, were rich and entertained constantly. President Grant could count wealthy friends by the score who were glad to do anything they could for him or his family. Nellie was so young and so much beloved by every one that, while they hated to think of her going to England, they were, in consequence, ready to lavish everything upon her. No bride was ever more beloved or received a greater number of magnificent presents than did Nellie Grant. The 21st of May, 1874, was a glorious spring day. The soft air was laden with the perfume of the magnolias and catalpas of the parks. Everything was full of life and hap-

piness. The executive mansion had been elaborately decorated. The crowd was not as great as at an evening reception, as only the most distinguished and special friends of
the President and Mrs. Grant were invited. Many members
of the cabinet, justices of the Supreme Court, senators, representatives, and distinguished officers of the army and navy
were there. Sir Edward and Lady Thornton were there as
friends and sponsors for the bridegroom. A dais had been
placed between the windows of the east side, above which
hung a floral bell with long smilax ropes attached. At eleven
o'clock Doctor Tiffany, of the Metropolitan Methodist Episco-
pal Church, entered and took his position on the dais. The
Marine Band played the wedding march and announced the
approach of the bridal party. All eyes were turned to the
entrance from the corridor. The bridegroom, Mr. Sartoris,
and Lieutenant-Colonel Fred D. Grant approached, followed
by Miss Edith Fish and Miss Frelinghuysen, Miss Sherman and
Miss Porter, Miss Drexel and Miss Dent. Next came Mrs.
Grant, attended on either side by her two sons, Ulysses and
Jesse. The President and the bride brought up the rear,
the bridesmaids separating so as to form a circle, the President and bride stepping on the platform where the bridegroom
advanced to meet the bride. Miss Edith Fish stood on the
other side as maid of honor, Mrs. Grant and her sons standing
immediately behind them. Doctor Tiffany, a man of imposing appearance, who had a fine voice, pronounced impressively the ceremony according to the ritual of the
Methodist Church, Mrs. Grant's tearful eyes betraying the
deep emotions of her mother's heart in giving up her daughter.
A superb breakfast was served in the State dining-room; the
customary boxes of bride's cake were distributed, after which
the guests made their adieus, and the bride and groom prepared for their departure for New York to sail on the *Baltic*
for England. The story of the life of Mrs. Sartoris, the death
of her husband, her return to her native land, and her recent

marriage to Mr. Jones of Chicago—a man of high standing and character—is well known. Of her three children, her son and one daughter reside in France; the other daughter lives in the United States.

Congress adjourned in June, and we returned to our home in Chicago. We had been away from southern Illinois for four years, and many of our interests there required General Logan's attention. He spent several weeks looking after our affairs and meeting old friends, and came home much rested from the fatigues of the long and trying session of Congress. We had the pleasure of enjoying our home for a longer time during the summer of 1874 than we were privileged to do afterward.

In October, 1874, we were summoned to attend the wedding of Lieutenant-Colonel Fred D. Grant, eldest son of General Grant, to the lovely Miss Ida-Marie Honoré. The Honorés had a beautiful house in the centre of South Park in Chicago, which was surrounded with grand old trees and was in every sense a charming summer home. It was ideal in its interior appointments. Mrs. Potter Palmer having previously lived in the house, it was filled with statuary and other articles of virtu, among them Miss Hosmer's "Puck," "The Veiled Cupid," or "Secret 7," "Love," by Rossetti, and a replica of Randolph Rogers's exquisite statue of "Nydia, the Blind Girl of Pompeii." The ceremony was performed by Reverend Mr. Errett, of the Christian Church, Mr. and Mrs. Honoré being members of that church. Miss Honoré was attended by Miss Levy, Miss Rucker, Miss Houston, and Miss Hall, while Lieutenant-Colonel Grant was attended by his brother Ulysses. The bride and groom left that afternoon for their bridal tour, Colonel Grant carrying away from Chicago one of its most attractive young women.

# CHAPTER XIV

GENERAL SHERMAN'S daughter Minnie was married October
1, 1874. Thus three important weddings had taken place in
the families of General Grant and General Sherman—those
of Nellie and Fred in Grant's family, and Minnie in Sherman's
family.

When we arrived in Washington early in December we
found that Colonel Fred and Mrs. Grant were ensconced in
the White House, and were to spend the winter with the President and Mrs. Grant, Colonel Fred being on duty in Washington. The presence of the fascinating Mrs. Grant, Jr.,
in the White House, and the promise that Nellie would soon
return for a visit to her native land, were a guarantee that
Mrs. Grant's receptions would be very brilliant during the
season. In fact, the society season began December 1, and
promised to be unusually gay.

King David Kalakaua and his suite arrived December 12.
Much ado was made over the fact that a real king was to

visit Washington. As I remember it, Congress made an appropriation of twenty-five thousand dollars for the entertainment of His Majesty during his stay. Secretary Fish, Secretary Belknap, and Secretary Robeson joined the committee to welcome the King on his arrival. He was escorted to his apartments which had been prepared for him in the Arlington Hotel. Unfortunately, on account of a severe cold which he had contracted, the King was unable to carry out part of the programme which had been arranged for him, but was able to attend the theatre to hear Clara Louise Kellogg in "Mignon." He displayed his gallantry by showering flowers on the prima donna. In appearance, the King was a fine specimen of a man. He was very tall, broad-shouldered, with a dark-olive complexion and very black hair and eyes. He looked more of a king than he was, and the devotees of titles went wild over this dusky sovereign. President Grant accorded him a brilliant reception and a state dinner. The Japanese minister and his lovely wife, Madame Yoshida, were among the guests who were invited to do honor to the King. A more magnificent costume was never worn in the White House than that of Madame Yoshida's. The material was of the rarest and most lustrous kind, and the gown had been made in the fashion of a full Japanese court dress. Mr. Yoshida, of course, appeared in the regulation court dress of his native country. King Kalakaua and his suite appeared in full-dress evening suits, except two of his generals, who wore the uniform of the Hawaiian Guards. General Logan and I attended both functions, and of the many occasions of this character at which I have been present at the White House none have been more attractive in the matter of appointments. Congress, and official and civilian Washington entitled to invitations to such affairs, were there in full force, the ladies rivalling each other in the splendor of their costumes. Very few who participated in the attentions to King Kalakaua anticipated what the future held for Hawaii, or that the King and the royal family were doomed to close their imperial careers in a few brief years.

There was an unusual number of famous people in Washington that year. Many of the houses, especially on K Street, were occupied by persons who had made their impress on the history of their country. Alas! the majority of them have passed away, and their places have not been filled by persons who are their equals in extending hospitality and cordial greetings. There was much excitement over the approaching centennial exposition in Philadelphia. Every one was busy with some feature which was to be used to add to the attractiveness of the celebration of our glorious victories one hundred years before. Among the entertainments which were given to raise money was a centennial tea in the rotunda of the Capitol on December 16, 1875, in which every person at all prominent in society took a very active part. There were thirteen tables to represent the thirteen original States, and it was gratifying to see the taste and the strict adherence to the custom and style of refreshments of Colonial days. The ladies who presided over these tables were attired in gowns of the days of seventy-six, many of the dresses belonging to the wardrobes of their illustrious ancestors. The tables of North and South Carolina were especially attractive, the ladies who presided being typical of their native State. The beautiful flowers and delicious fruits which characterized these States were in abundance, while Maryland and many of the other States had innumerable revolutionary relics displayed. The rotunda was decorated as never before. Boxes of tea in imitation of the Boston Tea Party were in evidence. Tea was served in cups marked George and Martha Washington. These were sold at one dollar apiece, and I have the pleasure of still retaining the one which I purchased. Liberty bells which had been rung in those historic days were on exhibition. On the committee of arrangements were prominent army and navy officers and officials of the Government.

Senator Hawley of Connecticut and Secretary Robeson made eloquent addresses, and the Marine Band discoursed patriotic music during the afternoon and evening.

At the opening of the exposition General Logan attended with the congressional committee, who were handsomely entertained by the commission at Horticultural Hall. In August I took our two children and their governess, Miss Parke, to Philadelphia, where we spent two weeks in seeing everything of interest at the exposition and enjoyed every moment. At the time I had not visited Europe, as I have done many times since, and therefore there were to me very many novelties and interesting exhibits. I had not previously appreciated the advancement of my own country and was delighted to find so many evidences that the wheel of progress had been busy developing our resources and bringing to our land the fruits of a higher civilization. The Centennial Exposition was a good thing for our country. If it did nothing else, it was the initiative in the opening of the way for its successors.

During the winter General Sherman's memoirs appeared and brought forth much adverse comment from various quarters, on account of the fact that they reflected strongly his natural prejudices and, it was frankly said, unjust criticism of distinguished officers under him in the service. He was especially severe on General Logan and General Frank P. Blair, two volunteer officers, whom he characterized as "political generals," notwithstanding the fact that they had arisen to the rank of major-general by their military skill in handling troops—many times in independent command —and their gallantry on the field of battle. While he had to comment favorably upon their action in battle and their soldierly conduct, he could not give them the praise they deserved because of the fact that they were not graduates of the military academy at West Point. If I remember correctly, Frank Blair died without Sherman ever having corrected his unfair estimate of Blair's military career.

In the case of General Logan it was different. There was an additional reason for Sherman's criticism of General Logan —on account of the fact that General Logan was the author of the bill for the reduction of the army after the close of the war, and had greatly offended Sherman by recommending a cut in his salary. Although Sherman wrote a very bitter letter to Congress denouncing the bill, the majority of Congress considered that its provisions were just, and General Sherman was unable to prevent its passage. This, in addition to the fact that General Sherman had recommended General Howard to supersede General Logan in command of the Army of the Tennessee, after General Logan had won the great battle at Atlanta, and after Sherman had assured Logan that he should retain the command, intensified the antagonistic feeling existing between General Sherman and General Logan. General Logan, however, was conscientious in the preparation of the bill and had not taken occasion to be revenged on account of General Sherman's unkind treatment of him. General Logan was entirely vindicated by the army, and was restored to the command of the Army of the Tennessee. He had no malice toward Sherman about the matter, because he felt that it all came from the prejudice existing against a man not a graduate of West Point. General Logan knew he had never lost a battle, or in any way failed in the execution of orders issued to him during the war, more than which could not be said of graduates of West Point. He never at any time felt that the latter had much the advantage over faithful, conscientious, brave volunteer officers, whose patriotism guided them in their services to the country. General Logan believed if a man were desperately in earnest in his desire to serve his country, he would not be long in mastering military tactics and in fitting himself for any emergency which might arise. There is no doubt at all that General Logan's military genius was inborn. General Grant was lavish in his praise of him as a soldier and commander, and would undoubtedly have retained him as commander of the Army of the Tennessee had he (Grant) been in command of the Western Army at the time. It was a source of gratification that the scene at the Corkhill Banquet, described in the earlier pages of this autobiography, was enacted, and that there was a reconciliation between General Logan and General Sherman before they passed to that land from which no one returns.

The New Year's reception of January 1, 1875, was in many respects more brilliant than any previous one. The New Year's reception at the White House was then, as now, the signal for the beginning of the round of social events for the winter. Dinners, luncheons, receptions—official and otherwise—were the rule. In January Mr. and Mrs. Sartoris returned and took up their abode in the White House, greatly to the delight of Mrs. Grant, who now had her daughter and Mrs. Fred Grant to assist in the discharge of her social duties. Her Saturday afternoons were especially attractive and, she often told me afterward, were really the most enjoyable social functions that were held in the executive mansion. Persons came in so informally and received such a cordial welcome that they were at once made to feel it a privilege to pay their respects to the occupants of the White House. People wandered about through the red room, blue room, green room, east room, and the beautiful conservatories then at the west end of the corridor, and the state dining-room. Mrs. Grant seemed very happy when she had Nellie standing beside her. Nellie had not contracted any European airs, but stood beside her mother the same unpretentious, lovely, girlish woman whom everybody was delighted to welcome back to Washington. Perhaps it is a matter of prejudice, but it seems as if the representative ladies in Washington in those days were far more attractive than the majority we meet now. I have sometimes thought that the frequent intercourse with Europe and the contracting of the habits of cocktail-drinking and cigarette-smoking have affected the cordiality and simplicity of the manners of American women. I can remember when the suggestion was made that the ladies of the White House and the wives of members of the cabinet and other officials should not shake hands with their callers because it was supposed to be a matter of too much fatigue. I confess that the custom which causes a hostess to stand erect with a bouquet in her right hand and a fan or something in her left, which prevents her from extending a more cordial greeting than a stiff bow to her callers, is not calculated to put people at their ease or make them feel that their calls are appreciated. There never was any reason why Americans should ape the airs and stiffness of any European court. We welcome to our shores people from all lands and extend to them the privileges of life, liberty, and the pursuit of happiness: and why we should erect a barrier against those of our kind whom we recognize as fitting persons to be invited across our thresholds is an incomprehensible question, which has not been satisfactorily answered. Cordiality and hospitality are supposed to be the chief characteristics of Americans, and I regret to see any departure from the customs and manners which have ever been the charm of our people. Of all women in the world, American women should be considered the most sincere and attractive as hostesses.

Every year it seems that attractive features of society grow fewer and fewer. Horatio King, John J. Nicolay, and Mrs. Dahlgren formerly had regular evenings in their homes, when musical programmes were rendered, impromptu papers read, and lectures delivered by able persons, among them General Garfield, General Logan, Librarian Spofford, Senator Ingalls, Jean Davenport Lander, and a daughter of Mrs. Scott Siddons, then a resident of Washington. Readings and recitations from Shakespeare and other classics were given, much to the enjoyment of the persons fortunate enough to be invited to these literary gatherings. The Schiller Bund gave delightful entertainments, when lectures were given, and the programme usually closed with amateur theatricals. Miss Edith Fish and Miss Nannie Jeffreys figured prominently in these plays. Miss Jeffreys won an enviable reputation as an amateur actress in her part in "Meg's Diversion."

When we came to Washington, early in December, General Logan was just recovering from a very serious attack of illness. He had been a victim of inflammatory rheumatism contracted at Fort Donelson and, after a political campaign, frequently was confined to his bed for weeks. The opening day of Congress the galleries of both houses were packed. Sir Edward and Lady Thornton and Hon. William M. Evarts were in the diplomatic gallery, as were also Mrs. Grant and Mrs. Fish. The people of the whole country were very much interested in the proceedings in Congress, as it was known that the matter of the reconstruction of the Southern States was still at white heat, and it was supposed that the Louisiana question would furnish food for many an exciting controversy in the Senate.

Mr. Pinchback had been elected United States senator from Louisiana, and was bitterly opposed because of the fact that it was said he had colored blood in his veins. Every day some member of the House or Senate was heard in denunciation of the privileges and protection extended to the colored men in the South. There were outbreaks of Indians in the West, and a serious controversy arose over the Black Hills Reservation, as gold had been discovered there, and the Indians sternly opposed the influx of gold-seekers into their domain.

There were constant charges and countercharges of corruption and defalcations of officials, the Whiskey Ring figuring conspicuously at this time. Charges of membership in the Whiskey Ring were made against persons in official positions under the very roof of the White House. Grant himself did not escape the insinuations on the part of these marplots that he, if not a member of the ring, was cognizant of the connection of those intimately associated with him; and his accusers went so far in their persecution as to make it necessary for General Babcock to demand an investigation of his conduct. He was, of course, exonerated, but the authors of these charges had accomplished their purpose of throwing discredit upon the administration. Men in the Republican party who advocated the election of Mr. Blaine, and other prominent men, took an active part in the warfare upon the integrity of the appointees of General Grant. The political campaign of 1876 may be said to have begun in 1875, since long before the holding of the convention for the election of delegates to the national convention, to be held at Cincinnati, the champions of candidates had exhausted much of their ammunition in trying to kill off the rivals of men whose cause they advocated. Men opposed to Mr. Blaine retaliated by making grave charges as to his connection with various questionable schemes. Blaine's reading of the Mulligan letters on the floor of the House of Representatives is perhaps the most remarkable incident of a personal explanation that has ever occurred in Congress. Subsequently Nast's caricature, appearing originally in a New York paper, showing Mr. Blaine as the "Tatooed Man," was without exception the most cruel persecution ever inflicted upon a public man.

There were innumerable resignations of men holding high positions by appointment. Some resigned from disgust and some to avoid the humiliation of investigations. Senators whose term expired March 4, 1877, were much concerned, as candidates for the members of the legislature would be elected on the ticket that would be nominated in 1876. Hence they had not only to be on the lookout in the interest of the candidates for the Presidency and Vice-Presidency, but had to watch every movement, politically, in their home States, to be sure that their party was successful.

The national convention was held in Cincinnati in June, 1876, and it was thought that Blaine, notwithstanding the intense abuse heaped upon him, had a majority. The convention was very largely attended by legions of Republicans who were not delegates, but who had gone there for the purpose of advocating or opposing Blaine's election. General Granville M. Dodge recently explained how Blaine's defeat was really brought about. He was a Blaine delegate in the convention and strongly advocated the election of Hon. James F. Wilson, of Iowa, as permanent chairman. Mr. Wilson was one of the ablest and most experienced statesmen of the nation. Don Cameron wanted McPherson, of Pennsylvania, then clerk of the House of Representatives and compiler of the "Political Hand Book of the Republican Party." Dodge worked very hard for Wilson and thought his election was agreed upon. He retired to get a few hours' sleep and rest, during which time the opponents of Wilson succeeded in electing McPherson as permanent chairman. This was the beginning of the blunders that led to Blaine's Waterloo. McPherson, as Dodge had suspected, was unequal to the position. He was too unsuspecting for the wily politicians who were inimical to Blaine, and at a critical moment entertained a motion to adjourn, which was followed by boisterous commotion and confusion, intensified by the trick of turning off the gas and enshrouding the hall in total darkness. Caucusing was the rule during the hours between the fatal adjournment and the meeting of the convention the following morning. No sleep was allowed to jeopardize the schemes of the anti-Blaine delegates, which culminated in nominating Rutherford B. Hayes, of Ohio, for President, and William A. Wheeler, of New York, for Vice-President. Mr. Hayes was the weakest man, save one, ever elected to the Presidency. His associate on the ticket, Mr. Wheeler, was really a nonentity.

It would not have been possible to have nominated two more non-committal, conservative men. They were the very antipodes of the candidates prominent before the convention met. They were the usual types of compromise candidates, and brought no strength to the ticket. As a matter of fact, no one anxious for the success of the party wanted either of them.

The whole campaign of 1876 was characterized by the most virulent abuse of the candidates, active persons of both parties striving with each other in making charges of fraud, irregularities, and malfeasance on the part of officials and members of their respective parties. Nominees on the tickets for the various offices from President down were anxious as to the results. In addition, reformers were busy advocating all kinds of isms and theories. The hapless farmers, the inevitable prey of political demagogues, came in for unusual attentions. They were persuaded that they were the victims of merciless injustice; that their only hope for relief was through the election of reformers to the house and senate of the legislatures of the States most interested in agriculture. Illinois, the great "Prairie State," was completely overrun by "Grangers," who were posing as the farmers' special friends. They declared, if they were put in power they would readjust the management of the railroads and secure a change in the freight schedules, so that the products of the farm could be set down at the great market points for half the rate then in existence. They would, in fact, procure high prices for every commodity the agriculturist had to sell. A majority of the Republican county conventions had instructed their nominees for the house and senate of the Illinois legislature for General Logan for re-election to the United States Senate, which event was dependent upon the election of these instructed candidates. Hence the campaign had scarcely begun when importunities came from every quarter urging General Logan to visit almost every county in the State to speak in behalf of the election of the candidates instructed for him. Congress was in session for some time after the adjournment of the Republican national convention.

Loyal and far-seeing Republicans realized the full force of

the mistake the national convention had made, but there was no alternative but to make the best of it, and if possible elect Hayes and Wheeler.  Strangely enough, it was during this campaign that the Democratic party, while boasting of Jeffersonian simplicity, began to intimate that Mr. Tilden's "barrels of money would enable them to win a Democratic victory all over the United States."  They claimed that the solid South, supplemented by the influence of money, would put their party in power—nationally and locally.  When the election returns were in the people were amazed to find that their predictions had come so near being true.  The election of President and Vice-President was in controversy and had to be finally settled by the famous Electoral Commission, under a special act to provide for the settlement of the important question as to who had been elected President and Vice-President in 1876.  Republican majorities had fallen off everywhere.  In Illinois the political complexion of the legislature was in doubt, depending largely upon the party—Republican or Democratic—with which the "Prohibitionists," "Grangers," "Reformers," and "Independents" would co-operate.

It would be difficult to imagine with what disgust General Logan confronted the situation in the legislature when he found that old farmers, who were supposed to be the soul of honor and integrity, and had been for years enthusiastic supporters of himself, had been changed by some surreptitious influence.  While they claimed to be undecided as to whom they would support for the Senate, nothing could induce them to commit themselves to General Logan.  Upon investigation later it was found that these men had received from three to five thousand dollars each, with which to lift the mortgages off their farms, from their Granger friends, who had been using the money of ambitious aspirants to the Senate.  So trustful was General Logan that it was some time before he could really credit the indubitable evidence that was laid before him of the dishonesty and duplicity of these old friends.

The designing political jugglers had skilfully bought up just enough of the senators and members of the house to prevent General Logan from having a majority in either. The legislature had not long been in session when it was found that a part of the scheme was to defeat General Logan by the election of Hon. David Davis as Associate Justice of the United States Supreme Court to prevent him from being chosen on the Electoral Commission. Somebody's barrel accomplished the purpose of defeating General Logan for re-election and put David Davis in the Senate in his place. Mr. Davis regretted this as seriously as any one else, and did not hesitate to maintain that both he and General Logan had been sacrificed to the stupendous scheme of political demagogues. For weeks the election of the United States senator from Illinois was in doubt. The action of the legislature was so uncertain because of the instability and lack of integrity on the part of members of both houses. This may be said to have been the beginning of the political demoralization of the great State of Illinois, and was, perhaps, the first instance of the flagrant use of money to influence the action of the legislature in the election of a United States senator. I was with General Logan at Springfield, and shall not forget to my dying day the deep humiliation and suffering which he experienced as day after day he discovered fresh evidences of the duplicity of men whom he had trusted in war and in peace. He felt that he had served his State honorably and acceptably from the day he took the oath of office as a member of the Illinois legislature in 1856, through all the trying years of the war, to that hour. Believing as he did that the people approved of everything he had done, and desired to reward him by a re-election to the United States Senate, he could not bear to think that their will was being thwarted by the use of money, a force which it was impossible for him to combat.

I hope it will not be considered indelicate to say that these reverses came at the most unfortunate time in our whole lives.

General Logan devoted every hour of his life and time to the discharge of his public duties, and therefore was obliged to neglect opportunities for money-making. It will be remembered that the salary of a United States senator was at that time only five thousand dollars a year. We had lived very prudently in inhospitable boarding-houses, and in many ways practised self-denial and economy. But the unavoidable demands that have always been made upon public men, for political and other purposes, including requests by individuals to whom public men consider themselves under obligations, for the indorsement of their notes for financial responsibilities —nine times out of ten the indorser having to pay these notes —all these things made accumulation almost impossible for a United States senator. General Logan, like many others, had encroached upon the savings of years to meet these various demands, and was at a loss to know just what he should do at the expiration of his term, March 4, 1877.

Prior to that time the Electoral Commission had declared Hayes and Wheeler elected President and Vice-President, and every one supposed that General Logan would be offered some position within the gift of the President. He received no such consideration, notwithstanding the fact that some of his friends had gone to the President and explained to him General Logan's necessities. We were both too proud to make any sign. After March 4 we went home to Chicago and finally solved the problem of what we should do. We had some land in southern Illinois which we were quite sure we could utilize in the payment of notes which were coming due in June. The general was too sensitive to go back to southern Illinois and make an appeal to his old friends for an extension of time, or to have them think that he was in the least discouraged by the temporary dislodgement from his seat in the Senate. I insisted that we had lived a long time before he was a senator, and that I was quite sure that we could manage in some way. I begged him to let me go down to southern

Illinois and dispose of some lands which we had owned for years. With great reluctance he agreed to let me try to see what I could do. When I arrived in Carbondale I was received with so many manifestations of genuine friendship and interest in our welfare that I felt no hesitancy in going to the substantial men who I thought wanted the property and could afford to buy the land which we had to sell. Memory will forever retain the tenderness with which these dear old men responded to my request that they buy this land and relieve our embarrassment. They gave me exactly what I asked for the property and said that they were ready to carry for an indefinite length of time any notes which General Logan had given, and would give him cash for his land beside. I could only express my gratitude by tears which they hastened to wipe away, and to say: "Be cheerful and happy. Your discomfiture is only a brief affair. Two years hence we will send him back to the Senate or die in the attempt."

General Logan had not quite forgotten the law which he knew so well before he took up his sword in the defence of his country. In the great State of Illinois there were grand men who knew what he had done. They came to him to place in his hands large legitimate claims which they wished him to collect, and he was soon happy in the possession of fees larger than his salary as a United States senator. As I look back upon it I feel that the two years intervening before he was again elected to the Senate were by no means the most unhappy years of our lives, and I am not quite sure but that, had he refrained from again taking an active part in politics, we should have been better off financially, and perhaps the days of his life might have been multiplied.

After General Logan became accustomed to being out of the treadmill routine and daily drudgery to which members of both houses of Congress are accustomed, he really enjoyed his freedom. He was not permitted, however, to remain long out of the political arena. Every day he received some communication from friends all over the country, urging him not to forswear politics; that there was much for him to do for his party and country that no other man could do. He employed his time in gathering up the threads of his private business affairs and in preparing to go to Washington in the winter of 1877-8 for some clients who had engaged his services as attorney.

November 27, 1877, on the twenty-second anniversary of our marriage, our only daughter was married to William F. Tucker of Chicago. Could we have known the sequel of this unfortunate alliance, General Logan and I would have suffered more keenly than we did in giving our only daughter into the hands of any man's keeping, as no one could have seemingly been more eligible for a trust so sacred than W. F. Tucker. It was arranged that our son, John A. Logan, Jr., then twelve years of age, should return to the Morgan Park Military Academy and that Mr. and Mrs. Tucker were to remain in our Chicago home, while I was to accompany General Logan to Washington.

We returned to Mrs. Rhine's boarding-house, 812 Twelfth Street, and were soon ensconced in our old quarters. Mrs. Edmund Miller, of Waterloo, Iowa, a cousin of the general's, was with us. Her husband had died, and she decided to join us for the winter. In reading over a diary kept that winter, I think it was perhaps one of the happiest we ever spent in Washington. Mrs. Rhine's boarding-house was composed of three private houses, 810–812–814 Twelfth Street, Northwest, and was one of the best of the old-time hostelries, having been the home of more prominent people than any other in Washington. Mrs. Mary S. Lockwood and Miss Ricksford were Mrs. Rhine's successors, and continued the establishment long after we moved away. General Logan was not at the beck and call of every one who needed a friend to intercede for him at the departments. His numerous constituents who had formerly deluged him with their correspondence requesting everything trom commissions from the State Department to seeds, plants, reports, and bulletins from the Department of Agriculture, realizing that he was an "ex," turned to his successor with indifferent success, that venerable ex-Associate Justice of the Supreme Court being disinclined to activities as an errand boy for his constituents.

We had many invitations for dinners and receptions. Mrs. Hayes sent me flowers and invited us to dine at state and informal dinners. She has had no superior and few equals as mistress of the White House. An unprejudiced, truthful historian would doubtless place the name of Lucy Webb Hayes at the head of the list of women who were most eminently qualified by nature and acquirement for the position of mistress of the White House. She was probably the only rival of the fame of Abigail Adams, the wife of John Adams, second President of the United States. Mrs. Adams's intellect, dauntless courage, and devoutly religious character may be said to have been repeated in the person of Lucy Webb Hayes.

Mrs. Hayes was born in Chillicothe, then the capital of Ohio. Her father, Doctor James Webb, was an eminent practitioner and very prominent in public affairs. He was an ardent Republican, after liberating the slaves which came to him through his North Carolinian ancestry. Mrs. Webb, her mother, was a remarkable woman, devoutly religious in character, and wonderfully well-informed for the epoch in which she lived. From her Mrs. Hayes inherited the best Puritan blood of New England. Being left a widow when her family was young, she removed to Delaware, Ohio, to be near the Wesleyan University, so that her children might be educated. Her sons were good students. Lucy, the only daughter, would not be outdone by her brothers. She therefore studied with them, and was tutored by the instructors of the college until prepared for the Wesleyan Female College, of Cincinnati, entering that institution at the same time her brothers began their studies in the Medical College of that city. She graduated from the Wesleyan Female College with high honors.

To her mother she gave all the credit for her splendid preparation for the sphere she was destined to fill.  She possessed a rare mind, and wonderful mental and physical strength.  She was of medium height, her complexion was a clear olive, and her abundant dark hair was always combed smoothly over her ears and wound into a coil quite low on the back of her head, and held in place by a beautiful comb.  Her glorious eyes were indescribable in their color and expression, ever reflecting the bright spirits which animated her whole soul.  Her face beamed with intelligence and happiness, and I am quite sure no one ever detected the slightest care, impatience, or unpleasantness in her countenance, as it was always full of tenderness and good humor.  Her winsome manners, sunny temperament, and cordial greetings vanquished all fear of the timid, and made them feel that they could tell her all their woes and be assured of sympathy.

Her inheritance and training seemed especially to fit her for the position she was to fill.  Her mother's example, care, and determination that her daughter should be educated beyond what was then thought necessary for girls; the excellent opportunities she had in the Female College at Cincinnati, under the guidance and tutelage of Reverend and Mrs. P. B. Wilbur, pioneer advocates of higher education of women in the West, developed her superior executive ability and well-balanced character.  Mrs. Hayes met her husband when she was a student in college at the Wesleyan, and they were married soon after they had both been graduated from their respective colleges.  Their marriage proved to be one that must have been made in heaven, if one may judge by its perfect happiness.  Mrs. Hayes, as all true wives should, immediately devoted herself to everything which tended to advance the interests of her husband.  She had absolute faith in his destiny, and unbounded confidence in his ability to climb to the topmost rung of the ladder of fortune and fame.  He had begun the ascent when the nation was startled by a call to arms of her loyal sons.  Rutherford B. Hayes could not turn a deaf ear to that call.    He helped to raise the 23d Ohio Volunteer Infantry, of which General Rosecrans was colonel, and the late Associate Justice Stanley Matthews, was lieutenant-colonel, going himself as major of that regiment. During the trying years of the varying fortunes of the Army of the Potomac, in which the 23d served, Mrs. Hayes was a frequent visitor to her husband in the field.    At South Mountain Major Hayes was badly wounded.    Mrs. Hayes appeared soon afterward to nurse him and many others back to health. When in camp, and it was possible to leave her husband, she spent her time in ministering to the Union and Confederate sick and wounded.    One might write a long story of the never-failing devotion of these men to this noble woman.

Colonel Hayes left the field a brigadier-general, promoted for gallantry on the field of battle, to become a member of Congress. After several years' service in that body he was chosen governor of Ohio.    From this position he was elected President of the United States.    President Hayes always accorded Mrs. Hayes a full measure of credit for his phenomenal advancement to the highest position within the gift of the people.    Her unselfish devotion to the unfortunate, her unceasing labors for the enlargement of the charities of Ohio, her arduous labors in church work, her womanly and wifely interest in her home and her husband, brought her a rich reward in the realization of all her hopes and aspirations.    Hence, when she came to be installed as mistress of the White House, she was well equipped by nature, training, cultivation, and unusual knowledge and long experience in official life for anything which might arise.    The sphere in which she had always moved had only been enlarged.

Her first appearance was eagerly awaited by the denizens of Washington and official representatives from all over the world.    They sought to criticise, but went away admiring and praising this gifted, accomplished woman.    The word was passed from mouth to mouth: "Mrs. Hayes is lovely." She was so radiantly happy herself that her gay spirits became infectious. She began her reign by giving an afternoon reception on a Saturday, soon after the inauguration, to which every one entitled to be received was invited. She had flowers and music and everything as elaborate as for an evening social function. Every one was charmed by the warmth of her greetings, which made them feel that she at least was destined to do her part toward making the new administration socially a success. Following this afternoon reception was a state dinner, given to the Russian Grand Dukes, Alexis and Constantine, to which were bidden diplomats, judges, senators, representatives, and many other distinguished persons, with their wives, including ourselves. The decorations of the house and table and everything connected with the magnificent entertainment were directed by Mrs. Hayes in person. Her triumph on this occasion convinced the critics that she was not a novice in social affairs of state.

Mrs. Hayes was much criticised by a certain class for the stand she took in banishing wine from the White House table, but even her severest critics have since come to laud and magnify her name for the wisdom and Christian firmness she displayed. She never discussed the question with the numerous officious and intrusive persons who are ever eager to talk, and especially with authors of innovations. She said to one friend: "Regarding the question of wine, it is true that I shall violate a precedent, but I shall not violate the Constitution, which is all that, through my husband, I have taken the oath to obey." To another she spoke of her sons and of her hesitancy in putting the wine before them, when it was in violation of her principles. She felt strongly her duty, and had the grace and courage to do it. From one of her addresses before the Home Missionary Society, of which she was an honored and useful member, I copy an extract, which was probably the foundation upon which she built her peerless character:

The corner-stone to practical religion is the Golden Rule. How best to obey its mandate is the vital question. Our conviction,

General John A. Logan in 1884.

our faith, is that the surest hope of mankind is in America. Within our limits, within our reach, are gathered representatives of all the races of mankind. . . . . That duty is of highest obligation which is nearest in time and place. With America and American homes what they should be, we need not greatly fear the evils that threaten us from other lands. We can easily shun or safely meet them, if our duty is faithfully done in behalf of the weak, the ignorant, and the needy of our country. If our institutions, social and political, are imperiled to-day, it is largely because of the wealthy and the fortunate. Engrossed as they are in the midst of our vast material progress and prosperity, they are not sufficiently mindful of what was taught by the words and life of the Founder of our blessed religion: "Whatsoever ye would that men should do to you, do ye even so to them."

Though a Methodist, she earnestly supported every movement for the advancement of religion and the betterment of the world.

General Logan having been returned to the Senate the winter of 1879, I saw much of Mrs. Hayes during President Hayes's administration, and am proud to repeat that I consider her to have been one of the noblest types of American womanhood, and beyond all question the ablest, and her influence for good the most abiding, of all the women who have ever presided in the White House.

During the winter we had delightful evenings in the parlor of the boarding-house, there being so many talented people in the house who were always ready to furnish papers, talks, recitations, and music. The regular residents in the house had guests from time to time, who frequently added interesting features to the programme. Reverend J. P. Newman was then filling the pulpit in the Metropolitan Church. His sermons were, without exception, full of inspired language. He made a study of the English language, and always used the exact word which would express his meaning most forcefully and beautifully. I once spoke to him about his peculiar gift. He said it was an acquisition rather than a gift. That he analyzed every word he used in writing and preaching, as he wished his readers or his hearers to have a clear comprehension of the subject he handled. He was a large man, with a big head full of brains, and it would have been impossible for him to be other than forceful. He was intensely patriotic and courageous, and there was never any doubt as to the meaning of his utterances. He was devoted to General Grant, and bore with ill grace the attacks upon his hero. Losing all patience with General Grant's detractors, he was ever ready to defend him valiantly. There is a pew in the Metropolitan Church assigned to the President of the United States. President Hayes being a Methodist, it was thought he would be Grant's successor in the occupancy of that pew, but for some unknown reason President Hayes had a prejudice against Doctor Newman, and decided to attend Foundry Church, then on the corner of Fourteenth and G Streets. I one day said to the wife of a member of President Hayes's cabinet: "Why do not the President and Mrs. Hayes attend the Metropolitan Church?" She replied: "Because Grant attended that church, and Doctor Newman is always defending Grant and all the 'skulduggery' of his administration." No further explanation was necessary. I have often wondered if President Hayes, after his retirement from the White House under the adverse criticism of the many, did not have a keener appreciation of the injustice heaped upon the chief magistrate by disappointed critics.

General Logan and I had a very happy winter, in that we were able to read aloud to each other, accomplishing more in that direction during this winter than we had been able to do for many years. We read a great many interesting books, and went to many lectures, dramatic performances, and social affairs. We had more time to enjoy our friends than we had ever had in Washington.

# CHAPTER XV

WHEN we arrived home we found that General Logan's
friends had been very busy in the matter of securing the members of the legislature who were favorable to his return to
the United States Senate. We found also that the many
letters which we had written from Washington in reply to
inquiries from General Logan's friends as to what he would
do had been most effective. At the November election,
although it was an off year (meaning that it was not a Presi-
dential-election year), the Republican party won many victories, and changed the complexion of Illinois politics completely. There was no longer any doubt as to which party
would control the legislature when it should meet in January,
1879, or who would succeed Senator Oglesby, whose time was
to expire March 4, 1879. Oglesby was a candidate himself,
but from written pledges sent to General Logan and his
friends it was well known that General Logan had a majority
of the legislature.

Although feeling confident of success, General Logan insisted that I should accompany him to Springfield, as he was loath to go into any contest unless I was near him. It was evident that there would be no such scenes as were enacted in the legislature of 1876-7, and that the "Reformers" had had their day, and had been retired to private life. The Republican and Democratic parties would have straight nominees for the senatorship; there would be no more mongrels with which to contend.

The legislature met January 1, and it was refreshing to us to be so cordially received when we arrived in Springfield, on January 4, accompanied by Doctor C. A. Logan, late American minister to Chile, and to be made to feel that there was a unanimous desire for General Logan's re-election. We were soon ensconced in the same old rooms in the Leland Hotel which we had occupied at the time of General Logan's first election to the Senate, and though we missed so many of the dear friends who were there at that time to lend their aid to the general's first election, we found their places had been taken by others who were equally enthusiastic and energetic in their daily efforts in my husband's behalf.

The legislature being strongly Republican, it was not long in organizing and settling down to business, the most important object being the election of the United States senator. The caucuses of both parties were held soon after the organization, and nominations were made for the officers of House and Senate. Naturally, General Logan had opposition, as, of course, it was impossible for any man to please everybody. The Chicago *Tribune* and *Times* fought him as usual. The *Times* because it was a Democratic paper, and the *Tribune* on the ground of free trade. Upright, patriotic men all over the State had arisen *en masse* to put down the men who had created so much trouble in the legislature in 1877. Senator David Davis was most enthusiastic in his support of General Logan, though he had himself been elected by a combination of the disgruntled elements of both parties, each claiming him as their own. It was soon discovered that it would be impossible for any malcontent to cause a postponement of the holding of the caucuses, the action of which was equivalent to an election in those days.

My observation has been that the old-fashioned conventions and caucuses were purer methods than the latter-day primaries and indifference to the mandates of a convention. If a man went into a convention and voted for a candidate, he regarded it as a pledge to support his candidate, and it was a rare thing for any man to take the chances of jeopardizing the confidence of his party and his friends by bolting a caucus or convention in which he had participated. It is impossible to account for the change in political affairs at the present day on any other theory than that the foreign elements that have crept into the party organizations are so impregnated with socialism and the various theories of socialists and anarchists that they wish to destroy rather than to build up.

The caucus for electing the officers of the legislature was held on January 7. There being little rivalry for the vice-presidency of the senate and the speakership of the house and subordinate offices, it passed off very harmoniously. Soon afterward it was agreed to hold, on January 17, the Republican caucus for nominating the United States senator.

When the time arrived there was not an absentee among those entitled to be present at the Republican caucus, which included every Republican member of the House and Senate, and there were but few who were disposed to disturb the harmony of the caucus. When the vote was taken it was as follows: total for General Logan—eighty; for General Oglesby—twenty-six. A legislature composed of more honorable men never met in the State of Illinois. Both candidates stood high in the estimation of the people of the State, but the majority were sure that General Logan could render the greater services to his State and country.

There were in Chicago at that time several aspirants for the Senate whose only foundation for such ambition was the fact that they had money, which had been inherited or made by devotion to private business, when men like Logan and Oglesby were serving their country in the field or forum. These men were unknown outside of the city and had nothing in common with the people. It was easy enough for them to promote the election to the legislature of impecunious men who, if they could do nothing else, could at least cause dissension in the party, and who had in the past aided in bringing about the defeat of the Republican party. They had done this, although they represented only the men who had caused their election for the purpose of promoting the aggrandizement of ambitions with no foundation except that of a financial nature. Mr. C. B. Farwell and E. B. Washburne, of the Republican party, and Lambert Tree and Franklin MacVeagh, of the Democratic party, were candidates from Chicago, while Hon. William R. Morrison and General John C. Black were candidates from the central and southern part of the State. General Logan, having had such an overwhelming majority of the party which controlled the legislature, was made United States senator as soon as all the forms prescribed by the Constitution were complied with. Mr. Frank Riddle and one or two others, without being able to give any legitimate excuse for their action, violently opposed General Logan's election while it was possible for them to make any trouble. When it became apparent that General Logan had such a large majority they were silenced and concluded that they would vote for him. It was always said that, having complied with the instructions of men whose creatures they were, they did not wish to be read out of the Republican party, so they came in and voted for General Logan at the last.

Everybody was so rejoiced over General Logan's election that a magnificent reception was tendered to us by the legislature and the citizens of Springfield, at the Leland Hotel, where we were stopping. At this reception I was assisted by Mrs. T. B. Needles, wife of Senator Needles; Mrs. James Shaw, wife of Speaker Shaw; Mrs. Joslyn, wife of Senator Joslyn; Mrs. White, wife of Senator White; Mrs. D. N. Bash, wife of Senator Bash; and Mrs. J. A. Connelly, wife of Major J. A. Connelly. A pleasant feature of this reception was the presentation to Hon. A. M. Jones, by Senator Hunt, on behalf of the State central committee and personal friends, of a magnificent silver tea-service in recognition of Mr. Jones's faithful and efficient services as chairman of the Republican State central committee.

We left Springfield for home under very different auspices from those of 1877. Everything looked bright and promising to us. Even though we knew that there was prodigious work awaiting General Logan as soon as he should enter the Senate, we were happy, as we felt that beyond any question he would be restored to the prominent places on the important committees in the Senate which he held when he retired from that body in 1877. The ovation tendered him on his arrival in Washington was most gratifying to both of us. We went back to our old quarters at 812 Twelfth Street, and took up the treadmill duties as if we had not been absent a day.

At the same time General Logan was elected to the Senate from Illinois, Senators Vest and Shields of Missouri; Daniel Voorhees of Indiana; Roscoe Conkling of New York; Platt of Connecticut; Hill of Colorado; Jones of Nevada; Governor Vance of North Carolina; Cameron of Pennsylvania; and Carpenter of Wisconsin were also returned. Many old colleagues greeted each other on the floor of the Senate March 4, 1879. Vice-President Wheeler was then in the chair. In the Senate there was Senator Thomas Bayard of Delaware, whose greatest pride was that he was a descendant of a long line of eminent statesmen. Senator Beck of Kentucky, that sturdy Scotchman who was never troubled by the Presidential bee because he was born in Scotland and thus disqualified for occupying the executive mansion, was one of the noblest and bravest men of the Senate, and his friendship was never bounded by the narrow limitations of partisanship. George H. Pendleton, of Ohio, the perfect opposite of his colleague, John Sherman, was a most ambitious man, and his elaborate manner was such that he had been given the cognomen of "Gentleman George." He was very polished in his manner, but never particularly forceful. The able Senator Pinkney Whyte of Maryland was in the Senate at this time. Cockrell of Missouri was a fine lawyer who, while having one of the bravest records among the officers of the Confederacy in the Senate, rarely boasted of it before that body. Senator Bruce, the colored Senator from Mississippi, was one of the most accomplished gentlemen in his manners and bearing in the Senate. He was a very agreeable man and conducted himself with the utmost propriety, winning the regard of his colleagues without distinction of party. L. Q. C. Lamar was one of the ablest men from the South. He had had a distinguished career during the war as a brave soldier. His manners were polished, and his ability as a debater and his sterling integrity made him very popular. He was subsequently named as associate justice upon the Supreme Bench. No one who ever saw Senator Vest of Missouri could forget him. He was a brave, conscientious representative of the State of Missouri, and was ever ready to enter into a discussion of any political question that arose in the Senate. Anthony and Burnside of Rhode Island, while of entirely different temperaments, were both able debaters and genial, companionable gentlemen. Senator Dawes of Massachusetts was probably the most perfect type of New England man in the Senate. He was conscientious and an earnest Republican in principle. He was not a brilliant man in any sense of the word, but a very hard worker on committees and for the best interests of Massachusetts. Plumb of Kansas, an able man without one particle of polish or appreciation of ceremony, was very careless in his dress and fearless in the advocacy of the principles of the Republican party.

General Logan's colleague, the Hon. David Davis, was ponderous in every sense of the word. He had a big head and a big body, a big brain and a big heart. He had been on the Supreme Bench so many years that he was well accustomed to listen; consequently he had very little to say in the Senate. He was always intensely interested in discussions, and now and again expressed himself in a forcible way which showed he was by no means a nonentity. Curiously enough he became so attached to General Logan that the general often said he had never had a more congenial colleague than David Davis. When the general's contest was going on in Springfield, David Davis assisted him greatly in the campaign and was among the first to congratulate the general on his election. His misfortune was that his aspirations to become President of the United States caused him to give up the position of Associate Justice of the Supreme Court for the position of United States senator, a position for which he was absolutely unfitted.

There is no disputing the fact that in those days, when men were elected on principle and on account of their fitness for the duties of statesmanship, we had greater men, especially in the Senate. Almost without exception, every man whose name is mentioned above made an enviable reputation during his term. Political problems affecting the welfare of the nation were as manifold then as now. Few men then in the Senate were connected with any business enterprise. Seemingly, they devoted all their time to the discharge of their public duties, rarely absenting themselves when Congress was in session. They were bitter partisans in politics, taking active parts in every movement affecting their party. "Independents," "Mugwumps," "Socialists," were few, the majority being loyal either to the Democratic or Republican party. Members of these two great parties entertained supreme contempt for renegades from their respective ranks.

Unfortunately for the peace and quiet of our country, there is continually some local, legislative, senatorial, or national election pending. A man is scarcely installed in the position to which he has been elected when he must begin to plan for re-election or to surrender his place to a successor. This constant revolution in offices deprives the country of the services of many good men; and there are so many safeguards that a bad man can not be ejected should one happen to be elected to office.

In addition to the momentous questions before Congress, the approaching Presidential election was causing more excitement, if possible, than that which preceded the nomination and seating by the Electoral Commission of Hayes and Wheeler, neither of whom had been satisfactory to the Republican party when they were nominated or after they were seated. President Hayes was too vacillating, too slow, to please either the radicals or conservatives. Mr. Wheeler was a good man, but far from brilliant. Candidates for the Presidency were daily springing up—Grant, Blaine, Washburne, Windom, Edmunds, Sherman, and Garfield. Garfield, under cover of being a Sherman man, was from the first thought to be working assiduously for his own nomination.

Naturally the prominence of these men for the nomination directed attention to their wives, any of whom would have made an acceptable mistress of the White House. Mrs. James G. Blaine was a tall, large woman with a distinguished carriage. She was a woman of rare intelligence, but was, unfortunately, very pronounced in her opinions. She was perfectly guileless in her character, and there was never any question as to Mrs. Blaine's approval or disapproval of political, social, or other matters. Great injustice has been done her by newspaper correspondents and other writers, as she was generally misunderstood. She was a devoted wife and mother, and no one in New England had a more conscientious appreciation of her duties as such.

Mrs. E. B. Washburne was one of the gentlest and most lovable women that I have ever known. She had a large family of children and a very imperious, irritable husband. Her cheery, amiable disposition was a panacea for all the ills of her family. She was so cordial and gracious in her manner that everybody loved her. When her husband assumed the duties of minister to France, it is said that Mrs. Washburne was the better diplomat of the two, and that she left behind her hosts of friends on the other side of the Atlantic, both in France and Germany.

Mrs. John Sherman was a woman of simplicity, but of intense sincerity of character. She was kind and considerate at all times, but was so modest and retiring that she was never properly appreciated. Mrs. Edmunds, wife of Senator Edmunds, one of the prominent candidates, was a perfect type of a New England woman in her domestic tastes and educational attainments. She was not at all fond of society, but devoted all of her time to her home and her brainy, ambitious husband. Mrs. William Windom of Minnesota was an active, intellectual woman, alive to all political conditions. She took part in all social affairs with enthusiasm. The world knows of Mrs. Garfield, the wife of the successful candidate. It is unnecessary to give a sketch of her, as so many have been written. Suffice to say that she is one of the most womanly of women, and would doubtless have filled the place of mistress of the White House with great credit to herself and satisfaction to the public had President Garfield lived to complete his term.

It would be well if, in the consideration of men for President, Vice-President, and members of the cabinet, some thought were given to the style of woman who is the candidate's wife. From time immemorial women connected with prominent men have been a power for good or evil. It is claimed that women are more subtle than men and that their machinations, when they are on mischief bent, have frequently resulted disastrously to friendly relations between individuals, governments, and nations. None of the wives of our Presidents have ever been accused of being mischief-makers, but some have accomplished much more than others in winning friends for the President and popularity for themselves, while wives of cabinet officers have broken up cabinets and defeated aspirants for the Presidency.

In a few brief weeks after his return to Washington General Logan had taken up many of the bills, a large number of which he had been interested in before his retirement, which were still on the calendar. It was not long before he had become wholly engrossed in the advocacy of the passage of these and many other measures which he considered important for the welfare of the nation. In the mean time the political pot was nearing the boiling-over point. General Grant had almost completed his tour around the world, and it was expected that he would be at home before the election of delegates to the national convention in 1880. As usual, a great warfare was being made on men who were to take an active interest in these political affairs. Among them General Logan came in for his share of abuse. One William H. Lowe, a member of Congress from Alabama, in making a political speech in the House, so far forgot himself as to make a personal attack upon General Logan, reviving the infamous slander that had been heaped upon him at the beginning of the war, when it was said that General Logan had attempted to raise a regiment for the Southern Confederacy. This old slander had been repeated at intervals ever since the beginning of the war, and had been over and over again disproved by men then living who were cognizant of all the facts in connection with the episode which led to this charge. It was to this effect: a number of young men from southern Illinois, led by Thorndike Brooks, a former resident of Baltimore, Maryland, and a man of some wealth but of a very reckless disposition, were induced to go South with Brooks who was an active secession sympathizer. Among the number of young men who joined Captain Brooks was H. B. Cunningham, my brother, who was then, as heretofore described, at school in Lebanon, Illinois. In his boyish sympathy with his Southern associates he had joined the Southern army without realizing that it meant treason against the Government, or that he was doing anything which he was destined to bitterly regret. Some ex-Confederates who had known Captain Brooks and his company in the South had greatly exaggerated the matter and had made charges that they were induced to go by General Logan. As a matter of fact, General Logan was in Washington at the time and knew nothing about their departure for the Southern Confederacy. General Logan lost all patience with Lowe, scorning a member of Congress who would so degrade himself as to be the author of such a villainous attack upon a member of the Senate. He denounced Lowe as a "poltroon and a coward." As every one knows, General Logan had at his command a strong vocabulary of invective when he wished to denounce a person who was guilty of slander or of repeating falsehoods. He caused Lowe to be posted as a "poltroon and a coward," and placed him in a very embarrassing position.

Lowe, following his Southern instincts, challenged General Logan to a duel. The excitement ran high among Lowe and his friends, but General Logan was perfectly indifferent to the matter. I must confess that I was very much distressed over it, not knowing what the outcome would be. General Logan contemptuously refused to accept Lowe's challenge, returning as his reply that he did not wish to see Lowe or any of his representatives, but that if Lowe did not retract the scandalous lies which he had heaped upon General Logan and should ever cross his (General Logan's) track, he would break his neck. This last message was sent the morning of

May 30. The weather was very hot, and the Hon. John R. Thomas and a number of friends invited us to accompany them to Fortress Monroe to stay over Sunday. It would have been delightful on the boat but for the great crowd, as it seemed that almost everybody had decided to go out of town over Sunday. We sat out on the upper deck in the bow of the boat until a very late hour, the party singing songs and telling stories and jokes, and having a good time. We knew that Colonel Lowe and his friends were on the boat, but as they were on the upper deck near the stern, we did not see them. Our stateroom was near the stern and Lowe's stateroom at the bow. Such a great crowd was on board that it had been necessary to lay mattresses end to end almost the whole length of the cabin. Some time after midnight we said good night to our friends and started for our stateroom, I leading the way through the narrow path between the staterooms and the edges of the mattresses. I was walking along in the very dim light in the cabin when I came face to face with Mr. Lowe, almost touching him before we recognized each other. Be it said to his everlasting credit that he bowed to me and turned about, going around the railing, that protects the stairway, to the other side of the cabin. Thus he and General Logan did not meet. I was never so frightened in my life, because I did not know whether he would have the politeness to move or not, and if he had not, I am quite sure there would have been a personal altercation between him and General Logan, which both of us would have regretted extremely.

A few days after our return from Fortress Monroe, Senator Spencer, of Alabama, came back to Washington, having been on a visit to his home. He was very much excited over what he called Lowe's foolhardiness. He hunted up Lowe and told him what he knew of the general's skill as a shot. He told Lowe how General Logan had a pair of the finest duelling pistols in the country, which he had won in a shooting contest, and that he used to practise, when they were all in the service together, shooting at a cap-box set on the head of a colored boy who thought it was a great thing to have General Logan shoot the box off his head. He said that Lowe turned very pale, and that after he had assured him that Logan would have no foolishness about anything of that kind, Lowe said he guessed he had made a fool of himself, and made haste to apologize to General Logan for making so vicious an assault upon him in the House. He said the story had been told him by a person he thought he could trust and that he had repeated it, believing that it was true.

Senator Lamar, Captain Thorndike Brooks, and a number of persons who knew about the facts in the case at once made affidavits which effectually silenced these detractors, and the matter was not again brought up after General Logan rose to a personal explanation in the Senate and put on record all these affidavits and statements. General Logan insisted that it was not necessary for him to meet anybody in personal combat to establish his reputation for moral courage, and he did his country a good service by taking advantage of this episode to bring the contempt of the whole country upon duellists and duelling. He succeeded because the press took up the matter universally and indorsed General Logan's action with enthusiasm. Poor Lowe suffered keenly from the criticism and execrations which were heaped upon him. I have two volumes of scrap-books containing editorials and articles on this subject, and I think that General Logan is entitled to great credit for aiding to put down forever a resort to "the code."

Among the public measures which General Logan advocated was that for devoting a certain percentage of the internal revenue to educational purposes. He had the opposition of the Prohibitionists and religious element, on the ground that the principal sources of the internal revenue were alcoholic liquors and tobacco and were therefore tainted, and the bill suffered defeat. From his first entrance into the House of Representatives after the war, General Logan had measures on the calendar for the relief of the Union soldiers, as also innumerable private bills for the relief of unfortunate persons who were unable to collect their just dues from the Government except by special act.

Congress adjourned quite late. We had a warm welcome when we arrived home. There was much excitement over the return of General and Mrs. Grant, who were expected to reach Chicago early in November from their trip around the world. Committees all over the State were busy arranging programmes with the various civil and soldier organizations to join the multitudes who were to welcome them home again. In Chicago, there were numerous committees hard at work in their efforts to make the many social functions successful. General Sherman, the president of the Army of the Tennessee, called a meeting of that society for the day of General Grant's arrival. At the same time he invited all other army societies to join them in the cordial welcome to the returning hero. The crowd was unprecedented. There were then in Chicago many persons who had formerly lived in Galena, among them Hon. E. B. Washburne. Mr. Washburne had resided in Galena, where General Grant lived when he joined the army under Mr. Lincoln's first call. Neither Mr. Washburne nor General Grant had been in Galena for years, and General Grant's home there had been closed during his entire absence.

The people of Galena were most anxious to accord General and Mrs. Grant as generous a welcome as the small city could afford. They enlisted the interest of Mr. and Mrs. Washburne in their project to make this the greatest event that had ever occurred in Galena. It was suggested that it would be a fine idea to open General Grant's house in Galena, put it in order, and have General and Mrs. Grant entertain a number of guests at dinner on the night of their arrival. The house was cleaned and heated. Many additions were

made to the furniture, abundant supplies were sent to the
larder, and efficient servants and caterers were installed.
There were many prominent persons then living in Chicago
who had formerly lived in Galena and who were much interested in the preparations.

The Illinois Central Railroad tendered a special car to a
number of guests who were to go on a special train to meet
General Grant's east-bound train from San Francisco and
transfer General and Mrs. Grant to the special train which
was to convey them to Galena. We were staying at the
Palmer House, our residence on Calumet Avenue then
being rented, and were invited to be of the party going
on the special train. It was a cold, raw day, but in the
comfortable train we soon forgot the weather, so jolly and
bright was the party, especially after General Grant came
on board. It was late in the afternoon when we reached
Galena. The citizens had decorated the whole city in bunting and every patriotic device conceivable, and had erected a
large platform in the centre of the square. It seemed as if
half the population of the surrounding country had assembled
there to extend a cordial welcome to the hero of Appomattox.
The address of welcome was made by State Senator McClellan; and a number of speeches followed. Governor Cullom of
Illinois; Governor Smith of Wisconsin; Governor Gear of
Iowa; General Logan, and a number of silver-tongued orators
of the State made glowing speeches. It was fully five o'clock
when the long procession, interspersed with brass bands, escorted General and Mrs. Grant and the Chicago delegation
to the old home.

The dinner was most delightful, every one being in high
spirits. The General and Mrs. Grant seemed for a moment
to have forgotten their long absence from this simple home.
Mrs. Washburne had made a visit to Galena a week before to
aid old friends in the work of renovating the Grant home. She
had assumed the direction of the workers, who were busy for

days, in the task of removing the accumulation of dust and cobwebs and making the old home ready for its aforetime occupants.

After dinner almost all the guests departed for the hotel. Mrs. Washburne had arranged for General Logan and myself, Mr. Washburne and herself, to spend the night in the Grant home, General and Mrs. Grant also insisting that we should remain. The day had been a busy, fatiguing one, but no one wished to retire. We six sat up until long after midnight listening to General Grant's description of the wonderful receptions he had had from the potentates of every land. His comparison of nations and many of the incidents of his journey were told to a charmed audience. I remember he expressed deep sympathy for the Italians as being more nearly without resources than any other people. He was greatly pleased with the Japanese and was sure that through them Western civilization would penetrate to the farthest boundary of the Orient. He was not much inclined to be a candidate for the Presidency, but did not like to refuse positively at that time because his friends insisted he was the man to insure the success of the Republican party. It was indeed a privilege to have been present on that memorable night. In his own home, surrounded by trusted friends, General Grant, although called the "Silent Man," was a fascinating talker. As I have already recorded, he enjoyed a joke at the expense of Mrs. Grant, who, in her guileless nature, was continually making mistakes and after realizing her blunders appealing to the general to extricate her from her dilemmas. The following morning the party returned, leaving General and Mrs. Grant to enjoy a few days' respite from the crowds so impatiently awaiting their arrival in Chicago. The welcome in Galena was the beginning of a series of demonstrations and entertainments such as had never before been paid to an American citizen. The honors tendered General Grant as the conquering hero of the Civil War could not compare with those proffered after he had borne himself so nobly as the guest of the rulers of the world.

On the twelfth of November the Army of the Tennessee convened at the Palmer House. This society had invited the members of all the other army societies to join them in welcoming home again their old commander. Many accepted the invitation and, as a result, there were more distinguished officers of the Union army present than had ever gathered since peace was declared. Each society had adopted a badge during the war and one could, therefore, tell by the badge to which army the officer belonged. Some of the badges were magnificently studded with precious stones. A number of the officers wore uniforms, and most of them wore the well-known army hat. General Sherman was beaming with high spirits and, as there were about him so many old comrades in arms, he was untiring in his efforts to keep everybody in good humor. Without exception they responded in like cordiality and good nature.

I have been in Chicago on very many memorable occasions, but I never saw such a crowd as there was on the day General and Mrs. Grant came into the city. Every street north of Twelfth and south of the north branch of the Chicago River was packed. Every hotel was full to overflowing, while private houses had been thrown open to guests. The whole police force, the Union Veteran's Club, and other organizations acted as guards of the city, while a portion of the Union Veteran's Club acted as special escort to General and Mrs. Grant. Their rooms were in the Palmer House, and it was simply impossible to cross the streets for blocks on either side of the hotel. It was with great difficulty that the distinguished party could get in or out of the hotel. A private luncheon in the red parlors had been arranged by Mr. Palmer for General and Mrs. Grant and other invited guests. It required masterly management on the part of Mr. Palmer and his assistants to serve the luncheon. Every time either door was opened by the servitors people peered in through the smallest opening to get a peep at the hero of the hour. At the public reception which followed the crowd was simply unmanageable, and the programme had to be abandoned on account of the pressure of ordinarily well-behaved, refined people who were determined to clasp the hands of General and Mrs. Grant. Strong men were unable to restrain the crowd. Finally, the receiving party made their escape through a window into a rear hallway, up a back stair to an upper story. It took some time to convince the mass of human beings jammed in the main halls, on the stairs, in the reception rooms and parlors, that General and Mrs. Grant had retired.

On the morning of the thirteenth, at ten o'clock, a superb reception was tendered General Grant by the Union Veteran's Club, at McVicker's Theatre, which was decorated from pit to galleries. The meeting was called to order by General Chetlain. On the platform stood a goddess of liberty surrounded by lovely young ladies, each representing a State and bearing a placard "Welcome." At the feet of the goddess sat five very small girls representing the territories. On the platform as speakers were General Logan, General Woodford, General Fuller, General Julius White, Reverend G. C. Trusdell, General R. J. Oglesby, Governor Cullom, John C. Barker, Colonel E. B. Sherman, Captain J. S. Curtiss, Colonel Mann, Emery A. Storrs, E. A. Filkins, Judge R. S. Tuthill, Mayor Harrison, Brigadier-General Pavey, Captain M. E. Ewing, J. H. Russell, and others. The old flag of the 21st Illinois Volunteers, Grant's original regiment, was brought out and three ringing cheers given. To hold aloft this tattered emblem during the war, seven color-bearers had laid down their lives. William Hendershott, "drummer-boy of the Rappahannock," gave a drum solo. After the speeches "taps" was sounded and the numerous guests took their departure.

On the evening of November 13 the Army of the Tennessee held a banquet in the large dining-room of the Palmer

House, which seated six hundred guests. From the long table across one end of the room the other tables extended like the four tines of a fork. The decorations were a matchless array of military insignia—miniature cannon, rifles, carbines, Minie balls—which, together with flowers, made a superb display. At each place there was a pasteboard tent, on the inside of which the menu was inscribed. These with narrow red-and-white ribbons and small silk flags were the souvenirs. The diners assembled in the large hall and parlors, and were arranged in line according to the position they were to occupy at the tables. At a bugle-call, the line moved to the dining-room, headed by Grant and Sherman, followed by Sheridan, Logan, Schofield, and the long list of illustrious soldiers and distinguished citizens. At the speaker's table, beginning at the south end, were Reverend David Swing, Reverend Doctor Thomas, Judge Dickey, Judge Drummond, Governor Cullom, Bishop Fallows, General R. J. Oglesby, General C. C. Auger, Senator Don Cameron, General Schofield, General W. Q. Gresham, General Logan, General Sherman, General Grant, General Sheridan, Rear-Admiral Stevens, Judge A. Taft, General Pope, General Crook, General Robinson, Governor Smith, Governor Gear, Hon. E. B. Washburne, Judge Howe, and Mayor Harrison, which brought Sherman in the middle with Grant and Sheridan on his right, Logan and Gresham on his left.

General Sherman was the toast-master, a position he filled admirably. The toasts, prepared mainly by Hon. Richard S. Tuthill of Chicago, were as follows: General Grant, "Our Country"; General Logan, "The President and Congress"; General Hurlburt, "Army of the Tennessee"; Colonel Vilas, "Our First Commander"; Admiral Stevens, "The Navy"; Leonard Swett, "The Mexican War"; General Wilson, "Army of the Cumberland"; General Pope, "The Other Armies"; Robert G. Ingersoll, "The Volunteer Soldiers"; Emery A. Storrs, "The Patriotic People"; General Thomas C. Fletcher,

"Woman"; Mark Twain, "Our Babies"; General Woodford, "Army of the Potomac"; General Schofield, "The Army."

After the cheering, as the speakers concluded, the bands gave some martial air, which frequently started the whole company to singing, and, as among so many there were fine voices, the effect was simply electrifying. Allusion to Grant brought them to their feet cheering vociferously. They waved their handkerchiefs and flags, making it almost impossible for Sherman to proceed with the programme. At its conclusion "Auld Lang Syne" was sung, the bugler sounded taps at three o'clock A. M., and this historic banquet was ended. Mr. Palmer had kindly arranged a place for the ladies in the gallery behind a curtain of smilax, through which they could see and hear everything. It would take a gifted pen and much space to describe the details of that marvellous series of receptions given in honor of Grant's return to his native land. Like all earthly things, they had to come to an end, but the celebrations left in their wake nothing but pleasant memories.

Every one was quite sure that General Grant would receive the nomination as Republican candidate for the Presidency. Mr. Washburne, usually a reticent man, was very outspoken for General Grant. Mr. Washburne himself had not long been at home from his diplomatic sojourn in Europe, and had not taken up any special work. Before our departure for Washington after Thanksgiving Day General Logan was in conference with the leading Republicans of the State in the interest of General Grant's nomination. He felt all was well, and did not anticipate the opposition which was brewing or the conspiracies that were being organized to defeat General Grant for the nomination.

We returned to No. 812 Twelfth Street, N.W., to the quarters we had occupied for years. We were scarcely unpacked and settled for the winter when a deluge of letters came pouring in from all over the country. Prominent and active Republicans in every State in the Union began to report that the

Blaine Bureau was secretly organizing the Republicans of their section in opposition to Grant and the third term and in favor of Mr. Blaine. Seemingly forgetting the storm of scandal and abuse through which Mr. Blaine had passed in 1872 and 1876, they revived all the scandals which had occurred during General Grant's eight years in the White House, and commenced a furor about "Cæsarism," "military despotism," and everything that could be conceived to create alarm and shake the confidence of the people in General Grant. Leading Republicans in the House and Senate allied themselves with the friends of Grant or Blaine. So intense was the excitement before the holidays that Conkling, Cameron, and Logan were called "The Triumvirate" because of their activities in the States they represented in the United States Senate.

Generally the month of December had very little of interest beyond the usual routine of calls and the constant employment of writing political letters. There was very little done in the House or Senate, as almost all the time was devoted to political rivalries over the nominations for President and Vice-President for 1880. Congress adjourned early for the holidays, but, as usual, we remained in Washington. There were not in those days so many opportunities for members of Congress and senators to enjoy their holidays by trips to Cuba, Bermuda, Panama, and other places which have been made so accessible in these days of progress. Besides this, General Logan always took advantage of what they called the "holidays" to bring up to date his reports on cases before the important committees on which he served.

One of the most brilliant receptions ever held in the White House took place January 1, 1880. Mrs. Hayes had done me the honor to invite me to assist in receiving on that day, and, as we had to reach the White House at ten o'clock, I arose at a very early hour to make the necessary preparations. The General, of course, joined the senators, and I had to go to the White House alone to be there before the forming of the receiving-line for the reception. The unpretentious and modest receiving costume which Mrs. Hayes wore at her first New Year's reception at the White House had been laid aside. She was beautifully gowned in a white-silk costume brocaded in gold figures and trimmed with beautiful lace. It was, indeed, a fitting gown for such an occasion, and was most becoming to Mrs. Hayes, with her glorious black hair and eyes. The diplomats were gorgeous in their uniforms, and the breasts of some of them were almost completely covered with magnificent medals studded with precious stones, while the ladies accompanying them were attired in the richest possible costumes.

The wives of the members of the cabinet were very retiring, unpretentious, modest women whose costumes attracted very little attention, and were usually of a correspondingly quiet character. Mrs. William M. Evarts was a motherly, gracious woman whose dress was always of the plainest possible type. She seemingly ignored the fiat that a person in certain positions should be richly gowned even if she wishes to observe the simplest style. Mrs. John Sherman was a lovely character, but she had very little interest in social affairs. While she could have boasted of a wardrobe worthy of the high position she occupied, her costumes were more simple than elegant. Mrs. George B. McCrary enjoyed her position as wife of the Secretary of War more enthusiastically than any lady whose husband has ever occupied this exalted position. The McCrarys were from Iowa, and Mrs. McCrary had about her all the breeziness of that Western State. She was a blonde, with blue eyes and fair complexion, and wore at all times the lightest possible colors. She had at her command a vocabulary of slang which she used sometimes very effectively, and she was reckless in her criticism of Grant and his administration. Mrs. Key, wife of the Postmaster-General, was a delightful woman and a great acquisition on New Year's Day on account of her brilliant conversational powers. She had three very interesting daughters, and their Wednesday receptions in their own home were the most agreeable of any of the cabinet on account of the genuine cordiality and hospitality they extended to all callers. Mrs. Carl Schurz, wife of the Secretary of the Interior, was one of the most delightful women ever in Washington. She was very stately and highly cultivated. Mrs. Schurz had a keen appreciation of her position and was always beautifully dressed, but sometimes greatly disturbed by the lack of dignity on the part of the ladies invited to assist in receptions and the rudeness of some of the callers. Attorney-General Charles A. Devens was one of the most distinguished men ever in the cabinet. He was a bachelor and was from Boston, Massachusetts, a man of rare ability and culture. The agricultural bureau was in those days a branch of the Interior Department, and thus was not of the cabinet as to-day.

As usual, New Year's Day was the beginning of the round of social functions including receptions, luncheons, and dinners by officials and prominent citizens of Washington. On January 22 General Logan and I attended a state dinner at the White House, and, while much has been said about the economy of President Hayes, there was no evidence of lack of liberality in the appointments of the dinner. There were thirty-six guests and the table never looked more resplendent than it did on that occasion. The wonderful set of china which Mrs. Hayes had caused to be made, illustrating the fauna and flora of the United States, executed by Theodore Davis, was a most artistic piece of work, and it is to be regretted that this magnificent set is no longer in use at the White House. I have never seen a greater profusion of flowers than there was at the state dinners and receptions in Mrs. Hayes's time. Every room on the first floor of the executive mansion was in each instance beautifully decorated, and the windows which formerly connected the greenhouse with the state dining-room were always thrown open and the conservatory brightly lighted so that the guests could not only enjoy the floral decorations in the mansion, but could look across at the profusion of flowers which were kept continually on the benches of the conservatory and throughout the White House. Mr. Pfister had been installed in the White House by Mrs. Hayes, who knew him in Ohio, and brought him here as White House gardener, and a better selection could not possibly have been made. I remember that Mr. John Sherman was my escort on that occasion, and, though known as a frigid man, he was, when he wished to make himself agreeable, one of the most delightful of dinner escorts. He had been so long in the public service and was so thoroughly acquainted with all the important events in the history of our country that it was a privilege to listen to his conversation.

Between making and receiving calls, and dictating and writing about forty letters a day to various people in the different States in his efforts to advance the interest of General Grant's nomination for the Presidency at the convention to be held in May, General Logan and I were kept busy day and night. The intervening months were devoted to the election of delegates in all the States; and I may be mistaken, but I think that more attention was devoted to the character of these delegates than is done at the present time.

On my own Thursdays at home during this winter the callers were numerous, including such well-known people as Vinnie Ream, the sculptor (now Mrs. Hoxie, wife of General Hoxie); Mary Clemmer Ames, Mrs. Claflin, Mrs. Ramsay, Mrs. James G. Blaine, the wife of the German ambassador, wives of members of the Supreme Court, cabinet, Senate, House of Representatives, and many others. On Saturday, February 7, we went to Mrs. Hayes's last Saturday-afternoon reception. We were courteously escorted by one of the ushers through the blue room by a circuitous route, and enjoyed seeing the stirring masses of people surge through the rooms. On February 9 we went to the reception tendered by the Mexican minister, Señor Zamacona, and his wife to President and Señora Diaz, of Mexico, who were visiting Washington. The costumes were superb. The ballroom—a marquee with a glass roof built especially for the occasion—was beautifully decorated with exotics. A long canvas extending nearly the length of the room, upon which was portrayed a view of Chapultepec, attracted universal attention. On the 10th of February we attended the reception to the foreign legations given at the White House. The decorations, refreshments, and every appointment of the reception were superb. In March our young son, John A. Logan, second, attended Marini's annual fancy-dress ball and had as his partner Fanny Hayes, daughter of the President and Mrs. Hayes.

Early in January General Logan began his work on the Fitz-John Porter case, usually taking it up after a seven-o'clock dinner, he having previously attended upon the sessions of Congress all day. It was a most voluminous affair, and frequently we were hard at work reading the testimony and reports of the court martial which had been held during the war, the original findings of which sentenced General Fitz-John Porter to be shot. Mr. Lincoln's great heart recoiled at the thought of executing Porter, and he sent for the eminent lawyer Leonard Swett, of Chicago, to come and stay in the White House, to see if it were not possible for him to find some way by which he might change the findings of the court martial. Lincoln wished to spare Porter's life, but to inflict such punishment as would satisfy the friends of the many men who had been sacrificed on account of Fitz-John Porter's alleged failure to obey orders and disloyalty to Pope.

Mr. Lincoln decided that this would be severe enough and returned the case to the court, who finally came to Mr. Lincoln's recommendation in the matter. Mr. Lincoln signed their second report, which deprived General Porter of his rank in the army and its pay and emoluments.

Fitz-John Porter was a man most prominently connected,

and felt keenly the humiliation of his position, and he and his friends never relaxed for one moment their efforts to set aside this verdict of the court martial, which had received Mr. Lincoln's approval, hoping that as time passed and many of the prominent actors in that tragedy were no more they might bring about the reinstatement of General Fitz-John Porter to the rolls of the army, and then secure his honorable retirement. They had succeeded in having a board of review, who recommended that his petition be granted.

General Logan differed with the findings of that board, and considered that it had been clearly established that Fitz-John Porter was responsible for the death of hundreds of men at the second battle of Bull Run, because of his failure to obey promptly the orders issued to him by General John Pope, who made charges against him. General Logan felt that it was an injustice to the victims of his blunder to allow him to escape all punishment. He further believed that Mr. Lincoln, through the legal advice of one of the greatest lawyers of the country, had exhausted every possible opportunity for the extension of leniency to Fitz-John Porter and justice to the memory of the dead. General Logan believed that Mr. Lincoln was perfectly conscientious and incapable of severity. If he had erred at all, General Logan felt it would have been on the side of being too lenient. While he had no personal prejudice against General Porter, he felt, nevertheless, that it would be a bad precedent if General Porter were restored to the place on the army list he would have occupied if his record had been clear.

The reports of the original court martial and the board of review were most ponderous documents. The reading of the testimony was a matter which consumed many hours, in fact days and weeks, so that society affairs had to be for a time completely laid aside to enable me to assist General Logan in reading this evidence and marking that which bore upon the side of the case which he had taken up. Almost every night we worked until two or three o'clock the following morning, General Logan in the mean time never failing to attend the sessions of Congress or the meetings of the committees of which he was a member, and which usually met at ten o'clock in the morning. He was then chairman of the military committee, second on appropriations, second on judiciary, and second on privileges and elections, also a member of the committee on Indian affairs.

On March 2, General Logan began his four days' speech in the Senate on the Fitz-John Porter case, in which he routed the enemy and made Senator Hill appear ridiculous, also discomfited Senators Kernan of New York and Randolph of New Jersey. Among the audience in the galleries sat Fitz-John Porter himself, listening attentively to everything which was said for and against the case. During the four days of his speech General Logan returned home at about six o'clock from an exhausting day in the Senate and usually found it necessary to lie down for a time to rest before dinner. Sometimes as late as nine o'clock the report of his speech of that day was brought him from the public printing-office for correction for *The Globe*, now called *The Congressional Record*. On the night of the second day, while I was reading aloud the proof of this report to him as he lay on the sofa, he discovered that the printers had confused the evidence of the original court martial, which was taken from the printed report, having mixed up the leaves of the report of the court martial, making "A" swear what "B" had sworn and "B" swear what "A" had sworn. These errors, if not corrected, would have placed General Logan in a most embarrassing position. Any one who has ever handled proof can appreciate what a stupendous job it was to get fresh reports and take pages from the court martial and board of review to be used in the report of General Logan's speech to appear in *The Globe* of the next day. Doctor Hamilton, then supervising surgeon of the Marine Hospital service, came in to look after General Logan. He, fortunately, had been an apprentice in a printing-office when quite a young man. He found General Logan not fit to do the laborious work of correcting the proof of the speech, and the doctor and I sat up all night long correcting this evidence, so that it would read properly in the columns of *The Globe*. After a brief sleep the general arose quite early to go over the proof himself to see that it was correct, had his breakfast, was ready to go before his committee and then take up the discussion of the Fitz-John Porter case after the morning hour in the Senate. Every night the report of his speech was brought from the public printing-office and we had to read it aloud and correct the proof for *The Globe*. The ten days devoted to the preparation and delivery of his argument in the Fitz-John Porter case was the greatest drain on his nervous system and the most onerous work of his life. After his speech it was said that it had been clearly demonstrated that Porter should have been shot for disobedience of orders at the battle of Manassas, August 27 to 29, 1862. This speech occupied eight hundred and ninety-one pages of manuscript, equal to fifty pages of *The Congressional Record*.

General Logan's regular work in the Senate was something tremendous, and at the same time he was doing far more than his share of the work in the political campaign. As I look back upon it now, it seems to me to be incredible that one man could have performed the amount of work he did during the whole year of 1880.

Early in April, Conkling, Cameron, Carpenter, Chandler, and other Republican senators with whom General Logan was co-operating, decided that so much agitation for Blaine was going on in Illinois as to make it necessary for General Logan to go to Chicago to do what he could to prevent the Blaine element from capturing the delegates for the national convention which was to be held in June.

The Illinois State convention of 1880 was the most remarkable one in the history of the State. A majority of the people strongly favored Grant's nomination, but through surreptitious means Blaine's agents had succeeded in procuring the active support of James P. Root, secretary of the State central committee, who was well known as an expert manipulator in political affairs. He had been clandestinely occupied for months proselytizing leading Republicans in different parts of the State in favor of James G. Blaine. Root and his employees had created an enthusiasm for the "plumed knight" on a purely fictitious basis which was incomprehensible. Mr. Blaine was never the author or the leader in the advocacy of any measure for the public welfare. There is no evidence in the records of Congress that he ever at any time took the initiative in the solution of any vexed problem in national affairs, his greatest services to his country consisting, eminently, in his wonderful diplomacy as an executive officer of the Government. At the time of his candidacy for the Presidency in 1880, his record was unenviable and would have deterred most men from seeking a nomination that would unavoidably lead to a revival of the scandals that cost him such a bitter experience before the national convention in 1876. His popularity could only be explained on the ground of his incomparable suavity of manner, brilliancy of intellect, marvellous memory, dashing alertness in taking advantage of individuals and situations, daring in political discussions, and his matchless diplomacy in utilizing every opportunity to advance his own political fortunes. These qualities drew about him friends who were ready to serve him to the bitter end in his overweening ambitions.

When the State convention met it seemed impossible to turn the tide from Blaine, and if General Logan had not been on the ground the convention would have been instructed for Blaine. Through General Logan's appeal and skilful management, Grant delegates were elected and instructed. Root, as secretary of the State central committee, issued to General Logan and nine other delegates "provisional tickets" of admission to the national convention. Root's plan was to cause in some way the credentials committee of the national convention to decide against General Logan and the nine other Illinois delegates being seated as delegates in the convention. General Logan was never so insulted during his whole political experience—an insult he would have resented had he not known that he could make better use of it in effecting Mr. Root's discomfiture and the defeat of his followers. The credentials committee shared General Logan's indignation at the action of Root, and accorded to General Logan and the discredited nine others every consideration.

Before going to Chicago General Logan had succeeded in obtaining a valuable list of names from every part of the State. He dictated notes from which I was to write letters to each of these men and forward to him the unsigned letters with an addressed envelope for each. Mr. Daniel Shepherd, then secretary of the Senate military committee, was to forward the letters after General Logan had read and signed them. After he had reached Chicago and entered earnestly into the fight, General Logan continued to send me lists and directions as to what to write. By reference to my diary I find that with the help of Miss Woodruff, our stenographer, we wrote on an average about fifty letters per day from the time General Logan went to Chicago until after the State convention. I hunted up also much information in the Congressional Library and from *The Globe*. I was busy all the time with matters which then seemed important, and which I now realize were vital and were a training which has been of incalculable value to me during the years since those eventful political times.

On May 22, after obtaining a suitable wardrobe, on the invitation of Mr. and Mrs. J. Donald Cameron, I accompanied them to Harrisburg, to make a visit as I went to join my husband in Chicago. Mr. and Mrs. Cameron were then staying in the home of Senator Cameron's father, Hon. Simon

Cameron, at their quaint old home, formerly that of Governor Harris of Pennsylvania. It was situated almost on the edge of the west shore of the Susquehanna River. Governor Harris's grave, enclosed by an iron fence, is located on a plot between the entrance to the Cameron mansion and the river, and can be seen by travellers on the Pennsylvania road as they approach the west end of the bridge over the river. Mrs. Cameron, Sr., and her venerable husband had lived at Willard's at the same time as we did when we went to Washington in 1867. We were intimate friends, General Logan being a special favorite of "Father Cameron's." They took me out to Lochiel, the home of Senator J. Donald Cameron, at that time one of the show-places of the country. It was one of the most charming places on the banks of the Susquehanna River. No more lovely spot could be found, with its perfection of natural beauty and the highest art of cultivation combined.

At three P. M., May 24, we boarded a director's car, used as such by Senator Cameron on the Pennsylvania Railroad. In the party were Senator and Mrs. Cameron (née Miss Elizabeth Sherman, niece of Senator John Sherman), Mr. and Mrs. L. P. Morton, Miss Emily Beale (the late Mrs. John R. McLean, and myself. At Pittsburg we were joined by Mr. and Mrs. "Chris" Magee, one of Senator Cameron's important political workers. The journey was delightful, every member of the party being in fine spirits. Senator Cameron was a lavishly hospitable host, and we had every luxury that could be procured. The scenery was enchanting, as every traveller over the Pennsylvania Railroad knows. We arrived in Chicago at four o'clock P. M. Tuesday, May 25. General Logan had been staying in the Palmer House, then the Grant headquarters, and we were soon alone in the suite we were to occupy till the convention was over. He told me of all his doubts and fears, hopes and plans. We had little opportunity for being by ourselves for the next ten days, as conferences were constantly going on between the leaders of the Grant wing. Rumors and proofs of disaffection and also of gains from various quarters were constantly being brought in. The mercurial temperaments of individuals had to be endured, cured, or handled with diplomacy. Many delegates and their friends were around with their open palms behind them, hoping and praying for their hands to be filled. Ambitious place-seekers were more numerous and insufferable. The former could be disposed of by skilful diplomacy and would go away empty-handed, but the latter were insinuating and disgusting. "Fool" friends were exasperating by their blunders in undoing something that had required time and patience to accomplish.

To add to the insufferable confusion and trying experience of every one however remotely connected with the convention, legions of men and women began an irrepressible clamor for tickets of admission to the convention. Mr. J. P. Root still had control of this important matter, and it was almost impossible for any one supposed to favor Grant's nomination to get one for himself or his friends. General Logan had to avoid contact with the suppliants for tickets, as he could do nothing for them and could not endure the ordeal of listening to their pleas when he was unable to comply with their requests. There was no alternative but for me to see them and explain the situation. Not infrequently the explanation I was able to give only served to intensify the bitterness they felt toward Root on account of his treatment of General Logan.

When the convention met at ten A. M. Wednesday, June 2, the fruits of Mr. Root's labor were evident, in the fact that the galleries were packed for Blaine, the clackers losing no opportunity to start a Blaine storm in obedience to their orders. The first session was very brief. Senator Cameron, chairman of the national committee, called the convention to order. Reverend Doctor Edwards invoked a blessing upon the convention in an earnest prayer. Mr. Hoar, of Massachusetts, was made temporary chairman, the committee on credentials was appointed, and the convention adjourned until ten A. M. the following morning.

The convention met at ten A. M. every day, but not until five P. M. on the third day did the credentials committee make its report, amid the wildest demonstrations—shouting, clapping of hands, waving of hats, handkerchiefs, and flags, on the floor and in the galleries. After the report the convention adjourned until eight P. M. On assembling at that hour the nominations began. The crowd, if possible, was greater than ever, and the hall was literally packed almost to suffocation. As soon as quiet reigned, Roscoe Conkling arose in his place and began his speech with the oft-repeated:

> "And when asked what State he hails from
> Our sole reply shall be,
> He hails from Appomattox,
> And its famous apple-tree."

This simply electrified the whole audience, bringing forth a whirlwind of applause. It was some minutes before he could proceed with his matchless speech, which in eloquence, perfect diction, and finished style was incomparable, and the like of it will not be heard again. Many, however, thought it was too well prepared and too soulless in its delivery.

A rousing speech that touched the hearts of men would have been far more effective, though it might have been punctuated with numberless grammatical errors and mispronounced words. Soul-inspired utterances bring soulful responses. Senator Conkling's speech, though a literary and oratorical triumph, lacked the fire and enthusiasm of a big heart overflowing with genuine love of mankind, and therefore did little to advance the cause of his hero, General Grant. Bradley, of Kentucky, seconded the nomination in a speech in striking contrast in style and delivery to that of Senator

Conkling, which was equally fruitless in its effect upon the convention. Mr. Joy, of Michigan, a man well known as a railroad magnate, nominated Mr. Blaine. It would have been a fine speech before a board of directors, but, from appearances, the convention was unmoved by it.

The consummate politician of the convention was James A. Garfield of Ohio. From the time of assembling it was evident to close observers that neither of the prominent candidates could be nominated. General Garfield, beyond question, had arrived at that conclusion and was the wise man of the hour. He had been chosen to nominate John Sherman of Ohio. Before the convention had reached the hour for nominations, General Garfield had managed to make himself the "dark horse." At every session after his delegation had been seated he came in alone, walking down the main aisle in stately dignity, smiling and bowing to acquaintances among the delegates. In an assemblage of so many thousands of people waiting breathlessly for momentous events, it was easy to start a cheer for anything or anybody. So every time General Garfield appeared some one in the gallery shouted "Garfield!" "Garfield!" the refrain being repeated first by a score of shouters and later by increasing numbers. Sitting in the gallery by Mrs. Chauncey I. Filley of Saint Louis, whose husband was on the national committee, I suggested that we should watch the Garfield by-play, which was apparently growing at every session.

The moment the nomination of Sherman was in order General Garfield arose with a ministerial air and began the discharge of a duty imposed upon him by Ohio Republicans in a speech colder toward Sherman than Sherman's own frigid temperament. Every brilliant phrase used by Garfield spelled "Garfield" when he mentioned Sherman as an eligible nominee for the Presidency. Almost every one detected the betrayal of Sherman, of which Garfield was openly accused by Sherman and his friends. Garfield had succeeded in accomplishing his purpose and was destined to win the nomination.

The nomination of Hon. E. B. Washburne fell flat, as it had been understood that Mr. Washburne was an ardent supporter of General Grant. General Logan had discovered before the meeting that Mr. Washburne had approached some of General Grant's friends, asking to have the Grant support if General Grant failed in being nominated. Washburne was unable to show that he had any strength outside of Grant's followers. In addition to this, Mr. Washburne provoked much criticism because of the discovery of his efforts to utilize Grant's strength in the convention for himself. Hence, when he actually allowed his name to be presented, there was no response.

Overtures were made daily to General Logan urging him to allow his name to be substituted for Grant's, and there is no doubt but that when it was discovered that Grant could not be nominated on account of the third-term cry, General Logan could have carried the nomination. He scorned the suggestion and could not see it in any other light than that it would be treachery to Grant. He preferred to go down with Grant rather than even seemingly to betray him.

It was midnight before the nominations were all made, and the convention adjourned until ten A. M. the following morning, when the balloting began. The balloting began on June 7, and continued for three days, with the most remarkable demonstrations and outbursts of enthusiasm that had ever been witnessed in a national convention.

After the convention had been in session for more than a week everybody was worn out and longed for relief. The deadlock was finally broken, and James A. Garfield and Chester A. Arthur were nominated. The disappointed and defeated men bravely made the nomination unanimous, and the historic convention adjourned *sine die*. The vast concourse of people dispersed almost in a twinkling. The national com-

mittee, a majority of whom had supported Grant, took up
the stupendous work of planning the campaign and electing
the nominees.  On the national committee, besides Mr. Cameron, chairman, there were John C. New, Chauncey I. Filley
of Missouri, General Powell Clayton of Arkansas, "Chris"
Magee of Pennsylvania, and other equally stalwart men.
Of the five named, three have passed to their reward.  General Logan was assigned to make speeches in Maine, New
York, Indiana, Ohio, Illinois, Nebraska, and Kansas between
the adjournment of Congress and the election, November 2.

Mr. Cameron being chairman of the national committee,
we were unable to leave Chicago until four P. M. on the afternoon of the 10th.  Mr. and Mrs. Morton, Miss Beale, Mr.
and Mrs. Cameron, General Logan, and I again boarded Mr.
Cameron's private car to make the return trip to Washington.  Considering the painful disappointment which had
come to all of us over the defeat of General Grant, we tried
to be as merry as possible, Mr. Cameron and General Logan
magnanimously endeavoring to work up for Garfield an enthusiasm which they did not feel, intending, of course, to do
everything they possibly could to secure his election.  We
had a delightful trip to Harrisburg, where we stopped over
for a day or two at "Father Cameron's."

It was fearfully hot in tropical Washington in June.  We
were glad, however, to be away from the turmoil and excitement in Chicago and were again established in our comfortable quarters at 812 Twelfth Street.  General Logan returned
to his duties in the Senate, and I busied myself with the correspondence and many other things that had to be disposed of
before adjournment.  After Congress adjourned, General
Logan went directly to New York to meet Garfield and the
Republicans, and I returned to Chicago to await the general's
home-coming before beginning the long list of appointments
the committee had made for him.  From July 1 to November 2, General Logan was canvassing almost every day,

many times making three, four, and five speeches a day from the platform of a special car which they used in going from place to place in filling his appointments. It was unfortunate that it took Mr. Conkling a long time to be reconciled to the nomination of Garfield and defeat of General Grant. His delay in making an earnest effort for the election of the ticket prevented him from accomplishing all he might had he more promptly indorsed Garfield and Arthur's nomination. As Senator Cameron was not a public speaker, the brunt of the indorsement of Garfield by the Grant men fell on General Logan. He acquitted himself nobly, as always, in his earnest advocacy of Garfield's election, many times addressing multitudes when he was physically unable to do so. Be it said to the everlasting credit of General Grant, that he, though in no sense a public speaker, appeared at many meetings and said a few words in commendation of the ticket. Probably the largest meeting and the most important one of the whole campaign was that held in Warren, Ohio, when a desperate effort was made to induce Mr. Conkling to appear with General Grant, thus committing himself to the support of Garfield and Arthur. This Conkling could not be induced to do. General Grant delighted the crowd by his cordial greeting to them and his acknowledgment of the honors he had received from the Republican party.

There were forebodings from time to time that the ticket might not be elected, but the Republicans were much encouraged by the victories of the October elections, and every one rejoiced when they read the returns of the election of November 2, 1880, which made James A. Garfield President and Chester A. Arthur Vice-President of the United States.

We returned to Washington, and, though still much exhausted from the labors of the campaign, General Logan began his usual treadmill duties in the Senate. There were many agreeable social features in December, General and Mrs. Grant making a visit to Washington in that month.

President Hayes gave a magnificent dinner in their honor, which General Logan and I attended. A curious list of guests had been invited to meet the General and Mrs. Grant, Chief Justice Waite and General Logan being the only two who had not in one way or another antagonized General Grant and opposed his nomination at Chicago. General and Mrs. Edward Beale, lifelong friends of the Grants, entertained them during this visit to Washington and gave, the morning after the White House dinner, a superb breakfast in their honor, to which were invited all the loyal friends of General Grant.

Before the adjournment of Congress there was as much discussion as to who would be in Garfield's cabinet as we heard recently about the prospective members of the cabinet of President Wilson. On account of the disaffection existing in the Republican party there was much fear that, by the appointment of his cabinet, Garfield might widen the breach already existing.

# CHAPTER XVI

INAUGURATION OF GENERAL GARFIELD — RUPTURE BETWEEN THE ADMINISTRATION AND SENATOR CONKLING — ASSASSINATION OF THE PRESIDENT — ADMIRABLE CHARACTER OF PRESIDENT ARTHUR'S ENTERTAINMENTS — VISIT OF FRENCH AND GERMAN OFFICERS — GARFIELD MEMORIAL MEETING OF CONGRESS — CAMPAIGN OF 1884 — NOMINATION OF BLAINE AND LOGAN — ACTIVITY OF GENERAL LOGAN ON THE STUMP — HIS RETURN TO THE SENATE — ENTHUSIASTIC RECEPTION AT SAN FRANCISCO — DEATH OF GENERAL LOGAN, DECEMBER 26, 1886 — FUNERAL HONORS PAID TO HIM — MARRIAGE OF OUR SON — I GO TO EUROPE — OUR STAY IN BERLIN AND SUBSEQUENT EUROPEAN TRAVEL — A SECOND TRIP ABROAD — DEATH OF MAJOR JOHN A. LOGAN, JR., IN THE PHILIPPINES — STATUES OF GENERAL LOGAN — RECENT ACTIVITIES

GENERAL LOGAN was much exhausted by the labors of the campaign of 1880, and had not fully recovered when we came to Washington for the convening of Congress in December of that year. When we arrived we found many of our old friends at Mrs. Rhine's. The month of December until the time of the adjournment of Congress for the holidays was a busy one socially and politically. The usual forebodings and anxiety of persons occupying appointive official positions and employees of the Government as to their fate in a change of administration made them active in trying to secure influence which would help them retain their positions. Another class who felt they had contributed to the election of Garfield and Arthur were equally impetuous in their efforts to secure appointments or employment.

Intense interest was aroused as to whom Garfield would select as cabinet officers. There was a particular desire to have Mr. Conkling return to the Republican fold that he might be counted upon to help carry out the policy of that party. Mr. Conkling's prejudices were very strong when he was against a man. He personally disliked Garfield, whom he accused of duplicity on several occasions when the Republican party had to hold confidential conferences to be sure of Garfield's attitude toward certain important measures.

The inauguration was, as so often has been the case, seriously marred by inclement weather. General Sherman was chief marshal of the procession and the whole parade moved with clockwork precision. Garfield was escorted by Senators Bayard and Anthony with the Columbia Commandery Knights Templar, of which he was a member, as a guard of honor. Vice-President-elect Arthur was escorted by Senator Pendleton. At the Senate chamber Mrs. Hayes and General Garfield's wife and mother were conducted to reserved gallery seats. Mrs. Hayes wore a sealskin coat and a black brocaded silk dress. "Mother" Garfield wore black silk trimmed with silver-fox fur. Mrs. Garfield, wife of the President-elect, wore a suit of dark-green velvet, while Miss Mollie Garfield wore a plum-colored woollen suit. General Garfield's first act after taking the oath of office was to kiss his mother and wife. After reviewing the inaugural procession Garfield lunched with Mr. and Mrs. Hayes, who soon afterward left the White House to spend the night with Secretary Sherman.

The inaugural ball was held in the new museum building. Mrs. Garfield wore light heliotrope satin with point lace, while Mrs. Hayes, who was escorted by the Hon. John B. Alley, wore a cream-colored satin dress trimmed with ermine. The preponderance of gold lace on the uniforms of the officers of the army and navy, marine corps, staffs of the governors and officers of the national guard from the various States, the court dress of the Diplomatic Corps, the magnificent costumes and resplendent jewels worn by the hundreds of ladies present, made the affair extremely brilliant.

The multitudes which had gathered for the inauguration

had hardly dispersed before legions of place-hunters made their appearance. James G. Blaine was made Secretary of State; William Windom of Minnesota was made Secretary of the Treasury; Robert T. Lincoln of Illinois was made Secretary of War; William M. Hunt of Louisiana, Secretary of the Navy; Samuel J. Kirkwood of Iowa, Secretary of the Interior; Thomas L. James of New York, Postmaster-General; and Wayne MacVeagh of Pennsylvania, Attorney-General. President Garfield had served in Congress with several of the members of his cabinet and naturally felt he knew them thoroughly and could depend upon their fidelity to him.

One of the most notable events in Congress at this time was the three hours' speech of Senator Mahone of Virginia. This speech was in reply to the bitter personal attacks which had been made on the senator from Virginia by the Democrats, and principally by Senator Ben Hill of Georgia, since he had acted with the Republican party. Altogether the session was a very stormy one.

Garfield's first appearance in public after his inauguration was at the unveiling of the Farragut statue, which had been executed by Mrs. Vinnie Ream Hoxie. A procession formed at the Capitol and marched to the statue. Speeches were made by Garfield, Horace Maynard of Tennessee, and Senator Voorhees of Indiana. Garfield also attended the commencement exercises and conferred the degrees at Kendall Green College for Deaf Mutes.

President Garfield had the largest family that had been in the White House since General Grant's administration. Having four sons, as well as one daughter, it was necessary to provide some amusement for the growing boys. The billiard table was accordingly restored, enabling General Garfield also to take much-needed exercise. The young daughter, Mollie, was the constant companion of her mother. The conditions under which wine was restored to the table of the

White House have never been known, as Mrs. Garfield was a very modest, quiet little woman, who made very few suggestions and gave no opinions for publication. She was gentle and ladylike, and always appropriately dressed. She gave only four receptions, and at these she acquitted herself with great credit. "Mother" Garfield received distinguished consideration, not only from the family but from all callers at the White House. She was a venerable, fine-looking old lady who was very positive in her convictions of right and wrong, but not at all intrusive in the advocacy of her own peculiar ideas of life, feeling that it was her duty to be loyal to whatever her son inaugurated at the Executive Mansion.

Vice-President Arthur avoided interfering in the matter of appointments, devoting himself exclusively to the mastering of the, to him, intricate parliamentary rules of the Senate. He had not previously had any experience in a legislative body or in any executive position.

At a special session of Congress, called after Garfield's inauguration, numerous changes were evident in the personnel of the Senate on account of the expiration of the terms of many of the members of that body. Senators Allen G. Thurman and Matthew H. Carpenter were missed by all their friends. Senator Carpenter, who died in April, 1881, was beyond question one of the ablest men ever in the United States Senate. Among the senators were General Logan, General Hawley, Senators Conger, Mitchell, Hale, and Fair, who was called the "Silver King of the Pacific Slope." As chosen, the Republicans had the majority of the Senate, but the transfer of Blaine, Windom, and Kirkwood to the cabinet gave the Democratic party a temporary majority until the arrival of successors to the senators who had been selected as cabinet officers made a tie, which the casting vote of Vice-President Arthur secured for the Republican party. One of the first occurrences to bring about a sudden rupture between Conkling and Garfield was the imbroglio about the appointment of Judge W. H. Robertson as collector of the port of New York. This appointment was strenuously opposed by Conkling but his opposition was in vain. President Garfield made the appointment and Judge Robertson was confirmed. Conkling immediately left the Senate taking with him his colleague Senator Platt, expecting to be returned to the Senate by the New York legislature, but in this he and his colleague were sadly disappointed.

A few months after its birth, in addition to the controversy between President Garfield and Roscoe Conkling, many vexatious problems confronted the administration. The "political mortgages" which some of the members of the cabinet had out and the forced exposure of the Star Route scandals added to the general ill feeling. Garfield soon began to suffer keenly from the lack of enthusiasm in his support by party leaders and from the demands of men who had precipitated his nomination and contributed to his election. Figuratively, he was between the horns of a serious dilemma.

General Logan believed that the majority should rule, and, if the majority decided adversely to the man or measure he advocated, he accepted the decision unqualifiedly. Therefore, after Garfield's nomination at Chicago, General Logan gave him his earnest loyal support. Garfield knew this and made haste to invite General Logan to Mentor early in February to confer about the appointments in his cabinet. General Logan wanted Mr. Robert T. Lincoln made Secretary of War and had induced a number of influential Illinois men to join in his request. General Garfield complied without hesitation. After the inauguration President Garfield frequently sent for General Logan, who never failed to respond and do his best to accomplish everything he could for peace and harmony between the administration and the Republican party in and out of Congress.

President Garfield had promised to deliver the commencement address at Williams College, his Alma Mater. On

July 2, 1881, the President and Secretary Blaine went together to the Baltimore and Potomac Railroad station, where Garfield was to take the train. While waiting there Charles Guiteau, the assassin, shot the President. The world knows what followed and of the long, painful weeks of illness of the President, vibrating between life and death for eighty-one days, until on September 19, 1881, he passed away. All nations had tendered their sympathy, and days of prayer and petition for the recovery of the President had been designated by Christian people throughout the nation. Garfield's body was brought back to Washington from Elberon, New Jersey, where the invalid had been carried during his last weeks, and lay in state in the rotunda of the Capitol for two days prior to being taken to Cleveland. Here, also, he lay in state for two days. The impressive ceremonies attending the funeral and the depositing of the remains of the lamented President in their last resting-place are too well known to be repeated.

No person in the nation was more deeply grieved over President Garfield's assassination than was General Logan. He stood aghast at the tragedy, and wondered if the anarchist organizations had on their list other men in authority. At the announcement of the deplorable deed, General Logan returned to Washington to lend his services in any way required. Meanwhile Guiteau had been confined in the District jail at Washington. The trial began soon after the funeral exercises were over and lasted eleven weeks, during which time there were some of the most dramatic scenes enacted that have ever characterized the trial of an assassin. Sentimental persons in the country made themselves supremely ridiculous by carrying flowers to this confessed criminal. Colonel Corkhill, the district attorney, was most vigorous in his prosecution, but gave the prisoner every possible chance to defend himself. Many persons regretted extremely the publicity given everything connected with the trial and the newspaper reports of the proceedings from day to day kept the country in a feverish state of excitement. This, however, served subsequently as a lesson, for in the case of Mr. McKinley's assassin the trial was conducted on a much more dignified and less sensational scale.

President Arthur was in New York and immediately on learning of Garfield's death, in order that the Government should not be without a Chief Magistrate for a single hour, he took the oath of office there. It was administered by Justice Brady. Immediately after returning to Washington he again took the oath of office, on September 22, in the Capitol. I have heard President Arthur say that he felt he was signing his own death-warrant, so acutely did he appreciate the responsibility which had fallen upon him. There was no further ceremony, and thus President Arthur succeeded President Garfield.

There had been such an interminable line of visitors passing in and out of the White House during President Garfield's long illness, that the carpets were worn threadbare, the furniture was dingy, and the curtains faded. The living-rooms on the second floor were in a direful condition from constant use by watchers, messengers, and privileged persons who were there day and night. The cabinet-room and library had been turned into consulting chambers for physicians and specialists. The whole house had, therefore, to be renovated before President Arthur could take up his permanent residence there. As Vice-President, he had been the guest of Senator and Mrs. Jones of Nevada, in the gray-stone residence across the street from the southeast corner of the House of Representatives, formerly the home of Benjamin F. Butler. He remained with them until an army of artisans had removed all traces of President Garfield's illness and had put everything in order, President Arthur personally directing the work. He displayed such exquisite taste in the changes he made that no one could believe but that some woman's taste and dainty fingers had given the delicate touches which lent to the staid old mansion such a homelike air. The Van Buren silver was given a new plating of gold, and all the service of china and glass was replenished. When it was ready for President Arthur's occupation every one declared the White House had never been before so fittingly furnished.

Mourning at the capital of a nation is brief at most, and in a few short weeks the soical season was again in full swing. President Arthur, without exception, was the most accomplished man ever in the White House and paid more attention to the observance of all the civilities and requirements of social etiquette than any of his predecessors. While he left on record no state papers which would give him credit for great ability, I have most delightful recollections of many charming entertainments which were given in the executive mansion during his administration. He spared no expense in the preparations for his social functions. He would have scorned the thought of inviting his guests to listen to the mediocre repertoire of local amateurs, and in arranging musical entertainments he availed himself of the presence of celebrated artists during their engagements in Washington. I never attended a single social affair in the White House during President Arthur's administration when refreshments of the rarest and most delicious kinds were not served. The President's sister, Mrs. John McElroy, wife of Reverend John McElroy, of Albany, New York, was with her brother much of the time during his occupancy of the White House. Her own daughter and Nellie Arthur were about the same age, and it was refreshing to see these beautiful, innocent young girls standing, simply gowned, behind the line at the receptions. There was never any discussion in the papers by the President or his sister as to the simplicity which should characterize social affairs in the White House, as they believed it should go without saying that everything done in the White House should befit the dignity of the home of the President of the United States.

The list of women prominent in society during this administration, all of whom were frequent visitors at the White House, was a long one. Among others there were Mrs. Hazen, wife of General Hazen, now Mrs. George Dewey, Mrs. John B. Henderson, wife of ex-Senator Henderson of Missouri, one of the most remarkable women of her time, Miss Taylor, Mrs. Beale, wife of General Beale, Mrs. Hill, wife of Senator Hill of Colorado, Miss Edith Harlan, Miss Schurz, Mrs. Schofield, wife of General Schofield, Mrs. Lord, Mrs. Shellabarger, wife of Judge Shellabarger, Mrs. Waite, wife of Chief Justice Waite, and Miss Waite, Mrs. Don Cameron, Mrs. Dahlgren, Mrs. and Miss Blaine, Mrs. Jewett, Mrs. John Davis, Olivia Briggs, Mary Clemmer Ames, the daughters of Senator Frelinghuysen, Mrs. Vinnie Ream Hoxie, and many of the wives of high officials, who were women of decided ability and rare accomplishments.

Under President Arthur foreign relations were conducted by Secretary Frelinghuysen in a friendly spirit. President Arthur favored reform in the civil service, but vetoed the Chinese bill and the bill making appropriations for rivers and harbors. The President convened the Senate on October 10, 1881, after President Garfield's death. The absence of the brilliant Roscoe Conkling was much felt, and the circumstances which had led to his untimely departure from the Senate were deplored by many. The ponderous Senator David Davis from Illinois, who was at this time sixty-seven years old and weighed three hundred and fifty pounds, was elected President *pro tem.* of the Senate. It was about this time that General Logan introduced his bill for the granting of a pension to Mrs. Lincoln of five thousand dollars a year, as well as his bill to amend the pension laws, increasing the fee of pension agents from ten to twenty-five dollars.

In October a number of French and German officers arrived, as the guests of the United States, to witness the dedication of the monument at Yorktown on the one hundredth anniversary of the victory which those nations had helped us to win. About forty officers were received at the State Department by Secretary Blaine. The procession formed and marched to the Capitol, which was still draped in black for President Garfield. Here they were received by President Arthur. The French minister, as dean of the Diplomatic Corps, introduced the French guests to the President, and afterward the German minister performed the same service for his countrymen. Later they were received by the Senate, and at night a great display of fireworks was made. The President and cabinet, with many senators, representatives, and visitors, went to Yorktown on a fleet of steamboats, where the governors of the original thirteen States, each with a militia escort and with a military and naval force of regulars, joined in the celebration.

Secretary and Mrs. Blaine entertained the guests at Wormley's Hotel, a large building which stood on the southwest corner of H and Fifteenth Streets, on the site now occupied by the imposing building of the Union Trust Company. This high-class hotel was conducted by Mr. Wormley, a colored man, who was then the leading caterer of the city of Washington. The cabinet, the Supreme Court, Senate, House, army, and navy were well represented. The supper-table was a thing of beauty, laid with the finest Dresden china. Low mounds of roses enhanced the brilliant effect of the china and cut glass. The different favorite dishes of the French and German visitors were bountifully supplied, and the stiff politeness of the diplomats was for a time laid aside, and cordiality of feeling indulged in. After the supper the guests danced until an early hour. The next day, while the German officers were in Baltimore, Mr. Blaine introduced the French visitors to the beauties of the capital of our nation. It was a noticeable fact that the French minister delayed tendering the reception to his countrymen until after the Germans had departed.

At the first session of the Forty-seventh Congress, December 5, 1881, the Republicans were again in power. President Arthur appointed Judge Folger Secretary of the Treasury, Frederick T. Frelinghuysen Secretary of State, Benjamin H. Brewster Attorney-General, and ex-Senator Howe, from Wisconsin, Postmaster-General. Mr. Conkling was tendered a seat on the Supreme Bench, but declined the honor. A committee of eight senators and a representative from each State was appointed to plan a fitting commemoration of the memory of Garfield. This they did, condoling with the widow and providing for an oration on his life, to be pronounced by James G. Blaine before the two houses of Congress and the high officials of the Government. The Garfield memorial meeting was held in the House of Representatives on February 27, 1882. Among those present beside the members of the cabinet, Senate, House, etc., were Generals Sherman, Sheridan, and Hancock, Admiral Porter, Rear-Admiral Worden, Frederick Douglass, General Schenck, and the historian George Bancroft, who himself had been the orator on the occasion of the Lincoln memorial meeting. Corcoran, the philanthropist, was there, as was Cyrus W. Field. Mr. Blaine, with great dignity, earnestness, and truthfulness, read impressively the voluminous pile of black-bordered manuscript which he had prepared, after which the assemblage, led by President Arthur, left the hall. I had the pleasure of hearing this fine oration.

President Arthur's first state dinner, which General Logan and I attended, was given in honor of General and Mrs. Grant, who were visiting General and Mrs. Beale. The table was laid for thirty-four guests and was decorated with roses and lilies of the valley. As usual, it was a great success, as the dinners given by President Arthur were at all times the most elegant of any ever given in the White House.

When the Forty-eighth Congress convened, December 3, 1883, Judge David Davis retired as President *pro tem.*, and

Senator Anthony, five times elected senator, was offered the chair. This he declined, and Senator Edmunds of Vermont, was finally elected. General Logan was placed on a committee to investigate the conditions existing on the Mississippi River and the Illinois and Hennepin Canal. With him were Senators Sawyer of Wisconsin and Walker of Arkansas. Mr. N. T. N. Robinson was secretary and an exhaustive examination was made into the condition of affairs on these two waterways.

The earlier candidates named for the Republican nomination in 1884 were Logan, Robert Lincoln, President Arthur, James G. Blaine, ex-Senator Conkling, General Grant, and Governor Foster, of Ohio; but when the convention met, in Chicago, June 3, 1884, the names put before the convention were Blaine, Arthur, Edmunds, Logan, John Sherman, Hawley, and William Tecumseh Sherman. On June 6 James G. Blaine was nominated, after many ballots had been cast, and General Logan's nomination for Vice-President followed by acclamation. The Democratic convention met at Chicago on July 6, and nominated Grover Cleveland for President and Thomas A. Hendricks for Vice-President. After the announcement of the nominations made at Chicago the people of Washington gave a magnificent reception to Mr. Blaine and also, on another evening, tendered one to General Logan. General Logan was very much disgusted because the speakers at the reception to Mr. Blaine, ratifying his nomination, began to explain and apologize for Mr. Blaine's record, in reply to charges that had been made against him by the opposition.

In addition to the reception tendered General Logan in Washington, thirty thousand citizens and ten thousand soldiers welcomed him in August to the city of Chicago. After a procession, in which thousands participated, speeches were made by General Logan, General Oglesby, Governor Cullom, and Colonel Carr. Early in October General Logan received an ovation in Philadelphia. After a parade in his honor, a great meeting was held in the Academy of Music, which was attended by an immense throng of people. In the latter part of October, on returning to Springfield, Illinois, he was also much honored. It was said that there were seventy thousand people in the city of Springfield at the time. General Logan and General Oglesby, who occupied a carriage together, were escorted to the hotel by thirty-eight ladies on white horses and thirty-eight gentlemen on black horses, to represent the thirty-eight States then in the Union. The ladies wore navy-blue riding-habits with red sashes, and the gentlemen wore dress suits with high black silk hats.

The campaign of 1884 was a strenuous one in every sense of the word. I accompanied General Logan, who travelled and spoke to great crowds almost daily from the adjournment of the national convention, in June, to the very night before the election. He filled appointments made for him in Maine, Vermont, Massachusetts, New York, New Jersey, Ohio, Indiana, Michigan, Wisconsin, Iowa, Kansas, Missouri, Nebraska, and Illinois. He did not agree with the policy of Mr. Blaine and his friends in their constant explanations and apologetic replies to the innumerable charges of fraud and corruption made against Mr. Blaine. General Logan insisted that an aggressive campaign was the only one sure to win. No charges were made against General Logan, for his record was an open letter and he invited a search-light investigation of his whole life. He defied the opposition in an aggressive campaign against the nominees of the Democratic party—Cleveland and Hendricks—but would not stoop to the personalities so wantonly and fatally indulged in during that campaign. He held the nominees responsible for the principles, methods, and deeds of the Democratic party, arraigning the party and not the nominees for its ruinous record and policy.

Through an arrangement of the national committee, Mr. Blaine came to Illinois about two weeks before the election, against General Logan's advice, as his presence revived many of the scandals charged against him which General Logan had silenced by ignoring. General Logan was obliged to lose all the time Mr. Blaine was in Illinois, as he could not continue his work elsewhere while his associate on the ticket was in his own State. Mr. Blaine closed in Illinois at Chicago. The committee had also planned that Mr. Blaine should go to New York State for the last week before the election, and that General Logan should canvass Indiana. Mr. Blaine left Chicago for New York in time to attend the famous banquet at which he received his quietus through the reckless Doctor Burchard's characterization of the Democratic party as standing for "Rum, Romanism, and Rebellion." General Logan had earnestly opposed the banquet proposition, anticipating some one's indiscreet utterances. He felt it would array many against Belshazzar's feast, to which only a few at most could be admitted. Unfortunately for General Logan, he had consented to allow his name to be used on the ticket with Mr. Blaine, hoping he could thereby save the Republican party from defeat. There is no gainsaying the fact that General Logan was the choice of the people for the Presidency in 1884, but Mr. Blaine had behind him the moneyed men, who saw in Mr. Blaine a more pliant character for their schemes than in General Logan, who steadily opposed all kinds of subsidies for railroads, steamships, and other gigantic enterprises based upon Government aid for their furtherance. He was known as an anti-monopolist and the enemy of "wildcat" schemes. He was, therefore, not a favorite with the class of men who all too frequently dictate nominations in spite of the expressed will of the people. Mr. Conkling and other influential men in the party declared their willingness to support the ticket if General Logan were at the head of it. They also avowed their uncompromising opposition to Mr. Blaine personally. Naturally, this aroused a feeling of distrust and jealousy in Mr. Blaine's mind toward General Logan, which, notwithstanding Mr. Blaine's efforts to conceal his real disposition, General Logan felt keenly. He tried by every possible means to convince Mr. Blaine of his loyalty to him as well as his deep concern for the success of the Republican party, but realized he was not always successful.

Failing in his attempts to change the programme of the committee, and with many forebodings, General Logan, accompanied by myself, proceeded to Indiana to fill the appointments which had been made for him there. He was joined by a number of prominent Republicans in a ten days' tour of the State, speaking night and day to very large crowds, which would have made most men sanguine of success. I tried to make him think all would be well, but it was impossible to dispel the depression of spirits which held him fast from the first.

We left Indianapolis the night before the election, reaching Chicago at seven the following morning. It was a raw, cold, cheerless day and the ground was covered with snow, which was still falling as we drove to our house on Calumet Avenue. General Logan scarcely spoke a word until I began to suggest that it would surely stop snowing soon; that it was not very cold, etc., thinking to dispel the gloom which seemed to have settled down upon him. He replied: "My dear, do not deceive yourself. It is all over, and we are defeated. It is pretty tough, though, to think that I must go down in defeat when I think of Hendricks's record as an enemy of his country, and remember the perils and hardships of the Civil War through which I passed in defence of my country."

When the returns were in and the result was announced, it was evident that the contest had been very close. Many good men doubted seriously the election of Cleveland and Hendricks if a fair count could be secured. At first Mr. Blaine thought of contesting the election and demanding a recount, especially in the State of New York. This State had been carried by such a small majority that it was the opinion of many that fraud had been perpetrated in counting the votes. But General Logan demurred. He was physically exhausted, and had before him a contest for re-election to the Senate.

It was discovered, after all the returns were in, that the Illinois legislature was again of doubtful political complexion. On account of the election of a number of men who had bolted their respective parties, it was doubtful with what party— Republican or Democratic—these independents would vote on the senatorial question.

General Logan had to be in Washington for the assembling of Congress. Hence we came on after Thanksgiving, going to No. 3 Iowa Circle, to which residence we had removed after General Logan's nomination at Chicago, feeling it necessary to have a house of our own to accommodate the ever-increasing number of callers and visitors. On January 1, 1885, we held a reception here. The house was beautifully decorated with flowers. In order to help entertain the constant stream of callers, I had with me Mrs. Cullom, wife of Senator Cullom, Mrs. George Upton, Miss Edith Andrews, later my son's wife, Mrs. Duval, wife of Lieutenant, now General Duval, Mrs. Rounds, Mrs. Moore, Miss Nash, Miss Eads, Miss Otes, Mrs. E. B. Wight, and Mrs. Stevenson, wife of Colonel Stevenson of the Geological Survey. Mrs. Stevenson is the author of the best book on the Indians ever written for that department of the Government.

Early in January General Logan had to go to Springfield, as his friends had informed him there were all sorts of combinations and conspiracies on foot. They had expected that General Logan would be returned to the Senate without opposition from his own party, and he would have been, without doubt, but for the mongrel condition of the legislature. Tree, Hoxie, and Morrison were candidates on the Democratic side, and the hope of success of any one of these lay in controlling the legislature. It was a bitter contest, the House and Senate voting daily without any one receiving a majority of either house. Old and tried Republican friends, it was found, had been completely demoralized by the use of money in the redemption of their farms and other financial inducements to vote for an independent or Democrat.

On April 12, 1885, Representative J. Henry Shaw, a Democrat of the Illinois legislature, died in Springfield, and the governor ordered the election of his successor on May 6. In the mean time, Mr. J. H. Craske conceived a plan by which the Republicans might elect Mr. Shaw's successor. It was this: that one man be selected in each county to manage said county; he in turn to select one man in each township of the county; he in turn to select one man in each school district, who in turn would select five others to assist him. All those engaged in the work were to be as secret as the grave. All were to start out on the morning of May 6, to see that all Republicans were at their respective voting-places promptly at 4 o'clock P. M., thereby insuring the election of a Republican representative.

The plan was submitted to General Logan, and there being nothing improper about it he gave it his approval. To some the success of the plan seemed impossible, but Craske was such a level-headed man and so sure of the success of the manœuvre that General Logan felt the chances were even. The next thing to do was to find the men to carry out the scheme, which Mr. Craske succeeded in doing. The secretary of the State central committee, Mr. Daniel Sheppard, and one or two friends of General Logan, went into the thirty-fifth district to help Mr. Craske, and to the amazement of the whole State they succeeded in electing a Republican to succeed Mr. Shaw. This closed the most remarkable senatorial contest that has ever been held in Illinois, as on the nineteenth day of May, after a struggle of four months and nineteen days, General Logan was re-elected to the United States Senate for six years. Many times during this trying and vexatious fight General Logan had felt inclined to withdraw and give up the contest, as it frequently seemed hopeless. The struggle was so remarkable, the climax so wonderful, that it attracted attention all over the nation, and General Logan was deluged with invitations to receive the homage of the different cities. He was entertained in Baltimore, Boston, and Chicago, the Republicans creating a jubilee over this remarkable victory. He returned to his seat in the United States Senate as soon as he could and took up his many duties with much zeal.

The session lasted until quite late. General Logan was much engrossed with his public duties and in the labor of writing his book, "The Great Conspiracy." He knew of General Grant's failing health and went to New York to see Grant before he was removed to Mount McGregor. General Logan was deeply grieved over General Grant's condition, which he realized was hopeless. He watched the daily bulletins with great solicitude until the announcement of the death of his beloved commander, July 12, 1885. General Logan went to New York to participate in the honors paid to the most illustrious soldier of the Republic. In September, 1885, at the meeting of the Army of the Tennessee in Cincinnati, that army mourned the death of their beloved General Grant. Resolutions of sympathy were adopted, and at the banquet which followed General Logan responded to the toast, "Statesmen and Statesmanship of the War."

We had experienced great discomfort for years by living in boarding-houses, and had so enjoyed having a house of our own after our removal to Iowa Circle, that I persuaded my husband to let me try to find a house which we might endeavor to buy, and in this way enjoy a home during the six years for which he had been re-elected to the Senate. Securing his consent, while he was busy writing "The Great Conspiracy," I made a tour of Washington, hunting property which

Mary Logan Tucker.

Major John A. Logan, Jr.

Mrs. John A. Logan, Jr.

John A. Logan III.

I thought suitable for our home. Confiding my wishes to a friend, he told me about the "Stone mansion" on Columbia Heights, which then belonged to Senator John Sherman. I found that Colonel M. M. Parker was the agent, and I induced him to go to see General Logan and offer the property to him. At first the general was afraid to undertake to buy this property, lest he might fail to meet the payments, but, after many interviews and thorough inspection of the premises, he purchased the place, notwithstanding its dilapidated condition. We christened our new home "Calumet Place," and during the winter of 1885 and spring of 1886 we had many valued friends with us. Our son was at home, and President Arthur had been good enough to cause Major Tucker, paymaster in the United States Army, to be placed on duty in Washington, which brought our daughter and her son home from Santa Fé, New Mexico. The outlook for the future seemed most propitious, and General Logan was supremely happy in having his family about him in a home of his own.

After the adjournment of Congress we returned to Chicago, having accepted an invitation from General Russell A. Alger, of Detroit, to accompany him and his family in his private car to San Francisco, where the national encampment of the Grand Army of the Republic was held. It was one continuous ovation for General Logan from the time we left Chicago until we reached San Francisco, the train stopping en route many times to allow the people to do him honor. When we reached San Francisco the reception he received was beyond description. It was impossible to get in or out of the Baldwin Hotel, where we stayed at the time. On the day of the procession the committee provided a magnificent landau with four beautiful horses, which General Logan, General Alger, and the chairman of the committee were to occupy in the procession. The parade ended at a great hall where there were to be speeches and addresses by the prominent men of the Grand Army. At that time there

were very many men surviving who had distinguished themselves in the service and made illustrious reputations after
their return to civil life. All joined in the demonstration accorded to General Logan. Some citizens of San Francisco
became so excited that they took the horses from the landau
and attached ropes by which they drew it themselves. So
many were anxious to reach the general and shake his hand
that they literally destroyed the top and the lining of the
landau, carrying away pieces as souvenirs, while the owner
stood by and laughed heartily to see the clamor to reach the
general, who was himself completely overwhelmed by the outburst of enthusiasm over him and returned to the hotel exhausted. I had to put him into bed and stand guard over
him myself until he could rest and recuperate for the exercises
of the evening. I have never seen such flowers, fruits, and
other courtesies as were showered upon us, each day's experience rivalling the preceding one in its programme of honors.

On our return journey the manifestations of regard of the
people which had characterized our outward trip were repeated, the crowds crying: "We'll have you for the Presidency
in 1888." It made General Logan very happy to know that
his record was so handsomely indorsed by the masses, whom
he loved dearly, and I have no hesitancy in saying that the
last few months of his life were the happiest he had ever known,
because he felt that he was through with the strenuous struggles which had characterized the contest he had made for
advancement. When callers would say to him, "Well, now,
general, take good care of yourself, we shall need you in 1888,"
he would say to me privately, "It is all right. I am entirely
satisfied, and it will be no matter which way things go in
1888."

In the fall, at the solicitation of friends, he accepted a number of invitations to different cities. We came to Washington
for the assembling of Congress on the first of December, but
the general had taken a cold and was not at all well, suffer-

ing acutely from rheumatism. In 1883 he had been to Hot Springs, Arkansas, and had received great benefit there. I was very anxious to have him go to Hot Springs at once, but he felt he had been away from his duties in the Senate long enough and was extremely desirous of securing the passage of his bill for the location of the military post north of Chicago now known as Fort Sheridan. He said he would wait until the Christmas holidays before going to the Springs. I wrote to Doctor Garnett, his physician there, and begged him to write to the general urging him to come to Hot Springs again. The general, however, persisted in attending to his duties for about two weeks, though suffering intensely from rheumatism.

I was much interested at that time in the building up of the Garfield Memorial Hospital, and was president of the ladies' board. I was then assisting the ladies of the society in getting up an entertainment for December 15, the proceeds of which were to be devoted to the support of Garfield Hospital. A meeting was held on Capitol Hill one morning, at the home of Mrs. T. L. Tulloch, the efficient treasurer of the society, and I went up to the Capitol with the general in the brougham, and from there went to Mrs. Tulloch's house to attend the meeting. I had not been there very long when some one, on looking out of the window, said that the general was in front of the door in the brougham. I rushed down to him, and he said he was suffering so severely that he was obliged to go home. I returned home with him and called his physicians—Doctors Baxter and Hamilton. They did everything possible, and we were untiring in our efforts to alleviate the rheumatic pains. The doctors succeeded in relieving him to the extent of his being able to sit up in an easy chair for an hour at a time for several days, and I was greatly encouraged until the morning of December 22, when a paroxysm of excruciating pain seized him in the arms and about the heart. Greatly alarmed, the doctors called in

Doctor Lincoln to confer with them.  Up to this time the
general's mind had been very clear.  I never left him for a
moment while he was confined to his bed, and through all of
this time he seemed perfectly rational, but I noticed that, although he recognized Doctor Lincoln, after the doctors left
the room for consultation his mind wandered.

From that moment until his brave spirit took its flight at
three P. M. on Sunday, December 26, 1886, while Bishop
John P. Newman stood beside his bed praying fervently for
the peace of his soul, he was only momentarily conscious, but
through it all he never for one moment failed to recognize
the members of his family or to respond correctly to their
inquiries.  The physicians decided a few days before that it
would make no difference if he were permitted to see some of
his friends who were anxious to speak with him once more.
Many of his colleagues of both parties in the Senate came to
the house to pay a tribute to him, each of whom he greeted
cordially.  The anguish of that hour is as vivid to me as if
twenty-six years had not come and gone with all their own sad
experiences.

A guard of honor was on duty in the house for two days,
when the casket containing his sacred remains was taken to
the rotunda of the Capitol, where, covered with marvellous
floral tributes, they lay in state for two days, during which time
a multitude paid its respects.  On the evening of the second
day his casket was returned to Calumet Place.  December 31,
1886, was the most stormy day I ever knew.  Sleet fell all
the night before, covering everything with a coat of ice.  It
was bitterly cold, and yet the streets were lined with people.
A long procession commanded by General Sheridan followed
the funeral train to Rock Creek Cemetery, two miles away,
where General Logan's casket was deposited in the vesti-
bule of the mausoleum of his friend Hutchinson, the use of
which was tendered by Mrs. Hutchinson.  General Sheridan
ordered a military guard of this tomb for many months.  As

soon as it was possible I erected a granite mortuary chapel in the Soldiers' Home Cemetery, and to this General Logan's casket was removed. The walls and ceiling of the chapel are covered with wreaths and other designs in immortelles.

And thus a great and spotless career was ended.

Stunned and almost paralyzed by the crushing blow which had fallen upon me, it took me some time to rally sufficiently to take up life's dreary duties. I could not forget the confidence reposed in me by him who had been taken away. I was ambitious for our children, and desired, if possible, to complete some of General Logan's unfinished work. At first it was an irksome task, but, as if guided by an unseen hand, little by little I took up what was before me to do and gradually became interested in life and its many problems. The kindness and generosity of friends who were ready to help me accomplish my desire to be of some use in the world sustained me until time enabled me to endure that which no human power could cure.

At the time of General Logan's death our son, John A. Logan, Jr., was engaged to be married to Miss Edith Andrews, daughter of Mr. and Mrs. Chauncey H. Andrews, of Youngstown, Ohio. Mr. Andrews was one of the noblest of men—an intensely patriotic citizen of the country he loved devotedly. He and General Logan had talked over the marriage of the young people, but General Logan's death changed all our plans. Much as I knew I should miss my son in such an hour, I would not allow his engagement to be disconcerted on my account, as I knew he would have to leave me sometime to live his own life. He was married on March 22, 1887. The pair went to Havana for their wedding-trip, and on their return went to Youngstown to live, as Mr. Andrews desired. Mr. Andrews had no son and at once adopted John A. Logan, Jr., as his own. Mr. Andrews survived General Logan but a few years, and my son continued to reside in the Andrews' home until a year or two prior to going into the service, in

1898, when he established his home on a farm near Youngstown.

Immediately after General Logan's death Senator Henry T. Harper introduced in the Illinois legislature a bill providing for the erection of an equestrian statue of General Logan in the State of Illinois, at the same time providing that I should be allowed the honor of selecting the location of this statue. A committee was appointed consisting of Judge William H. Blodgett, Richard S. Tuthill, Judge Harker of Carbondale, Illinois, Hon. John R. Walsh, and Hon. Robert T. Lincoln. Hon. John R. Walsh was appointed treasurer, and the award for this statue was given to Augustus Saint-Gaudens. He had at this time a number of orders and found it very difficult to get himself into a satisfactory spirit to execute such a statue as he desired. Therefore the committee indulged him very much in his delays in furnishing the model of his conception of the statue. Finally he succeeded in making the great statue which is erected in Michigan Avenue Park, on the lake front in Chicago. It was unveiled by John A. Logan III, grandson of General Logan, on July 22, 1903, on the anniversary of the fall of McPherson in the battle of Atlanta, July 22, 1864. No work of this illustrious artist has been more universally praised. John A. Logan, Jr., was intensely interested in the erection of the statue and presented to Mr. Saint-Gaudens a magnificent Russian stallion, from which the horse was modelled.

Before General Logan's death I had contracted to write a book on Washington for one Mr. Brodix, then an agent for subscription-books. General Logan wrote the contract and encouraged me to write the book. I had almost completed the manuscript for the prospectus setting forth the scope of the work, which I was to deliver January 1, 1887. It was impossible for me to fulfil my contract at that time, and Mr. Brodix, recognizing the impossibility, kindly suggested a postponement for a year or two until I could settle up my husband's affairs, which was no easy task, and bring myself to think of something besides the unspeakable affliction which had fallen so suddenly upon me.

In the autumn of 1887 Mr. and Mrs. George M. Pullman, of Chicago, urged me to chaperon their charming daughters to Europe for as long a stay as I desired to remain on the other side of the Atlantic. It was a cold November day when Miss Florence S. Pullman and her sister Harriet S. Pullman and I embarked on the North German Lloyd steamer *Trave* for Bremen, Germany. It was my first voyage and I had made every preparation for much unhappiness from the effects of *mal de mer*. Through Mr. Hudson, who had sailed many times with Captain Villergorod of the *Trave*, we had the pleasure of having the jovial captain with us at dinner at the Buckingham Hotel the night before sailing. Mr. Pullman was delighted that we were to be in the care of Captain Villergorod, who had crossed the ocean seventy-five times without ever having any serious accident. After the ship was under way and the captain's duties were disposed of, he called to us saying his first duty was to teach us how to walk on deck. Taking one of us on each side of him and drawing our hands through his arm, he bade us put forward our right foot as he put his. We soon found ourselves launched in a true sailor's gait, swinging, following the rolling of the ship with rapid strides. The bracing salt air was delightful, and all thought of seasickness disappeared.

There were on board the usual cosmopolitan group of passengers, a few of whom were interesting people. Many amusing incidents occurred at the expense of first voyagers. On the North Sea we ran into a frightful storm, which lasted thirty-six hours, before we reached Bremen. Ice and sleet covered everything; consequently the passengers were sent down below and the hatches closed. Opposite our cabin was Mr. C. of New York, and his family. On my way to our cabin during the raging of the storm I met Mr. C. going forward. He had on his overcoat and stovepipe hat, carried his hand-bag in one hand and an umbrella in the other. I inquired: "Where are you going, Mr. C?" "Madam, are you aware that we are liable to go down at any moment?" he asked. "I suppose that is true, but why take your hand-bag, hat, and umbrella?" "One might be picked up, you know, and why lose more than you have to in such a case?" His appearance in the salon served to amuse the anxious passengers and break the tension of the inexpressible suspense as the roaring waves beat upon the tossing vessel. Some one discovered that Captain Villergorod had been seized with an acute attack of a chronic trouble from which he had suffered for years, and that the second officer had allowed the ship to wander out of her course. The dear old captain realized the trouble as he lay in his berth, and made the steward strap him to a cot and carry him to the bridge. There his cot was fastened to the iron framework, and he directed the ship into the right course, or Mr. C.'s fears might have been realized. After port was finally reached and all the passengers safely landed, we were allowed to call upon Captain Villergorod at his home in Bremen to bid him goodby, as he was to sail no more and was retired soon afterward.

Frederick III had not been long dead when we arrived in Berlin. The funeral wreaths used when the great Kaiser Wilhelm I died had not withered. Berlin was in deep mourning for the two emperors, Frederick III having followed his illustrious father to the tomb within a few brief months. Bismarck was then occupying his palace in Berlin, and we saw him frequently walking in the park. Princess Bismarck gave the use of their drawing-rooms for a charity fair in which she took an active part, receiving every one in a most gracious manner. The young Prince and Princess Bismarck were residing with their father and mother, and were seen at the opera and concert after the season began. Count and Countess Waldersee we met on several occasions, while the octogenarian General von Moltke was among the interesting persons then in Berlin. His wonderful achievements, great age, and marvellous activity frequently made him the central figure of assemblages. The Empress Frederick was also in Berlin at that time and was probably the most talked-of person there. Her son was about to ascend the throne. She had been watched by jealous eyes because of her supposed English influence over Frederick III, and it was feared, should she remain in Berlin, near Wilhelm II after he ascended the throne, she might exercise undue influence over him. Her aged mother, Queen Victoria, it was then thought, might abdicate in favor of her son, Prince of Wales, later King Edward VII; and some alliance might be established between the rulers which would surrender to England power over Germany, which would be very distasteful. Bismarck had ever been a bitter enemy of Victoria from the time of her marriage to Frederick III, then Crown Prince of Germany. She was a brilliant woman, with all the sturdiness of character of her queenly mother, and was progressive in every sense of the word. She was very popular with the people because of her philanthropy and interest in everything which affected their welfare. She personally interested herself in every movement for their advancement and the development of the resources of the empire. It was said that it was at the behest of Bismarck and those who were influenced by him, whose support the young Emperor felt he must have in the beginning of his reign, that Wilhelm II insisted upon his mother leaving Berlin. She was not in good health and in a few years followed her husband to the grave. Her daughters were interesting young women, who have since made marriages befitting their station.

Finally the day arrived for the delivery of the proclamation, or rather coronation address, of Emperor Wilhelm II in the throne-room of the Emperor's palace. Mr. George H. Pendleton, the American minister to Germany (it was before we had ambassadors) caused tickets to the gallery to be sent us, and the second secretary, Mr. Crosby, did us the honor to escort us to our seats. It was an imposing spectacle and one never to be forgotten. On one side of the room with its many white columns and marble floor was a canopied throne, with two white chairs upholstered in red. Battalions of cuirassiers, uhlans, and many crack regiments of the German army, with their resplendent uniforms, took their places. Then came the Emperor, walking with solemn tread, dressed in the full white uniform of the cuirassiers, with the helmet. He was escorted to the throne by four of his staff, two in front and two in the rear, a form recently adopted by an American President. After the prayer by an eminent divine the Emperor began to read his address from manuscript. It was in German, naturally, and as we did not understand the language, we had to depend upon friends for its interpretation. It was pronounced admirable by many, but no one, on looking at the youthful soldier on that day, would have predicted that he was to become such a powerful ruler. There was nothing about him which betrayed strength of character or the indomitable will he has since displayed. We lived at the Fürstenhof Hotel in Leipziger Platz, and he passed under our windows on his frequent trips to Potsdam. He was always attended by officers of his staff, and was rather democratic in his salutations and responses to salutes given him.

We were invited to attend the opening of the Reichstag, and saw Bismarck and other illustrious German officials and statesmen. We heard the discussions on the condition of the German colonies, which was taken up after what we should call "the morning hour." At the time the colonial question was of grave importance to the German people. We were fortunate in knowing a Mr. Chrisman who had once lived in Chicago, but who had returned to his native land and occupied a prominent position in the government. He secured for us many privileges we should not otherwise have enjoyed.

We spent five delightful months in Berlin, the intelligent and interesting companionship of these lovely young women serving as a benediction to me in winning me away from the gloomy thoughts which would have intensified my desolation. Miss Florence, the elder, as the wife of Hon. Frank O. Lowden, of Illinois, has made for herself an enviable reputation as one of the most charming women ever at the national capital, her keen intelligence, gracious manners, and perfect poise fascinating all who knew her. Harriet, now Mrs. Frank Carolan, of Burlingame, California, is also one of the most brilliant and beautiful of women, her kind heart and generous sympathetic nature endearing her to many who have been the recipients of her bounty.

In March we began an interesting itinerary which took us first to Prague in Bohemia, a quaint old city which I can not believe has changed much in the elsewhere progressive intervening years. From there we went to Vienna, to my mind one of the most beautiful cities in Europe. We were greatly interested in the grand Ring Strasse, the magnificent buildings, fine parks, and, best of all, the superb-looking people. The court is said to be the most exclusive and at the same time the most demoralized in the world. This may be true, but certain it is that the people you see at the assembling-places bear no marks of degeneracy.

From Vienna we went to Budapesth, in Hungary, where the peasant class seemed to predominate. One of their annual festivals was at its height when we were there, and we saw the young girls sitting on their highly colored and decorated boxes or chests, which contained their treasures, waiting for swains to sue for their hands in marriage. Their costumes and handiwork were all of very bright colors. Returning to Vienna we passed through the Austrian Tyrol to Trieste and thence to Florence, Rome, the Riviera, and to Nice, where Mrs. Pullman met us. After a delightful stay of two or three weeks, we went via Como through the Saint Gotthard tunnel to Lucerne, Geneva, and thence to Paris, where we were joined by Mr. Pullman.

From Paris we went to London. Hon. Robert T. Lincoln was our American minister to England, and it goes without saying that we had every consideration and enjoyed many invitations to social functions. We attended the garden party given by Queen Victoria to the Shah of Persia at Marlborough House. We were greatly impressed by the simplicity of the dress of the Queen. She wore a plain black silk and on her head was a lace cap, the counterpart of those worn by English matrons. She received the guests sitting under a canvas pavilion, which was carpeted with red. The decorations were not unusual for such occasions and nothing like as handsome as we see many times at private garden-parties in our own country. The refreshments were extremely simple. When the Queen walked away, on the arm of the Prince of Wales, later King Edward VII, she used a cane. She was much heavier than we expected to see her, though we knew she was a large woman. We were glad to have seen the most remarkable woman of the time, and could understand the loyalty of her subjects, over whom she reigned so many years.

We completed our sojourn in England by a trip around the English lakes, and had a most delightful coaching-tour through the lake region, enjoying every moment of the time. We then returned to London, and sailed for home, which we reached in July, 1890. In our nine months of study and travel, we had allowed nothing of historic or other interest to escape us, and felt we had spent the time profitably as well as delightfully.

Before I left Washington for Europe Mr. Brodix had formed a copartnership with Mr. J. H. McGowan, one of God's noblemen, for the purpose of starting the *Home Magazine*, which was to be founded on my name. I was to be the editorial writer, and was to be responsible for all manuscript accepted. They were to pay me a good salary, and engaged an assistant who was to take my place in the management while I was absent in Europe, during which time I was to send editorials and other matter for the magazine. Being obliged to do this work, and finding myself in an interesting channel which supplanted the melancholy thoughts suggested at every turn at home, I became absorbed in the delightful occupation and expected to improve steadily, so that for the remainder of my days I should conduct the *Home Magazine*. From the first issue it was a phenomenal success. I worked on it for seven years. But finally, owing to financial complications quite foreign to the conduct of the magazine, and though our subscription and advertising lists were rapidly multiplying, the enterprise failed. In the crash I lost more than a year's salary, simply because I failed to draw it regularly, thinking I was letting it accumulate to insure permanent employment.

In May, 1891, my son and his wife, my son's wife's sister, Miss Andrews, and Mr. Leslie Bruce and I sailed for England. We had a most enjoyable summer, visiting first in the delightful English country homes of which so much has been written. My son's mission was to buy hackney horses. Consequently, we visited the most notable estates upon which they were raised, or places where they were on exhibition. After spending much time in going from one place to another, we went to Scotland and made a tour of the lakes. Much has been written of the delights of a trip through the Trossachs, made famous by the pen of Sir Walter Scott. We concluded our tour at Edinburgh, and visited Melrose Abbey, near Abbotsford. There is a little inn at the entrance of the abbey, where we went to arrange for our dinner at five o'clock. My son called out: "Look on the wall over the door opening to the dining-room." I looked, and imagine my surprise to see a framed copy of Brady's celebrated photograph of "Sherman and His Generals," General Logan being in the centre of the group. We were curious to know how the photograph had found its way to the place where it hung, and the proprietor told us his father had been a soldier in our Civil War and had sent the picture home for his son to see his generals. We lingered long to gaze upon the familiar picture.

From Scotland we returned to London and across the English Channel to fascinating Paris. As it was midsummer, the races were in progress and there was much gayety during our stay. The environment of Paris is full of historic interest. It is little wonder that, with its innumerable fascinations, Paris is the most demoralizing city in Europe. The people live in the parks and on the boulevards, many of them taking their meals on the sidewalk in front of the restaurants. The city has little of the charming home life of French families in the country. It was a delightful summer's outing and enjoyable to me in having my son and his wife with me.

In 1893 I had the honor to be appointed by Hon. William A. Britton as representative of the District of Columbia on the Board of Lady Managers of the Chicago World's Columbian Exposition. The women had a more conspicuous part in this exposition than in any previous one. As a matter of fact, the exposition was the greatest, most complete, best located and appointed of any ever held. Royalty and distinguished personages took active part. The daily programme was something which has never been equalled. The untiring, indomitable energy of the men of the State of Illinois and the city of Chicago in making the exposition a success was marvellous, and their friends were abundantly rewarded. Every nation and race on the globe was represented, especially in the Congress of Religions, which brought together the finest scholars and most learned men in the ecclesiastical world. It is unfortunate that the reports of the proceedings, speeches, declarations of faith and creed could not have been more generally distributed, although they were preserved in a limited form. This broadened the views of every nation, particularly our own, and the results have since been fruitful.

In 1896 Major Tucker was ordered to Saint Paul, Minnesota, and my daughter had to leave me absolutely alone to accompany her husband to his new post. During President Harrison's administration, on the retirement of Corporal Tanner as commissioner of pensions, without my knowledge I was strongly recommended as his successor. President Harrison sent for me and said it would give him great pleasure to appoint me commissioner of pensions if I desired the position. I realized the grave responsibilities attached to it and felt unequal to assuming them. I none the less appreciated the honor which had been done me by the recommendations of my friends and President Harrison's willingness to comply with their request.

January 19, 1895, I again sailed for Europe, this time on the *Kaiser Wilhelm II*, accompanied by Mrs. George M. Pullman, her son Sanger, and Miss Nina Gillett. There was on board an unusual number of charming people, among them General and Mrs. Blackmar, Miss Brewer, sister of Mrs. Blackmar; Elihu Vedder, the artist; Professor Agassiz, of Boston; Mr. and Mrs. Currey, Doctor Schultz, and Mr. and Mrs. Converse. My companions were obliged to remain in their cabins on account of indisposition. Fortunately, I could sit on deck, read, write, and enjoy my friends. I was especially entertained by the interesting conversation of Professor Agassiz, who, in addition to his wonderful knowledge, had a fund of anecdote and real wit, and told good stories with inimitable drollery. The usual concert given in going and coming from Europe was given for the benefit of the Sailors' Home on each side of the Atlantic, the generous passengers being willing to pay for some diversion, albeit their contributions might never reach the treasury of the Homes.

For six long days we sailed on the broad ocean with only the horizon to break the boundless expanse. The skies were fickle. Flitting clouds brought us sunshine and shadow. The air was cold at times, but not enough to mar the delight of the voyage. The ship rolled but little, as it was a steady steamer which made no effort at speed, but moved quietly and majestically through the sea like a thing of life. Between walking the deck, resting on the chairs all wrapped up in the comfortable robes, and visiting with interesting people, we thought little of the flight of time until, Friday A. M., January 25, the mountain peaks of the Azores could be seen through the fleecy clouds that were passing over the sky. Nearer and nearer we came until three P. M., when the captain sent for me to come on the bridge. I shall never forget the glory of the view. First Fayal, with its mountainous centre and rugged shores, with innumerable white villages all along on the side of the mountains. Church-spires innumerable and quaint old windmills added picturesqueness to the landscape. The harbor of Fayal is evidently an extinct crater of a volcano, with the side next the sea worn away by the action of the water. Opposite the lower end of Fayal lies Pico.

A few days later the impregnable Rock of Gibraltar rose majestically before us, and at last under a lowering sky we sailed into the Bay of Naples. Notwithstanding the fact that Vesuvius was covered with snow and everything looked wintry enough, the spectacle was grand, the sapphire blue of this enchanting bay being always the same. We spent several days in Naples enjoying every moment of our stay. I left my party to make a flying trip to Rome to criticise the sculptor Simmons's work on General Logan's statue for the city of Washington and found everything very satisfactory.

Shortly afterward we embarked on the *Hesperides* for Alexandria, Egypt. There were on board a number of agreeable passengers, some of them distinguished people, among them Colonel Logan, of the English Artillery, and Sir Frederick Harrison, the writer.

On the morning after our arrival in Alexandria, which might be called the "City of Obelisks," we started out to see the sights. The Pharos (one of the wonders of the world) has passed away, but on the ruins a modern lighthouse has been erected, which is one of the first objects in view near this ancient city. We had delightful drives through the fine gardens which seemed elysian in their beauty.

From Alexandria to Cairo the journey is uninteresting, but the moment you enter Shepheard's Hotel in Cairo, you feel that you are in a cosmopolitan city; and if you will sit on the veranda an hour, you will see representatives from every nation on the face of the globe wearing costumes of their native land. Smart turnouts from England and France side by side with those of the Khedive, with the sâis running in front dressed in bright colors, their lithe, bare limbs carrying them as swiftly as the four-footed animals behind them can trot. Americans, Englishmen, Frenchmen, Germans, Arabs, Nubians, Turks, Greeks, Jews, Indians, rush up and down the streets as if bent on some important business. English soldiery, infantry and cavalry, are in evidence everywhere, as England holds a mortgage on Egypt that will not be paid for many generations.

While in Cairo, we visited the Pyramids which rise like gigantic mountain peaks from the boundless desert, and were so much impressed with their magnitude and grandeur that I had no words with which to express my admiration. We went to the bazaars and found them as (so often described) revoltingly dirty and unattractive. We visited the grounds and museum of Gizeh, the citadel of the old prophets of the dervishes, the tombs of the Khalifs, the Egyptian cemeteries, and the ostrich farms, attended the ball given by the Khedive in the magnificent Palace of Abdin, and went to Sakhara to visit the step Pyramid and the Mosque of Amir, on all hands being beset by the dirtiest and most repulsive of beggars.

Our party decided against a trip up the Nile, a pleasure to be enjoyed a few months later. In February we sailed for Brindisi, Italy. Thence, via Rome and the Riviera, to Paris and London, and from London home. My daughter, Mrs. Tucker, having remained in Saint Paul, I yielded to the importunities of friends to play chaperon to a party of young ladies. The Misses Koon, of Minneapolis, the Misses Dousman and Miss Paul, of Wisconsin, were of the party—and five more intellectual, companionable young women could not be found in any country. On November 6, 1895, I again embarked for Europe. Our itinerary was via the Mediterranean. Landing at Naples, we visited Rome, Florence, and Milan in Italy; thence to Brindisi, en route to the Holy Land, via Greece and Turkey. Passing the beautiful island of Corfu, we landed to visit the lovely palace of Elizabeth, Empress of Austria. The exquisite gardens, magnificent statuary and appointments made this an enchanting retreat. Our ship was abominable, and we breathed a sigh of relief when we landed at Patras. We hurried to Athens for a sojourn of several weeks, each day furnishing something more interesting than the preceding. One who has not visited Athens can form no idea of the impression made by actually seeing the specimens of the masterful art that once made Greece the queen of art.

A short journey by train brings you to the ruins of Olympia. The German Government has made extensive excavations, rescuing the most exquisite specimens of Greek art from the bosom of mother earth, where they have been buried for so many years. The careful study of these indefatigable scientists and archæological students who have made such wonderful and laborious investigations enables one, in imagination, to rebuild and repeople the lost city which once occupied the devastated area. The American and Russian legations, through Mme. Bakmeteff (*née* Miss Beale of Washington), bestowed upon us such generous hospitality that we were loath to take our departure.

We left Patras in the early morning on board a very uncomfortable ship bound for Alexandria, thence to Cairo. After enjoying Cairo for some weeks, we decided to go up the Nile on a Cook steamer as far as Assuan. We contemplated chartering a dahabiyeh, but after investigating the condition of these "house-boats," we concluded we would not endure the discomforts, bad table, the proximity of the Arab boatman, and the reported vermin which infest these antiquated vessels. Cook's boats were delightful—clean, comfortable, and with a good *menu* every day. As we passed the dahabiyeh and realized the tediousness of a trip on them, we congratulated ourselves on the decision we had made. The Misses Koon, the Misses Dousman, Miss Ann Paul, and myself, with Doctor J. D. Rushmore, Mr. Taylor, Mr. Curtis, and Mr. Dodge made a delightful party of ten. Our itinerary provided for a stop at every interesting point between Cairo and Assuan. It would take volumes to describe in detail the ruins of the marvellous temples, cities, and tombs on either side of the slow-flowing Nile. Many of them were some miles from the river whose shifting sands have changed the channel of this desert stream. One looks many times in wonder at the tombs of the sacred bulls made of almost black granite, the dimensions of which are astonishingly great, and immediately begins to conjecture how these huge blocks of granite could have been transported to their present position from the quarries above Luxor or Assuan, the nearest possible point at which granite appears in the desert waste of upper Egypt.

Returning to Cairo from Assuan, where we spent a few days, we proceeded to Alexandria, where we embarked on a very good steamer for Spain, making a tour of that country just prior to the Spanish-American War. We visited the Alhambra, arriving in Seville in time to witness the ceremonies of the church during Holy Week, and spent Easter Sunday attending the bull-fight, witnessing its revoltingly brutal features. From Seville we went to Cordova to visit the famous church of many arches. From Cordova we journeyed to Madrid, the most interesting city in Spain, where there are many art treasures. From Madrid we went to Paris, where we were joined by my son, John A. Logan, Jr., and his family, my son's friend Gallonay, and Mrs. Washington A. Robeling, *née* Emily Warren, sister of General Warren, of Gettysburg fame. From Paris our party, with the exception of my son's family, who went to Switzerland, went to Moscow, Russia, to attend the coronation of the Czar and Czarina in May, 1896. This was one of the most remarkable events of the nineteenth century, which beggars description. From Moscow we went to Saint Petersburg, and thence via the Gulf of Finland and the Gottenborg Canal to Stockholm, Sweden, Norway, Denmark, and to The Hague, Holland. From Holland we went to London, and finally reached home safely after an experience of nine months of consuming interest and great profit, intellectually and physically.

In 1898 war was declared in Cuba. My son determined to enter the service. He was appointed an adjutant-general on Major-General John C. Bates's staff and he served in that capacity until hostilities ceased in Cuba, having taken part in the battles of San Juan Hill, Santiago, and other engagements. He was attacked with malarial fever and I met him at Montauk Point. While waiting for his arrival I tried to do all I could for the returning troops, many of whom were in a wretched condition from malarial diseases. In May, 1898, Dewey having sunk the Spanish fleet and captured Manila, it became necessary for the Government to occupy the Philippine Islands. At first it seemed there was to be no resistance, but Aguinaldo renewed hostilities, and my son again entered the service as major of the 3d Battalion, 33d Infantry, commanded by Colonel Hare. He liked the service in the line better than that of the staff. In August he joined his regiment at San Antonio, Texas, where they were ordered to San Francisco to sail for Manila in October. On their arrival in Manila he found General Lloyd Wheaton, an aid on his father's staff at the close of the Civil War, watching for his arrival, as General Wheaton wanted my son's regiment to join his command. He desired to have Major Logan with him, as he was greatly attached to Jack as the son of his old commander. Major Logan helped get General Otis to make the assignment and they embarked for northern Luzon in a few days with General Wheaton's command. Major Logan was impatient for active service and was very ambitious to capture Aguinaldo. General Wheaton allowed him to make the first reconnoissance the night after they landed. The next morning, November 11, 1899, he begged General Wheaton to allow his battalion to have the advance. He was on the point, gallantly leading his battalion of the 33d Infantry against Aguinaldo's intrenched troops at San Jacinto, northern Luzon, when a Filipino hidden by the dense foliage of a cocoanut-tree, shot one of his sergeants. Major Logan stooped over to administer the first aid to the brave sergeant, when the same man in the tree fired the fatal shot which instantly killed our only son.

This shock again prostrated me for a long time. After his father's death all my ambitions centred in my idolized son, and could he have lived I am quite sure he would have fulfilled all my expectations. He was the counterpart of his father in appearance, temperament, and aspirations. He was but thirty-six years old, but had a well-thought-out plan to add to the glory of the name he bore. He left a lovely wife and three children—two daughters and a son—all of whom are now grown to manhood and womanhood. The eldest, a daughter, is married and lives abroad, greatly to my distress. John A. Logan III bids fair to be a worthy scion of his illustrious grandfather and father. He is a graduate of Yale, and was married September 2, 1913, to Miss Margaret Powell of Saint Joseph, Missouri. He has established his home at Youngstown, Ohio. He is patriotic in the highest degree, a member of the Ohio national guard, ready and anxious for orders should his State or country need his services. The youngest child, Edith Josephine Logan, has a decided talent for sculpture, and has already modelled some fine works. Unfortunately, we must live each his own life and can not always have about us the few dear ones whom death has not claimed.

President McKinley, in trying to comfort me at the time of my son's death, said: "Dear Mrs. Logan, do not forget that in that brief moment he immortalized himself more than he could have done had he lived fifty years. His father, could he have chosen his end, would rather have had him die gallantly leading his command in battle than in any other way." John Hay, America's peerless diplomat, wrote me: "Dear Mrs. Logan: It should be some consolation to you that few women have had such a husband and such a son to lose."

That my son immortalized himself and added lustre to the name of Logan could but gratify the heart of a doting mother, but could not fail to deepen the incurable wound of his untimely death. Bereft of father, husband, and son, I had to face the world alone with no one to whom I could appeal for advice and assistance in times of trouble. But good friends came to me in my desolation, and to them I owe everything that I am and have achieved.

General Logan's statue in Washington was being made by Franklin Simmons in Rome. As soon as Mr. Simmons could complete the statue, which, as I have already said, I had seen and criticised in Rome, he brought it to Washington. It is an unusual statue, as the pedestal is in bronze as well as the figures of the horse and man. There are bas-reliefs on either side of the pedestal, showing the dual career of General Logan as soldier and statesman. On the west side of the pedestal is represented a council of war, composed of such distinguished officers as Blair, Mower, Leggett, and Dodge, who are considering the topography of the country about Atlanta from a map which lies on the table. A young staff-officer is also in the group. On the south end is the female figure representing "War," and on the north end another graceful figure representing "Peace." The senatorial group, showing Voorhees, Thurman, Vice-President Arthur, Conkling, Cullom, Miller, and Slocum, depicts General Logan in the act of taking the oath of office as a senator.

The preparations for the unveiling of this monument were planned by General Bingham, superintendent of public grounds, and Frederick Owen; and a more complete programme could not possibly have been arranged. President McKinley delivered the oration of the day, and addresses were made by Senators Shelby M. Cullom and Chauncey M. Depew, while the members of President McKinley's cabinet occupied the platform.

This is without question the finest statue in this country because of its repose and artistic merit, to say nothing of the fine likeness to General Logan and the well-modelled horse. It was unveiled by General Logan's grandson, George Edwin Tucker, the little son of Mrs. Mary Logan Tucker. The family of Major Logan was then in Europe and were not present at the unveiling. It was infinitely gratifying to me to have been spared to witness the completion of Saint-Gaudens's equestrian statue in Michigan Avenue Park, Chicago, erected by the State and personal friends of Illinois, and the one in Logan Circle in the national capital erected by Congress, the Society of the Army of the Tennessee, the Grand Army of the Republic, and personal friends as a tribute to General Logan as the "greatest volunteer soldier" of the Civil War and an incorruptible statesman.

The Spanish-American War was fortunately of brief duration, but, like all wars, brought daily its sorrows and anxieties, especially to the big-hearted President McKinley, who was wholly engrossed with the prodigious affairs affecting our nation, our army, our navy, and the people in whose behalf we had interfered. Mrs. McKinley being an invalid, there was really little attention paid to social or frivolous affairs.

Before peace was actually established in the Philippines President McKinley's term was nearing its close. He was renominated for President with Theodore Roosevelt as candidate for the Vice-Presidency, both of whom were elected in November. Alas! President McKinley did not long survive his second inauguration, but was assassinated while extending the hand of cordial greeting to a brute in human form. His death added one more to the list of martyred Presidents, each of whom were men of kindly spirit and generous impulses and who were governed by the Golden Rule in all their relations with mankind. Their charity and generosity were boundless, their patriotism broad, their courage unflinching, and yet demons in human form cut them down and ended in a twinkling their great work for humanity.

In 1902 Mr. Hearst urged me to accept a position on the syndicate staff of his newspapers. For seven years I furnished them two manuscripts per week on various topics. From Mr. Hearst and the manager of the syndicate, Mr. C. J. Mar, I at all times received the most distinguished consideration. After Mr. Hearst's rescue of Evangeline Cisneros from the Spanish prison in Cuba, I became her guardian under the laws of the District of Columbia and kept her with me constantly until her marriage to Mr. Carbonell, of Havana. I have always considered it a special providence to have had this employment, which prevented me from dwelling upon the melancholy events that seemed to pursue me.

Since I severed my connection with the Hearst syndicate in 1909 I have contributed to various papers and magazines. In 1910–11, assisted by my daughter Mrs. Mary Logan Tucker, I wrote the large volume entitled, "The Part Taken by Women in American History," intending by it to accord to all American women of every creed and condition their full credit for work actually done in the advancement and welfare of mankind and the progress of their country. In 1913 I contributed to the *Cosmopolitan* magazine in a series of ten articles the first part of this Autobiography under the title "The Story of a Soldier's Wife."

Under the brightest and darkest of skies I have passed more than a half-century at the national capital, surrounded all the while by the most illustrious people of my own and other countries. I have been familiar with the great events and movements that have made America and Americans what they are, and I honor the men and women great and small who have had a part in the building of this peerless Republic, which guarantees to all men life, liberty, and the pursuit of happiness.

# INDEX

453

JOHN Y. SIMON, professor of history at Southern Illinois University at Carbondale, is the editor of *The Papers of Ulysses S. Grant* and a founder of the Association for Documentary Editing. He has published more than sixty articles in such journals as *Military Affairs, Journal of American History, Ohio History, Journal of the Abraham Lincoln Association,* and *Journal of the Illinois State Historical Society.* The editor of *The Personal Memoirs of Julia Dent Grant* and the coeditor of *Ulysses S. Grant: Essays and Documents* and *The Continuing Civil War: Essays in Honor of the Civil War Round Table of Chicago,* Simon has held office in national professional associations and has served as a consultant for federal and state agencies, university and commercial presses, and other editorial projects.

**A SHAWNEE CLASSIC**

A Series of Classic Regional Reprints for the Midwest

*Personal Memoirs of John H. Brinton*
*Civil War Surgeon, 1861–1865*
John H. Brinton

*Stagecoach and Tavern Tales of the Old Northwest*
Harry Ellsworth Cole
Edited by Louise Phelps Kellogg

*The Great Cyclone at St. Louis and East St. Louis, May 27, 1896*
Compiled and Edited by Julian Curzon

*"Black Jack"*
*John A. Logan and Southern Illinois in the Civil War Era*
James Pickett Jones

*A History of the Ninth Regiment Illinois Volunteer Infantry,*
*with the Regimental Roster*
Marion Morrison

*The Outlaws of Cave-in-Rock*
Otto A. Rothert

*A Woman's Story of Pioneer Illinois*
Christiana Holmes Tillson
Edited by Milo Milton Quaife

*Army Life of an Illinois Soldier*
*Including a Day-by-Day Record of Sherman's March to the Sea*
Charles W. Wills